Professional Web APIs with PHP: eBay®, Google®, PayPal®, Amazon®, FedEx®, plus Web Feeds

Professional
Web APIs with PHP: eBay®, Google®, PayPal®, Amazon®, FedEx®, plus Web Feeds

Paul Reinheimer

Wiley Publishing, Inc.

Professional Web APIs with PHP: eBay®, Google®, PayPal®, Amazon®, FedEx®, plus Web Feeds

Published by
Wiley Publishing, Inc.
10475 Crosspoint Boulevard
Indianapolis, IN 46256
www.wiley.com

Published by Wiley Publishing, Inc., Indianapolis, Indiana

Published simultaneously in Canada

ISBN-13: 978-0-7645-8954-6
ISBN-10: 0-7645-8954-7

Manufactured in the United States of America

10 9 8 7 6 5 4 3

1B/RS/QX/QW/IN

About the Author

Paul Reinheimer (Ontario, Canada) is a Zend Certified Engineer and principal member of the PHP Security Consortium (PHPSEC). He is currently developing Share The Beat (`www.sharethebeat.com`), an online music portal developed extensively in PHP. Paul has been programming in PHP for the last three years on a multitude of professional and personal projects.

Credits

Acquisitions Editor
Kit Kemper

Development Editor
Ed Connor

Technical Editor
Chris Shiflett
David Mercer

Production Editor
Pamela Hanley

Copy Editor
Kim Cofer

Editorial Manager
Mary Beth Wakefield

Production Manager
Tim Tate

Vice President and Executive Group Publisher
Richard Swadley

Vice President and Executive Publisher
Joseph B. Wikert

Graphic and Production Specialists
Jennifer Click
Joyce Haughey
Alicia B. South
Julie Trippetti

Quality Control Technician
Jessica Kramer

Project Coordinator
Ryan Steffen

Proofreading and Indexing
Techbooks

For my loving parents

Acknowledgments

It wasn't until I started writing that I realized that the name on the front cover of a book is just the tip of the iceberg when it comes to significant contributions. Thanks to Chris, David, Debra, Ed, Kit, and Scott for not losing faith in me when my first chapters came back more wrong than right, and for helping me find "right" each step of the way. And a very special thanks to Laura for supporting me throughout this journey.

Contents

Introduction

With the growing popularity of the Internet, not merely as a research tool or toy, but as a bona fide business communication tool, groups are finding new ways to communicate with each other. Initially (mirroring the vendor-based communication protocols that ran rampant before standardized open protocols were introduced) they communicated via proprietary closed protocols. Fortunately, technologies like XML feeds and broader web services are allowing communication frameworks to be built faster, and allowing more groups to participate.

In this book, feeds are introduced first. These XML documents are used to pass information off from one party to others. These feeds are frequently used by news sites (both professional and amateur) to pass off their stories to interested third parties. Feeds are frequently used to mirror content available on the general website. By providing this same information in a convenient XML format, users are able to easily integrate it into their own site without resorting to cumbersome (and often unreliable) scraping techniques. Both aspects of feeds are discussed—producing the feeds to provide your users with your content in an easy-to-use format, and consuming those feeds to present external content to your users.

Second, APIs are introduced. Whereas feeds provide the same document to all requestors, the response an API provides is very dependent on the requestor and the specifics of the request. Allowing the user to request specific information opens a whole new world of opportunities, where detailed information can be requested on anything the server offers, or frequently, to push information to the server itself. APIs often allow users to connect to the server via a secure channel, which allows confidential transfers such as money transfers or bidding on auctions. A series of existing APIs are presented, complete with working code.

Although these topics are nothing new to the bookseller's shelf, I have often been frustrated with the common approach of exploring a single problem in a variety of languages. As a PHP programmer, I read the PHP sections and skip the rest. This leaves me paying for a whole book, but only reading a quarter of it. While you may have bought this book with a specific API or project in mind, my hope is that by covering a variety of things in a single language, you will not only find a more detailed coverage of that specific topic, but will also find other topics of interest, which you can hopefully use later.

Who This Book Is For

This book was written with the beginner to intermediate PHP programmer in mind, and as such a good understanding of PHP is assumed throughout the book. That being said, complicated concepts or code examples that make use of PHP's more arcane features are explained carefully.

Both feeds and APIs communicate primarily in XML, so a good understanding of XML would be beneficial. XML is introduced and discussed in Chapter 2; you may want to read that section before proceeding elsewhere if you have not previously examined XML.

How This Book Is Structured

This book has two sections, Web Feeds and APIs. Logically enough the first section discusses web feeds, from both the production and consumption angles. As such, the section is divided into three chapters, covering the introduction, consumption, and production of web feeds. The second section examines APIs. Past the introductory chapter there are four chapters, each delving into a single API. Following that there is a chapter that briefly examines three other APIs, followed by a chapter that examines APIs from the other side, producing an API to offer to your users. Each section and chapter stands on its own, with few exceptions. XML is introduced in Chapter 2, as are the basic formats for web feeds. The basic structure for REST and SOAP APIs are introduced in Chapter 5, useful things to know while working with APIs. For both the feeds and API sections, I would recommend reading at least one of the chapters that concentrates on consumption before moving onto the production side of things. This will help ensure you have a good grounding

What You Need to Use This Book

The code in this book was written for PHP5, and it is strongly recommended that you upgrade to PHP5 if you haven't already. That being said, with the exception of the examples using `SimpleXML()` the code will run under PHP4 (and even in those cases, similar functionality is available from third-party libraries). The examples in this book that require a database use either MySQL or SQLite, so having them available on your test machine would be a good idea (PHP5 includes SQLite in a default install).

Unfortunately, PHP doesn't ship with all of the things required for some of the examples in this book. Appendix C outlines all of the options PHP was built with to develop the code shown within these pages.

Finally, a few of the examples in this book make use of some of the tools that come with the OpenSSL package under Linux to create certificates for authentication purposes. If you do not have access to a machine with this package, you will need to find another way to create these certificates.

Conventions

To help you get the most from the text and keep track of what's happening, we've used a number of conventions throughout the book.

> **Boxes like this one hold important, not-to-be forgotten information that is directly relevant to the surrounding text.**

Tips, hints, tricks, and asides to the current discussion are offset and placed in italics like this.

As for styles in the text:

- We *highlight* new terms and important words when we introduce them.
- We show keyboard strokes like this: Ctrl+A.
- We show file names, URLs, and code within the text like so: `persistence.properties`.
- We present code in two different ways:

```
In code examples we highlight new and important code with a gray background.
```

```
The gray highlighting is not used for code that's less important in the present
context, or has been shown before.
```

Source Code

As you work through the examples in this book, you may choose either to type in all the code manually or to use the source code files that accompany the book. All of the source code used in this book is available for download at `http://www.wrox.com`. Once at the site, simply locate the book's title (either by using the Search box or by using one of the title lists) and click the Download Code link on the book's detail page to obtain all the source code for the book.

Because many books have similar titles, you may find it easiest to search by ISBN; for this book the ISBN is 0-7645-8954-7.

Once you download the code, just decompress it with your favorite compression tool. Alternatively, you can go to the main Wrox code download page at `http://www.wrox.com/dynamic/books/download.aspx` to see the code available for this book and all other Wrox books.

Errata

We make every effort to ensure that there are no errors in the text or in the code. However, no one is perfect, and mistakes do occur. If you find an error in one of our books, like a spelling mistake or faulty piece of code, we would be very grateful for your feedback. By sending in errata you may save another reader hours of frustration and at the same time you will be helping us provide even higher quality information.

To find the errata page for this book, go to `http://www.wrox.com` and locate the title using the Search box or one of the title lists. Then, on the book details page, click the Book Errata link. On this page you can view all errata that has been submitted for this book and posted by Wrox editors. A complete book list including links to each book's errata is also available at `www.wrox.com/misc-pages/booklist.shtml`.

If you don't spot "your" error on the Book Errata page, go to `www.wrox.com/contact/techsupport.shtml` and complete the form there to send us the error you have found. We'll check the information and, if appropriate, post a message to the book's errata page and fix the problem in subsequent editions of the book.

p2p.wrox.com

For author and peer discussion, join the P2P forums at `p2p.wrox.com`. The forums are a Web-based system for you to post messages relating to Wrox books and related technologies and interact with other readers and technology users. The forums offer a subscription feature to e-mail you topics of interest of your choosing when new posts are made to the forums. Wrox authors, editors, other industry experts, and your fellow readers are present on these forums.

At `http://p2p.wrox.com` you will find a number of different forums that will help you not only as you read this book, but also as you develop your own applications. To join the forums, just follow these steps:

1. Go to `p2p.wrox.com` and click the Register link.
2. Read the terms of use and click Agree.
3. Complete the required information to join as well as any optional information you wish to provide and click Submit.
4. You will receive an e-mail with information describing how to verify your account and complete the joining process.

You can read messages in the forums without joining P2P but in order to post your own messages, you must join.

Once you join, you can post new messages and respond to messages other users post. You can read messages at any time on the Web. If you would like to have new messages from a particular forum e-mailed to you, click the Subscribe to this Forum icon by the forum name in the forum listing.

For more information about how to use the Wrox P2P, be sure to read the P2P FAQs for answers to questions about how the forum software works as well as many common questions specific to P2P and Wrox books. To read the FAQs, click the FAQ link on any P2P page.

Part I
Web Feeds

1

Introducing Web Services

I imagine you picked up this book for a reason.

Perhaps you've built a fantastic website for your organization, but now that it's done, you want more: more ways to view the information, more ways to alter the information, more ways to share the information. Web services can help.

Maybe you run a small business through eBay and want better ways to manage the items you are selling. Web services can help.

You could be a student, a teacher, or an institution wanting to leverage the vast wealth of information compiled by Google. Web services can help.

Web services can help you use the information on the Web in new ways, from simply allowing someone to subscribe to pockets of information so that they can be immediately notified when new information is available, to creating complex business applications that can manage complex real-time supply chains.

Before digging in to how to use web services in the following chapters, this chapter presents you with the following:

- What web services are
- Why web services are used
- How web services work
- Who uses web services
- And finally, why you should use web services

Defining Web Services

Web services are a collection of protocols that are used to exchange data between disparate applications or systems. The essence of web services is the open standards on which they are built, by leveraging public and common protocols like HTTP, along with the XML document model. Web services are easy to implement with existing technologies. Not only are you (as a PHP developer) already familiar with many aspects of web services and the tools required, but you already have the facilities required to deploy them.

Why They Are Used

Simply put, web services allow information to easily pass from those who have it to those who desire it. Both feeds and APIs allow the requestor to obtain information from the service, regardless of the information type. Web services allow customers to access the information they desire, without the extraneous information generally presented on web pages. For example, running a search for a book on Amazon.com will yield several relevant results, generally (under the current layout) in the center column of the page. The right and left columns will contain other information, not directly related to your search (recommended titles, recently viewed items, and so on). Performing the same search via the API will yield the same results, but without that extraneous information.

This points to a key factor in web services — they are used to obtain specific information, or complete specific tasks. Unlike people, the automated processes that utilize web services don't make impulse decisions (like choosing a recommended title from Amazon), so there is no point in presenting them with those types of options.

How They Are Used

Web services generally present information already available via another method (that is, a website). The advantage in the services is the consistent presentation of the information (in stark contrast to methods like screen scraping) in an easy-to-parse format. Here are some examples:

- Federal Express — Allows customers to do rate lookups and schedule shipments after logging into its online system. These same tasks can be accomplished via its API; as such, customers with larger shipping needs can integrate the API with their own systems to quickly automate shipping, and allow customers to determine how much it will cost to ship a particular product.
- Amazon — Allows customers to search for products via its website, and similar tasks can be accomplished via its API (often with more granularity than the traditional web interface provides). Using the API allows small booksellers to transparently integrate with Amazon to offer additional books and apply their own pricing.
- My Personal Blog — Allows people to read my thoughts on various professional matters. The feeds provided by my blog allow those people to read the posts on their own terms, within their own client, without ads or cute pictures of my cat.

It's important to recognize both types of interaction presented here. In some cases the web service is accessed directly by the end user (as is often the case with blogs and feeds). In other cases the service is consumed by an intermediate service, then presented (through various means) to its users.

Who Uses Them

If you accept my broad definition of web services, including both feeds and APIs, the answer is almost everyone. Most news sites offer at least some of their information via an XML feed. Blog sites almost without exception include some form of feed, and APIs are becoming more prevalent offerings from businesses of all sizes.

Also keep in mind that the scope of web services varies widely depending on who offers them. Many are merely informational in nature (such as the National Weather Service API), providing read-only access to information. Others, however, allow you to present information to the server; this could be purely digital in nature (such as adding a bookmark to your del.icio.us account), or it could set into motion a series of physical events (like scheduling a package pickup through FedEx).

Why You Should Use Web Services

There are two main reasons to use web services, both remarkably straightforward: someone else has information you require, or you have information you wish to provide to others. When planning a new web service, remember that servers can either provide or accept information. Remember that web services can provide any level of security, from a completely open service open to all who request it, to a private service with transfers happening over SSL and client-side certificates to validate identities.

Convincing the Boss

Here are a few more tidbits that should help convince the boss (or you) that web services are a route to look into:

- Web services make use of technology you already have deployed—you already have a web server, you already have a database, and so on. Why not provide another way to access the data?
- Web services fit into the security scheme you are already employing. Careful deployment will keep security concerns in line with regular web access.
- Technically savvy users will find a way to access the information they desire. Without web services they will need to resort to methods like screen scraping, which is more difficult to control and can be unreliable (and providing unreliable access to your information is worse than providing none at all).
- Web services can help manage costs; easy integration with companies (like FedEx) that offer services to you can result in lower variable costs for your transactions.
- Web services will allow your business to scale; allowing clients to integrate their systems with yours will help encourage continued relationships, and avoid devoting resources to creating systems for specific clients.

Summary

This chapter answered some basic questions about web services that should allow you to do the following:

- Explain what web services are and how they work
- See the value in utilizing web services in your own projects
- Convince others that it's definitely worth the effort to build and use web services

In the next chapter, you start working with web feeds, a simple but useful form of web services. As you progress through the book, you'll start getting into more complex uses of web services and eventually create your own web service APIs.

2

Introducing Web Feeds

Web feeds (or simply feeds) are a quickly growing, easy-to-deploy technology that allows both providers and users of the feed easy access to the relevant information. Feeds are regularly updated eXtensible Markup Language (XML) documents, generally containing some basic information about the site or group offering the feed, followed by a group of items containing whatever information the feed producers want to disseminate.

Of course, there are a whole host of different uses for web feeds. For example, you could stick a work-related feed onto your intranet site to keep employees up to date on industry news, or you could combine the feeds from various blogs and websites to create a personal start page containing all the sites you read in a condensed format. Just find the feeds you're interested in and away you go!

Obviously, having the ability to view the latest information, in a given subject area and in an easily readable format, can be a huge bonus for a host of businesses and people. Accordingly, this chapter looks at the following:

- What web feeds are
- Important considerations when using feeds
- Key differences between HTML and XML
- Who provides web feeds
- What software uses web feeds

You might be asking yourself whether there are other ways to get information from the Web. Well, in general, feeds are the only reliable (and legal) way to obtain many types of information from other websites in an automated manner. Other methods, such as scraping HTML pages, are not only frowned upon, but may be illegal (if you choose to present this information to others).

What Are Feeds?

You can think of feeds as small modules of information that can be plugged into existing websites, consumed by clients on their desktop, or consumed by aggregators to be presented by users with other feeds. Aggregators also offer searching functionality to users, allowing new users to locate your site and feed (a great reason to provide a feed in the first place).

- Websites such as Yahoo! produce web feeds.
- Software that downloads and uses feeds is said to consume or aggregate feeds.
- Sites such as Google News that retrieve feeds from a number of sources and display selected items are called aggregators.

Figure 2-1 shows feeds in action.

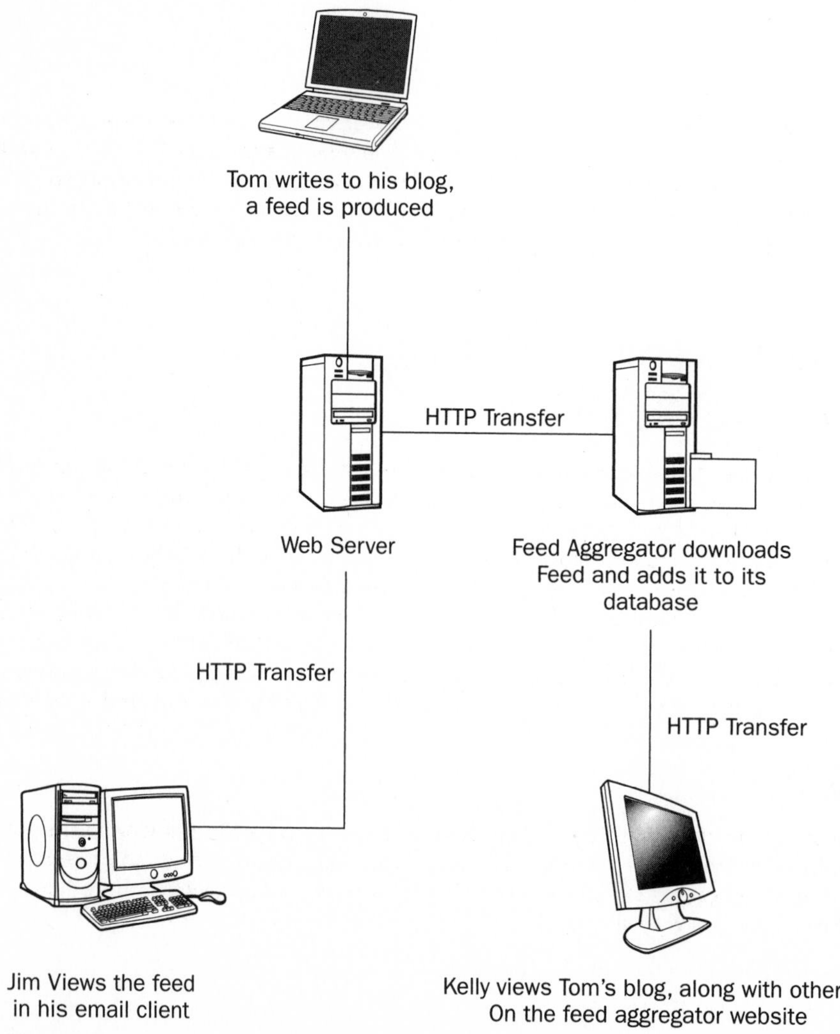
Tom writes to his blog,
a feed is produced
HTTP Transfer
Web Server
Feed Aggregator downloads
Feed and adds it to its
database
HTTP Transfer
HTTP Transfer
Jim Views the feed
in his email client
Kelly views Tom's blog, along with others
On the feed aggregator website

Figure 2-1

Most feeds are provided in one of two formats, either RSS (Rich Site Summary, or RDF Site Summary, depending on who you ask) or Atom. These formats provide standardized ways for information to be presented, such as templates for the content providers to stick their information into. The use of these standard display formats by different (and otherwise competing) websites has been a major component of the success of feeds, because a piece of software need only be written once, and it can consume the relevant information from a wide variety of different sites.

RSS

RSS is likely the more prevalent format on the Web. It was originally developed by Netscape to give content providers an easy way to have their information plugged into their My Netscape portal (a user-configurable homepage that contains news sources selected by the user). Further versions were developed by others until the 2.0 specification was released and declared to be the final version in the series. Most sites using RSS either provide a feed in 0.91 or 2.0—I have yet to find a site only providing a feed in the 1.0 version of the spec. The full specification for all three versions is available in Appendix B.

Atom

Atom was developed after RSS to resolve perceived failings of the now complete RSS specification. It makes more extensive use of namespacing for all of its elements, and currently sits at predraft status for its 0.3 state, where it has sat since late 2003. Despite all the warnings in the specification about not using it until it is officially released, most sites and aggregators offering Atom support make use of the 0.3 version of the spec. You can find the 0.3 version of the specification in Appendix B.

Important Considerations When Using Feeds

XML feeds provide a great resource of information, but their use is not without its own special considerations. Security and legal concerns go hand in hand whether you are producing or consuming feeds. Consider if you will the implications of going away for the weekend, only to discover that your aggregator has been attacked, your site is now displaying wildly inaccurate information provided by the attacker, and your legal department is fielding not-so-nice phone calls regarding the current content of your homepage. Also consider how often the information in the feed will be updated; frequently updated feeds will require the user to download and parse the document frequently, so the load on the server to create and serve the feed will be much greater still. Finally, a good understanding of XML is required—XML is the structure of which feeds are formed. Don't worry, XML is discussed shortly.

Security

When you include information from an XML feed in your site (regardless of whether or not the information is displayed publicly), you need to remember that all data received from an external source must be filtered. Feeds are at least as vulnerable to a cross-site scripting attack (XSS) as form data, and as such, all data must be examined carefully.

Cross-site scripting attacks are commonly executed when an attacker convinces a site to display his own code on the site. Without any filtering on your site, an attacker could place JavaScript code into a feed you consume, which would then be presented to your users. This JavaScript code would then be executed by your users, where it could send cookie data (such as user information) to remote sites, or even rewrite portions of your pages to accomplish even more nefarious deeds.

Finally, it is likely that the feeds you consume will be stored in a database; just because you expect (or feed specifications require) that certain characters will be escaped, it isn't always the case. SQL Injection attacks can occur in this manner, so ensure all data entered into your database is escaped properly.

Legal Concerns

The existence of a feed does not give one free reign to use it at will. Certain feeds (especially those from commercial sources) may have specific restrictions on their use, commercial or otherwise. Be sure to research the feeds you want to use before going live with any site using them.

Some specific restrictions are mentioned in more detail in Chapter 3, but common restrictions include that information may not be redistributed at all, information may only be redistributed for noncommercial purposes, and (often with either of the previous two restrictions) frequently that appropriate credit must be given to the source. Failing to meet any of these restrictions could result in your attempt to request the feed being blocked or even legal action.

Legal concerns don't stop with consuming feeds; presenting a feed has a few of its own concerns. Most of the concerns (accuracy and timeliness of information) are identical to those of a regular website, so don't forget that. Also remember that regardless of the restrictions you place on your feed, it is likely that it will be consumed by aggregators and presented to others outside the confines of your website (where those disclaimers may not be prominent or even visible). Many people are of the opinion that merely by creating a feed you have tacitly agreed to allow people to aggregate and re-present your content. If selling information (a subscription news site, for example) is a major part of your business, you may want to reconsider offering a feed at all.

Update Frequency

The frequency with which a feed is updated is an important item to consider when writing your code. Do a little background research to determine how often a feed is updated — a feed updated many times an hour may require slightly different handling from a feed updated only a few times per week (or month) on predictable dates.

The level of concurrency you require for your own site may also come into play. Some items, such as product reviews, can probably be updated on a pretty lenient schedule. If the site updates the feed daily, you can update your cached copy once a day as well (rather than many times throughout the day, trying to catch that update as soon as it happens). For some items such as stock prices, you would probably want to update on a more aggressive timeline, regardless of how often the price actually changes.

Be considerate when consuming feeds — read them only as often as is actually necessary because many feed providers have begun to express concern over the amount of bandwidth shifting away from their primary website (and hence money-generating revenue) to their feeds. You may want to consider using a service such as rsscache to reduce the load on the feed provider.

Now that you are aware of the major issues behind using live web feeds, you are almost ready to begin looking at how they are put together in PHP. Before doing so, however, one important topic needs to be discussed first.

A Crash Course in XML

Before feeds can be examined in detail, a basic understanding of the language they are provided in is needed. XML should look familiar to anyone with experience with HTML because they both follow a similar set of rules. The primary difference in application is that HTML was designed to be used for the Web, whereas XML was designed to be used with anything, and only incidentally is of great use on the Web.

XML is a textual format for describing data, currently being used everywhere, for nearly everything. HTML (Hypertext Markup Language) is converting to an XML-compliant format with XHTML— publishers are using XML to store data internally, content providers are using XML to provide their users with easy-to-consume data, and web service providers are using XML to allow complex transactions to occur between disparate systems.

As you might suspect, XML documents have to follow certain rules in order to be considered what is known as *valid* and *well formed*. As well as these two terms, XML, like any other technology, has its own special lingo. This section gets you up to speed on all the rules and terminology you will need to be able to use web feeds competently.

Terminology

The best way to learn all the terminology associated with XML is to look at a simple XML document, like the one shown here:

```
<bookshelf>
  <book>Professional PHP 4</book>
  <book price="$9.99CDN">Learn how to program PHP poorly in 24 minutes</book>
  <magazine>PHP|Architect</magazine>
</bookshelf>
```

In this instance you can say the following:

- **bookshelf** is the root element for this XML document
- **bookshelf** is the parent of **book**
- **book** is an element within this XML document
- **book** is the child of **bookshelf**
- **price** is an attribute within the **book** element

You should be able to tell that the names given in bold in the preceding list are pretty intuitive, assuming you look at them in the context of the structure of the document. The *root* element contains all other elements; it is therefore the *parent* of the elements contained within. An element that has a *parent* (is contained by a higher-level XML tag) is called a *child*, and tags can contain *attributes*, which describe their properties.

That covers most of what you will need to know in terms of how the structure of an XML document is thought of. However, you still need to understand the concepts of validity and well-formedness.

Well-Formed XML

There are three key rules for creating well-formed XML: It must have a single root-level element, tags must be opened and closed properly, and entities must be well-formed.

A Single Root-Level Tag

Every XML document has a single root-level element. This element must contain all other elements within the document.

An example of not well-formed XML:

```
<book>Professional PHP 4</book>
<book>Beginning PHP 4</book>
```

Here is an example of well-formed XML:

```
<bookshelf>
  <book>Professional PHP 4</book>
  <book>Beginning PHP 4</book>
</bookshelf>
```

The first example has two root elements, both titled `book`. The second example has a single root element, titled `bookshelf`. The first is not well-formed because XML documents can have only a single root element. In the second example, the `book` elements are enclosed within a single `bookshelf` element, making the `bookshelf` element the single root tag and fulfilling the first condition for well-formedness in the process.

> *XML is used to add a logical structure to information. Invariably, you need to structure information to indicate or reflect a real-life situation. In this case, a library has bookshelves, which contain books, so it makes sense that the* `bookshelf` *tag contains* `book` *elements. You wouldn't really want a* `book` *root tag containing* `bookshelf` *elements.*

Tags Must Be Opened and Closed Properly

Each and every element within the XML document must be opened and closed properly.

An XML tag is considered closed if it has a matching, closing tag. You can also open and close the tag at once by placing a forward slash immediately before the closing brace. In contrast, HTML often has tags that are left open, (`img`, `p`, `hr`, `br`, and so on).

This is not well-formed XML:

```
<bookshelf>
  <book>Professional PHP 4
  <book>Beginning PHP 4
</bookshelf>
```

This is well-formed XML:

```
<bookshelf>
  <book>Professional PHP 4</book>
  <book>Beginning PHP 4</book>
  <book title="Learning PHP 4" />
</bookshelf>
```

It should be obvious to you that the first example document is not well-formed because neither of the `book` tags is closed. The second example shows two closed `book` tags and one empty, closed `book` tag. Why is the final tag empty? Well, if you look closely, the final `book` tag has a `title` attribute and is closed immediately after this. In this instance, the attribute tells you about the book's title.

A tag opened within another tag must close before its parent. Similar rules exist for HTML, which are often ignored when the situation suits the coder. Whereas most programs that deal with HTML are forgiving in this respect, XML parsers, generally, are not.

This is not well-formed XML:

```
<bookshelf>
  <book>Learn PHP for only <price>$9.99</book>CDN</price>
</bookshelf>
```

This is well-formed XML:

```
<bookshelf>
  <book>Learn PHP for only $9.99</book>
  <price>$9.99CDN</price>
</bookshelf>
```

Here is another example of well-formed XML:

```
<bookshelf>
  <book price="$9.99CDN">Learn PHP for only $9.99</book>
</bookshelf>
```

In the first incorrect example, the `book` tag is opened, then the `price` tag is opened, then the `book` tag is closed, and finally the `price` tag is closed — these tags overlap. The second and third examples show valid ways to record the information. The last example is preferable because it properly demonstrates the relationship between the book and its price.

Entities Must Be Well-Formed

Entities accomplish several things within XML. At their most basic level they provide a method to encode several characters to avoid confusion (<, >, &, ', "), as well as represent nonstandard characters such as ©. They can also be used to represent user-defined text (entire sentences or paragraphs). The first use is the only method discussed here because it is critical in creating well-formed XML.

Encoded XML entities all take on a similar form: `&entity` identifier;. The appropriate encoding for an ampersand is `&`, which is a special named entity. XML has five named entities, as described in the following table.

Entity Name	Value	Example
lt	Less than <	6 < 7
gt	Greater than >	7 > 6
amp	Ampersand &	Tom & Jerry
apos	Single quote or apostrophe '	Kelly's Car
quot	Double quote "	100% "Secure"

Each of these five named entities must be used within your documents to be considered well formed.

This is invalid XML:

```
<bookshelf>
  <book>Tom & Jerry's, a history of</book>
  <book>2 + 2 < 5, Math for beginners</book>
</bookshelf>
```

Here is an example of valid XML:

```
<bookshelf>
  <book>Tom &amp; Jerry&apos;s, a history of</book>
  <book>2 + 2 &lt; 5, Math for beginners</book>
</bookshelf>
```

The transition between the two should be obvious; the named entities were encoded as necessary in the second example. This encoding is necessary for each of the five named elements for the XML to be considered well-formed.

Encoding other characters (such as ©) is similarly easy; the format is &#Unicode character number;. So © is `©`. You can also use the hexadecimal representation of the number by prefixing it with an x: `©`.

Valid XML

Valid XML is the next step from well-formed XML. As such, before an XML document can be considered valid, it must first be well-formed. A document can be well-formed while still not being valid.

Valid XML references a Document Type Definition (DTD), which may either be contained within the document itself or, more likely, an external resource. In order for the document to be valid, it must follow the rules outlined by that DTD. Here is an example DTD from an RSS feed:

```
<!DOCTYPE rss SYSTEM "http://my.netscape.com/publish/formats/rss-0.91.dtd">
```

With that declaration in place, the program that parses the XML can retrieve the DTD and ensure it is valid before attempting to process it.

Fully exploring the relationship between DTDs and XML documents is beyond the scope of this book — for now it should suffice to accept that valid XML documents have a DTD and follow the rules outlined within it (all of the feed examples presented within this book are valid).

Additional Considerations

You should be mindful of two additional items when creating XML documents.

Capitalization Matters

In HTML, capitalization is irrelevant. That is not the case with XML; for example, `bookShelf` is different from `bookshelf` or `BookShelf`.

This is not well-formed XML:

```
<bookShelf>
  <book>Professional PHP 4</BOOK>
  <book>Beginning PHP 4</BOOK>
</bookshelf>
```

This is well-formed XML:

```
<bookshelf>
  <book>Professional PHP 4</book>
  <book>Beginning PHP 4</book>
</bookshelf>
```

White Space Will Remain

White space within HTML is stripped out or ignored. Repeated spaces, new lines, and so forth are all removed by the browser, but this is not the case with XML. In XML, white space characters are considered as much of the data as any other character, so they remain. This isn't to say that a web browser displaying the XML won't try and do something funny with the characters (such as displaying white space in a manner identical to its treatment of HTML), but just that XML does recognize those characters.

Now that you have a pretty good idea of XML, the underlying technology behind web feeds, the next section talks about what a web feed looks like in the flesh. Having put in the hard work learning how XML works, you should find that the content of a web feed is pretty easy to understand.

Looking at a Basic Feed

To tie together everything you have learned so far, the following code is a stripped-down feed from ZDNet's Web Services channel. Recall from earlier that XML's structure can be used to describe any given entity's logical structure in a hierarchical format. In ZDNet's case, we are talking about articles of some sort so you would expect, among other things, to see tag elements like `title`, `language`, and `description` because the XML will be used to describe the properties of an article. Of course, you don't have to take my word for it; you can take a look for yourself:

```
<rss version="0.91">
<channel>
<title>ITPapers.com - Recent Web Services White Papers</title>

<description>Recent Web Services White Papers Added to ITPapers.com</description>
<language>en-us</language>

<item>
<title>MSDN Webcast: How to Design Your Web Services For Successful
Interoperability</title>
<link>http://www.itpapers.com/abstract.aspx?scid=436&amp;docid=117431&amp;tag=rss&a
mp;promo=100112</link>
<description>Beginning in early design stages and throughout the development
process, you must make decisions that affect the ability of your Web service to
interoperate. Join us for this webcast as we offer proven strategies for maximum
interoperability and highlight what practices to avoid while designing and building
interoperable Web services.
</description>
</item>

<item>
<title>MSDN Webcast: Web Services (Level 300)</title>
<description>Web Services offer a vision of interoperability between multiple
platforms, applications and vendors. But what is the reality? What are the tips and
tricks for developing seamless Web Services between Microsoft .NET, IBM WebSphere
and BEA WebLogic? How are vendors contributing to the WS-* process, and what does
this mean to you? In this Webcast we'll answer these questions and more - showing
the promise of interoperability using Web Services and discussing best practices
for implementing these in your own applications.
</description>
</item>

</channel>
</rss>
```

In this example, `rss` is the root-level element, and the version for it is 0.91. The first six elements (up to and including `language`) introduce the feed, its homepage, and the language in which it is provided. These elements introduce the whole feed, like a header. The feed has a repeating element entitled `item`, and each story is contained within its own `item` tag. Each `item` tag contains the same three elements: `title`, `link`, and `description`. According to the RSS specification, the `channel` element can have any number of `item` elements (though a maximum of 15 is recommended) so the feed can provide a large number of stories to interested parties. That's pretty much it—quite simple really! In the next chapter you learn how to make use of web feeds such as this one, but first take a quick look at the formatting behind the common feeds.

Standard Feed Formats

In order for a feed to be useful to the general public, it needs to be in a format their software already understands; the two most common types of formats are RSS and Atom. Both types are already supported by a wide range of aggregators and are produced by numerous blogs and news sites.

A brief introduction to the feeds is presented here, with sample code from each of the major formats use today. Don't get bogged down reading into the details; the next two chapters take a more in-depth look.

There are more versions of both the RSS and Atom specifications than are presented here, but this book concentrates on the versions most often used.

RSS

One of the most popular formats for syndicating information is RSS. Currently, three versions are widely used: 0.91, 1.0, and 2.0, all of which present varying levels of compatibility. Most aggregators, whether stand-alone client or web-based, can support all three versions, so it really comes down to what you and your users need. As with any project, examine the specific capabilities of your users before making any decisions. (For example, if this is for a corporate intranet, examine the software and versions common throughout the organization. Frequently, Information Technology departments run a version or two ahead of the rest of the organization, and hence the target market for your feed must be closely examined.)

For all three revisions of the RSS schema, the height and width elements for an image are considered optional. However, note that the assumed values are a width of 88 px and a height of 31px (this is approximately the size of those "web buttons" you see on various sites promoting software or other sites).

RSS 0.91

RSS 0.91 is commonly used by many blogs and news sites. It allows basic textual information syndication, without too many required tags. For a basic news site, this allows a base `channel` tag to describe the site (`name`, `description`, `language`, `webmaster`, `copyright`, `logo`, and so on), and then an `item` tag for each individual story containing further information (`title`, `link`, `description`). The link in each `item` should be to the page containing the story itself, not the root page for the site.

```
<?xml version="1.0"?>
<!DOCTYPE rss SYSTEM "http://my.netscape.com/publish/formats/rss-0.91.dtd">
<rss version="0.91">
  <channel>
    <language>en</language>
    <title>Example News.com</title>
    <description>News and commentary from the example community.</description>
    <link>http://www.example.com/</link>
    <image>
      <title>Wrox News .com</title>
      <link>http://www.example.com/</link>
      <url>http://www.example.com/pics/button.png</url>
    </image>
    <item>
      <title>Feed usage up 1000%!</title>
      <link>http://www.example.com/story2/index.html</link>
      <description>Feed usage has increased a dramatic 1000% in the past 48hrs
alone, this may...</description>
    </item>
    <item>
      <title>RSS Feed Goes Live!</title>
      <link>http://example.org/story1/index.html</link>
      <description>Example.com is proud to announce the launch of our premier RSS
service...</description>
    </item>
  </channel>
</rss>
```

RSS 1.0

The 1.0 version of the specification changed to allow for forward flexibility by adding namespaces to the document; these changes presented a few incompatibilities with previous versions of RSS. The goal with version 1.0 of the specification was to lock down core functionality, and allow everything else to be expanded with new namespaces.

```
<?xml version="1.0"?>
<rdf:RDF
  xmlns:rdf="http://www.w3.org/1999/02/22-rdf-syntax-ns#"
  xmlns="http://purl.org/rss/1.0/">
  <channel rdf:about="http://www.example.com/xml/news.rss">
    <title>Example News.com</title>
    <link>http://example.com/news</link>
    <description> News and commentary from the example community.</description>
    <image rdf:resource="http://www.example.com/pics/button.png" />
    <items>
      <rdf:Seq>
        <rdf:li resource="http://www.example.com/story1/index.html" />
        <rdf:li resource="http://www.example.com/story1/index.html" />
      </rdf:Seq>
    </items>
  </channel>
  <image rdf:about="http://www.example.com/pics/button.png">
    <title>Example.com promotional button</title>
    <link>http://www.example.com</link>
    <url>http://www.example.com/pics/button.png</url>
  </image>
  <item rdf:about="http://example.org/story2/index.html">
    <title> Feed usage up 1000%!</title>
    <link> http://example.org/story2/index.html </link>
    <description>
      Feed usage has increased a dramatic 1000% in the past 48hrs alone, this
      may...
    </description>
  </item>
  <item rdf:about="http://www.example.com/story1/index.html">
    <title>RSS Feed Goes Live!</title>
    <link>http://www.example.com/story1/index.html</link>
    <description>
      Example.com is proud to announce the launch of our premier RSS service...
    </description>
  </item>
</rdf:RDF>
```

RSS 2.0

This is where the real fun begins. The biggest change you will notice is with the introduction of many much-needed tags in the `item` element, including `enclosure` (to attach a file with the specific item), `author`, `category`, `comments`, `pubDate`, and so on. These additions will probably serve to make RSS 2.0 the schema of choice if it is available to your audience.

This example builds on the one presented for version 0.91 by adding a third item and fleshing out the information provided. Because the information permitted in RSS 0.91 is a subset of 2.0, it is a good idea to provide both 0.91 and 2.0 feeds if you decide to go with 2.0.

```
<rss version="2.0">
  <channel>
    <language>en</language>
    <title>Example News.com</title>
    <description>News and commentary from the cross-platform scripting
      community.</description>
    <link>http://www.wroxnews.com/</link>
    <image>
      <title>Example News.com</title>
      <link>http://www.wroxnews.com/</link>
      <url>http://www.wroxnews.com/pics/button.png</url>
    </image>
    <item>
      <title>Feed usage up 1000%!</title>
      <link>http://www.wroxnews.com/story2/index.html</link>
      <description>Feed usage has increased a dramatic 1000% in the past 48hrs
        alone, this may...</description>
     <enclosure url="http://www.wroxnews.com/feedusage.pdf" length="38642"
      type="application/pdf" />
    </item>
    <item>
      <title>RSS Feed Goes Live!</title>
      <link>http://wroxnews.org/story1/index.html</link>
      <description>Wroxnews.com is proud to announce the launch of our premier RSS
        service...</description>
     <enclosure url="http://www.wroxnews.com/feedlive.pdf" length="28646"
      type="application/pdf" />
    </item>
  </channel>
</rss>
```

Expanding RSS

RSS provides a mechanism for adding tags to an RSS document. This can be done by adding additional XML namespaces to the document in the rss tag. The syntax is relatively simple. For example:

```
<rss version="2.0" xmlns:cc="http://backend.userland.com/creativeCommonsRssModule">
```

This defines the document as being RSS 2.0, adds an additional namespace (cc) to the document, and indicates where to find more information about the namespace. In this case, the cc namespace is for the Creative Commons license. Adding this tag will allow inclusion of several cc tags to define the copyright restrictions (or lack thereof) placed on the document. To declare a tag within the cc namespace, just prepend the tag with cc. For example:

```
<item>
  <title>RSS Feed Goes Live!</title>
  <link>http://wroxnews.org/story1/index.html</link>
  <description>Wroxnews.com is proud to announce the launch of our premier RSS
service...</description>
```

```
    <cc:license>http://www.creativecommons.org/licenses/by-nc/1.0<cc:license>
  </item>
```

This extensibility allows feed creators to include any desired information with their feed in a recognizable way. Before defining your own namespace, look at the ones already available. Using the same namespaces as other similar sites will allow users to consume your feed more easily (because their aggregation software will likely already support your added namespace).

You will often see namespaces referencing a URL beginning with `http://purl.org/`. *Purl offers a Permanent URL for resources that might move around in the future (saving everyone the headache of changing their links, as well as providing a short URL in place of a cumbersome one).*

Atom 0.3

Atom was created to resolve some perceived ambiguities within the RSS specification (RSS 2.0 was declared to be the final version, so these issues can't be resolved by releasing new versions of RSS). This section covers Atom 0.3, which is the latest version as of print time, but is still in beta.

```
<?xml version="1.0" encoding="utf-8"?>
<feed version="0.3" xmlns="http://purl.org/atom/ns#">
  <title>dive into mark</title>
  <link rel="alternate" type="text/html" href="http://diveintomark.org/"/>
  <modified>2003-12-13T18:30:02Z</modified>
  <author>
    <name>Mark Pilgrim</name>
  </author>
  <entry>
    <title>Atom 0.3 snapshot</title>
    <link rel="alternate" type="text/html"
     href="http://diveintomark.org/2003/12/13/atom03"/>
    <id>tag:diveintomark.org,2003:3.2397</id>
    <issued>2003-12-13T08:29:29-04:00</issued>
    <modified>2003-12-13T18:30:02Z</modified>
  </entry>
</feed>
```

As you can see, although the Atom specification may use different terms for several of the elements, there really isn't too large a difference between the specifications. Personally, I appreciate the addition of the modified tag to remove some of the ambiguity associated with posts that were later updated. That being said, I prefer the date format used in the RSS feeds. Beyond that, which feed formats you decide to produce is entirely dependent on what your user base desires or is able to interpret. When unsure, produce both. The full Atom spec, for versions 0.1–0.3, is available in Appendix B.

The Atom 0.3 specification calls for the Content-Type header to be set to `application/atom+xml`. *However, while I am debugging feeds with a browser, I find it convenient to set the Content-Type header* to `text/xml`, *because most browsers will attempt to locate an external registered handler for* `application/atom+xml`, *but will display* `text/xml` *themselves.*

Summary

This chapter introduced the concept of web feeds, providing you with a basic understanding of what they are and what they can mean to your organization. Important things to consider before either offering or consuming feeds, such as security, legal concerns, and server load, were introduced.

XML, the language that presents feeds, was introduced, along with the accompanying terminology (root element, parent, child, valid, and well-formed). Keeping these rules in mind will be vital when producing feeds, because errors may not be immediately apparent but will make your document inaccessible to the public. Two additional considerations were also mentioned as a contrast to HTML: Capitalization counts with XML and repeated white space characters are not ignored.

Finally, the most common feed formats were introduced—RSS 0.91, 1.0, and 2.0, along with Atom 0.3. These formats (and often RSS in particular) are often treated as synonyms for web feeds, so at least a passing understanding of their layout is required. These specifications continue to be discussed in the next few chapters.

Overall, the major goals of this chapter were as follows:

- Introduce the concept of feeds as well as their use
- Present major considerations when using feeds
- Provide enough information on the XML format to allow you to continue to use XML in future chapters
- Introduce major feed formats

The next few chapters all build on the knowledge gained here. Chapter 3 concentrates on retrieving data from feeds provided by others, and Chapter 4 introduces the concepts involved in developing your own feed.

3

Consuming Web Feeds

The programs that can use or "consume" a web feed are almost as numerous as the sites that provide the feeds themselves. Because the entire feed structure was designed to be easy to read and utilize, many different types of software have added feed capability to their feature set. You can take a look at software such as Trillian (Instant Messenger) at `www.ceruleanstudios.com/learn/` or Mozilla Firefox (web browser) at `www.mozilla.org/products/firefox/` to get a feel for what's out there.

Having seen how basic feeds are put together, and the role XML plays in delivering the feeds and their information, you probably want to dive into building your own aggregator. That's exactly what you are going to do now. Along with consuming your first feed, you also learn the following topics:

- Feed consumption in detail
- Feed structure in detail
- Making your feeds even more secure
- Images in feeds
- Dealing with broken HTML from feeds
- Recording feeds

Of course, consuming feeds is only one side of the coin. Chapter 4 discusses how you go about building your own feed, but for now, get familiar with making use of what is already out there.

Consuming Your First Feed

Yahoo! produces a plethora of web feeds available to the world at large, so the first example looks at one of the Yahoo! feeds: `http://rss.news.yahoo.com/rss/software`. Take a quick look at that page in your browser and you will see the now familiar sight of an XML document that provides a live feed. Apart from the bits and bobs at the top of the feed, which provide information about the Yahoo! channel, you will see something like this:

```
...
- <item>
  <title>Astaro rolls out new spyware (InfoWorld)</title>

  <guid isPermaLink="false">infoworld/20050308/57432</guid>
  <pubDate>Tue, 08 Mar 2005 12:00:55 GMT</pubDate>
  <description>InfoWorld - Astaro on Tuesday released an improved version of its
Linux-based security package that now includes gateway-based spyware protection
against malware and the ability to block and removed infected software already on a
system.</description>
  </item>
- <item>
  <title>Google Preps Enterprise-Ready Desktop Search (Ziff Davis)</title>

  <guid isPermaLink="false">zd/20050308/147231</guid>
  <pubDate>Tue, 08 Mar 2005 07:52:45 GMT</pubDate>
  <description>Ziff Davis - As free desktop search tools raise corporate security
and policy concerns, Google says it wants to reach enterprises with its software
for searching local data.</description>
  </item>
...
```

Obviously, by the time you read this, the actual feed items will have changed, and the start and end bits of the feed have been left out for brevity's sake. The important things here to note are `item` tags, which enclose, among other things, `link`, `pubDate`, and `description` tags. This repetitive type of structure is obviously a good candidate for an iterative process. But what do you do with it now? Somehow you need to take that XML and process it so that you can present it on your own web pages.

Luckily, PHP5 makes it pretty easy to consume web feeds using SimpleXML. Take a look at the following program:

```
<?php
  $request = "http://rss.news.yahoo.com/rss/software";
  $response = file_get_contents($request);
  $xml = simplexml_load_string($response);
  echo "<h1>{$xml->channel->title}</h1>";
  foreach($xml->channel->item AS $story)
  {
    echo "<a href=\"$story->link\" title=\"\">$story->title</a><br>";
    echo "<p>$story->description</p><br><br>";
  }
?>
```

You begin by defining the request string, which is the URL of the web feed you want to consume. The call to `simplexml_load_string()` takes the document returned by `file_get_contents()` and creates an easily accessible object, whereby each element of the XML document can be accessed directly through the object references. As you can see, you can even iterate through the various `item` elements with a `foreach` loop, printing out each item's pertinent information in turn. This process is discussed in more detail later; this is just a basic demo for now.

As you can tell, SimpleXML is pretty neat; it deals with the XML, and provides you with a clean interface to use it all. Unfortunately, it didn't come around until PHP5, so if you are still using PHP4, it isn't available to you. You do have some alternatives, however. MiniXML does the same sorts of things for you; however, the interface it provides is a bit different. Here is the preceding example, converted to use MiniXML:

```
<?php
  require("./minixml.inc.php");
  $request = "http://rss.news.yahoo.com/rss/software";
  $response = file_get_contents($request);

  $parsedDoc = new MiniXMLDoc();
 $parsedDoc->fromString($response);
  $rootEl =& $parsedDoc->getRoot();

  $title = $rootEl->getElementByPath('channel/title');
  echo "<h1>" . $title->getValue() . "</h1>";

  $returnedElement =& $rootEl->getElement('channel');
  $elChildren =& $returnedElement->getAllChildren();

for($i = 0; $i < $returnedElement->numChildren(); $i++)
{
  if ($elChildren[$i]->name() == 'item')
   {
    $link = $elChildren[$i]->getElementByPath('link');
    $title = $elChildren[$i]->getElementByPath('title');
    $desc = $elChildren[$i]->getElementByPath('description');
    echo "<a href=\"" . $link->getValue() . "\">" . html_entity_decode($title-
        >getValue()) . "</a><br>";
    echo "<p>" . html_entity_decode($desc->getValue()) . "</p><br><br>";
   }
}
?>
```

Throughout the book I have attempted to keep included files in the same directory as the script itself. This is done for simplicity but is actually a poor security practice. Allowing included files to exist within your document root can be a large problem, because executing those scripts outside of their normal context can have unexpected consequences on your site as a whole. Play it safe and keep include files outside of the document root; just give Apache (or whatever web server you are using) access to the directory in question.

As you can see, the interfaces are in fact quite different, but the net result is the same. MiniXML is distributed under the GPL license, something to keep in mind if you intend to distribute projects based upon it. Psychogenic (creators of MiniXML) does have other licenses available if you need to distribute a project using it under other terms. The output for both scripts is identical (see Figure 3-1).

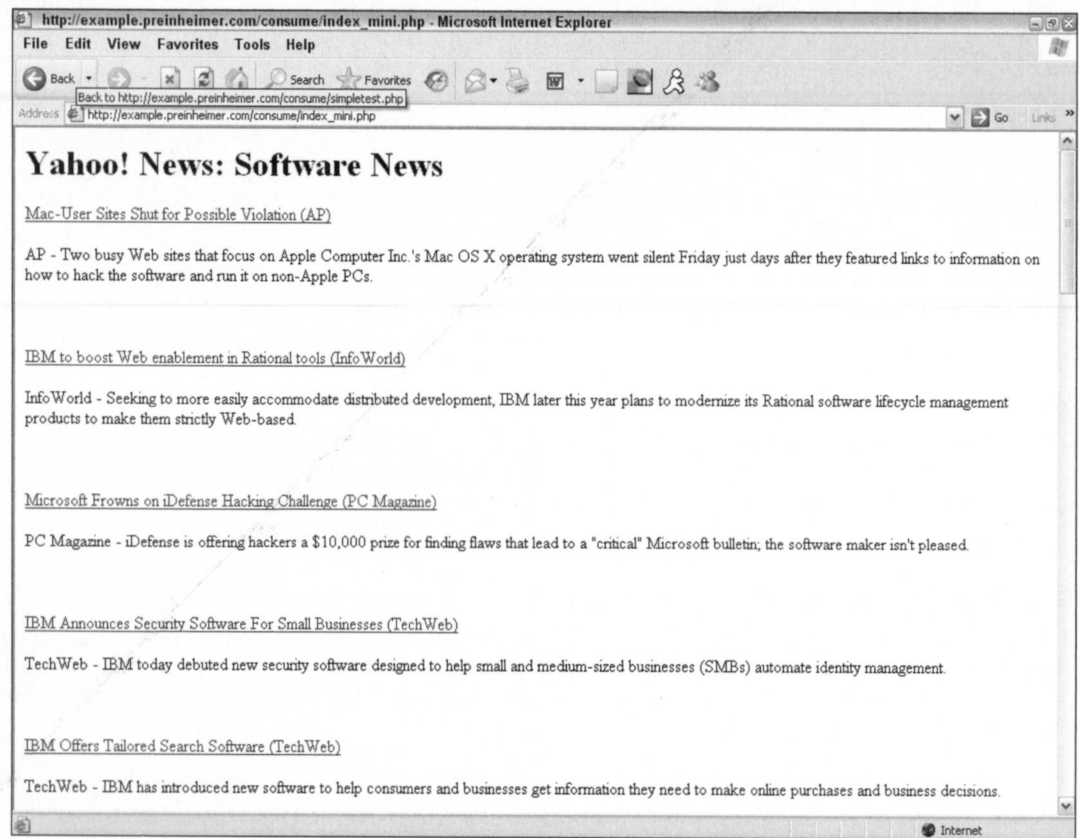

Figure 3-1

In-Depth Feed Consumption

So far, you have looked at only the very basics of consuming feeds. The devil is really in the detail when it comes to making a robust aggregator, because quite a number of factors can come into play.

Know Thy Elements

In this section, you continue to consume the Yahoo! Software feed, found at `http://rss.news.yahoo.com/rss/software`. Having viewed the feed in your browser (or a text editor for that matter), you can be sure you have the exact URL, as well as familiarize yourself with the content of the feed. You may have been lured into a false sense of security by the specifications presented thus far — it looks simple enough, after all. Unfortunately, this isn't quite the case; different programmers interpret the specifications differently, and add their own elements via namespacing. Some feeds (even major ones) don't actually follow any of the specifications at all, resulting in quite a few details that may require a special case in your code. Understanding exactly how the feed you are about to consume works is critical if you want your aggregator to work properly, so always look for edge cases (the really long or really short entries, or entries that have other unique characteristics). The following sections discuss some important things to note.

Which Elements Do You Want?

Chances are you aren't going to need the entire feed, but only certain elements of it. In this case, you want to grab the `<title>` for the feed itself, as well as the `<link>` of the web page for the feed. The `lastBuildDate` tag can be used to check to see if anything new has been posted, and the `ttl` (Time To Live) tag notes that the feed should be cached for 5 minutes. You won't save the TTL, but keep it in mind when figuring out how often to hit the page. The `image` tag can be ignored; you don't need that for now. Finally, you want the `item` tag and everything underneath it (`title`, `link`, `guid`, `pubDate`, `description`).

Which Elements Repeat?

Some elements will repeat in the feed (`item`, for example, in RSS feeds), whereas others will only have one instance. Some subelements may usually only be there once, but may repeat in some instances (think of a listing of books — most only have one author, but some (like this one) have more than one), so your code should be ready to deal with this. Because this is indeed an RSS feed, the `item` tag repeats.

Plain Text versus HTML Encoded Data?

Look at what type of data the feed is providing. You may need to either add tags yourself (encapsulate the content of a feed in `<p></p>` tags, for example), or strip tags to be better displayed within your templates. Remember to view the document's source for this, because your browser will automatically turn things like `&` into just `&`.

The Yahoo! feed appears to provide all of its data in plain text, with appropriate characters encoded into HTML entities. Running strip tags on all of the data should be fine because there isn't any meaningful links in the content. It is interesting to note that this feed presently sends its root link as shown here:

```
http://news.yahoo.com/news?tmpl=index&amp;cid=1209
```

You will need to change `&` to simply `&` if you want this to be a functional link.

Am I Using UTF-8 Encoding? Is The Feed Really Encoded That Way?

Document encoding is rather important; often (thanks to the magic that is PHP) we pretty much ignore it and trust that everything will work well, when in fact, using things like SimpleXML, this simply (if you will pardon the pun) isn't the case. Content providers are often careful with the information they provide, to ensure it is of the appropriate type, but often still manage to send characters encoded in another format when including user-submitted text (such as product reviews on Amazon, or posts in a forum). SimpleXML will return errors and warnings if it receives such incorrectly formatted data; in these cases you may need to either massage the data yourself or contact the provider of the feed and inform them of the encoding issues.

For your purposes, the Yahoo! feed declares itself to be ISO-8859-1, and all the content provided appears to be encoded correctly.

Don't kid yourself and think that big professional sites don't make these mistakes — they do! While writing this book, Amazon corrected an error where it was returning ISO-8859-1 characters in its REST-based API while declaring the stream to be UTF-8. Test your script well, trap errors, and if the script fails while trying to grab a feed, have it notify someone, and continue to use the cached copy. Don't trust foreign data, ever!

Browse the Site Providing the Feed

Look around the site for copyright information and restrictions regarding the feed you want to consume. Also look to see if there is more detailed information with regards to what will be included in the feed (in terms of HTML formatting, content-type, and so on).

Browsing the Yahoo! site indicates that the feed will be provided in the RSS format, and lays out the terms of use for the content of the feed. You can view this information here: `http://news.yahoo.com/rss`.

Reuters also provides a feed, as well as clear terms of use. If you are planning to make use of a feed in any commercial context, be especially careful when consuming feeds. You (or someone from the legal department) would be well advised to contact the feed provider to request permission before coding. Here is what Reuters spells out as its terms of use:

> ***What are the terms of use?***
> *Reuters offers RSS as a free service to any individual user or non-profit organization that would like to access it for non-commercial use. For all other usage requests, contact us. By accessing our RSS service you are indicating your understanding and agreement that you will not use Reuters RSS for commercial purposes. Reuters requests that your use of our RSS service be accompanied by proper attribution to Reuters as the source. Reuters reserves the right to discontinue this service at any time and further reserves the right to request the immediate cessation of any specific use of our RSS service.*

Keep a Copy of the Feed Structure

Drop the feed into either a SimpleXML or MiniXML construct, and use `print_r()` to view the contents. From here you should be able to spec out your code in detail. Keep `print_r()` handy while coding because it is a great tool to re-examine the branch of a feed you are working with when you are having problems. I often like to keep a hard copy of a `print_r()` dump handy while playing with an XML document.

Doing a quick dump of the Yahoo! feed results in the following (some items have been shortened for space — the description tag for one, to fit on one line and the indenting has been modified):

```
SimpleXMLElement Object
(
 [channel] => SimpleXMLElement Object
 (
  [title] => Yahoo! News: Technology - Software
  [copyright] => Copyright (c) 2004 Yahoo! Inc. All rights reserved.
    [description] => Technology - Software
  [language] => en-us
  [lastBuildDate] => Fri, 26 Nov 2004 18:50:07 GMT
  [ttl] => 5
  [image] => SimpleXMLElement Object
  (
   [title] => Yahoo! News
   [width] => 142
   [height] => 18
      [url] => http://us.i1.yimg.com/us.yimg.com/i/us/nws/th/main_142.gif
  )
```

```
    [item] => Array
    (
     [0] => SimpleXMLElement Object
     (
      [title] => Recording Industry, File-Share Face Off (AP)
      [link] => http://us.rd.yahoo.com/dailynews/rss/software/*
        http://story.news.yahoo.com/news?tmpl=story2&u=/ap/20041126/
        ap_on_bi_ge/kazaa_trial
      [guid] => ap/20041126/kazaa_trial
      [pubDate] => Fri, 26 Nov 2004 18:50:07 GMT
      [description] => AP - The next chapter in the global legal battle between...
     )

     [1] => SimpleXMLElement Object
     (
      [title] => Britons Offered 'Real' Windows XP (AP)
          [guid] => ap/20041126/britain_microsoft_piracy
      [pubDate] => Fri, 26 Nov 2004 16:25:12 GMT
      [description] => AP - Owners of pirated copies of Microsoft Corp.'s Windows...
     )

     ...

     [49] => SimpleXMLElement Object
     (
      [title] => GPL 3 to Take on IP, Patents (Ziff Davis)
          [guid] => zd/20041122/139714
      [pubDate] => Mon, 22 Nov 2004 06:21:23 GMT
      [description] => Ziff Davis - With a relatively hostile environment that has...
     )
    )
   )
  )
```

Note that running `print_r()` *on a SimpleXML object will not reveal attributes, which are used in several places throughout feeds. If something seems to be missing, go back and look at the original source.*

Looking at the feed in this manner, it is obvious not only where loops belong (a `foreach` around the `item` tag would work perfectly), but what the syntax should be to access any element in particular (`$xml->item[0]->pubDate` to get the publication date of the most recently posted item).

As an additional piece of wisdom to make your life easier, I suggest you grab the feed once (I like to use `file_get_contents()` then `file_put_contents()` myself, to avoid any encoding "fun" taking it on and off my Windows box) and save it on your test server. There is simply no need to pester the source of the feed constantly while testing everything. In this instance, a copy of the feed was saved with the `file_` functions and as `yahoo.xml`.

Retrieving and Storing the Feed

This section looks at a more advanced script, which makes use of a database to store feeds. Obviously, the table used will need to reflect the structure of the feed.

A Basic Storage Script

First, you need to create a mysql table that will be populated with the information from the feed when the `aggregateFeeds.php` script is run:

```
  `id` varchar(32) NOT NULL default '',
  `source` varchar(75) NOT NULL default '',
  `title` varchar(255) NOT NULL default '',
  `date` timestamp(14) NOT NULL,
  `content` text NOT NULL,
  `link` varchar(255) NOT NULL default '',
  PRIMARY KEY  (`id`)
) TYPE=MyISAM;
```

The ID field will contain an MD5 hash, which is 32 hex characters long. The source field will contain the URL of the feed in question. Title, date, content, and link will all come from the feed:

```
<?php
  include ("../common_db.php");
  $request = "http://rss.news.yahoo.com/rss/software";
  $response = file_get_contents($request);
  $xml = simplexml_load_string($response);
  echo "Updated " . processRSSFeed($xml, $request) . " feeds";
```

The URL for the feed is declared and the feed is retrieved. The feed is then processed into the SimpleXML object. The feed is sent for processing, and the total number of feeds updated is printed (this script would most likely be run by a cron job, or other timed construct, so a detailed output isn't really required). Updating is done by a `processRSSFeed()` function, which looks like this:

```
function processRSSFeed($xml, $source)
{
  $updatedStories = 0;
  foreach($xml->channel->item AS $story)
  {
    if (saveFeed($story->guid, $source, $story->title, $story->pubDate,
      $story->description, $story->link) == 2)
    {
      break;
    }
    $updatedStories += 1;
  }
    return $updatedStories;
}
```

`ProcessRSSFeed()` takes the input RSS feed as a SimpleXML object, as well as the source URL of the feed provided. The `foreach` loop provides an easy method to access each element in the `item`; rather than `$xml->channel->item[#]->title`, you can simply use `$story->title`. Each story is saved in turn, and the output indicates whether this was an addition to the database or merely an update to one already present in the database. If the story was merely an update, you can stop processing other items because it is likely that they are already present. The function returns the total number of elements updated.

This method assumes that the feed is provided in reverse chronological order (as is the standard), with the most recent additions posted at the top. It also assumes that any updates to previous stories will be re-seeded at the top of the feed, rather than updated in their current position (a standard reporting practice is to report any corrections or updates in the same manner as the original story). Depending on how the feed you are consuming operates, you may want to process the entire feed regardless.

Finally, to actually save the feed to the database, use the following code:

```
function saveFeed($guid, $source, $title, $date, $content, $link)
{
  if (strlen($guid) > 0)
  {
    $pk = md5($source . $guid);
  }else
  {
    $pk = md5($source . $title);
  }
```

A primary key is generally a good idea when storing data into the database; in this case it is a good idea to create one of your own. GUID could be used—however, it isn't always provided, and although sites guarantee theirs to be unique on their own site, there are no claims of cross-site uniqueness (there are likely several home-brewed RSS feed providers out there with GUIDs starting at 1, incrementing as appropriate), so you prepend the source URL to the GUID. In cases of feeds that do not provide the GUID field, the title is used—date or link would be another good choice. In either case, the primary key is the MD5 (a one-way hashing algorithm that generates a key 32 hex characters long) of the resultant string:

```
  $linkID = db_connect();
  $title = mysql_real_escape_string(strip_tags($title));
  $content = mysql_real_escape_string(strip_tags($content));
  $link = mysql_real_escape_string($link);
  $source = mysql_real_escape_string($source);
```

A connection is established to the database, the strings are stripped of any HTML encoding, slashes are added to avoid SQL Injection attacks, and the variables are ready to be saved to the database.

It is considered a best practice to escape all data to be saved to the database with the database-specific function, rather than simply using `addslashes()`. This ensures that all characters that the specific database requires are escaped, rather than simply ', ", \, and NULL (`mysql_real_escape_string()` also escapes `\x00`, `\n`, `\r`, and `\x1a`). Other databases have similar functionality.

```
  $date = strtotime($date);
  if ($date == -1)
  {
    $date = date();
  }
```

To process the date, you rely on the `strtotime()` function. It will make every effort to interpret the date presented, and result in a date in the UNIX format. Although the RSS specification requires the date to be in a specific format (ISO 8601), using `strtotime()` is not only easier than writing your own function, but it also understands most other textual date formats. If, however, the format is not understood, or simply not there, the current date is used instead.

```
      $query = "REPLACE INTO 03_feed_raw
   (`id`, `source`, `title`, `date`, `content`, `link`)
   VALUES
   ('$pk', '$source', '$title', FROM_UNIXTIME('$date'), '$content', '$link')";
   return replaceQuery($query, $linkID);

}
?>
```

The `REPLACE INTO` syntax in MySQL is a real timesaver in this case, though it only works because you have a primary key. If the query is run, and no existing record has the same primary key, it will insert the record, and `mysql_affected_rows()` will return 1. If, however, a record exists with that primary key, it will be deleted, a new record will be created with the information in the query, and `mysql_affected_rows()` will return 2.

If your database system doesn't support a `REPLACE INTO` syntax (or MySQL's alternative `INSERT ... ON DUPLICATE KEY UPDATE`) or something to that effect, you still have a few choices. You can check for an existing record in each instance with a `SELECT` query, and create it if it doesn't exist. You could simply compare the most recent date in your database, and only insert queries from feed elements that came afterwards, and so on.

As mentioned earlier, this feed was designed to be called by a cron job, or other automated process (Windows Scheduled Tasks, for example). The `$request` variable could be turned into an array and iterated through to grab multiple feeds and so on.

Extending the Script to Include Atom Support

Extending the script to grab other feed types should be trivial. This function (in place of the preceding `processRSSFeed()` function) will grab the specified Atom feed and save it. This script was tested against the Google Blog (`www.google.com/googleblog/atom.xml`) where Google employees post on a semiregular basis.

Here is a snippet of Google's Blog for reference (trimmed for space):

```
<?xml version="1.0" encoding="UTF-8" standalone="yes"?>
<?xml-stylesheet href="http://www.blogger.com/styles/atom.css" type="text/css"?>
<feed xmlns="http://purl.org/atom/ns#" version="0.3" xml:lang="en-US">
  <link href="http://www.blogger.com/atom/10861780" rel="service.post"
title="Google Blog" type="application/atom+xml"/>
  <link href="http://www.blogger.com/atom/10861780" rel="service.feed"
title="Google Blog" type="application/atom+xml"/>
  <title mode="escaped" type="text/html">Google Blog</title>
  <tagline mode="escaped" type="text/html"></tagline>
  <link href="http://googleblog.blogspot.com" rel="alternate" title="Google Blog"
type="text/html"/>
  <id>tag:blogger.com,1999:blog-10861780</id>
  <modified>2005-06-16T21:33:27Z</modified>
  <generator url="http://www.blogger.com/" version="5.15">Blogger</generator>
  <info mode="xml" type="text/html">
    <div xmlns="http://www.w3.org/1999/xhtml">This is an Atom formatted XML site
feed. It is intended to be viewed in a Newsreader or syndicated to another site.
Please visit the <a href="http://help.blogger.com/bin/answer.py?answer=697">Blogger
Help</a> for more info.</div>
```

```
  </info>
   <entry xmlns="http://purl.org/atom/ns#">
     <link href="http://www.blogger.com/atom/10861780/111775901581356827"
rel="service.edit" title="Dot what?" type="application/atom+xml"/>
     <author>
       <name>A Googler</name>
     </author>
     <issued>2005-06-03T13:03:00-07:00</issued>
     <modified>2005-06-06T13:32:53Z</modified>
     <created>2005-06-03T00:36:55Z</created>
     <link href="http://googleblog.blogspot.com/2005/06/dot-what.html"
rel="alternate" title="Dot what?" type="text/html"/>
     <id>tag:blogger.com,1999:blog-10861780.post-111775901581356827</id>
     <title mode="escaped" type="text/html">Dot what?</title>
     <content mode="escaped" type="text/html"
xml:base="http://googleblog.blogspot.com" xml:space="preserve">&lt;span
class="byline-author"&gt;Posted by Tom Stocky, Product Marketing Manager
&lt;/span&gt;&lt;br /&gt;&lt;br /&gt;There's been a lot of talk lately about
ICANN's preliminary approval of some new top level Internet domains (.cat, .jobs,
.mobi, .post, .travel, and .xxx),...
<content>
  </entry>
</feed>
```

```
function processAtomFeed($xml, $source)
{
  $updatedStories = 0;
  foreach($xml->entry AS $story)
  {
    if (saveFeed($story->id, $source, $story->title, $story->issued,
      $story->content, $story->link) == 2)
    {
      break;
    }
    $updatedStories += 1;
  }
  return $updatedStories;
}
```

As you can tell, changing the script to allow different feed types to be retrieved is quite simple. Examine the feed in question, determine your needs, and modify the loop, database tables, whatever.

It may seem like a neat idea to have your script autodetect the encoding used in the specified feed (RSS versus Atom), but in the majority of cases, it isn't too useful. The frequency with which new feeds will be added for retrieval is generally low, so you might as well have the user specify the feed type. If you do require auto detection of feed type, do it once, when the feed is added to the retrieval list, rather than on each run of this script.

Retrieving Enclosures

The RSS specification includes the `enclosure` element, which is a subelement of `item`. It contains the `filesize`, `type`, and `URL` for a file attached to the `item` element. This would commonly be used to attach a song to a post by a band, or an image related to a specific post. Updating the `processRSSFeed()` function to retrieve and save the specified enclosure is also relatively painless.

```
function processRSSFeedWithEnclosure($xml, $source)
{
  $updatedStories = 0;
  $MaxSize = 1000000;
  foreach($xml->channel->item AS $story)
  {
    if (saveFeed($story->guid, $source, $story->title, $story->pubDate,
      $story->description, $story->link) == 2)
    {
      break;
    }else if (isset($story->enclosure['url']) && isset($story->enclosure['length'])
      && ($story->enclosure['length'] < $MaxSize))
    {
      $filename = basename($story->enclosure['url']);
      $file = file_get_contents($story->enclosure['url']);
      file_put_contents("/tmp/" . $filename, $file);
    }
    $updatedStories += 1;
  }
  return $updatedStories;
}
```

The check for an enclosure with the particular item is done after the save attempt for a couple reasons, primarily to avoid repeatedly downloading the same enclosure for an unchanged lead item. This also ensures that the file is downloaded again if the story is updated. The `if` portion of the `else if` statement is a little tricky:

```
if (isset($story->enclosure['url']) && isset($story->enclosure['length'])
      && ($story->enclosure['length'] < $MaxSize))
```

First, check for the existence of the `url` element of `enclosure` (note the different syntax for attributes), then the existence of the `length` attribute, and finally ensure that the `length` attribute indicates a file size less than the specified max size. This works because conditionals are checked in order — when one fails (in this case, with all AND operations), the rest are ignored.

Assuming that the enclosure exists and is of an appropriate size, it is downloaded with `file_get_contents()` and saved to disk. Depending on how the feed and enclosures are used, you will want to add at least one additional step, saving information on the enclosures to a separate table or to the same table, moving files somewhere "safer" on disk, running a virus scan, double-checking the encoding of the file, and so forth. You could also add additional logic to retrieve only certain file types (in other words, only images, or everything but `.pdf` files). As with anything, the possibilities are endless.

The file in this example was saved to `/tmp`*, and though this works great for an example, it is a bad idea in any real-world application. Save your files to a directory where only your web server has access, outside the document root. Have the files virus-scanned and moved elsewhere by a batch process called after all feeds have been updated.*

Dealing with XML Namespaces

Many feeds that you will encounter will likely include some form of XML namespacing; you can recognize namespaces by two elements within the document. First, within the declaration of the root element, as seen here for an RSS blog:

```
<rss version="2.0"
   xmlns:rdf="http://www.w3.org/1999/02/22-rdf-syntax-ns#"
   xmlns:admin="http://webns.net/mvcb/"
   xmlns:dc="http://purl.org/dc/elements/1.1/"
   xmlns:slash="http://purl.org/rss/1.0/modules/slash/"
   xmlns:wfw="http://wellformedweb.org/CommentAPI/"
   xmlns:content="http://purl.org/rss/1.0/modules/content/">
```

The document declares itself as RSS version 2.0, then proceeds to define each of the XML namespaces (XMLNS) that the document will make use of. In this sample, the namespaces are rdf, admin, dc, slash, wfw, and content, respectively (the portion after the colon).

You will also notice the namespacing within the document itself, because there will be elements containing a colon:

```
<dc:language>en</dc:language>
```

This is an element within the dc namespace named language, with content of en. This declares the language of the document to be English.

In order to interact with namespaced elements within the document, and through SimpleXML, the namespaces will need to be properly declared in the document and you will need to access it specifically with the children method. For example:

```
$dc = $xml->children("http://purl.org/dc/elements/1.1/");
$language = $dc->language
```

The first line extracts all of the dc namespaced children of the root node, and the second line accesses the language element.

Further Securing Your Feeds

In the previous examples, all recorded data was completely cleaned by replacing all HTML entities (such as < and >) with their encoded counterparts (such as > and <, respectively), thus ensuring that any inline HTML is displayed to the end user, rather than interpreted by the user agent. Taking some action is imperative, because every cross-site scripting (XSS) attack that can be performed via data entry on a form can also be performed by simply providing a feed to be consumed.

Link Utility Functions

These functions will come in useful for handling tags that contain links, which may need to be rewritten entirely or modified slightly to be contained within your feed.

Strip URLs of Filenames

Retrieving the path using parse_url() makes it easy to obtain the path and filename portion; however, splitting the filename off to retrieve only the path component isn't quite as easy. At first glance the dirname() function seems appropriate because it accomplishes basically the same task. However, it assumes that the last portion of the string is a filename, unless it contains a trailing slash, which doesn't generally hold true for URLs:

```
    function getPathOnly($path)
    {
      if(substr($path, -1, 1) == "/")
      {
        return $path;
```

If the path in question ends with a forward slash, there is no filename present and the path may be returned as is:

```
      }else
      {
        $pathComponents = explode("/", $path);
        $count = count($pathComponents);
        $last = $pathComponents[$count - 1];
        if (substr_count($last, ".") > 0)
        {
           array_pop($pathComponents);
        }
```

Explode the path using the forward slash into an array, and check the last element of the array (and hence the path). If it contains a period, assume it is a filename and pop it off the array to remove it. If no period is found, assume it is a directory and leave the last element as is:

```
        $final = implode("/", $pathComponents);
        return $final . "/";
      }
    }
```

Put the path back together using the forward slash as glue, and finally, append a forward slash to the end to return a properly formatted path.

Combine URLs

Many bloggers only consider their own website when blogging, not their feed and how it might be used. As such, you will occasionally see relative URLs used in images, or anchor links found in a feed. Obviously, when presenting the feed to users on your site these links won't work, which is far from desired. What to do? Ideally, you somehow need to be able to replace the relative URLs with an absolute URL, which should allow your aggregator to retrieve the images just fine.

The following function takes two URLs, the URL from which the feed was retrieved and the URL found in the content of the feed, and returns an absolute URL. This absolute URL may just be the URL found within the content of the feed, or some work may be done to interpret the link:

```
    function relativeToAbsolute($sourceURL, $link)
    {
     $sup = parse_url($sourceURL);
```

`relativeToAbsolute()` is called with the source URL and the link in question. The source URL is then divided into parts with `parse_url()`. The source URL needs to be worked with because it may include a script name (such as `http://example.org/feed.php`) or even query elements (`http://example.org/feed.php?format=rss&sort=desc`), which need to be removed. This is where the previous function comes in.

```
if (!isset($sup['scheme']))
{
 $sourceURL = "http://" . $sourceURL;
 $sup = parse_url($sourceURL);
}
```

If the source URL didn't contain a scheme (`ftp://`, `http://`, `https://`), prepend the http scheme and re-parse the URL. This needs to be done because running `parse_url()` on URLs without a scheme yields undesirable results:

```
$sourceURL = $sup['scheme'] . "://" . $sup['host'] . getPathOnly($sup['path']);
```

Using the scheme and host from `parse_url`, combined with the path run through the previous function, should result in a nice clean URL to work with, with a trailing slash.

```
$start = substr($link, 0, 1);
```

The first character of the passed link will be used a few times, so it is saved.

```
if($start == '.')
{
 if (substr($link, 0, 2) == "./")
 {
    $final = $sourceURL . substr($link, 2);
```

If the link starts with a period, and indeed starts with period slash, the absolute URL for the link in question is simply the source URL, followed by the link (period and slash removed).

```
 }else if (substr($link, 0, 3) == "../")
 {
   $sup = parse_url($sourceURL);
   $pathParts = explode("/", $sup['path']);
   array_pop($pathParts);
   while ((substr($link, 0, 3) == "../") & (count($pathParts) > 0))
   {
     $x = array_pop($pathParts);
     $link = substr($link, 3);
   }
    $final =  $sup['scheme'] . "://" . $sup['host'] . implode("/", $pathParts) "/"
      . $link;
```

If the link starts with `../` the source URL must be traversed upwards, the source URL is again parsed into its parts, and the path is exploded into an array. `array_pop()` is used to remove the last element of the array (the leading and trailing slashes in the path result in the first and last array elements being empty; this doesn't matter when the `implode()` function is called, but it comes into play when a content filled element must be removed from the end). By placing the logic to traverse the path one directory up, and removing the `../` from the link in a loop, relative links such as `../../logo.png` can be processed.

```
 }else
 {
   $final = $sourceURL . $link;
 }
```

If the link begins with a period, but not ./ or ../, it is assumed that the period is merely part of the filename, and the final URL is created as such.

```
  }else if ($start == "/")
  {
   $final =  $sup['scheme'] . "://" . $sup['host'] . $link;
```

If the link begins with a leading slash (/), the final URL is simply the scheme, the host, and the link appended together. In this case the leading slash in the link is needed.

```
  }else if (substr_count($link, "/") == 0)
  {
   $final = $sourceURL . $link;
```

If the link contains zero forward slashes, it is assumed to be the filename (for example, logo.png), and the final URL can be created merely by appending the link to the source URL.

```
  }else
  {
   $final = $link;
  }

  return $final;
}
```

Finally, if none of the other situations has been appropriate, the link is assumed to be complete on its own and is not touched, and the resultant string from whatever operation was performed is returned.

Image Tags

The image tag is often considered rather benign and thus safe to allow through and shown to the end user, but this couldn't be further from the truth. The request that a browser generates when you click a link is identical to the request it generates when it attempts to load an image for you. Consider the following HTML document:

```
<html>
<head>
<title>Example Page</title>
</head>
<body>
<img src="http://www.google.ca/search?q=Paul+Reinheimer">
<a href="http://www.google.ca/search?q=Paul+Reinheimer">Search Again!</a>
</body>
</html>
```

When the document is loaded, my browser generates the following request:

```
GET /consume/security.html HTTP/1.1
Host: example.preinheimer.com
User-Agent: Mozilla/5.0 (Windows; U; Windows NT 5.1; en-US; rv:1.7.5)
Gecko/20041107 Firefox/1.0
```

```
Accept:
text/xml,application/xml,application/xhtml+xml,text/html;q=0.9,text/plain;q=0.8,ima
ge/png,*/*;q=0.5
Accept-Language: en-us,en;q=0.5
Accept-Encoding: gzip,deflate
Accept-Charset: ISO-8859-1,utf-8;q=0.7,*;q=0.7
Keep-Alive: 300
Connection: keep-alive
```

Then, immediately thereafter (without clicking anything), it generates this request:

```
GET /search?q=Paul+Reinheimer HTTP/1.1
Host: www.google.ca
User-Agent: Mozilla/5.0 (Windows; U; Windows NT 5.1; en-US; rv:1.7.5)
Gecko/20041107 Firefox/1.0
Accept: image/png,*/*;q=0.5
Accept-Language: en-us,en;q=0.5
Accept-Encoding: gzip,deflate
Accept-Charset: ISO-8859-1,utf-8;q=0.7,*;q=0.7
Keep-Alive: 300
Connection: keep-alive
Referer: http://example.preinheimer.com/consume/security.html
```

Clicking the link on the page generates this request, and the Google search results page loads:

```
GET /search?q=Paul+Reinheimer HTTP/1.1
Host: www.google.ca
User-Agent: Mozilla/5.0 (Windows; U; Windows NT 5.1; en-US; rv:1.7.5)
Gecko/20041107 Firefox/1.0
Accept:
text/xml,application/xml,application/xhtml+xml,text/html;q=0.9,text/plain;q=0.8,ima
ge/png,*/*;q=0.5
Accept-Language: en-us,en;q=0.5
Accept-Encoding: gzip,deflate
Accept-Charset: ISO-8859-1,utf-8;q=0.7,*;q=0.7
Keep-Alive: 300
Connection: keep-alive
Referer: http://example.preinheimer.com/consume/security.html
```

The only difference is in the `Accept` line. The request generated by the image tag indicates that it is expecting a png, but will also accept anything else (`*/*`). As far as Google is concerned, the first request is no different from the second, and as such, will respond to both requests the same (by sending the search results page). In this case, nothing really happened. Requesting search results is pretty benign (though in some corporate environments, sending out search requests on, shall we say, more colorful topics may get someone in trouble), however the same technique could be used in hundreds of other places.

For example:

```
<img src="http://my.stockbroker.com/buyshares?ticker=SCO&lot=2000">
```

The user's browser makes a request to a stockbroker, purchasing 2,000 shares of SCO—a charitable activity, but not one someone is likely to want to engage in while reading your feed aggregation site.

```
<img src="http://www.amazon.com/oneclickbuy?isbn=0764589547&number=10">
```

A more useful image tag, this one orders multiple copies of this book from Amazon.

```
<img src="http://my.florist.com/sendflowers?product=deluxe&address=home&from=Liz">
```

Finally, this image tag orders flowers to be sent to one's home, from Liz—not terrible, unless your significant other sees these and her name isn't Liz."

All of these URLs are completely fictional, and are merely presented to try and make clear the dangers presented by these normally ignored tags.

These attacks may seem humorous, but they are a lot closer to reality than you might think. "Advances" such as remembering login information and single-click purchases are quite convenient, but are what allow attacks like these to take place. The original architects of the HTML specification considered this (and things like this) and as such, `GET` requests are to be considered "safe," in that they should not generate any lasting action. Lasting actions, such as purchasing shares, ordering books or flowers, and such should be done with `POST` requests, which cannot be created with the same ease.

Many developers and development teams ignore these safety precautions, however, and allow "unsafe" transactions to occur over `GET` requests. Some of these vulnerabilities may stem from improper use of constructs such as `$_REQUEST` in PHP, which allows developers to easily access passed information from either request type. The problem is, however, that it doesn't specify from which request type the information came. It is usually safer to explicitly use either `$_GET` or `$_POST` for this reason.

In the majority of circumstances I feel it is often permissible to strip all image tags from a given feed, and provide either a link to the images (URL shown) or just simply a link back to the original source. However, you may disagree. The next few sections discuss a few of the available options.

Retrieve All of the Image Links within a String

Retrieving all of the image links within the string (feed) isn't too difficult, with some regular expression (regex) fun. The following expression can be used to process HTML image tags, and it is also used, in this case, to take the opportunity to provide a crash course in regular expressions:

```
$processedFeed = preg_replace('/<img\s+.*?src="([^\"\'
>]*)"\s?(width="([0-9]*)")?\s?(height="([0-9]*)")?[^>]*>/ie',
            "cleanImage('$sourceURL', '\\0','\\1','\\2','\\3','\\4', '\\5\)",
            $feed);
```

The function `preg_replace()` will perform a regex search and replace on the given string. The form is `preg_replace(pattern, replacement, subject, [limit])`. So the pattern for this regex is as follows:

```
/<img\s+.*?src="([^\"\' >]*)"\s?(width="([0-9]*)")?\s(height="([0-9]*)")?[^>]*>/ie
```

The first forward slash and last forward slash are the delimiters, setting the left and right limits of the pattern. The last `ie` indicates that this should be a case-insensitive match, and that the compiler should execute the `replacement` as PHP, so you can call a function (in this case, `cleanImage()`).

This regex pattern uses several special characters, as outlined in the following table.

Character	Meaning
`\s`	This matches white space, like spaces or tabs.
`.`	This matches any single character except line breaks.
`*`	This applies to the previous character. It may be repeated 0 or more times.
`?`	This applies to the previous character. It may be present 0 or 1 times.
`+`	This applies to the previous item. It may be present 1 or more times.
`()`	This groups a segment of the pattern together. This affects what is returned, and can be used to mark a portion of the expression as optional, repeating, and so on.
`[]`	The contents define a character class. [0-9] will match any digit from zero to nine, [a-zA-Z0-9] will match any single lowercase letter, uppercase letter, or digit, and [a-zA-Z0-9] will match any number of them.
`^`	This is when the first character of a character class negates anything within the class, so [^0-9] will match anything that is not a number.

So, with this newfound knowledge in mind, you can examine the pattern:

- `<img\s+.*?` — This seeks out `<img`, followed by white space (there must be at least one white space character, followed optionally by any other character any number of times).
- `src="([^\"\' >]*)"\s?` — This seeks out the source portion of the tag. `src=""` is sought, with anything but a single or double quote or a right caret, repeated zero or more times. All of that can optionally be followed by white space.
- `(width="([0-9]*)")?\s?` — This seeks out an optional width parameter, in which any number of digits are sought. The width parameter should be followed optionally by white space characters.
- `(height="([0-9]*)")?` — This seeks out an optional height parameter in the same manner.
- `[^>]*>` — This matches anything but a right caret any number of times, followed by the right caret to close the image tag.

This regex pattern will return up to six separate items, the entire match, followed by whatever matched inside each set of parentheses. Running the regex on the following string:

```
Hi <img src="./logo.png" width="23" height="66"> Logo
```

results in the following:

```
0 <img src=\"./logo.png\" width=\"23\" height=\"66\">
1 ./logo.png
2 width=\"23\"
3 23
4 height=\"66\"
5 66
```

Each of those six returned elements are passed to the `cleanImage()` function, as well as `$sourceURL` (which is another variable not related to the regex expression). Whatever `cleanImage()` returns will be put in place of the entire match.

```
function cleanImage($sourceURL, $entireMatch, $link, $widthE, $w, $heightE, $h)
{
   $link = relativeToAbsolute($sourceURL, $link);
   return "<img src=\"$link\" height=\"$h\" width=\"$w\">";
}
```

While the function initially doesn't seem to do much, because it merely replaces one properly formatted image tag with another, consider the following image tag:

```
<img src="./logo.png" width="178" height="60" border="0" alt="Logo"
onClick="window.alert('Click');">
```

If a string containing that image tag was run through this function, the JavaScript (remember, other more malicious code could just as easily take its place) would be stripped, as would the `border` and `alt` tags, and the `src` attribute would be set to the absolute URL, based on the URL the feed was received from.

This brief introduction to regex should be sufficient for the following examples to make sense. For a more in-depth look at regex (the more you learn about regex the more powerful it becomes and the more you want to learn), take a look at this excellent tutorial online: `www.regular-expressions.info/tutorial.html`.

Replace Images with Links

Replacing inline images with links to the image in question is trivial with the previous example:

```
function replaceImages($sourceURL, $entireMatch, $link, $widthE, $w, $heightE, $h)
{
   $link = relativeToAbsolute($sourceURL, $link);
   return "<a href=\"$link\" title=\"Inline Image\">(image)</a>";
}
```

Pro

Lessened XSS vulnerability.

Cons

Removing images may destroy the layout of the text.

Images very pertinent to the story aren't immediately available.

Retrieve and Serve the Image in Question

Upon aggregation of any feed, the content is examined for embedded `<img>` tags. When found, the images in question are retrieved and saved on the server, and the image tags are rewritten to point to the new local location:

```
function retrieveImages($sourceURL, $entireMatch, $link, $widthE, $w, $heightE, $h)
{
  $localSavePath = "/www/domains/feedimages.preinheimer.com/";
  $localImageURL = "http://feedimages.preinheimer.com/";
```

The destination path for retrieved images, as well as the eventual URL for those images, is specified.

```
  $link = relativeToAbsolute($sourceURL, $link);
  $image = file_get_contents($link);
```

An absolute URL for the image is created (or merely confirmed) and the image is retrieved.

```
  $filename = md5($link);
  $filepath = $localSavePath . $filename;
```

A unique filename for the file is generated; if the remote filename was used (and feeds from multiple locations were aggregated), collisions would be likely. This also saves you from any sort of filename filtering — the MD5 string will be safe. The file is saved to the specified directory.

```
  file_put_contents($filepath, $image);
  $image = null;
  @list($lwidth, $lheight, $ltype, $lattr) = getimagesize($filepath);
```

The image is saved to disk, and the variable that contained the image is destroyed because it is no longer needed. Variables with information regarding the image are populated with `getimagesize()`.

```
 if ($lwidth * $lheight == 0)
 {
   return "";
```

If either the width or height specified by `getimagesize()` is not present, the image is invalid (as would be the case in a cross-site scripting attack) and an empty string is returned. This effectively removes the image tag from the feed.

```
 }else
 {
  if ($w < 1)
  {
    $w = $lwidth;
  }
  if ($h < 1)
  {
    $h = $lheight;
  }
  return "<img src=\"" . $localImageURL . $filename . "\" width=\"$w\"
height=\"$h\" alt=\"Original Source: $link\">";
 }
```

If either the width or height variable is not present in the original feed, it is set to the correct value from `getimagesize()`. This should help speed page loads for users, because their browsers can make intelligent decisions about page layout. The correct height and width variables are simply not used, because many people still use the height and width tags to stretch images (either smaller or larger), even though there are far more effective alternatives. The `alt` tag is set to the original full URL of the image in question, giving credit where credit is due.

Pros

No XSS vulnerabilities.

Predictable image availability.

Images will show even for users who have instructed their browser not to load images from external sources.

Some sites block remote image loads when they are noticed.

Cons

There could be copyright issues. The owner of the image may not take kindly to your display of it outside its original source (this person may or may not be the one providing the feed).

You may find you end up with images of questionable moral values. Depending on the content of the image, you or your users may not desire to have it hosted or displayed on your site.

Some methods employed to prevent cross-site image linking may also prevent your script from retrieving the image in question, though it is quite likely that your users would have been able to load the image themselves if this is the case.

Retrieve Image Once, and Confirm It Is an Image

Download the image once to the server (when the feed is aggregated) and use a tool such as imagemagik to examine the image. If it loads properly, it is likely safe to assume that it is not in fact an XSS attack.

Updating the previous script to point to the original URL and deleting the local file are trivial.

```
unlink($filepath);
return "<img src=\"" . $link . "\" width=\"$w\" height=\"$h\">";
```

`unlink()` is PHP's delete function, which removes the file in question, and returns the correct (absolute) image source. Note that this will still remove broken image links from feeds, and will set correct width and height values if they are not present.

Pros

Lessened XSS vulnerability.

Images don't have to be served locally (no bandwidth usage, fewer copyright concerns).

Con

Attacker could merely examine request headers for the image to see if it comes from a known aggregator (or doesn't specify a user agent, or a referrer, like an automated download might do) and return an image. If not, do a header re-direct to the targeted XSS site. This is definitely more complicated, but not outside the realm of possibility.

Link Tags

Allowing use of the `<a href>` tags will probably be required for any major aggregation, because the links themselves may often provide as much "content" as the rest of the feed. There are a few things to consider when allowing these tags to be used.

First, consider the following HTML snippet:

```
<a href="home.php" onclick="window.open(this.href, 'home',
'width=480,height=480,scrollbars=yes'); return false;">Comments (0)</a>
```

The JavaScript possibilities within a link tag are endless. In short, you don't want them.

Second, titles can be misleading. Just because a link says it points somewhere doesn't mean it does. Consider this:

```
... Today we got a new puppy <a href="http://www.playboy.com">rover</a> he is cute!
```

Nothing tragic; the user merely ends up at a site different from the one they expected, but keep in mind the URL doesn't have to be that benign. Consider the example URLs provided in the image example. Yes, in this case the user would be aware that shares were purchased, books or flowers were ordered, or whatever, but in many cases canceling such transactions has repercussions (stock trades), or may in fact be impossible (some forum packages do not allow retraction of posts).

Although your technical users likely glance at the URL shown in the status bar of their browser before clicking on a link (and thus immunizing themselves against such an attack), the less technically minded rarely do, and as such, these things should be considered.

The regex pattern used to pull links out of the feed is quite similar to the one used for images.

```
$teststring = preg_replace('/<a\s+.*?href=[\"\']?([^\"\'
  >]*)[\"\']?\s?(title=[\"\']?([^\"\'>]*)[\"\']?)?[^>]*>(.*?)<\/a>/ie',
              "cleanHREF('$sourceURL', '\\1', '\\3', '\\4')",
              $teststring);
```

The returns for this regex are as follows:

0 – Entire match
1 – URL in question
2 – Title match
3 – Title in itself
4 – The name for the link

Note that this regex is a little more flexible than the previous example. Rather than specifying that double quotes must encase all of the variables, `[\"\']?` is used, which allows either type of quote to be used, or none at all.

While writing the examples for this book, "The Regex Coach" was a great tool. It shows the results to specific regex patterns against given text, highlights specific returns, and so on. If you are going to be using regex for long, I would recommend using this free tool.

The corresponding function returns the cleaned link:

```
function cleanHREF($sourceURL, $link, $title, $name)
{
    $link = relativeToAbsolute($sourceURL, $link);
    return "<a href=\"$link\" title=\"$title\">$name</a>";
}
```

To deal with the possible issue of a misleading title, a small substitution can be made:

```
function cleanAndDisplayHREF($sourceURL, $link, $title, $name)
{
    $link = relativeToAbsolute($sourceURL, $link);
    return "<a href=\"$link\" title=\"$title\">$name</a> ($link)";
}
```

Although these methods effectively deal with additional JavaScript elements that may be added to the tag, JavaScript can also be added to the `href` attribute. There are a few options to deal with this possibility.

IFrames

It really seems like the concepts of IFrames and feed syndication are in opposition to each other. A feed seeks to present all of the relevant information cohesively in one spot, whereas an IFrame functions to reference external information and present it internally. When presented with an IFrame in a feed to be consumed, you have a few attractive options:

1. Strip the IFrame. IFrames were designed with backward compatibility in mind, so they should include content between the frame tags that can be substituted when the IFrame itself is not loaded.
2. Retrieve the content of the IFrame and display it inline.
3. Provide a link to the content in question.

Fortunately, IFrames in feeds remain quite rare. If you notice that one of the feeds you are consuming is using the IFrame tag, the previous examples should be easily modified to meet your needs.

Formatting Tags

Formatting tags include `h1`, `h2`, `. . .`, `h5`, `p`, `b`, `i`, and so on.

These tags in themselves rarely present any security risk. A best practice would be to use html_entities() on the feed, then use str_replace() on the feed to replace the entities with allowed strings. For example, take the following string:

```
<h1>Hi!</h1> my name is <b>paul</b>
```

Run htmlentities() on it, and you receive this:

```
&lt;h1&gt;Hi!&lt;/h1&gt; my name is &lt;b&gt;paul&lt;/b&gt;
```

Use str_replace() to replace <b> and </b> with <b> and </b>, respectively, and you have this:

```
&lt;h1&gt;Hi!&lt;/h1&gt; my name is <b>paul</b>
```

The allowed tags make it through, and the other ones just get left behind.

That concludes the section on how you can increase the security of your feeds. Of course, doing things like ensuring the feed provider is a legitimate business, that the feeds are administered, or that they are simply well-known names can go a long way to ensuring you avoid the snares and pitfalls of using external content. Alas, security is not the only thing you need to worry about when obtaining information from other people or sites. Look at another consideration.

Dealing with Broken HTML

Like it or not, someone is going to send you broken HTML at some point, and unless you decided to strip all HTML tags from the feeds, this is going to adversely affect your site. Luckily PHP and HTML Tidy make a great pair, and make dealing with broken HTML a breeze.

There are two versions of Tidy: 1.0 and 2.0. Version 1.0 is used with the 4.3.x tree of PHP, and the 2.0 release is used with the 5.x tree. You can check to see if you have Tidy installed with your version of PHP with the phpinfo() command. You should be able to locate a "tidy" section in the output if it is present.

Installing Tidy

Assuming you don't already have it, installing Tidy under PHP4 should be pretty easy. If your system includes pear, you can download the pecl package with one command (from a suitable account):

```
pear -v install tidy
```

Failing that, you will need to download the package directly from the pecl repository at http://pecl.php.net/package/tidy.

Tidy support is built into PHP5. It just needs to be enabled either at compile time or runtime, depending on the host operating system. Getting Tidy to run just involves that you uncomment the following line in your php.ini file:

```
extension=php_tidy.dll
```

Then restart your web server for the changes to take effect. You can confirm that Tidy is present by checking the output of `phpinfo()`.

Installing Tidy on a Linux system will require that you (or your host) recompile PHP to include Tidy. This can be done with the `-with-tidy` configure option. Don't just type `./configure -with-tidy` to get it to work, because chances are that several other configure options are already present, and doing this will lose them. The `phpinfo()` command will display your current configure options — use this as a base and add `-with-tidy` to it.

If tidylib is not installed on the machine in question (you will know because the configure returns an error telling you so), you will need to download and install tidylib. You can get tidylib from `http://tidy.sourceforge.net/`. Grab the source package, not the compiled binary (it won't have the libraries PHP will need). Build from the source package as you normally would. Then reconfigure php and install. Finally, restart your web server for the changes to take effect.

Cleaning Broken HTML

Take the following sample output:

```
<html>
<head>
<title>This is a horrible page</title>
<body>
<h1>This is a broken snippet
<p>Notice the poor use of tags, leaving tags open, links left
<a href="open.html">open
<p>All in all, this is a horrible piece of <b>code!
</html>
```

Although it is unlikely that anyone will ever provide you with a piece of code quite that bad, you need to be prepared for tags to be left open at the termination of the feed. Viewing that in a browser yields a broken HTML sample, as shown in Figure 3-2.

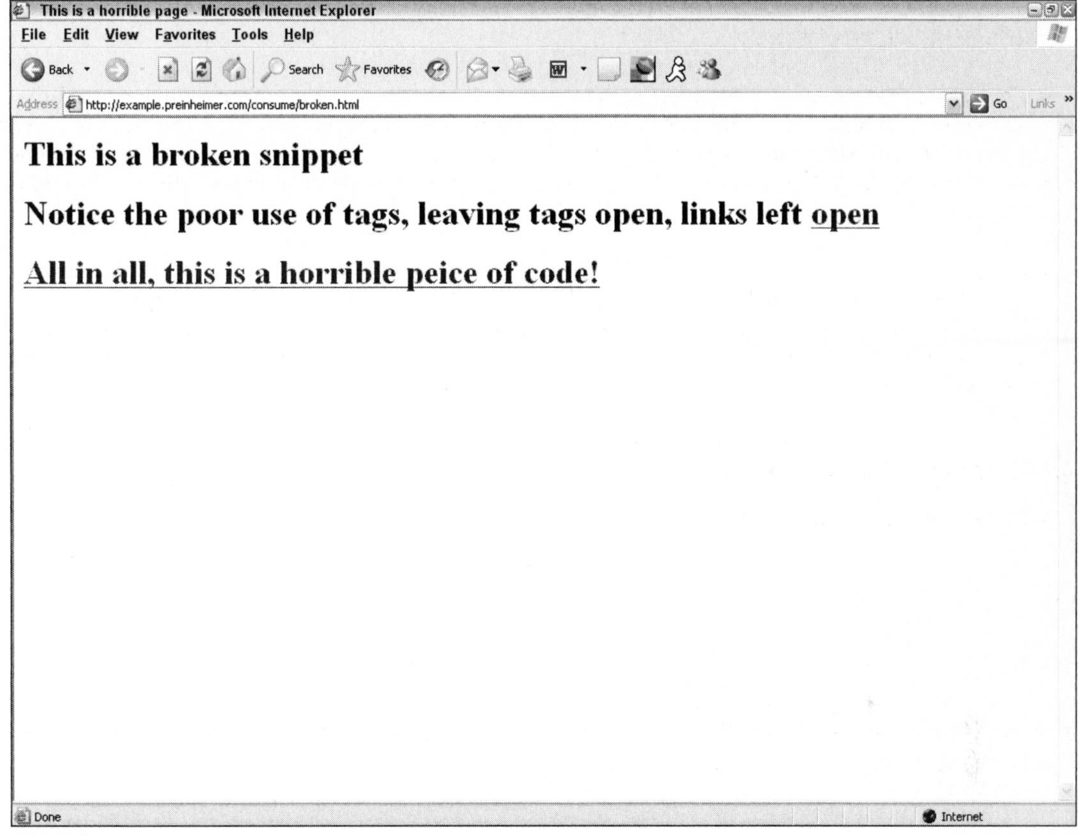

Figure 3-2

Giving it a quick run through HTML, Tidy results in the following code:

```
<!DOCTYPE html PUBLIC "-//W3C//DTD HTML 3.2//EN">
<html>
  <head>
    <title>
      This is a horrible page
    </title>
  </head>
  <body>
    <h1>
      This is a broken snippet
    </h1>
    <p>
      Notice the poor use of tags, leaving tags open, links left <a
href="open.html">open</a>
    </p>
    <p>
      All in all, this is a horrible piece of <b>code!</b>
    </p>
  </body>
</html>
```

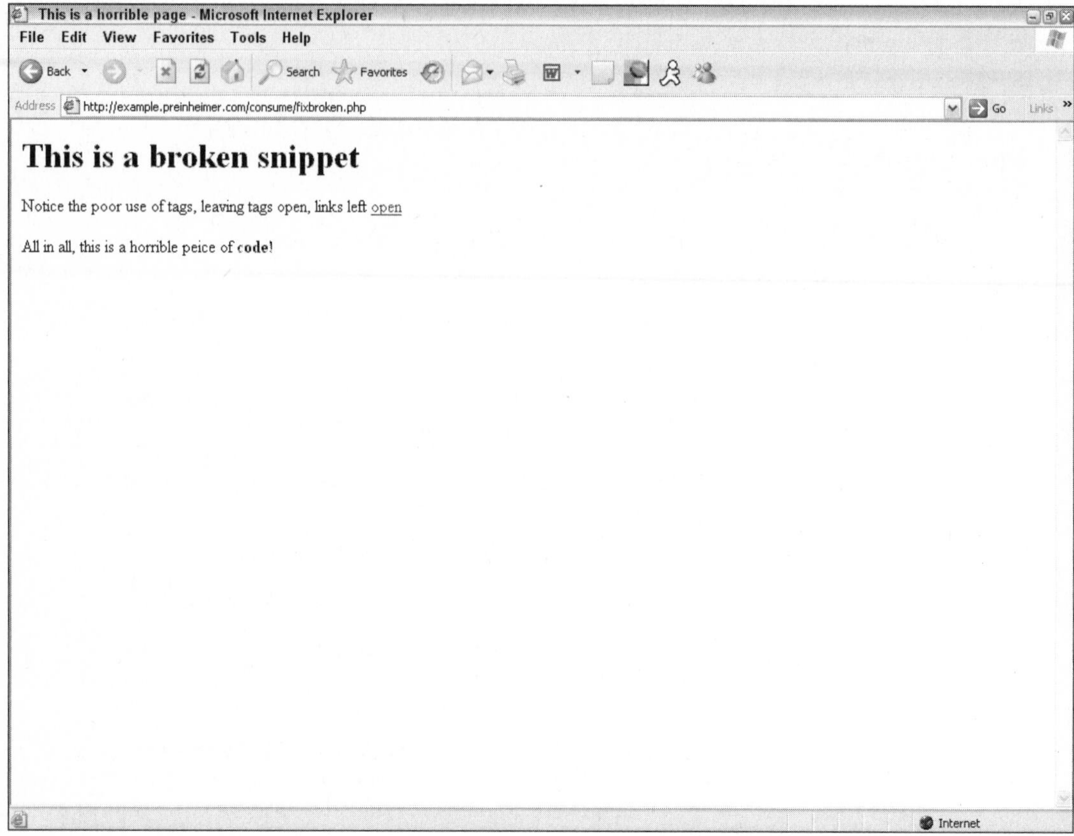

Figure 3-3

The code involved was as follows:

```
$brokenHTML = file_get_contents('./broken.html');
$config = array('indent' => TRUE,
                'output-html' => TRUE,
                'wrap' => 200,
                'clean' => TRUE);
$tidy = tidy_parse_string($brokenHTML, $config, 'UTF8');
tidy_clean_repair($tidy);
echo tidy_get_output($tidy);
```

The broken HTML page is loaded into the appropriate variable, and then a few configuration options are set (this is covered in greater detail in a moment). The broken HTML is given to Tidy to be parsed, along with the configuration options and desired output. Finally, Tidy is asked to clean and repair the document in question and output the result. These few simple steps can save major headaches down the road when your site design is thrown out the window by a few unclosed tags floating around your displayed feeds (see Figure 3-3).

The configuration options available are quite expansive; one of particular interest when dealing with feeds is `show-body-only`. Using that option against the earlier example would yield the following:

```
<h1>
  This is a broken snippet
</h1>
<p>
  Notice the poor use of tags, leaving tags open, links left <a
href="open.html">open</a>
</p>
<p>
  All in all, this is a horrible piece of <b>code!</b>
</p>
```

This would obviously be necessary or there would be one HTML document declared for every feed shown on your page. Configuration options of particular note are shown in the following table.

Option	Action
`Output-html`	This option specifies that the output should be presented as HTML, in contrast to the following two options.
`Output-xml`	This option specifies that output should be XML.
`Output-xhtml`	This option specifies that output should be XHTML.
`Wrap`	This specifies the maximum line length before Tidy will line-wrap to the next line. A good thing to keep in mind for consistency among the code generated by your site.
`Clean`	This option instructs Tidy to strip out surplus presentation tags (think about the code generated by nearly every automated tool out there) and attributes, replacing them with style rules or structural markup as required.
`Hide-comments`	Specifies whether Tidy should print out comments.
`Css-prefix`	This is the prefix Tidy will use for all of its css classes. Keep in mind the css classes used in the rest of your site to avoid conflict.
`Drop-empty-paras`	This option specifies whether empty paragraphs should be dropped entirely or replaced with ` ` tags. The HTML 4 specification does not allow for empty paragraph tags.
`Enclose-text`	Tells Tidy to enclose any text in the body within a `<p>` element. Useful if you want all text to be enclosed for css reasons.
`Fix-backslash`	Defaults to yes, but tells Tidy to replace backslashes in URLs with forward slashes. Internet Explorer generally allows either, while backslashes confuse everything else (and rightly so).
`Indent`	Instructs Tidy to properly indent the code; helps keep it all readable.
`Show-errors`	Whether or not Tidy should display errors with the output.
`Show-warnings -`	`Whether warnings should be displayed.`

Table continued on following page

Error-file	By default errors go to stderr; use this option to have them saved to a file.
Force-output	With this option you can force Tidy to give some output in all circumstances. This is not recommended, however, because the attempts that may be made in order to give some output may result in a very odd-looking result.

Generally I am a large proponent of storing all data in a state as close to its original or provided state as possible, then doing any necessary modifications at page time. This allows changes to formatting preferences and the like as needed. In this case, however, as a concession to performance issues, I would recommend dealing with proper formatting of consumed feeds at the time of consumption. If you do want to record the original form of the data (escaping it for safe SQL entry, of course), do it in a separate table.

Putting It All Together

Using the aforementioned methods, this section illustrates a cohesive method of retrieving and recording a foreign feed. In this case the script was run against several RSS-based blog feeds. After examining these feeds, it was noted that they did not provide a description element as the earlier Yahoo! samples did, so the `content:encoded` element was used in its place:

```
function processRSSFeed($xml, $source)
{
  $updatedStories = 0;
  foreach($xml->channel->item AS $story)
  {
    $content = $story->children( "http://purl.org/rss/1.0/modules/content/" );
    $storyContent = $content->encoded;
```

In this case, the `content:encoded` element is needed, so the namespace is accessed directly.

```
    if (saveFeed($story->guid, $source, $story->title, $story->pubDate,
$storyContent, $story->link) == 2)
    {
      break;
    }
    $updatedStories += 1;
  }
  return $updatedStories;
}
```

As you can tell, there haven't been many changes to the `processRSSFeed` function.

```
function saveFeed($guid, $source, $title, $date, $content, $link)
{
  if (strlen($guid) > 0)
  {
    $pk = md5($source . $guid);
  }else
```

```
    {
      $pk = md5($source . $title);
    }
```

The big plus with the use of MD5 (or any other hashing algorithm, for that matter) is that no matter what the input is, you are guaranteed a predictable length and a predictable content string as output, so this is one case where no changes are needed.

```
    $linkID = db_connect();
    //We still don't want any HTML tags in the title of the item
    $title = mysql_real_escape_string(strip_tags($title));

    //Clean broken HTML first, to avoid problems with other steps
    $config = array('indent' => TRUE,
               'output-html' => TRUE,
               'wrap' => 200,
               'clean' => TRUE,
               'show-body-only' => TRUE);
      $tidy = tidy_parse_string($content, $config, 'UTF8');
      tidy_clean_repair($tidy);
      $content = tidy_get_output($tidy);
```

You want HTML output, wrapped at 200 lines, cleaned up, and you only want what would be contained within the body element, rather than an entire page.

```
      //Confirm HTML links are absolute, and append the url to the link
      $content =
  preg_replace('/<a\s+.*?href=[\"\']?([^\"\'>]*)[\"\']?\s?(title=[\"\']?([^\"\'>]*)[\
"\']?)?[^>]*>(.*?)<\/a>/ie',
               "cleanAndDisplayHREF('$source', '\\1', '\\3', '\\4')",
               $content);

      //Display images as images, but load from local server
      $content = preg_replace('/<img\s+.*?src="([^\"\'
>]*)"\s?(width="([0-9]*)")?\s?(height="([0-9]*)")?[^>]*>/ie',
               "retrieveImages('$source', '\\0','\\1','\\2','\\3','\\4', '\\5')",
               $content);

      $content = mysql_real_escape_string(strip_tags($content, "<p><img><a>"));
```

Deal with any and all links or images within the provided text, then strip out any HTML tags that aren't images, links, or paragraph markers. It is strongly advisable to take a strict whitelist approach to which tags you want to allow, especially if the content will appear nested within other items. Having a first-level header appear in the middle of what should be smooth text can ruin your day and your page layout.

```
      $link = mysql_real_escape_string($link);
      $source = mysql_real_escape_string($source);

      $date = strtotime($date);
      if ($date == -1)
      {
```

```
      $date = time();
    }

    $query = "REPLACE INTO 03_feed_raw
    (`id`, `source`, `title`, `date`, `content`, `link`)
    VALUES
    ('$pk', '$source', '$title', FROM_UNIXTIME('$date'), '$content', '$link')";
    return replaceQuery($query, $linkID);
  }
```

Finally, using the escaped link and source information, along with the now properly formatted date, the information is replaced in the database for future use.

Using Your Recorded Feeds

The feeds have been found, cleaned, and prepared, then recorded. Now comes the time to use these feeds. The options are nearly endless; the goal here is merely to present a few attractive options.

Email Mailing List

Although having target individuals use feed aggregators themselves is the common practice, it may not always be appropriate. Many corporate environments maintain strict control over which applications are permissible on client PCs, or may not want to burden nontechnical staff with the task of installing and configuring a feed aggregator. This also presents a bandwidth advantage, because the feed is downloaded once by the server and then emailed to the appropriate staff members, rather than having each staff member in turn make use of the Internet connection to download the feed.

```
<?php
  include ("../common_db.php");
  $subscribers = array();
  array_push($subscribers, array('email' => "paul@example.com", 'format' => 1));
  array_push($subscribers, array('email' => "joe@example.com", 'format' => 0));
```

For this example, recipients of the message are set initially in an array. If you have a large or dynamic set of recipients, this data could just as easily be pulled from a database.

```
  $query = "SELECT id, source, title, DATE_FORMAT(date,'%a, %d %b %Y %T EST') as
    date, link, content FROM 03_feed_raw WHERE (NOW() - `date`) < 86400";
  $updatedFeeds = getAssoc($query);
```

Set the query to select all updates completed in the past day (60 seconds Mlti 60 minutes Mlti 24 hours = 86,400 seconds in a day). The date will be formatted nicely (Tue, 14 Dec 2004 17:19:32 EST).

```
  //Produce HTML Version
  $htmlUpdate = "<html><body>";
  foreach ($updatedFeeds as $item)
  {
    $htmlUpdate .= "<h3>{$item['title']}</h3>\r\n";
    $htmlUpdate .= "<font size=-1>{$item['date']}</font>\r\n";
    $htmlUpdate .= "<p>{$item['content']}<br>\r\n";
```

```
    $htmlUpdate .= "<a href=\"{$item['link']}\" title=\"Full
Story\">{$item['link']}</a></p>\r\n";
    $htmlUpdate .= "<br><br>\r\n";
  }
  $htmlUpdate .= "<p>This email is sent as a service of example-corp. If you no
longer wish to receive it, or wish to change subscription options please contact
the help desk</p>";
  $htmlUpdate .= "</body></html>\r\n";

  //Produce Plain Text Version
  $plainUpdate = strip_tags($htmlUpdate);
```

Generate two different versions of the email, one for those who wish to receive (or are capable of receiving) an HTML formatted document, and one for those who would prefer a plain text version.

```
  $htmlHeaders  = "MIME-Version: 1.0\r\n";
  $htmlHeaders .= "From: Daily Feed Updates <dailyfeed@example.com>\r\n";
  $htmlHeaders .= "Content-type: text/html; charset=UTF-8\r\n";
  $plainHeaders = "MIME-Version: 1.0\r\n";
  $plainHeaders .= "From: Daily Feed Updates <dailyfeed@example.com>\r\n";
```

Generate headers for both types of email; note the Content-Type header added for the HTML formatted message.

```
  $error = "";
  foreach($subscribers as $individual)
  {
    if($individual['format'] == 1)
    {
      if (!mail($individual['email'], "Daily Feeds", $htmlUpdate, $htmlHeaders))
      {
        $error .= "Error To:{$individual['email']}, Content: $htmlHeaders\n";
      }
    }else if ($individual['format'] == 0)
    {
      if (!mail($individual['email'], "Daily Feeds", $plainUpdate, $plainHeaders))
      {
        $error .= "Error To: {$individual['email']}, Content: $plainUpdate\n";
      }
    }
  }
```

Each recipient is iterated through, and a message is sent. If the `mail()` function returns an error, save that separately. Note that the `mail()` function will only return an error if it is unable to contact the MTA, any other possible problems with the message are ignored (for example, an invalid destination address). As such, it is likely that if one message fails to go through they all will.

```
  if (!($error == ""))
  {
    $error = "Messages could not be delivered because the MTA could not be
contacted\r\n" . $error;
    file_put_contents("/tmp/feederrors.txt", $error);
    echo "$error";
  }
?>
```

If errors are encountered they are saved to a local file. Note that it would be pointless to attempt to email the error messages because it has already been determined that the MTA is unreachable. If the automated process used to call the script has a better way to contact a human operator, for example, page to console, and save file to specific web directory, and so on, it would make for an easy replacement. Generally speaking, when one major error has already been encountered it is good practice to first make an attempt to save information about the error in as simple a manner as possible (in other words, dump to a file or output to console), then try the more complicated methods such as paging.

This example uses PHP's mail function to transport the mail to the MTA. Each message that is sent will require a separate connection to the MTA, because the process is (for each function call) to connect, communicate, and disconnect. As an example, sending 100 messages to a local MTA from PHP took 216 seconds during testing.

If you are planning on sending a large amount of mail, say over 1,000 recipients, you may want to look into either directly connecting to the MTA with streams or, as mentioned earlier, using a dedicated piece of mailing list software.

On Page Widget

Generating a small on page widget (suitable for use in a sidebar, for example) should be rather trivial once you have recorded the feeds. These two short example functions should provide you with some ideas:

```
function getStories($count, $source = "")
{
  $titleLength = 25;
  $storyLength = 100;
  if($source == "")
  {
    $query = "SELECT `title`, `content`, `link` FROM 03_feed_raw ORDER BY `date`
DESC LIMIT $count";
  }else
  {
     $query = "SELECT `title`, `content`, `link` FROM 03_feed_raw WHERE source =
'$source' ORDER BY `date` DESC LIMIT $count";
  }
  echo $query;
  $stories = getAssoc($query);
  foreach($stories as &$story)
  {
    $story['title'] = substr(strip_tags($story['title']), 0, $titleLength);
    $story['content'] = substr(strip_tags($story['content']), 0, $storyLength);
    echo ".";
  }
  return $stories;
}
```

This function retrieves the most recent stories (up to the supplied maximum) either from any source, or optionally a specific source. It also strips all HTML tags from the elements in question and trims them down to a preset length. Note the use of the ampersand before `$story` in the `foreach` loop. It is important to remember that `foreach`, by default, works on a copy of the given array. The ampersand directs the loop to work directly with the array in question. This option is new to PHP5, so if a previous version is still in use, a different method of array iteration will need to be used.

You will note that the table name used in the previous several examples has been `feed_raw`—that's exactly what it contains, raw feed data. If you intend to use other formats of the data throughout your site (as is done in this example), it would be best for you to use multiple tables, one containing raw data, the others containing specifically formatted versions of that data for use elsewhere:

```
function printWidget($count, $source = "")
{
 $stories = getStories($count, $source);
 foreach($stories as $story)
 {
   echo "<a href=\"{$story['link']}\">{$story['title']}</a><br>\n";
   echo "<p>{$story['content']}</p>\n";
 }
}
```

Using the preceding function prints out the specified number of stories in a simple HTML format. Assuming some sort of stylesheet is inherited from the page in question, it actually works out rather well.

> *Notice that no validation was ever done to the* `$source` *variable. Keep that in mind while coding, you will need to ensure that it is specified by code, not by the user. For example, it could be populated either statically or from a generated array, where the user gives the index to select the desired element. It should not, however, be given directly by the user (or allowed to be given on a request URL) because it is vulnerable to a SQL Injection attack.*

Customizable Portal Page

Using the preceding code, it is trivial to create a portal page that looks suspiciously like Slashdot or Netscape:

```
<html>
<head>
<title>Example Portal Page</title>
</head>
<table width="100%" border="1">
<tr>
  <th width="15%">Paul's Blog</th>
  <th width="70%">Yahoo! Technology</th>
  <th width="15%">Chris's Blog</th>
</tr>
<tr valign="top">
  <td><?php printWidget(3, "http://www.preinheimer.com/rss.php?version=2.0");
?></td>
  <td><?php printWidget(7, "http://rss.news.yahoo.com/rss/software"); ?></td>
  <td><?php printWidget(3, "http://shiflett.org/rss"); ?></td>
</tr>
</table>
</body>
</html>
```

Taking that code as a base, and with a little tweaking of the maximum length from `getStories()` earlier, you have a reasonable looking portal, as shown in Figure 3-4.

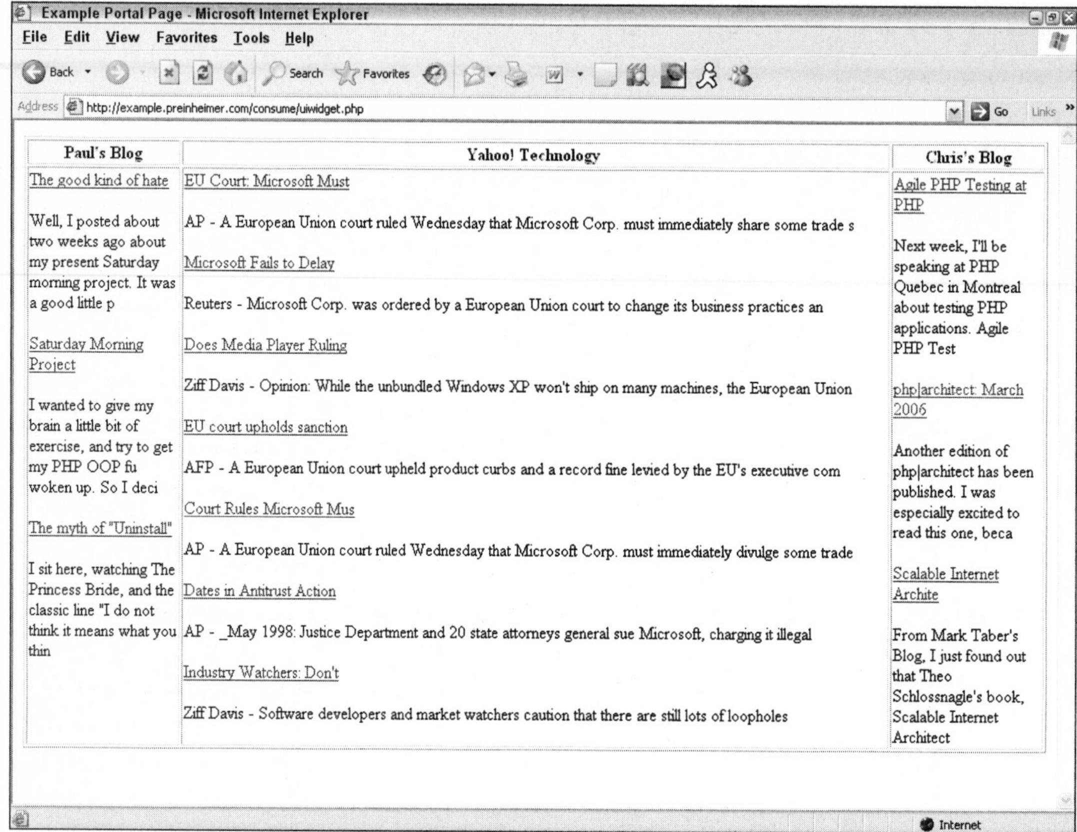

Figure 3-4

Improving the Portal Page

Naturally, there is always room for some improvement, so here are a couple of suggestions to get you going.

You could use cookies to allow users to select which elements they want to see and where. For example, add a few drop-downs to your existing user admin page to allow the users to select among your available feeds, and then display those feeds when they view the index page.

Use caching to reduce load. If the page is dynamically generated each time it is loaded, you may soon bring the server to its knees—plan ahead and cache content. In this context it probably makes the most sense to cache each feed you provide in a "nugget form" ready to be plugged into any page as required, and also cache the default page in its entirety because most users will probably not bother to change the defaults. Several caching methods are discussed in the next chapter.

Display the total number of items available from any particular feed. Underneath each feed provide a `More` option, indicating the number of additional items available from that feed. You may want to provide only current items (in other words, the last 10–25 depending on feed update frequency), or simply allow access to every item in your database.

Some Web Feed Providers

You now know what you're dealing with, so here is a small list of some feeds you may find interesting:

Site	Feed Address
BBC	`http://news.bbc.co.uk/rss/newsonline_world_edition/americas/rss091.xml`
CBC	`http://www.cbc.ca/rss/`
Reuters	`http://www.reuters.co.uk/newsrss.jhtml` `http://www.reuters.com/newsrss.jhtml`
Slashdot	`http://slashdot.org/index.rss`
BBC	`http://news.bbc.co.uk/rss/newsonline_uk_edition/world/rss091.xml`
ZDNet	`http://itpapers.zdnet.com/rsslist.aspx`
Google Blog	`http://www.google.com/googleblog/atom.xml`
New York Times	`http://www.nytimes.com/services/xml/rss/nyt/HomePage.xml`

These sites are just a small sample of what is out there. To see literally hundreds of others, just type "rss" or "atom" into a search engine.

Summary

This chapter covered a lot of ground, starting with a brief look at a basic web feed in RSS format. Now a little more familiar with the format of the feed, a more in-depth examination was undertaken, including a detailed examination of critical feed elements, as well as some tips to keep in mind when examining a feed for the first time. Retrieving feeds is all well and good, but it's impractical to do on page load, and as such the code required to store those feeds was presented, including some extensions to look at Atom feeds. Next, namespaced elements require some special code to be accessed with SimpleXML; the code required and some reasoning behind the namespacing was discussed. Consuming feeds and re-displaying their content is all well and good, but it can expose your site to security vulnerabilities, so methods of mitigating or lessening this risk were discussed. A less sinister but still worrisome problem is broken HTML in feeds. Using HTML Tidy resolves the problem nicely. Building on previous examples was a complete set of functions, designed to consume a feed and safely store it in a local database to be used in the next example. Finally, some possible uses for your retrieved feeds were suggested, along with some possible feed sources.

Overall, the major topics covered in this chapter were as follows:

- ❑ Examining remote feeds, determining which elements are of particular use to your project
- ❑ Retrieving remote feeds, including looking at the code, pulling it into a SimpleXML object, and caching a local copy

- Dealing with namespaces in SimpleXML
- Securing your feed handling
- Handling broken HTML code within your feeds
- Presenting your feeds to users

This chapter examined the processes involved in retrieving a feed presented elsewhere. The next chapter looks at things from the opposite perspective: how to present your data in a feed to others. The skills and knowledge you gained here will prove invaluable when developing your own feeds.

4

Producing Web Feeds

The process of consuming web feeds was discussed in the last chapter; here the process of producing those feeds is examined in detail. Producing feeds, from a technical perspective, is simply taking the content you already have, and instead of encapsulating it in HTML, encapsulating it in XML following a specified format.

This chapter covers the following:

- Why feeds are important
- Standard feed formats
- Testing feeds
- Caching
- Blog feeds
- Trackbacks

The chapter then provides a simple real-world example of providing feeds for a sample retail store.

Why Do You Need to Produce Feeds?

Feeds have several advantages, primarily related to consumption, over traditional HTML formats. Many desktop applications are devoted to reading feeds at regular intervals, and many of the new batch of web browsers include features for reading feeds. These free the user from manually checking various sources (websites) for new information. Instead, the automated tool checks the subscribed feeds every few minutes and presents them to the user (usually organized in a user-configurable manner). The standard and predictable format makes this a much easier task than traditional page scraping methods that parse HTML. Feed aggregators are also coming to popularity on the Web with sites such as Planet PHP (www.planet-php.org/) and Feedster (www.feedster.com/). Finally, popular news sites (Google News, for example) compile the feeds of various news outlets to provide a single source of current news.

By simply updating a corporate news/public relations page to provide a web feed, a company suddenly finds new outlets for its information, and by adding feeds to your own pages, you can make it easy and convenient for your audience to keep up to date with your content.

Additional Considerations When Producing a Feed

Once you discover how easy it is to produce a web feed and how easy the plethora of feed readers out there makes it for your users to consume your feed, you may have some inner drive to produce feeds for everything. Don't.

First, as with any project, consider how useful the feed will be to outside users, what new information it will provide, and how it will be used. If this is a business site, consider how the feed will help achieve your corporate goals. Sure it would be cool to have a feed that ran the current weather in your office's city, but A) chances are you have windows (the look outside kind, not the operating system kind), B) a variety of sites already provide exactly this service, and C) is this something worth devoting resources toward?

Second, consider the load requirements of generating the data. Remember that feeds are usually consumed by software automatically, at preset intervals. Many preset to small increments such as half an hour. Users who may have visited a given page once per day are now downloading the feed up to 48 times per day! Multiply that by the number of potential users, and you have a lot of additional traffic, and, unless you play your caching cards right, a lot of load on the server. Some of this, however, is negated by the smaller document size overall. For example, visiting http://slashdot.org/ involves a total of 23 HTTP requests, and a total size (images and all) of 21,819 bytes, whereas visiting http://slashdot.org/index.rss involves only one HTTP request, and only 4,515 bytes—definitely a significant savings.

Finally, do consider the usefulness of this feed to your competitors. Placing all of your current pricing information or weekly production schedules in a feed may seem like a great boon internally (especially to upper management), but consider the repercussions if that URL becomes known to your competitors! Because feeds are generally consumed by software automatically, it can be more difficult to secure access. I strongly recommend against providing confidential data in a feed without first undergoing a strenuous security audit and seriously considering the alternatives.

Publicizing Your Feed

As with any web project, your work is worthless unless you publicize it to your target audience. This is becoming easier and easier with some recent developments in the browser world. Mozilla in particular has made this quite easy in recent releases. When the browser sees the appropriate alternate link code in a document header, it presents an RSS icon in the lower-right corner of the browser window to inform the user, who may then create a "Live Bookmark" to monitor the feed. For example:

```
<LINK REL="alternate" TITLE="Slashdot RSS" HREF="//slashdot.org/index.rss"
TYPE="application/rss+xml">
```

However, publicizing your feed involves at least one more step. Create at least one page for your site that lists the URLs for the various feeds you will be providing, as well as what format the feeds will follow (RSS, Atom, and so on). You should also consider offering more detailed information about what type of content should be expected within the feed itself — what HTML tags should be expected, maximum length, and so on. This is important, because responsible, security-conscious users of your feed will need to filter the information they receive, and can make a much more intelligent decision about how to do that if you let them know what to expect. The topic of filtering feeds is covered in greater detail in the previous chapter.

Standard Feed Formats

You can slap some XML together, update the document regularly, and then call it a feed, but it would serve limited usefulness. Luckily (or not), you can choose from a wide range of standard feed formats out there already, supported by a wide range of aggregators. I have included the specifications for the main feed formats in Appendix B as well as the URLs where current versions of the specifications can be found. You can also find some code that generates dates in the required format in Appendix A.

RSS

One of the most popular formats for syndicating information is RSS. There are currently three versions: 0.91, 1.0, and 2.0. All of the versions are forward compatible, so a feed created with the 0.91 specification will be readable by an aggregator created with 1.0 or 2.0 in mind. Most aggregators, whether stand-alone client or web-based, can support all three versions, so it really comes down to what you and your users need. As with any project, examine the specific capabilities of your users before making any decisions (for example, if this is for a corporate intranet, examine the software and versions common throughout the organization. Frequently, Information Technology departments run a version or two ahead of the rest of the organization, and hence the target market for your feed must be closely examined).

> *Current work on refining and expanding the RSS specification is outlined at* `www.rssboard.org/`. *This website provides the specifications for past and present versions of the RSS specification as well as useful discussion about various features.*

The following sections introduce the three versions of the standard, explaining what tags are available in each, then go through some examples using different versions of the standard. For the basis of explanation, producing a feed for a news site is discussed. This is merely for simplicity because the paradigms match closely.

> *For all three revisions of the RSS schema, the height and width elements for an image are considered optional. However, note that the assumed values are a width of 88 px and a height of 31px (this is approximately the size of those "web buttons" you see on various sites promoting something).*

RSS 0.91

RSS 0.91 is commonly used by many blogs and news sites. It allows basic textual information syndication, without too many required tags. For a basic news site, this allows a base `channel` tag to describe the site (name, description, language, webmaster, copyright, logo, and so on), then an `item` tag for each individual story containing further information (title, link, description). The link in each item should be to the page containing the story itself, not the root page for the site.

```
<?xml version="1.0"?>
<!DOCTYPE rss SYSTEM "http://my.netscape.com/publish/formats/rss-0.91.dtd">
<rss version="0.91">
  <channel>
    <language>en</language>
    <title>Example News.com</title>
    <description>News and commentary from the cross-platform scripting
community.</description>
        <image>
      <title>Wrox News .com</title>
      <link>http://www.wroxnews.com/</link>
      <url>http://www.wroxnews.com/pics/button.png</url>
    </image>
    <item>
      <title>Feed usage up 1000%!</title>
      <link>http://www.wroxnews.com/story2/index.html</link>
      <description>Feed usage has increased a dramatic 1000% in the past 48hrs
alone, this may...</description>
    </item>
    <item>
      <title>RSS Feed Goes Live!</title>
      <link>http://wroxnews.org/story1/index.html</link>
      <description>Wroxnews.com is proud to announce the launch of our premier RSS
service...</description>
    </item>
  </channel>
</rss>
```

RSS 1.0

The 1.0 version of the specification didn't really change much; it adds a few restrictions to ensure compliance with RDF, and that's about it. The restrictions it imposes aren't a big deal—just a few subtle changes to ensure things happen nicely.

RSS 2.0

This is where the real fun begins. The biggest change you will notice is with the introduction of many much-needed tags in the `item` element, including `enclosure` (to attach a file with to the specific item), `author`, `category`, `comments`, `pubDate`, and so on. These additions will probably serve to make RSS 2.0 the schema of choice if it is available to your audience.

This example builds on the one presented for 0.91 by adding a third item and fleshing out the information provided. Because the information permitted in RSS 0.91 is a subset of 2.0, it is a good idea to provide both 0.91 and 2.0 feeds if you decide to go with 2.0.

```
<rss version="2.0">
  <channel>
    <language>en</language>
    <title>Example News.com</title>
    <description>News and commentary from the cross-platform scripting
community.</description>
    <link>http://www.wroxnews.com/</link>
    <image>
      <title>Example News.com</title>
```

```
        <link>http://www.wroxnews.com/</link>
        <url>http://www.wroxnews.com/pics/button.png</url>
      </image>
      <item>
        <title>Feed usage up 1000%!</title>
        <link>http://www.wroxnews.com/story2/index.html</link>
        <description>Feed usage has increased a dramatic 1000% in the past 48hrs
alone, this may...</description>

      </item>
      <item>
        <title>RSS Feed Goes Live!</title>
        <link>http://wroxnews.org/story1/index.html</link>
        <description>Wroxnews.com is proud to announce the launch of our premier RSS
service...</description>

      </item>
    </channel>
</rss>
```

Expanding RSS

RSS provides a mechanism for adding tags to an RSS document. This can be done by adding additional XML namespaces to the document in the `rss` tag. The syntax is relatively simple. For example:

```
<rss version="2.0" xmlns:cc="http://backend.userland.com/creativeCommonsRssModule">
```

This defines the document as being RSS 2.0, adds an additional namespace (`cc`) to the document, and indicates where to find more information about the namespace. In this case, the `cc` namespace is for the Creative Commons license. Adding this tag will allow inclusion of several `cc` tags to define the copyright restrictions (or lack thereof) placed on the document. To declare a tag within the `cc` namespace, just prepend the tag with `cc`.

For example:

```
<item>
  <title>RSS Feed Goes Live!</title>
  <link>http://wroxnews.org/story1/index.html</link>
  <description>Wroxnews.com is proud to announce the launch of our premier RSS
service...</description>
  <cc:license>http://www.creativecommons.org/licenses/by-nc/1.0<cc:license>
 </item>
```

This extensibility allows feed creators to include any desired information with their feed in a recognizable way. It may be tempting to define namespaces as required to fit your data, but don't. Chances are good (especially by the time this book goes to print) that there is already one defined way, if not several, to get your information across. It may not be quite the format you were hoping for (possibly a different date format, or different nesting rules), but it is worth the effort. The Internet really doesn't need more incompatible standards with similar data.

You will often see namespaces referencing a URL beginning with `http://purl.org/`. *This is not a central repository of XML namespaces; instead it offers a way to offer a Permanent URL to a specific resource located elsewhere.*

Atom

Atom was created to resolve some ambiguities within the RSS specification (RSS 2.0 was declared to be the final version, so these issues can't be resolved by releasing new versions of RSS). This section covers Atom 0.3, which is the latest version.

```
<?xml version="1.0" encoding="utf-8"?>
<feed version="0.3" xmlns="http://purl.org/atom/ns#">
  <title>dive into mark</title>
  <link rel="alternate" type="text/html" href="http://diveintomark.org/"/>
  <modified>2003-12-13T18:30:02Z</modified>
  <author>
    <name>Mark Pilgrim</name>
  </author>
  <entry>
    <title>Atom 0.3 snapshot</title>
    <link rel="alternate" type="text/html"
     href="http://diveintomark.org/2003/12/13/atom03"/>
    <id>tag:diveintomark.org,2003:3.2397</id>
    <issued>2003-12-13T08:29:29-04:00</issued>
    <modified>2003-12-13T18:30:02Z</modified>
  </entry>
</feed>
```

As you can see, while the Atom specification may use different terms for several of the elements, there really isn't too large a difference between the specifications. Personally, I appreciate the addition of the modified tag, to remove some of the ambiguity associated with posts that were later updated. That being said, I prefer the date format used in the RSS feeds. Beyond that, which feed formats you decide to produce is entirely dependent on what your user base desires/is able to interpret. When unsure, produce both. The full Atom spec for versions 0.1–0.3 is available in Appendix B.

The Atom 0.3 specification calls for the Content-Type header to be set to application/atom+xml. However, while I am debugging feeds with a browser, I find it convenient to set the Content-Type header to `text/xml`*, because most browsers will attempt to locate an external registered handler for that type.*

Testing Your Feed

It is probably safe to assume that most web programmers have interacted with some semblance of an HTML validator (because you always write valid HTML, right?). There are similar sites devoted to testing feeds in the common formats. It is a good idea to run your feed through one of them for testing. You can access one at `http://feedvalidator.org/`. It is capable of checking both RSS and Atom feeds.

Producing a Feed with Basic Content

The first stage in producing a feed is choosing a format to provide the feed in. For the purpose of examples in this book RSS 2.0 is used. Figure out what you need from your feed (do you need to attach files, what can your users support, and so on), look at the options, and pick one. From a production standpoint, it doesn't really matter that much, you are still just producing XML in a basic repeating format.

```
<?php
 header("Content-Type: text/xml");
?><rss version="2.0">
  <channel>
    <language>en</language>
```

```
    <title>Easy Recipes</title>
    <description>Easy recipes for the computer hacker/culinary
slacker.</description>
    <link>http://example.preinheimer.com/feed1.php</link>
    <image>
      <title>Easy Recipes</title>
      <link>http://example.preinheimer.com/feed1.php</link>
      <url>http://example.preinheimer.com/feed1.png</url>
    </image><?php
    include("./common_db.php");
    $query = "SELECT title, link, description, author, category,
      DATE_FORMAT(pubdate,'%a, %d %b %Y %T EST') as pubdate
      FROM 11_basic_feed";
    $recipes = getAssoc($query);
    foreach($recipes AS $item)
    {
      echo "<item>\n";
      echo "<title>{$item['title']}</title>\n";
      echo "<link>{$item['link']}</link>\n";
      echo "<description>{$item['description']}</description>\n";
      echo "<author>{$item['author']}</author>\n";
      echo "<category>{$item['category']}</category>\n";
      echo "<pubdate>{$item['pubdate']}</pubdate>\n";
      echo "</item>\n";
    }
?></channel>
</rss>
```

As you can see, producing the feed is pretty simple. There are several places that code can be trimmed down, but that should serve for easy readability. Note that `header("Content-Type: text/xml");` is critical; you need to set this up before you send any other type of output. You will also notice that there is no white space between the opening and closing of the php tags (`<?php ?>`) and the following XML tag. This is because XML does not ignore white space (unlike HTML). One final element I would like to bring to your attention is the definition of the SQL query, namely `DATE_FORMAT(pubdate,'%a, %d %b %Y %T EST') as pubdate`. This instructs MySQL to give the date in the RFC 822 format, rather than the MySQL internal timestamp format. Whenever you have the option of either formatting information in PHP, or having your database engine doing it for you, I would recommend the latter. It is likely more efficient (it is, after all, working with one of its internal formats), and will avoid further processing either with a loop or `array_walk`. Also note that as per the format, the `<author>` tag *must* contain an email address. Many individuals I have spoken to consider this to be one of the weak points in the spec, because the format is very easily scraped by automated spiders looking to spam the world. Because the spec requires a syntactfully valid email address, normal tricks like `paul (at) example (dot)` org and the like won't work. Since the `author` tag is optional, you may want to encapsulate further information within a namespace.

The output of the script is as follows:

```
<rss version="2.0">
  <channel>
    <language>en</language>
    <title>Easy Recipes</title>
    <description>Easy recipes for the computer hacker/culinary
slacker.</description>
```

```
      <link>http://example.preinheimer.com/feed1.php</link>
      <image>
        <title>Easy Recipes</title>
        <link>http://example.preinheimer.com/feed1.php</link>
        <url>http://example.preinheimer.com/feed1.png</url>
      </image><item>
  <title>Waffles</title>
  <link>http://example.preinheimer.com/feed1.php?item=2</link>
  <description>1. Take box out of freezer
  2. Remove two waffles from box
  3. Place waffles in toaster
  4. Depress button
  5. Wait for toaster to pop
  6. Remove waffles from toaster, place on plate
  7. Pour Canadian Maple Syrup on waffles
  8. Enjoy</description>
  <author>Paul</author>
  <category>Breakfast</category>
  <pubDate>Tue, 02 Nov 2004 20:28:15 EST</pubDate>
  </item>
  <item>
  <title>Chocolate Chip Cookies</title>
  <link>http://example.preinheimer.com/feed1.php?item=1</link>
  <description>1. Take the tube out of the fridge
  2. Place the cookie sheet on the counter
  3. Cut the tube open
  4. Slice the cookie batter into 12 equally sized pieces
  5. Place each slice on the cookie sheet
  6. Preheat the oven to 350F
  7. Place cookie sheet on center rack
  8. Wait 20 minutes
  9. Remove cookies from oven
  10. Burn fingers and enjoy</description>
  <author>Paul</author>
  <category>Baking</category>
  <pubDate>Tue, 02 Nov 2004 20:28:15 EST</pubDate>
  </item>
  </channel>
  </rss>
```

Note that you do not see the results of the Content-Type header tag; this is an HTTP header that is interpreted by the browser, and (unless you have something like Live Headers in Mozilla Firefox enabled) not shown to the end user.

The database used to provide this example is trivial, but for completeness sake, here it is (just a little reminder: all of this code is online at `www.wrox.com` for download, so don't waste your time typing this in manually):

```
CREATE TABLE `11_basic_feed` (
  `id` int(11) NOT NULL auto_increment,
  `title` varchar(100) NOT NULL default '',
  `link` varchar(100) NOT NULL default '',
  `description` text NOT NULL,
  `author` varchar(50) NOT NULL default '',
  `category` varchar(25) NOT NULL default '',
```

```
  `pubdate` timestamp(14) NOT NULL,
  PRIMARY KEY  (`id`)
) TYPE=MyISAM;

INSERT INTO `11_basic_feed` VALUES (1, 'Chocolate Chip Cookies',
'http://example.preinheimer.com/feed1.php?item=1', '1. Take the tube out of the
fridge\r\n2. Place the cookie sheet on the counter\r\n3. Cut the tube open\r\n4.
Slice the cookie batter into 12 equally sized pieces\r\n5. Place each slice on the
cookie sheet\r\n6. Preheat the oven to 350F\r\n7. Place cookie sheet on center
rack\r\n8. Wait 20 minutes\r\n9. Remove cookies from oven\r\n10. Burn fingers and
enjoy', 'Paul', 'Baking', '20041102202815');
INSERT INTO `11_basic_feed` VALUES (2, 'Waffles',
'http://example.preinheimer.com/feed1.php?item=2', '1. Take box out of
freezer\r\n2. Remove two waffles from box\r\n3. Place waffles in toaster\r\n4.
Depress button\r\n5. Wait for toaster to pop\r\n6. Remove waffles from toaster,
place on plate\r\n7. Pour Canadian Maple Syrup on waffles\r\n8. Enjoy', 'Paul',
'Breakfast', '20041102202815');
```

Caching Your Feed

As mentioned earlier with the frequent page loads common to feeds, caching is a really good idea. Just as an example, I update my blog about five times a week; several people appear to have their feed aggregators (mis)configured to grab the feed every 5 minutes. There are two main ways to go about caching. You can either take care of caching on the side of the feed script itself, or you can move the feed generation logic to the script that allows users/administers to add data to the feed. The latter is more efficient, but also more restrictive. These methods are called feed-side caching and generation-side caching, respectively.

Feed-Side Caching

The essence of feed-side caching is for the script being called to generate the feed to handle caching on its own. This has several advantages. First, it fits with the paradigm most of us are comfortable with: The user visits a page, and the page generates and returns the appropriate result. Second, it allows for greater flexibility in terms of how the feed itself is updated. The output of these cached pages is identical. During development and thereafter you may want to consider adding an XML comment to your feed to mark whether it was a cached copy (and if so, the time at which it was cached) or freshly generated.

To update the earlier simple feed script to allow for feed-side caching, you just need to add a few function calls:

```
<?php
 header("Content-Type: text/xml");
 include("./feedcache.php");
 if (cacheIsRecent())
 {
   echo getCache();
 }else
 {
   ob_start();
?><rss version="2.0">
  <channel>
    <language>en</language>
```

```
        <title>Easy Recipes</title>
        <description>Easy recipes for the computer hacker/culinary
    slacker.</description>
        <link>http://example.preinheimer.com/feed1.php</link>
        <image>
          <title>Easy Recipes</title>
          <link>http://example.preinheimer.com/feed1.php</link>
          <url>http://example.preinheimer.com/feed1.png</url>
        </image><?php
        include("./common_db.php");
        $query = "SELECT * FROM 11_basic_feed";
        $recipes = getAssoc($query);
        foreach($recipes AS $item)
        {
          echo "<item>\n";
          echo "<title>{$item['title']}</title>\n";
          echo "<link>{$item['link']}</link>\n";
          echo "<description>{$item['description']}</description>\n";
          echo "<author>{$item['author']}</author>\n";
          echo "<category>{$item['category']}</category>\n";
          echo "<pubdate>{$item['pubdate']}</pubdate>\n";
          echo "</item>\n";
        }
        echo "</channel>\n</rss>";
      updateCache(ob_get_contents());
      ob_end_flush();
    }
    ?>
```

The use of a few function calls to manage the cache allows you to use the same basic file for all the feed-based cache examples.

Timed Cache Release

This method checks for the existence of and the timestamp on the cached data every run. If it exists, and was written less than a specified number of minutes ago, it is sent to the users. If the cache doesn't exist, or is too old, the script runs as earlier and updates the cache. Using a flat file can be tempting because of its simplicity; however, you will likely quickly encounter race conditions where more than one invocation of your script begins trying to update the cache simultaneously. You could solve this problem with file locks and timeouts; however, it is probably easier to use a tool explicitly designed for the purpose, a database. SQLite is a perfect choice, lightweight and fast.

Creating the SQLite database, and table:

```
<?php
$db = new SQLiteDatabase("/tmp/11.timedcache.sqlite");
$db->query("BEGIN;
  CREATE TABLE timedCache(id INTEGER PRIMARY KEY, cache BLOB, tstamp TEXT);
  COMMIT;");
?>
```

As you can see, you don't need the table to hold much, just an ID to serve as a primary key, the cache itself, and the timestamp for when it was created.

Checking to see if the cache is recent:

```
function cacheIsRecent()
{
  $db = sqlite_open("/tmp/11.timedcache.sqlite");
  $query = "SELECT tstamp FROM timedCache WHERE id = 1";
  $result = sqlite_query($db, $query);
  $row = sqlite_fetch_array($result);
  if (time() - $row['tstamp'] > (60 * 10))
  {
    return false;
  }else
  {
     return true;
  }
}
```

Loading data into the cache:

```
function updateCache($body)
{
  $db = new SQLiteDatabase("/tmp/11.timedcache.sqlite");
  $time = time();
  $query = "REPLACE INTO timedCache (id, cache, tstamp) VALUES (1, '$body',
'$time')";
  $db->query("BEGIN; $query; COMMIT;");
}
```

Retrieving data from the cache:

```
function getCache()
{
  $db = sqlite_open("/tmp/11.timedcache.sqlite");
  $query = "SELECT cache FROM timedCache WHERE id = 1";
  $result = sqlite_query($db, $query);
  $row = sqlite_fetch_array($result);
  return $row['cache'];
}
```

This method can definitely be improved. It uses two queries against the same record when the cache is old. Moving the checking and retrieval logic together (return the row if the cache is current, or null if it is not, for example) and working with that would see some savings.

It should also be noted that during benchmarking, this method of caching actually performed worse than no caching at all! You will likely see similar results if you benchmark against such a contrived dataset (two records in one table designed only to hold feed information). In real-world cases, the query probably spans at least two tables and returns many rows. This leads into a route to performance enhancement not covered here: changing your database structure. Keeping all of the applicable fields in one table would certainly show a performance improvement over cross-table queries. If you are using a database package that supports triggers, these can be used to automate the process (also beyond the scope of this book).

Update Cache at Specified Intervals

If your feed receives sufficient traffic, you can realize significant savings over the previous example by working with the current time, and ignoring any cached data until you need it. Note that under this specific example all requests occurring over the one-second target will refresh the cache:

```
function cacheIsRecentTimeOfDay()
{
  if ((time() % (10 * 60)) == 0)
  {
         return false;
  }else
  {
         return true;
  }
}
```

Update Cache Randomly

The entire point of a cache is to be fast. Any solution involving database queries to determine if the cache is old will lose a few cycles to perform that check. Doing some quick math based on the number of hits your feed receives per day, you can use random numbers to update the cache, on average, throughout the day. Say the feed receives 10,000 hits per day. With 86,400 seconds in a day, that means that your feed receives a hit every 8.4 seconds (assuming queries are evenly distributed throughout the day, which they aren't). If you want the cache to be updated every 10 minutes or so, that means that you should update the cache approximately once for every 71 hits.

```
function cacheIsRecentRandom()
{
  if (rand(0, 71) == 42)
  {
    return false;
  }else
  {
    return true;
  }
}
```

Once the feed has been public for a while, take a look at the number of hits generated per hour throughout the day. It may be wise to refine your algorithm to update less often (say, 1 in 200 hits) during peak hours, and more often (say, 1 in 40 hits) during the slow hours. This can help reduce load during peak times, and still ensure that the feed is as up to date as possible during the slow times.

Update Cache on Update

This method compares the timestamp in the cache and the timestamp on the most recent post. If the post is newer, the page is generated as shown earlier and saved to the cache. This method doesn't present much in the way of savings for this simple example. However, in real-world feeds, where the data needs to come from several tables and be massaged into the appropriate format before display, it does have some use.

```
function cacheIsRecent()
{
  $db = sqlite_open("/tmp/11.timedcache.sqlite");
  $query = "SELECT tstamp FROM timedCache WHERE id = 1";
  $result = sqlite_query($db, $query);
  $row = sqlite_fetch_array($result);
  if (time() - $row['tstamp'] > (60 * 10))
  {
    return false;
  }else
  {
     return true;
  }
}
```

Generation-Side Caching

Generation-side caching utilizes scripts to update the cache whenever new content is added to the feed. Though this almost always guarantees the cache is up to date, it can limit the ways that new content can be added.

Cache Deletion on Update

This is probably the most efficient method that still relies on the feed page itself to generate the page. This method assumes you have a script that is used to update the feed, and when it does so, it deletes the cache. The feed script detects this and re-creates the cache. This method will require its own `CacheIsRecent` function similar to the previous examples, as well as some code in the page to be executed after the database containing the feeds is updated.

```
function cacheIsRecentExists()
{
  $db = sqlite_open("/tmp/11.timedcache.sqlite");
  $query = "SELECT tstamp FROM timedCache WHERE id = 1";
  $result = sqlite_query($db, $query);
  if (sqlite_num_rows($result) == 1)
  {
    return true;
  }else
  {
    return false;
  }
}
```

As with previous examples, this one can be greatly improved by combining the check for data, and when it exists, returning it directly.

Feed Pre-Generation

If you are going to go as far as to involve the script that creates the feed information and deletes the record, why not just create a flat file, and keep all the logic off the heavily trafficked page? This is the most efficient method in terms of server load for each hit against the feed. However, with this and the previous method, you need to ensure that all updates to the feed data are done through capable scripts — no cheating and posting directly to the database. Accomplishing this should be pretty easy, especially with previous code examples. At the end of the script being used to update the feed, tack on code that would generate the feed itself, encapsulated in output buffering. Save that output buffer either to a database as shown earlier, or to a flat file. You can either pass that file through with `readfile()`, or (for much improved performance) just configure your web server to serve the flat file directly with the appropriate Content-Type header.

Under Apache, you can save the file with a specified extension, configure that extension under the Apache configuration file `mime.types`, and then restart Apache:

```
text/xml      xml
```

Second, you can save all of your feeds from a specific directory, and use `ForceType` in that directory to ensure the Content-Type header is set correctly:

```
<Location /www/feeds/>
  ForceType text/xml
</Location>
```

Finally, you can use the `AddType` directive to set the type for a specified file type. This has the advantage of being configurable on a VirtualHost, directory, or .htaccess level:

```
AddType text/xml .xml
```

Caching Summary

As you can tell, your options for caching are extensive. Because many of the options presented here can be combined (for example, check for an updated document randomly, or check time since feed was updated randomly), your full set of options is almost endless. Important metrics to consider when trying to choose a caching method include the following: How resource intensive is generating the feed, how often is the feed updated, how is the feed updated, and how many hits does the feed receive? Take a look at what you have and the pros and cons of the various caching options to choose one that is best for you.

Blogs

If you own this book, you know what a blog is. Writing your own blogging software is a common trait among PHP programmers; however, as with all things, the devil is in the details, and there are quite a few things to consider. Feed production is only one of them.

Some of the examples here differ little from the previous examples; however, they go the additional step to provide an example of a standard HTML output for the purposes of exploring trackbacks later in the chapter. The examples continue to use RSS 2.0; converting these to other formats should be trivial.

> *Often when reading a blog post, one is inspired to write their own, possibly on a related title. Trackbacks are the method used for the second blogger to inform the first of the link. For example: Tim writes a blog post about baking cookies. Bob reads this post, and decides to post his own blog about baking cookies. The use of trackbacks will allow readers of Tim's blog to know that Bob also wrote about a similar topic, and depending on the software used at both ends, readers of both blogs may be informed of the relationship between the posts.*

Simple Blog Example

This example uses three files: `admin.php`, `index.php`, and `feed.php`. Each is introduced initially with basic capabilities, and will be expanded to include more advanced features as the example progresses.

First, here is the code for the Database:

```
CREATE TABLE `03_simple_blog` (
  `id` int(11) NOT NULL auto_increment,
  `email` varchar(70) NOT NULL default '',
  `subject` varchar(50) NOT NULL default '',
  `category` varchar(50) NOT NULL default '',
  `post` text NOT NULL,
  `date` datetime NOT NULL default '0000-00-00 00:00:00',
  `name` varchar(50) NOT NULL default '',
  PRIMARY KEY  (`id`)
)
```

This is the `admin.php`:

```
<?php
include("./common_db.php");
if ($_POST['name'] != "")
{
  $name = $_POST['name']; $email = $_POST['email'];
  $subject = $_POST['subject']; $category = $_POST['category'];
  $post = $_POST['post']; $date = date('Y-m-d G:i:s');
  $query = "INSERT INTO_03_simple_blog
   (`id`, `name`, `email`, `subject`, `category`, `post`, `date`)
   VALUES (null, '$name', '$email', '$subject', '$category', '$post', '$date')";

   $id = insertQueryReturnID($query);
   $messages = "Post added, Post id <a href=\"./index.php?entry=$id\">$id</a>";
}
?><html>
 <head>
  <title>Simple Blog</title>
 </head>
 <body>
  <?php echo $messages; ?>
  <form action="#" method="post">
   Name: <input type="text" name="name"><br>
   Email: <input type="text" name="email"><br>
   Subject: <input type="text" name="subject"><br>
   Category: <input type="text" name="category"><br>
   Post:<br><textarea name="post"></textarea><br>
   <input type="submit" value="Submit">
  </form>
 </body>
</html>
```

This is your basic, zero-security admin page. This will suffice to allow you to add entries to your basic blog, as long as they don't contain any quotes or other things that could confuse the simple script. The same `common_db.inc` file used in previous examples has been used here; you can view the full code of this file in Appendix A.

Figure 4-1 shows how the sample administration page should look.

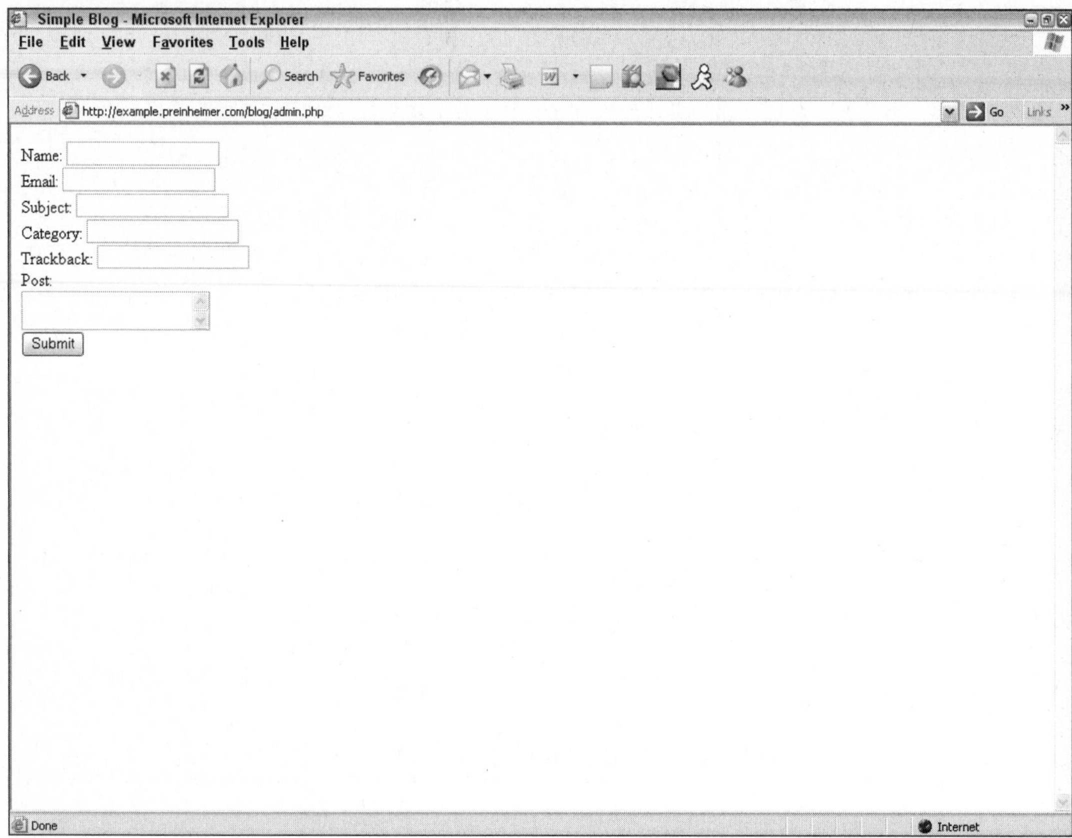

Figure 4-1

Here is the code for the index.php file:

```
<!DOCTYPE HTML PUBLIC "-//W3C//DTD HTML 4.01 Transitional//EN"
   "http://www.w3.org/TR/html4/strict.dtd">
<html>
<head>
 <META HTTP-EQUIV="Content-Type" CONTENT="text/html; charset=iso-8859-1">
 <title>My Sample Blog</title>
 <link rel="alternate" type="application/rss+xml" title="RSS"
  href="http://example.preinheimer.com/blog/feed.php">
</head>
<body>
<h1>Sample Blog</h1>
<?php
  include("./common_db.php");
  if (is_numeric($_GET['entry']))
  {
    $query = "SELECT * FROM 03_sample_blog WHERE id = '{$_GET['entry']}'";
  }else
  {
    $query = "SELECT * FROM 03_sample_blog ORDER by `id` DESC";
```

```
    }

    $blogEntries = getAssoc($query,2);
    foreach($blogEntries AS $entry)
    {
      echo "<h2><a href=\"./index.php?entry={$entry['id']}\">
        {$entry['subject']}</a></h2>\n";
      echo "<b>{$entry['category']}</b>\n";
      echo "<p>{$entry['post']}</p>\n";
      echo "<a href=\"mailto:{$entry['email']}\">{$entry['name']}</a>\n";
      echo "({$entry['date']})\n";
    }
  ?>
  </body>
  </html>
```

Again, note that this example as it stands contains major security flaws, primarily the use of unfiltered data from a GET request in a SQL query. Using this script on a live web server is just asking to be the target of a SQL Injection attack. This script includes the ability to load a specific post, rather than all of them, so this should assist in ensuring that links created from the feed can point to a relevant page.

Figure 4-2 shows a sample index page.

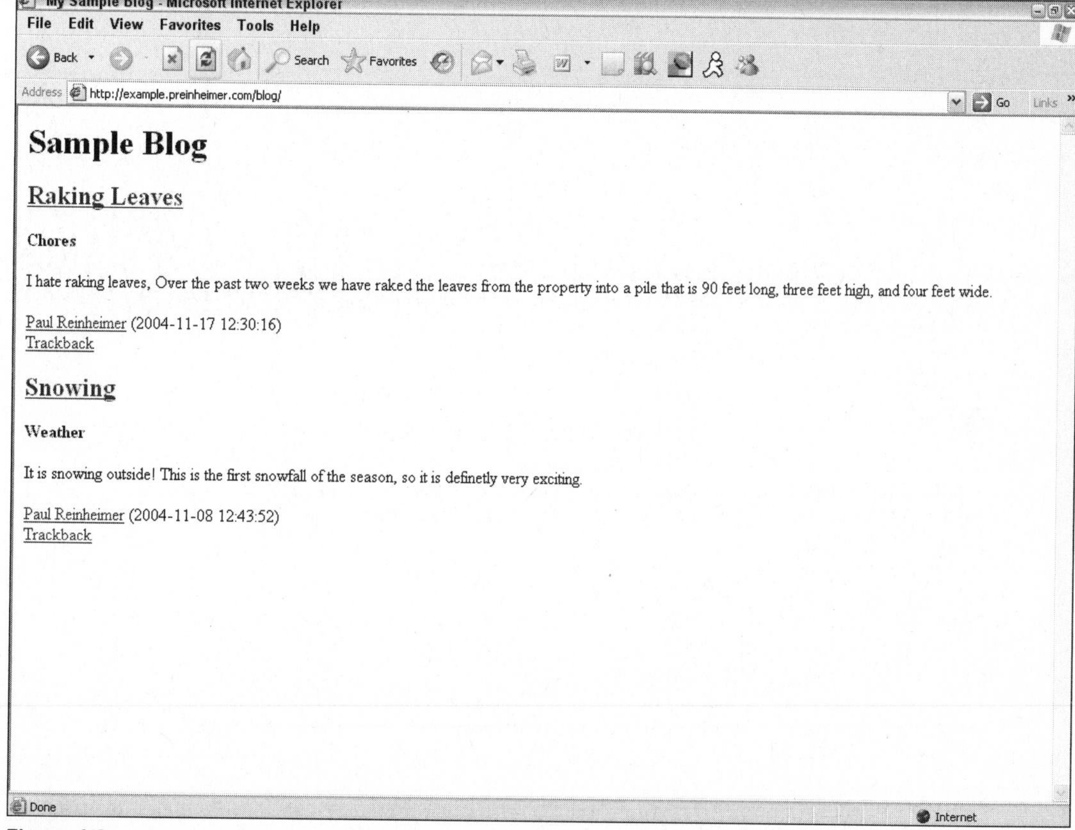

Figure 4-2

Finally, here is the code for the `feed.php` file:

```
<?php
 header("Content-Type: text/xml");
?><rss version="2.0">
  <channel>
    <language>en</language>
    <title>Sample Blog</title>
    <description>My Sample blog example.</description>
    <link>http://example.preinheimer.com/blog/</link>
    <image>
      <title>Sample Blog Logo</title>
      <link>http://example.preinheimer.com/feed1.php</link>
      <url>http://example.preinheimer.com/feed1.png</url>
    </image><?php
    include("./common_db.php");
    $query = "SELECT subject, id, post, email, name, category,
      DATE_FORMAT(date,'%a, %d %b %Y %T EST') as date
      FROM 03_simple_blog ORDER BY id DESC";
    $recipes = getAssoc($query);
    $url = "http://example.preinheimer.com/blog/index.php?post=";
    foreach($recipes AS $item)
    {
      echo "<item>\n";
      echo "<title>{$item['subject']}</title>\n";
      echo "<link>$url{$item['id']}</link>\n";
      echo "<description>{$item['post']}</description>\n";
      echo "<author>{$item['email']}</author>\n";
      echo "<category>{$item['category']}</category>\n";
      echo "<pubDate>{$item['date']}</pubDate>\n";
      echo "</item>\n";
    }
    echo "</channel>\n</rss>";

?>
```

Here is the sample output for the `feed.php` file:

```
<rss version="2.0">
  <channel>
    <language>en</language>
    <title>Sample Blog</title>
    <description>My Sample blog example.</description>
    <link>http://example.preinheimer.com/blog/</link>
    <image>
      <title>Sample Blog Logo</title>
      <link>http://example.preinheimer.com/feed1.php</link>
      <url>http://example.preinheimer.com/feed1.png</url>
    </image><item>
<title>Raking Leaves</title>
<link>http://example.preinheimer.com/blog/index.php?post=2</link>
<description>I hate raking leaves. Over the past two weeks we have raked the leaves
from the property into a pile that is 90 feet long, three feet high, and four feet
wide. </description>
<author>paul@preinheimer.com</author>
```

```
<category>Chores</category>
<pubDate>Wed, 17 Nov 2004 12:30:16 EST</pubDate>
</item>
<item>
<title>Snowing</title>
<link>http://example.preinheimer.com/blog/index.php?post=1</link>
<description>It is snowing outside! This is the first snowfall of the season, so it
is definately very exciting.</description>
<author>paul@preinheimer.com</author>
<category>Weather</category>
<pubDate>Mon, 08 Nov 2004 12:43:52 EST</pubDate>
</item>
</channel>
</rss>
```

This code example should look remarkably similar to the one earlier. Different database, some different fields, but not much of a real change.

Trackbacks

To empower trackbacks, you need to add capability to both the admin and index scripts. This will allow the author to send trackbacks to other blogs while posting, and to receive trackbacks via the index page for their own posts. Trackbacks were invented by the authors of Moveable Type to allow bloggers to source the ideas for their comments.

Trackbacks to Other Blogs

The following code includes a `sendTrackBack` function within the `admin.php` script. This will allow the administrator to send trackbacks for his/her posts.

```
function sendTrackBack($url, $title, $excerpt, $postURL)
{
  $blogname = urlencode("Sample Blog");
  $title = urlencode($title);
  if (strlen($excerpt) > 252)
  {
    $excerpt = substr($excerpt, 0, 252) . "...";
  }
  $excerpt = urlencode($excerpt);
  $url_info = parse_url($url);
  $host = $url_info['host'];
  $path = $url_info['path'] . "?" . $url_info['query'];
  $url = urlencode($url);
$data="tb_url=$url&url=$postURL&blog_name=$blogname&title=$title&excerpt=$excerpt";
```

First, you should declare the function to initialize the blog name (this is probably going to remain the same for all trackbacks; if not, it can be added to the function's variable list). The excerpt should be no longer than 255 characters, so it is trimmed if necessary, and all appropriate variables are URL encoded. The HTTP request requires different parts of the trackback URL to be used differently, so the host must be specified on its own in the request, as must the path and query. The `parse_url()` function makes this a snap. The `$data` variable contains all the information that will be passed with the request; it should be constructed in advance, so that the appropriate Content-Length header can be passed.

```
    $fp=fsockopen($host, 80);
    fputs($fp, "POST " . $path . " HTTP/1.1\r\n");
    fputs($fp, "Host: " . $host ."\r\n");
    fputs($fp, "Accept:
  text/xml,application/xml,application/xhtml+xml,text/html;q=0.9,text/plain\r\n");
    fputs($fp, "Accept-Charset: ISO-8859-1,utf-8;q=0.7,*;q=0.7\r\n");
    fputs($fp, "Connection: close\r\n");
    fputs($fp, "Content-Type: application/x-www-form-urlencoded\r\n");
    fputs($fp, "Content-Length: " . strlen($data) . "\r\n\r\n");
    fputs($fp, "$data");
```

A socket is opened to the specified URI, headers are passed, as is the data from the request. Note that the `Connection: close` header does not close the connection; it is an HTTP header that indicates that the connection should be closed after this request (as opposed to `Connection: keep-alive`). Also note the `Content-Type` header, letting the server/script know that the data is going to be URL encoded.

```
    $response="";
    while(!feof($fp))
    {
      $response.=fgets($fp, 128);
    }
    fclose($fp);
```

Retrieve all of the response information from the host, and then close the connection.

```
    list($http_headers, $http_content)=explode("\r\n\r\n", $response);

    if (substr_count($http_content, "<error>0</error") > 0)
    {
      return "Trackback Successful";
    }else if (substr_count($http_content, "<error>1</error") > 0)
    {
      return "Trackback Failed";
    }else
    {
      return "Unrecognized response, Bad URL?";
    }
  }
```

Split the response into its header and content portions, then determine if the request was successful. A more robust (but more difficult to read) method of checking the response would be with regex, to allow for new lines before and after the response code. If the response doesn't contain either of the expected responses, it is likely that a bad URL was entered.

Changing the existing `admin.php` file to make use of the trackback function is trivial. Add the appropriate function call:

```
    $postURL = "<a href=\"./index.php?entry=$id\">$id</a>"
    $messages = "Post added, Post id $postURL";
    if ($_POST['trackback'] != "")
    {
      echo sendTB($_POST['trackback'], $_POST['subject'], $_POST['post'], $postURL);
    }
```

And the appropriate form element:

```
Category: <input type="text" name="category"><br>
Trackback: <input type="text" name="trackback"><br>
Post:<br><textarea name="post"></textarea><br>
```

That's it. Trackbacks are a useful tool for bloggers to communicate with each other and reference sources. There is also the added benefit of increased visibility for each link. Note that you didn't save the trackback URL to be displayed with the post. When sending a trackback, it is generally desirable to either list the trackbacks you sent at the end of the post, or (more commonly) just to reference the original source for your ideas inline with the rest of your post. If you choose to specifically list which trackbacks were sent at the end of a post, just record the URL into the database when the trackback succeeds, and add the element to your `index.php` script.

Receiving Trackbacks

You can send trackbacks, so why not return the favor by receiving them? Receiving trackbacks is simpler than sending them, because you do not need to generate a raw HTTP request to accomplish the results. A few changes to `index.php` is all that is required. You need to store these trackbacks in a separate table because it will likely end up being a one-to-many relationship between the post and associated trackbacks.

```
SQL-query:
CREATE TABLE `03_simple_blog_trackback`
(
  `blog_id` INT NOT NULL ,
  `blogName` VARCHAR( 80 ) NOT NULL ,
  `title` VARCHAR( 80 ) NOT NULL ,
  `url` VARCHAR( 150 ) NOT NULL ,
  `excerpt` VARCHAR( 255 ) NOT NULL
);
```

The field values should be pretty self-explanatory; the excerpt field is 255 characters long (as is specified by the spec), and the rest were pretty arbitrary. While I am generally a fan of studlyCaps over underscores, I feel using underscores in field values is an effective way to indicate relationships.

Updating `index.php` will require three changes: an addition to provide for receipt and receipt acknowledgment of trackbacks from remote scripts, a minor addition to display trackback links for each story, and finally to display trackbacks to users viewing the page normally.

```
if ($_GET['action'] == "trackback")
  {
    echo "Trackback";
    if ($_POST['url'] == "")
    {
      echo '<?xml version="1.0" encoding="iso-8859-1"?>
      <response>
        <error>1</error>
        <message>URL required</message>
      </response>
      ';
      exit;
```

Under the trackback specification, a URL is required; if one is not received, return the appropriate error code.

```
}else if (!is_numeric($_GET['id']))
{
  echo '<?xml version="1.0" encoding="iso-8859-1"?>
  <response>
    <error>1</error>
    <message>Invalid Trackback ID</message>
  </response>
  ';
  exit;
```

If the ID that the remote user is attempting to trackback is non-numeric, it cannot be valid (in this instance), so an error should be returned. This check could be extended to ensure that the ID was numeric, and that being a valid post for accepting trackbacks.

```
}else
{
  $id = $_GET['id'];
  $blogName = mysql_escape_string($_POST['blog_name']);
  $title = mysql_escape_string($_POST['title']);
  $excerpt = $_POST['excerpt'];
  if (strlen($excerpt) > 252)
  {
    $excerpt = substr($excerpt, 0, 252) . "...";
  }
  $excerpt = mysql_escape_string($excerpt);
  $query = "INSERT INTO 03_simple_blog_trackback
  (`blog_id`, `blogName`, `title`, `url`, `excerpt`) VALUES
  ('$_GET[id]', '$_POST[blog_name]', '$_POST[title]', '$_POST[url]',
  '$_POST[excerpt]')";
  insertQuery($query);
  echo '<?xml version="1.0" encoding="iso-8859-1"?>
  <response>
    <error>0</error>
  </response>
  ';
  exit;
 }
}else if (is_numeric($_GET['entry']))
{
  $query = "SELECT * FROM 03_simple_blog WHERE id = '{$_GET['entry']}'";
}else
```

Finally, at this point assume that the trackback is valid, and insert the appropriate data (after escaping any quotes, and trimming the excerpt if necessary) into the database.

Publicizing Trackback URL

In this section, you declare the existence and location of the trackback URL in two different manners: first in regular HTML for a human-readable form, and secondly using XML/RDF to support auto discovery of the trackback URLs.

The human-readable link is trivial, continuing with the earlier `index.php` example:

```
echo "<a href=\"mailto:{$entry['email']}\">{$entry['name']}</a>\n";
echo "({$entry['date']})\n<br>";
echo "<a href=\"http://example.preinheimer.com/blog/index.php?
  action=trackback&id={$entry['id']}\">Trackback</a>";
```

The auto discovery declaration is a little more complicated. You will recognize the rdf declarations from the discussion on extending RSS feeds. The completed `foreach` loop to display each of the entries looks like this:

```
foreach($blogEntries AS $entry)
  {
    $pageURL = "http://example.preinheimer.com/blog/index.php";
    echo "<h2><a href=\"$pageURL?entry={$entry['id']}\">
      {$entry['subject']}</a></h2>\n";
    echo "<b>{$entry['category']}</b>\n";
    echo "<p>{$entry['post']}</p>\n";
    echo "<a href=\"mailto:{$entry['email']}\">{$entry['name']}</a>\n";
    echo "({$entry['date']})\n<br>";
    echo "<a href=\"$postURL?action=trackback&id={$entry['id']}\">Trackback</a>";
    echo '<!--\n<rdf:RDF xmlns:rdf="http://www.w3.org/1999/02/22-rdf-syntax-ns#"
       xmlns:dc="http://purl.org/dc/elements/1.1/"
       xmlns:trackback="http://madskills.com/public/xml/rss/module/trackback/">
     <rdf:Description
       rdf:about="$pageURL?entry=' . $entry['id'] . '"
       dc:identifier="$pageURL?entry=' . $entry['id'] . '"
       dc:title="' . $entry['subject'] . '"
       trackback:ping="$pageURL?action=trackback&id=' . $entry['id'] . '" />
     </rdf:RDF>\n-->';
  }
```

The addition of the `$pageURL` variable was necessary to ensure the lines of code fit on this page. It also helps separate the URLs that are local and the RDF declarations that point to external sites.

The XML code shown here is exactly what the spec specifies — nothing too drastic.

You can also publicize your trackback links in the RSS feed for your document. Here is some example output. Changes required to output this document should be obvious based on previous examples.

```
<rss version="2.0"
  xmlns:trackback="http://madskills.com/public/xml/rss/module/trackback/" >
 <channel>
  <language>en</language>
  <title>Example News.com</title>
  <description>News and commentary from the cross-platform scripting
community.</description>
  <link>http://www.wroxnews.com/</link>
  <image>
   <title>Example News.com</title>
   <link>http://www.wroxnews.com/</link>
   <url>http://www.wroxnews.com/pics/button.png</url>
  </image>
```

```
    <item>
      <title>Feed usage up 1000%!</title>
      <link>http://www.wroxnews.com/story2/index.html</link>
      <description>Feed usage has increased a dramatic 1000% in the past 48hrs alone,
this may...</description>
      <trackback:ping rdf:resource=" http://www.wroxnews.com/story2/tb.cgi?tb_id=2"/>
    </item>
    <item>
      <title>RSS Feed Goes Live!</title>
      <link>http://wroxnews.org/story1/index.html</link>
      <description>Wroxnews.com is proud to announce the launch of our premier RSS
service...</description>
      <trackback:ping rdf:resource=" http://www.wroxnews.com/story2/tb.cgi?tb_id=2"/>
    </item>
  </channel>
</rss>
```

Trackback Spam

Unfortunately, trackback spam is slowly becoming more widespread. The point with trackback spam is not usually to generate clicks, but instead to assist with search engine indexing by creating thousands of links from hundreds of different domains to specific pages using certain keywords. This widespread linking can improve the search engine ranking of a particular site considerably. The attack is quite similar to those used in comment spam — some automated crawler searches the Web for URLs matching a certain pattern (often seeking specific blogging software, but occasionally not) and uses a pregenerated GET or POST request against the URL to advertise its wares. Unfortunately, my favorite defense against comment spam (using a Completely Automated Public Turing Test to Tell Humans and Computers Apart (CAPTHCA)) doesn't work with trackbacks, as both desired and undesired trackbacks will be generated by automated scripts. You do, however, have a few options.

Check for Links

First, recognize what trackbacks are for, and hence a common attribute that most valid trackbacks should have, and their site should link to yours. If Sally read your blog and decided to comment on it, it is probably a reasonable assumption that she posted a link to your original story somewhere within her blog, either in the post itself or underneath where her software lists outgoing trackbacks. This function is designed to be used after determining that the trackback is valid (contains a URL and such), but before the data is placed in the database. It simply downloads the remote page and checks for a link back to your page. Upon discovery, it returns true; if it is missing, it returns false.

```
function checkLinkBack($remoteURL, $localURL)
{
  $page = implode('', file($remoteURL));
  if (stristr($page, $localURL) != FALSE)
  {
    return true;
  }else
  {
    return false;
  }
}
```

This method does have a few failings:

- The remote software package might send trackback pings before saving the post, and as such the URL containing the post might not be available or might not contain the URL to your blog yet, for entirely valid reasons.
- It could provide an easy method to launch a denial of service attack against your blog, making repeated trackbacks indicating a URL that either resolves to a really long page or a particularly slow connection, wasting resources on repeated requests.
- The author of the post might only refer to your site in a textual manner; for example, "I was reading Paul's blog today," rather than actually containing a link.

That being said, the method is still worth consideration. The first failing could be mitigated by having your blog software check trackbacks in the database after the fact (say, 24 hours later), or when instructed to do so by an administrator.

Blacklisted Words

The comment and trackback spam I receive on a regular basis generally contains one of a few keywords over and over again. By checking for the presence of commonly spammed words, you can likely detect trackbacks without having to download a remote page.

```
function checkBadWords($excerpt)
{
  $wordList = array('debt',  'poker', 'weight-loss', 'phentermine', 'diet');
  foreach($wordList as $word)
  {
    if (stristr ($excerpt, $word) != FALSE)
    {
      return false;
    }
  }
  return true;
}
```

You should of course change the wordlist to match your own experiences with spammers. They appear to work in phases, sending a lot of spam of a certain type for a while and then moving on. As with the previous method, this one contains a few weaknesses:

- If this method of blacklisting becomes common, trackback spammers will follow the lead of those who send email spam, and begin misspelling words, encoding characters, and so on.
- Valid posts could contain one of those words, and thusly be ignored.
- Trackback spam changes over time, so you will need to update the word list to stay current.

URL Dissection

When sending a trackback, the trend is to link to a specific post rather than to the root domain of a page. The reasons behind this are obvious—the referenced post will not be on the front page anymore, so following trackback links would be pointless. Comment and trackback spam, however, often link to the root domain, and as such, should be identifiable.

```
function checkURL($remoteURL)
{
  $urlInfo = parse_url($remoteURL);
  if (str_len($urlInfo['path'] > 1))
  {
    return true;
  }else
  {
    return false;
  }
}
```

The `parse_url()` function makes this process trivial, splitting the URL into its separate segments for you (those being scheme, host, path, query). You want the path portion of the URL to be longer than a single character (`www.wrox.com/` would have a path of "`/`") to indicate that a more complex path was used. As always, this method does have its weaknesses:

- The spec for trackbacks is pretty loose; someone could send you a trackback to their root page.
- Trackback spammers could start linking to pages deeper within their domains.

Ultimately, the methods you decide to run with will depend on how big a problem trackback spam becomes for you. None of these methods are terribly complex, and should any particular spammer decide to investigate your blog, they can be easily broken. That, however, usually isn't the problem. Spammers use automated software to deluge tens or hundreds of blogs. The fact that your blog in particular is resistant likely won't be noticed. A longer-term solution (and more advanced one) could use some combination of the previous methods together with admin intervention.

Retail Store Example

This example takes an imaginary store, Tom's Garden Shed, and creates a sample RSS feed that the store could use to inform its eager public. The store will actually offer several feeds: a product feed (including pricing information), a weekly garden tip feed, and a weekly sale item feed. These three feeds will make use of both the RSS and Atom specifications, and will extend where appropriate via XML namespacing. I'm going to ignore the data entry side of these feeds to concentrate on the ways the feeds can be produced. As such, I have included some sample data with the table specs. Please remember that all this code is available online, at www.wrox.com, so don't type this in if you can avoid it.

Here's the product table:

```
CREATE TABLE `03_store_products` (
  `id` int(11) NOT NULL auto_increment,
  `name` varchar(50) NOT NULL default '',
  `description` text NOT NULL,
  `category` varchar(25) NOT NULL default '',
  `price` decimal(5,2) NOT NULL default '0.00',
  `unit` varchar(25) NOT NULL default '',
  PRIMARY KEY  (`id`)
) TYPE=MyISAM;

INSERT INTO `03_store_products` VALUES (1, 'Marigolds', 'Beautiful perennial
flower', 'perennial', 0.99, 'pack of 100 seeds');
```

```
INSERT INTO `03_store_products` VALUES (2, 'Tulip', 'Beautiful flower with two
lips', 'Annual', 3.69, 'bulb');
```

Here's the sale table:

```
CREATE TABLE `03_store_sales` (
  `week` int(11) NOT NULL default '0',
  `product_id` int(11) NOT NULL default '0',
  `sale_price` decimal(5,2) NOT NULL default '0.00',
  `sale_unit` varchar(25) NOT NULL default '',
  `blurb` text NOT NULL
) TYPE=MyISAM;

INSERT INTO `03_store_sales` VALUES (1, 1, 0.69, 'pack of 100 seeds', 'Marigolds
are on sale this week only!');
INSERT INTO `03_store_sales` VALUES (1, 2, 4.59, 'Twin pack of 2 bulbs', 'Our
supplier sent us the wrong shipment, so we can pass on the savings of these great
twin packs on to you!');
```

Finally, here's the tips table:

```
CREATE TABLE `03_store_tips` (
  `id` int(11) NOT NULL auto_increment,
  `week` int(11) NOT NULL default '0',
  `name` varchar(25) NOT NULL default '',
  `email` varchar(50) NOT NULL default '',
  `title` varchar(50) NOT NULL default '',
  `tip` text NOT NULL,
  PRIMARY KEY  (`id`)
) TYPE=MyISAM;

INSERT INTO `03_store_tips` VALUES (1, 1, 'Tom', 'tom@tomsgardenshed.com',
'Landscaping a shady hill', 'One question I often get asked is, Tom, how can I get
the grass to grow on the top of, and the slope of, a small shaded hill on my
property? No matter what I try it dies off mid season!.<br><br>My Answer: You
don't. Yes, there are hardier strains of grass out there, but with the combination
of shade, poor irrigation and the packed clay soil prevalent in the area you are
going to waste a lot of time on a small portion of your yard. You do however have
several options. Ground covering ivy, or other low to ground shrubs will thrive in
this environment, and should have shallow enough roots to avoid damaging your
trees. ');
```

Feeds

You will start off with one of the easier feeds, the tip feed. This feed is designed to provide customers with a weekly garden tip. With rapid adoption of feed support (both RSS and to a lesser extent Atom) into mainstream email clients, feeds are quickly becoming an attractive alternative to mailing lists.

Advantages of providing a feed versus running a mailing list are as follows:

- Feeds require no administration; users handle registration and removal on the client side.
- Users may forget they subscribed to a particular list and mark the message as spam, placing delivery of messages from your entire domain (not just your mailing list) at risk. Once you are listed as a sender of unsolicited mail, it can be very difficult to lose that label.

- No stress on your mail server; sending a large batch of messages out on a weekly basis can delay delivery of regular email.

Disadvantages of providing a feed versus running a mailing list are as follows:

- Users may be unfamiliar with the feed concept, even though they likely own software that supports reading it. Down the road it will likely become possible to create a link with a registered protocol that will automatically create a subscription in the appropriate software, but it isn't here yet.
- You can't forward a feed. Often mailing list recipients will forward a particular message to a friend. This may not work quite like they expect in the average client.
- Repeated pointless loads. Even if you only update your feed once a month, most clients will probably hit your feed at least once an hour, even if your feed indicates the appropriate update interval.

With these points in mind, Tom still wants a feed for his weekly tips. He will use some of the lessons learned in Chapter 3 to present the most recent tip on his homepage.

Because Tom wants to provide for both Atom and RSS users, one script will provide for both types of output:

```
<?php
 include("../common_db.php");
 switch ($_GET['format'])
 {
  case "atom":
   displayATOM();
   break;
  case "rss":
  default:
   displayRSS();
   break;
 }
```

The feed gets off to an easy start—it expects to be called with either `?format=atom` or `?format=rss`, and will use that information to decide with which format to answer the request.

This is the Atom format:

```
function displayATOM()
{
 header("Content-Type: application/atom+xml");
 $url = "http://example.preinheimer.com/store/index.php";
 $query = "SELECT id, name, email, title, tip,
  DATE_FORMAT(pubDate,'%Y-%c-%dT%H:%i:%S-04:00') as pubDate
  FROM 03_store_tips ORDER BY pubDate";
```

The date format shown here differs greatly from the one seen in RSS feeds because the requirements are quite different. Other than that, the code required so far differs little from an RSS feed.

```
    $tips = getAssoc($query, 2);
    ?><?xml version="1.0" encoding="utf-8"?>
    <feed version="0.3" xmlns="http://purl.org/atom/ns#">
     <title>Tom's Garden Shed</title>
     <link rel="alternate" type="text/html"
      href="http://example.preinheimer.com/store/index.php" />
     <modified><?php echo $tips[0]['pubDate'] ?></modified>
     <author>
      <name>Tom's Garden Shed</name>
     </author>
```

Notice the XML namespace declaration, but unlike previous examples, it isn't prefixed with a namespace (they often read `xmlns:namespace`). As such, elements within the namespace may also forgo the usual namespace prefix.

```
     <?php
     foreach($tips AS $item)
     {
      if (strlen($item['tip']) > 252)
      {
       $item['tipTrim'] = substr($item['tip'], 0, 252) . "...";
      }else
      {
       $item['tipTrim'] = $item['tip'];
      }
```

As usual, we will trim the tip to provide a summary field. A more professional feed would likely have a true summary, rather than the first X characters from the feed. Further enhancements might include stripping any HTML tags from the summary to ensure it displays properly in non-HTML environments.

```
      echo "<entry>\n";
      echo "<title>{$item['subject']}</title>";
      echo "<link rel=\"alternate\" type=\"text/html\"
  href=\"$url?entry={$item['id']}\" />";
      echo "<id>$url?entry={$item['id']}</id>";
      echo "<summary>{$item['tipTrim']}</summary>\n";
      echo "<content>{$item['tip']}</content>";
      echo "<issued>{$item['pubDate']}</issued>";
      echo "<modified>{$item['pubDate']}</modified>";
      echo "</entry>\n";
     }
     echo "</feed>";
  }
```

The issued and modified dates are both populated from the same database field. Again, in a more professional feed these would likely be independent elements to allow for updates to be appropriately declared.

Sample output of code:

```
  <?xml version="1.0" encoding="utf-8"?>
  <feed version="0.3" xmlns="http://purl.org/atom/ns#">
   <title>Tom's Garden Shed, Weekly Tips</title>
```

```
<link rel="alternate" type="text/html"
href="http://example.preinheimer.com/store/index.php" />
 <modified>2004-10-31T23:59:59-04:00</modified>
 <author>
  <name>Tom</name>
 </author>
 <entry>
  <title>Planting Tips</title>
  <link rel="alternate" type="text/html"
href="http://example.preinheimer.com/store/index.php?entry=2" />
  <id>http://example.preinheimer.com/store/index.php?entry=2</id>
  <summary>I often get called in to examine a garden that the owner feels is
performing poorly. The most common problem is usually over crowding. Don't forget
to space your plants adequately, the seed package, or the information packet that
comes with a bulb for a...</summary>
  <content>I often get called in to examine a garden that the owner feels is
performing poorly. The most common problem is usually over crowding. Don't forget
to space your plants adequately, the seed package, or the information packet that
comes with a bulb for appropriate spacing information.

As a general rule of thumb you should plant two items no closer than half of its
fully grown height. </content>
  <issued>2004-10-31T23:59:59-04:00</issued>
  <modified>2004-10-31T23:59:59-04:00</modified>
 </entry>
 <entry>
  <title>Landscaping a shady hill</title>
  <link rel="alternate" type="text/html"
href="http://example.preinheimer.com/store/index.php?entry=1" />
  <id>http://example.preinheimer.com/store/index.php?entry=1</id>
  <summary>One question I often get asked is, 'Tom, how can I get the grass to grow
on the top of, and the slope of, a small shaded hill on my property? No matter what
I try it dies off mid season'.

My Answer: You don't. Yes, there are hardier strains of grass ...</summary>
  <content>One question I often get asked is, 'Tom, how can I get the grass to grow
on the top of, and the slope of, a small shaded hill on my property? No matter what
I try it dies off mid season'.

My Answer: You don't. Yes, there are hardier strains of grass out there, but with
the combination of shade, poor irrigation and the packed clay soil prevalent in the
area you are going to waste a lot of time on a small portion of your yard. You do
however have several options. Ground covering ivy, or other low to ground shrubs
will thrive in this environment, and should have shallow enough roots to avoid
damaging your trees. </content>
  <issued>2004-11-07T23:59:59-04:00</issued>
  <modified>2004-11-07T23:59:59-04:00</modified>
 </entry>
</feed>
```

The RSS feed isn't too different from the Atom example, nor from previous examples.

```
function displayRSS()
{
  header("Content-Type: text/xml");
  $query = "SELECT id, name, email, title, tip,
```

```
    DATE_FORMAT(pubDate,'%a, %d %b %Y %T EST') as pubDate
    FROM 03_store_tips ORDER BY pubDate";
    $tips = getAssoc($query, 2);
  ?><rss version="2.0" xmlns:content="http://purl.org/rss/1.0/modules/content/">
  <channel>
    <language>en</language>
    <title>Tom's Garden Shed, Weekly Tips</title>
    <description>Weekly gardening tips from Tom</description>
    <generator>Tom's Feed Generator, v0.01b</generator>
    <ttl>1440</ttl>
```

Notice the content XML namespace. This allows you to include the entire post, not just a summary within the feed. I've also included the `TTL` declaration in this script; aggregators should notice this and refresh the feed only once a week. You could also look into the `skipDays` and `skipHours` elements to further define this more clearly.

```
    <pubDate><?php echo $tips[0]['pubDate'] ?></pubDate>
    <link>http://example.preinheimer.com/store/</link>
    <image>
      <title>Tom's Garden Shed</title>
      <link>http://example.preinheimer.com/store/</link>
      <url>http://example.preinheimer.com/store/tom.png</url>
    </image><?php

    foreach($tips AS $item)
    {
      $url = "http://example.preinheimer.com/store/index.php";
      if (strlen($item['tip']) > 252)
      {
        $item['tipTrim'] = substr($item['tip'], 0, 252) . "...";
      }else
      {
        $item['tipTrim'] = $item['tip'];
      }
      echo "<item>\n";
      echo "<title>{$item['title']}</title>\n";
      echo "<link>$url?item={$item['id']}</link>\n";
      echo "<description>{$item['tipTrim']}</description>\n";
      echo "<content:encoded>{$item['tip']}</content:encoded>";
      echo "<author>{$item['email']}</author>\n";
      echo "<pubDate>{$item['pubDate']}</pubDate>\n";
      echo "</item>\n";
    }
    echo "</channel>\n</rss>";
}
```

Overall the script shouldn't be that confusing.

Sample output:

```
<rss version="2.0" xmlns:content="http://purl.org/rss/1.0/modules/content/">
  <channel>
    <language>en</language>
    <title>Tom's Garden Shed, Weekly Tips</title>
    <description>Weekly gardening tips from Tom</description>
```

```
    <generator>Tom's Feed Generator, v0.01b</generator>
    <ttl>1440</ttl>
    <pubDate>Sun, 07 Nov 2004 23:59:59 EST</pubDate>
    <link>http://example.preinheimer.com/store/</link>
    <image>
      <title>Tom's Garden Shed</title>
      <link>http://example.preinheimer.com/store/</link>
      <url>http://example.preinheimer.com/store/tom.png</url>
    </image><item>
<title>Landscaping a shady hill</title>
<link>http://example.preinheimer.com/store/index.php?item=1</link>
<description>One question I often get asked is, 'Tom, how can I get the grass to
grow on the top of, and the slope of, a small shaded hill on my property? No matter
what I try it dies off mid season'.

My Answer: You don't. Yes, there are hardier strains of grass ...</description>
<content:encoded>One question I often get asked is, 'Tom, how can I get the grass
to grow on the top of, and the slope of, a small shaded hill on my property? No
matter what I try it dies off mid season'.

My Answer: You don't. Yes, there are hardier strains of grass out there, but with
the combination of shade, poor irrigation and the packed clay soil prevalent in the
area you are going to waste a lot of time on a small portion of your yard. You do
however have several options. Ground covering ivy, or other low to ground shrubs
will thrive in this environment, and should have shallow enough roots to avoid
damaging your trees. </content:encoded><author>tom@tomsgardenshed.com</author>
<pubDate>Sun, 07 Nov 2004 23:59:59 EST</pubDate>
</item>
</channel>
</rss>
```

One of the items from this output has been cut to save on space.

Product Feed

Just to keep things interesting, Tom's product feed will use the Smarty Templating System.

If you are interested in learning more about Smarty, take a look at `http://smarty.php.net/`*. It serves to facilitate separation of business and presentation logic. A detailed exploration of Smarty's feature set is beyond the scope of this book.*

Here is the product template:

```
<rss version="2.0"
  xmlns:content="http://purl.org/rss/1.0/modules/content/"
  xmlns:plantInfo="http://example.preinheimer.com/store/plantInfo">
  <channel>
    <language>en</language>
    <title>Tom's Garden Shed, Weekly Tips</title>
    <description>Weekly gardening tips from Tom</description>
    <generator>Tom's Feed Generator, v0.01b</generator>
    <ttl>1440</ttl>
    <pubDate>Sun, 07 Nov 2004 23:59:59 EST</pubDate>
    <link>http://example.preinheimer.com/store/</link>
    <image>
```

```
        <title>Tom's Garden Shed</title>
        <link>http://example.preinheimer.com/store/</link>
        <url>http://example.preinheimer.com/store/tom.png</url>
      </image>
       {section name=tip loop=$tips}
        <item>
          <title>{$tips[tip].title}</title>
          <link>http://example.preinheimer.com/pinfo.php?item={$tips[tip].id}</link>
          <description>{$tips[tip].name}</description>
          <content:encoded>{$tips[tip].description}</content:encoded>
          <pubDate>{$tips[tip].pubDate}</pubDate>
          <plantInfo:type>{$tips[tip].category}</plantInfo:type>
          <plantInfo:price>{$tips[tip].price}</plantInfo:price>
          <plantInfo:unit>{$tips[tip].unit}</plantInfo:unit>
         </item>
        {/section}
    </channel>
  </rss>
```

Here is the `product.php` file:

```
<?php
  header("Content-Type: text/xml");
  include("../common_db.php");
  require('Smarty.class.php');
  $smarty = new Smarty;
  $smarty->template_dir = '/www/smarty/example.preinheimer.com/templates/';
  $smarty->compile_dir = '/www/smarty/example.preinheimer.com/templates_c/';
  $smarty->config_dir = '/www/smarty/example.preinheimer.com/configs/';
  $smarty->cache_dir = '/www/smarty/example.preinheimert.com/cache/';

   $query = "SELECT id, name, description, category, unit, price
    FROM 03_store_products ORDER BY id";
    $tips = getAssoc($query, 2);

   $url = "http://example.preinheimer.com/store/index.php";


  $smarty->assign('url', $url);
  $smarty->assign('tips', $tips);
  $smarty->display('product.tpl');
?>
```

And here is the sample output:

```
<rss version="2.0"
  xmlns:content="http://purl.org/rss/1.0/modules/content/"
  xmlns:plantInfo="http://example.preinheimer.com/store/plantInfo">
 <channel>
  <language>en</language>
  <title>Tom's Garden Shed, Weekly Tips</title>
  <description>Weekly gardening tips from Tom</description>
  <generator>Tom's Feed Generator, v0.01b</generator>
  <ttl>1440</ttl>
  <pubDate>Sun, 07 Nov 2004 23:59:59 EST</pubDate>
```

```
    <link>http://example.preinheimer.com/store/</link>
     <image>
      <title>Tom's Garden Shed</title>
      <link>http://example.preinheimer.com/store/</link>
      <url>http://example.preinheimer.com/store/tom.png</url>
     </image>
     <item>
        <title></title>
            <link>http://example.preinheimer.com/pinfo.php?item=1</link>
            <description>Marigolds</description>
            <content:encoded>Beautiful perennial flower</content:encoded>
            <pubDate></pubDate>
            <plantInfo:type>perennial</plantInfo:type>
            <plantInfo:price>0.99</plantInfo:price>
            <plantInfo:unit>pack of 100 seeds</plantInfo:unit>
           </item>
                <item>
            <title></title>
            <link>http://example.preinheimer.com/pinfo.php?item=2</link>
            <description>Tulip</description>
            <content:encoded>Beautiful flower with two lips</content:encoded>
            <pubDate></pubDate>
            <plantInfo:type>Annual</plantInfo:type>
            <plantInfo:price>3.69</plantInfo:price>
            <plantInfo:unit>bulb</plantInfo:unit>
           </item>
            </channel>
  </rss>
```

Summary

This chapter concluded the coverage of web feeds. Specifically, this chapter covered the following:

- The process of taking content from the web page and putting it into the XML format required by one of the common feed specifications.
- The topic of caching with a variety of different techniques. Some of the methods likely seemed trivial, but I believe they are worthwhile to examine just to get the mind started on different alternatives.
- How to create a simple blog, taking the blog data from the database and presenting it to the user.
- Trackbacks as they are often listed in feeds along with comments, and methods of defeating trackback spam.
- An example of a feed centering on a fictional gardening store.

The next part of the book focuses on web APIs, the process of web-based applications trading information back and forth.

Part II
APIs

5

Introduction to Web APIs

Web APIs are the other essential component under the web services umbrella. Like web feeds, they are provided in a clearly defined manner by many of the top web-aware firms. The primary difference between web APIs and web services is the level of interaction available — feeds are relatively static; you get one page, and it's the same page everyone else gets. APIs, on the other hand, are entire programs, ready to provide information, ship products, or query databases, all depending on your request. From an object-oriented (OO) standpoint, dealing with an API is much like dealing with a class. It receives your request, and then, based entirely on the information you gave it (it cannot come back and request information), it returns a result.

Although numerous APIs are used today, for the purposes of this book the focus here is on the two most popular. The first, Representational State Transfer (REST), uses long GET requests to indicate exactly what action is desired. Requests performed using REST look identical to the request seen after filling out a form that uses the GET method, and you can in fact perform REST requests in that exact manner. The second, Simple Object Access Protocol (SOAP), posts XML objects to the server and receives a similarly fashioned XML object as a response.

This chapter covers the following topics:

- The choice between using REST and SOAP
- An introduction to REST and SOAP
- How REST and SOAP both work
- How to generate SOAP and REST requests
- Handling REST and SOAP responses

REST or SOAP?

When interacting with web services, generally the choice of which method to use will be made for you. The majority of services operate in either REST or SOAP, not both (Amazon is a notable exception to this rule). When given the choice, however, there are several points to consider:

- **Overhead** — REST requests are relatively slim. SOAP requests, on the other hand, contain a lot of additional information, which can really add up.
- **Transparency** — With REST requests (even when completed over HTTPS), all request information is sent in the clear; with SOAP only the end point (URL) is visible. This may sound like a clear-cut win for SOAP, but not quite. When requests go in the clear, they can easily be monitored by the relevant IT departments and screened by firewalls. REST requests can also be easily cached (when this is marked as allowable by the server) by existing infrastructure, reducing server load and bandwidth costs.
- **Ease of use** — Many developers have indicated a preference to develop for REST servers, because the requests can be quickly generated without all the extra encapsulation required by SOAP. Amazon, for example (offering both REST and SOAP interfaces), has 85 percent of its requests occur over REST.
- **Service definition** — SOAP services are defined by Web Services Description Language (WSDL) files, which contain all the information required to make a request. In fact, generic SOAP clients are available that will allow you to make any request provided by a service given nothing but the address of the WSDL file. There is no equivalent for REST services.
- **Encapsulation** — SOAP requests are encapsulated within an XML `envelope`. The body of the request itself is then again encapsulated within a `body` element. The addition of namespacing within the document goes further to clearly define exactly what each element is describing. There are several excellent tools out there to assist document creation, which can take the tedium out of creating these longer requests.

Overall, there is no clear winner (if there was, I wouldn't need to introduce both). The choice will depend on the particular application and the tools available to build it. Generally speaking, when given the choice, I prefer to use SOAP in my web service communications. I feel that the service definition and encapsulation provided by SOAP outweighs the additional overhead and lack of protocol-level transparency.

One other common web service API is XML-RPC. Although XML-RPC is quite simple to learn and use, it lacks the features of SOAP while retaining a much higher overhead than REST. Therefore, depending on your purposes, choosing REST or SOAP would almost always be a better choice.

Introducing REST

REST was described as an architectural style by Roy Thomas Fielding as part of his doctoral dissertation in the year 2000 (Architectural Styles and the Design of Network-based Software Architectures, Chapter 5). For the curious, it is available online at `www.ics.uci.edu/~fielding/pubs/dissertation/rest_arch_style.htm`.

For the focus of this chapter, REST is discussed as per its application to web services.

REST is a stateless method for applications to present requests to the required service. Each request has two essential parts: the endpoint (usually a URL) and the message indicating the requested action. That might sound scary, but realistically it isn't so different from a web browser requesting a web page — it knows the endpoint (the URL for the web page in question) and it knows what action it would like to perform (download the page in question). Also just like web browsing, there are methods to mimic a stateful connection — with web browsing these are called sessions; REST has similar constructs.

While architecturally speaking REST can take place over any transport medium (not just HTTP/HTTPS), in the context of APIs, HTTP is *the* logical choice. We (the programmers) already have great experience dealing with communications over HTTP, and have suites of tools at our disposal to aid development and problem resolution.

How REST Works

Generally speaking, a REST request will involve sending a request to a special URL (similar to what you would see after filling out a form using the GET method), then receiving an XML document containing the server's response. The XML response is then parsed, and the desired information is extracted and acted upon.

Each REST request generally has several common elements:

- **Endpoint URL** — The full address for the desired script. A REST service might have only a single script that handles all request types, or different scripts for different request types.
- **Developer ID** — Most REST services require some sort of developer ID or key to be sent with each request. This identifies the origin of the request and is generally used for tracking purposes. Some services may use this value to limit the number of queries run during a given timeframe.
- **Desired action** — Few servers have a unique endpoint for all possible requests. As such, it is generally required to include the desired action in the request.
- **Parameters** — Several parameters will need to be included with the request to provide the requested action with some context (for example, the desired action might be a search; the parameters might be a type, and the keywords values of book and style).

With those elements in mind, you can create a theoretical request:

```
http://library.example.com/api.php?devkey=123&action=search&type=book&keyword=style
```

Here a request is sent to the endpoint `http://library.example.com/api.php`, with a developer key of `123`. The desired action is `search`, and `type` and `keyword` parameters are included with values of `book` and `style`. Given that request, the response would look something like this:

```
<?xml version="1.0" encoding="UTF-8"?>
<LibraryAPI xmlns="http://library.example.com/api/spec">
<Request>
 <RequestId>123a456</RequestId>
 <Parameters>
  <Argument Name="devkey" Value="123" />
  <Argument Name="action" Value="search" />
  <Argument Name="type" Value="book" />
```

```
    <Argument Name="keyword" Value="style" />
  </Parameters>
 </Request>
 <Response>
  <ResultCount>2</ResultCount>
  <Item>
   <Title>Style Book Vol 1</Title>
   <Status>Out</Status>
   <Holds>3</Holds>
   <CopiesOnHand>2</CopiesOnHand>
   <Author>Jon Doe</Author>
  </Item>
  <Item>
   <Title>Style Book Vol 2</Title>
   <Status>In</Status>
   <Holds>0</Holds>
   <CopiesOnHand>1</CopiesOnHand>
   <Author>Jon Doe</Author>
  </Item>
 </Response>
 </LibraryAPI>
```

You can see that the response has several structural elements. First, it declares itself to be XML 1.0 and uses UTF-8 for encoding. The LibraryAPI element is the root element of this document and includes the specified namespaces. Second, the `Request` section; it is common for REST requests to include all information sent with the request in the response. This adds clarity, and can ease programming on the requestor's end. Here you see each of the four elements passed to the service.

Finally, looking a bit closer, you will notice that in this case the response has returned some metadata about the results, shown in the `ResultCount` tag, along with the result items themselves. For this request you see each book is encapsulated within an `Item` element, which has five children that describe specific attributes of the books.

Implementing REST

Now that you know basically how it works, it's time to look at how to use REST for your own purposes. There are two sides to this tale, the first is how to generate legitimate REST requests, and the second is how to handle the responses correctly.

Generating Requests

When it comes to generating the request, you have three main options. First, you can generate the request manually, using PHP's header functions. This gives you complete flexibility in generating the request, but does involve the most coding. Second, you can use one of PHP's built-in request functions such as `file_get_contents()` or `file()/fopen()`, `fread()`, and `fclose()`. With this method, a lot of the detailed information is handled automatically by PHP, and you receive the same response. Finally, you can use a custom class designed to be used with the API in question. Generally these classes require nothing more than the parameter list, and will return the results in the form of a custom object or make them accessible through a class.

Manual Generation

Generating requests manually is only tricky the first time, after that, code-reuse and modularity kick in. Conceptually the function that will generate the request is pretty basic. First, all the request parameters are prepared to ensure proper transmission. Next, the URL for the endpoint is generated, then parsed and broken up into its component parts. Finally, the request itself is sent using sockets:

```
function callAPI($endpoint, $devkey, $action, $type, $keyword)
{
  $action = urlencode($action);
  $type = urlencode($type);
  $keyword = urlencode($keyword);
```

Three of the passed parameters are URL encoded. This is necessary to ensure they are passed properly over the URL. In the previous example, a search for "style" was performed; if the search had instead been "style book," the space would have required encoding, resulting in `style%20book`. I have neglected encoding the `devkey` variables, trusting that the issuing authority took how it would be used into consideration when creating them.

```
  $url = $endpoint . "?devkey=$devkey&action=$action&type=$type&keyword=$keyword";
  $url_info = parse_url($url);
  $host = $url_info['host'];
  $path = $url_info['path'] . "?" . $url_info['query'];
  $data = "";
```

Here the URL itself is generated, including the now URL-encoded parameters. The URL needs to be deconstructed down to its component parts for use in the raw socket connection.

```
  $fp=fsockopen($host, 80);
  fputs($fp, "POST " . $path . " HTTP/1.1\r\n");
  fputs($fp, "Host: " . $host ."\r\n");
  fputs($fp, "Accept: */*\r\n");
  fputs($fp, "Accept-Charset: ISO-8859-1,utf-8;q=0.7,*;q=0.7\r\n");
  fputs($fp, "Connection: close\r\n");
  fputs($fp, "Content-Type: application/x-www-form-urlencoded\r\n");
  fputs($fp, "Content-Length: " . strlen($data) . "\r\n\r\n");
  fputs($fp, "$data");
```

Here the information generated by previous code is finally sent. The first `fputs()` line sends the path to the requested document, and the second line specifies the desired host.

```
  $response="";
  while(!feof($fp))
  {
    $response.=fgets($fp, 128);
  }
  fclose($fp);
  list($http_headers, $http_content)=explode("\r\n\r\n", $response);
  return $http_content;
}
```

Finally, the response is retrieved and the content of the response is returned. You learn how to handle responses in the sections dealing with that side of things shortly.

Quick Generation

Utilizing PHP's built-in file functions, the same process can be completed with much less code (though you do have less flexibility). Conceptually this function works the same as the previous one, except all the file socket calls are replaced with one call to `file_get_contents()`:

```
function callAPIQuick($endpoint, $devkey, $action, $type, $keyword)
{
  $action = urlencode($action);
  $type = urlencode($type);
  $keyword = urlencode($keyword);
  $url = $endpoint . "?devkey=$devkey&action=$action&type=$type&keyword=$keyword";
  $response = @file_get_contents($url);
  return $response;
}
```

There really isn't much to explain with this example. The URL encoding was discussed previously, and the single `file_get_contents()` call handles all the magic. The ampersand in front of the function call is used to suppress any warnings that may arise from a non-existent file or URL, because these should be handled by the calling function (`file_get_contents()` will return false in these instances). In pre-PHP5 environments you will need to use `fopen()` instead of `file_get_contents()`. Some flexibility is lost with this request type, because you can no longer set custom headers or optional headers, which may be required or very desirable depending on the API with which you are interacting.

Automated Tools

As the popularity of web services increases, so will the prevalence of prebuilt classes to handle the dirty work of actually interacting with the server. If the service you want to interact with has a class available, it is definitely worth looking into. Accessing the class will of course be dependent on the class itself. It should come with sufficient documentation, and access will likely not differ too much from the earlier examples—just with a little more error checking (you hope). Something to keep in mind is that many prebuilt modules are developed and maintained by third parties, and as such you might have to wait a while after new features are released on the API for them to become available with your class.

Handling the Response

How you deal with the response depends on which method of sending the request you choose. If you generated the request either manually or with the aid of one of PHP's built-in functions (like `file_get_contents()`) you will also need to manually handle the response. If you used a third-party module, it will have its own interface for retrieving results.

Manually Parsing the Response

The response provided by the server should be an XML document; luckily, XML was designed to be easy to parse. Unfortunately, no matter how it was designed, manually parsing anything usually isn't a lot of fun. PHP5 comes with SimpleXML, which makes handling XML documents a breeze. PHP4 users don't have SimpleXML; however, a few third-party modules like MiniXML are available that perform similar functions. MiniXML was explored in Chapter 3, so take a look back if you skipped it—the interface is a little different but structurally you should be able to use it the same way.

Once you have received the response, sticking it into a SimpleXML object should be a breeze. Using the previous library example and request function, you end up with something like this:

```
$response = callAPIQuick('http://library.example.com/api.php', '123', 'search',
'book', 'style');
if ($response)
{
  $xml = simplexml_load_string($response);
  print_r($xml);
}else
{
  echo "Error loading feed";
}
```

Here, the response is not false (and hence something, presumably the XML you were hoping for, was returned). Note that this assumption is generally pretty valid. When a server providing an API encounters an error, it should provide the error in a nice XML format. The `simplexml_load_string()` function takes the response and turns it into an XML object that can be directly accessed, iterated through, and so on. Finally, the `print_r()` function results in a user-friendly output showing the contents of the object, shown here:

```
SimpleXMLElement Object
(
  [Request] => SimpleXMLElement Object
  (
    [RequestId] => 123a456
    [Parameters] => SimpleXMLElement Object
    (
      [Argument] => Array
      (
        [0] => SimpleXMLElement Object
        (
        )
        [1] => SimpleXMLElement Object
        (
        )
        [2] => SimpleXMLElement Object
        (
        )
        [3] => SimpleXMLElement Object
        (
        )
      )
    )
  )
  [Response] => SimpleXMLElement Object
  (
    [ResultCount] => 2
    [Item] => Array
    (
      [0] => SimpleXMLElement Object
      (
        [Title] => Style Book Vol 1
        [Status] => Out
        [Holds] => 3
        [CopiesOnHand] => 2
        [Author] => Jon Doe
```

```
        )

        [1] => SimpleXMLElement Object
        (
          [Title] => Style Book Vol 2
          [Status] => In
          [Holds] => 0
          [CopiesOnHand] => 1
          [Author] => Jon Doe
        )
      )
    )
  )
```

Looking at that output, a couple things should be immediately obvious:

- SimpleXML does a lot of really useful things for you very quickly.
- The resultant objects don't display attributes (see the argument list under parameters). The data is in there, it just isn't shown with a `print_r()`.
- Arrays start counting at 0 (just like everywhere else in PHP, it's just something to keep in mind).
- The `Item` array is just begging to be handled with a `foreach()` loop.

Bearing all that information in mind, a couple of quick lines of code are all that is required to explore the content more fully.

```
echo "You searched for: {$xml->Request->Parameters->Argument[3]->Value}<br>";
echo "Here are your {$xml->Response->ResultCount} results<br>";
foreach($xml->Response->Item AS &$item)
{
  echo "{$item->Title} by {$item->Author}<br>";
}
```

Here the search query and result count is presented, and then the results themselves are iterated through. The syntax gets a little weird when dealing with arrays (as demonstrated when the search query is printed), so it is often sensible to iterate through them for clarity.

REST is an effective method of querying remote APIs when it is permissible for the request portion of your transaction to take place in the clear. Creating REST queries is as easy as URL-encoding the required parameters and specifying an endpoint for the call. Dealing with REST responses can be a little trickier; however, by leveraging tools like SimpleXML, it too can be completed quickly.

Introducing SOAP

SOAP started off as a Microsoft initiative (pause for the collective gasp from the anti-MS community) in 1997 with the goal to implement remote procedure calls over HTTP. DevelopMentor and Userland joined the discussions and the term SOAP was coined in 1998. Internal politics delayed release of the specification, until Userland broke ranks and published the specification as XML-RPC in the summer of 1998. A flurry of releases and revisions took place over the next few years (incorporating revisions and extensions to the XML specification itself) to arrive at SOAP 1.2 in 2001.

SOAP (like REST) allows a program to request data from a remote server using HTTP. Unlike REST, the request itself is not sent in the request header, but instead within the body of the message. The message itself is an XML document with the root element being an `Envelope`, which in turn contains a `Body` element. The `Envelope` declaration defines the namespaces to be used, and the `Body` contains the request itself. This additional encapsulation adds transmission overhead, but does provide the benefits of namespacing and variable scope.

The services provided by a SOAP server, as well as the request parameters to make any available calls, are specified within a WSDL file provided by the server. Many modules designed to assist with SOAP development will require this file (either locally, or a link to it), and in fact several generic SOAP clients are out there that can make calls and return results given that file.

How SOAP Works

A SOAP request will involve creating and populating a request envelope, which contains all the required information (as specified by the WSDL document), transmitting that envelope to the API server, and handling the response.

A SOAP request generally contains all of the following elements:

- **SOAP Envelope** — With namespace inclusions.
- **SOAP Body** — Possibly defining additional namespaces.
- **Desired Action** — How the desired action is represented will depend on the API in question. It may be as simple as a parameter, or involve additional namespaces.
- **Developer Key** — A unique identifier assigned by the server to the requestor.
- **Request Parameters** — Detailing the request being performed.

With that information in mind, a SOAP request, equivalent to the REST request performed in the previous section, can be generated.

```
<?xml version="1.0" encoding="UTF-8" standalone="no"?>
<SOAP-ENV:Envelope
  xmlns:SOAP-ENV="http://schemas.xmlsoap.org/soap/envelope/"
  xmlns:xsd="http://www.w3.org/2001/XMLSchema"
  xmlns:xsi="http://www.w3.org/2001/XMLSchema-instance">
  <SOAP-ENV:Body>
    <devkey xsi:type="xsd:int">123</devkey>
    <action xsi:type="xsd:string">search</action>
    <type xsi:type="xsd:string">book</type>
    <keyword xsi:type="xsd:string">style</keyword>
  </SOAP-ENV:Body>
</SOAP-ENV:Envelope>
```

The parameters included in the request are easy to pick out, and though the variable typing isn't of great importance for PHP development, it does come in handy for more strongly typed languages. The missing item here is the endpoint, made clear in the REST example because it was the URL to which the request was posted. SOAP requests, of course, are run against specified URIs, which do not need to be re-specified within the request itself.

Given that request and the responses presented in the previous section, the SOAP response would look like this:

```
<?xml version='1.0' encoding='UTF-8'?>
<SOAP-ENV:Envelope
  xmlns:SOAP-ENV="http://schemas.xmlsoap.org/soap/envelope/"
  xmlns:xsi="http://www.w3.org/1999/XMLSchema-instance"
  xmlns:xsd="http://www.w3.org/1999/XMLSchema">
 <SOAP-ENV:Body>
 <LibrarySearchResponse xmlns="http://library.example.com/api/ns">
  <RequestInfo>
    <devkey xsi:type="xsd:string">123</devkey>
    <action xsi:type="xsd:string">search</action>
    <type xsi:type="xsd:string">book</type>
    <keyword xsi:type="xsd:string">style</keyword>
  </RequestInfo>
  <ResponseInfo>
   <ResultCount>2</ResultCount>
   <Item>
    <Title xsi:type="xsd:string">Style Book Vol 1</Title>
    <Status xsi:type="xsd:string">Out</Status>
    <Holds xsi:type="xsd:int">3</Holds>
    <CopiesOnHand xsi:type="xsd:int">2</CopiesOnHand>
    <Author xsi:type="xsd:string">Jon Doe</Author>
   </Item>
   <Item>
    <Title xsi:type="xsd:string">Style Book Vol 2</Title>
    <Status xsi:type="xsd:string">In</Status>
    <Holds xsi:type="xsd:int">0</Holds>
    <CopiesOnHand xsi:type="xsd:int">1</CopiesOnHand>
    <Author xsi:type="xsd:string">Jon Doe</Author>
   </Item>
  </ResponseInfo>
 </LibrarySearchResponse>
 </SOAP-ENV:Body>
</SOAP-ENV:Envelope>
```

The SOAP response isn't too different from the REST response shown earlier. In fact, much of the namespacing could actually be omitted (though it is rare to see a SOAP response without it), at which point, with the exception of the additional encapsulation, the two documents would be very similar.

As you should be able to discern from the response shown, it declares itself to be XML 1.0 and uses UTF-8 for encoding. The `SOAP-ENV:Envelope` element is the root element for the document, and has three namespaces, including the `SOAP-ENV` namespace. The `Body` then contains the `LibrarySearchResponse` element among other things, which also defines its own namespace.

The `RequestInfo` parent follows after, and this contains the request parameters that generated the response that follows on from there. Returning request parameters with the response is a common occurrence in SOAP.

Finally, the response itself is returned. Notice that the `ResultCount` element sits as a direct child of `ResponseInfo`, and the result items themselves are again stored under a repeating element, `Item`.

Implementing SOAP

Like REST, implementing SOAP involves both generating requests and then handling the response. Whereas handling the SOAP response is similar to the REST result, generating the SOAP request is quite different.

Generating Requests

Unlike REST, it is rather uncommon to see requests generated manually, though it can still be done. Generally, SOAP requests are either generated with a generic tool (like NuSOAP or Pear:SOAP) or with an application-specific class or module. Manual generation is covered here (a good understanding of how it works will come in useful), as well as NuSOAP.

Application-specific tools are going to be ignored, for a couple reasons. By definition they are application specific, and therefore not very useful in this generic chapter. Secondly, the tools have varying interfaces and functionality levels, and in order to do the topic justice it would require an in-depth look. Finally, I am firmly of the opinion that if you can figure out how to make it work with NuSOAP (or raw, for that matter), you can get the application-specific tool to work too.

Manual Generation

Generating SOAP requests manually isn't too different from generating REST requests. The process of generating the request and actually transmitting it is split into two separate functions, for demonstrating purposes.

For generating the request itself, I have chosen to use a pregenerated string, and merely populate the required values at runtime. There are more complex options (such as creating the document within SimpleXML, or creating it from scratch each run), but they aren't really required:

```
function createRequest($devkey, $action, $type, $keyword)
{
  $request = "<?xml version=\"1.0\" encoding=\"UTF-8\" standalone=\"no\"?>
<SOAP-ENV:Envelope
  xmlns:SOAP-ENV=\"http://schemas.xmlsoap.org/soap/envelope/\"
  xmlns:xsd=\"http://www.w3.org/2001/XMLSchema\"
  xmlns:xsi=\"http://www.w3.org/2001/XMLSchema-instance\">
  <SOAP-ENV:Body>
    <devkey xsi:type=\"xsd:int\">$devkey</devkey>
    <action xsi:type=\"xsd:string\">$action</action>
    <type xsi:type=\"xsd:string\">$type</type>
    <keyword xsi:type=\"xsd:string\">$keyword</keyword>
  </SOAP-ENV:Body>
</SOAP-ENV:Envelope>";
  return $request;
}
```

As you can tell, the function is just about as simple as it can get. Note that the variables haven't been URL-encoded; that's because they aren't being sent in the URL (sounds obvious, but it's also easy to miss).

Actually, calling the API to transmit the request involves borrowing some code from the first REST example, because the request will be sent raw this time.

```
function callSOAPAPI($data)
{
  $url = "http://library.example.com/api/soap/search";
  $url_info = parse_url($url);
  $host = $url_info['host'];
  $path = $url_info['path'];
```

I could have just populated the `$host` and `$path` variables at the start, but this should be clearer. In a production system, you could save a few CPU cycles by hardcoding these elements.

```
  $fp=fsockopen($host, 80);
  fputs($fp, "GET " . $path . " HTTP/1.1\r\n");
  fputs($fp, "Host: " . $host ."\r\n");
  fputs($fp, "Accept: */*\r\n");
  fputs($fp, "Accept-Charset: ISO-8859-1,utf-8;q=0.7,*;q=0.7\r\n");
  fputs($fp, "Connection: close\r\n");
  fputs($fp, "Content-Type: application/soap+xml\r\n");
  fputs($fp, "Content-Length: " . strlen($data) . "\r\n\r\n");
  fputs($fp, "$data");
```

This block is nearly identical to the previous example. The previous example was a POST request, whereas this is a GET request, a change that will be dictated by whatever API you are working with. The Content-Type header is different to accurately reflect what you're sending and this time of course you have `$data` to send, so Content-Length won't be 0.

```
  $response="";
  while(!feof($fp))
  {
    $response.=fgets($fp, 128);
  }
  fclose($fp);
  list($http_headers, $http_content)=explode("\r\n\r\n", $response);
  return $http_content;
}
```

This section is also identical to the REST example. Wrapping both those functions to retrieve a response is only barely worth mentioning:

```
$request = createRequest('123', 'search', 'book','style');
$response = callSOAPAPI($request);
```

Wasn't too hard!

Unlike REST, you can't just use `file_get_contents()` to hit the API, because you need to send the XML body with the request. `file_put_contents()` wont work either, because you need the response (`file_put_contents()` returns an `int`), but there are other options. Pear (`http://pear.php.net`), for example, has a bunch of HTTP-specific functions that can take some of the headache of manually creating the request off your hands, but still allow you all the flexibility you get with manual creation.

Generation with NuSOAP

For anything other than a one-shot program, I would definitely recommend going with some sort of a SOAP module to make your coding life easier. Although, if you run into problems, tracking them down can be a bit of a pain. I like using a local development box during development, so should things start going awry I can use a packet sniffer to look at the request/response in its raw form.

Conceptually, using NuSOAP isn't too different from completing the task manually. The object is initialized, the payload is created, and the request is sent. The key difference here is that NuSOAP is doing all the dirty work.

```
require('../lib/nusoap.php');
$client = new soapclient("http://library.example.com/api/soap/wsdl/", true);
```

Here the `$client` object is created. Two options are available when creating a new soapclient: You can either specify the `wsdl` file for the service (and set the second parameter to true), or specify the endpoint for the call (and set the second parameter to false). Whenever possible, I like to use the `wsdl` file; the NuSOAP module can catch some of your mistakes that way, and it ensures that different request types all go to the correct endpoint.

```
$params = array(
  'devkey'    => '123',
  'action'    => 'search',
  'type'      => 'book',
  'keyword'   => 'style'
);
```

Preparing the parameters for transmission is a bit easier than earlier methods.

```
$namespace = 'http://library.example.com';
$action = 'http://library.example.com/api/soap/search';
$method = "SearchRequest";
$result = $client->call($method,
  array('SearchRequest' => $params),
  $namespace, $action);
```

Finally, the last few parameters are set, and the call itself is made. The resulting object is discussed in the next section.

Handling the Response

Handling a response from a SOAP request is again not too different from the REST response—both are provided in similar XML formats. The SOAP response carries the additional `Envelope` and `Body` elements, but often present data in a similar manner within those elements. There is of course some variation between handling the response from a manual request and from a NuSOAP request. Both methods are presented here.

Manually Parsing the Response

Mimicking the output generated with the REST request uses similar code, with a few modifications for the encapsulation scheme used with SOAP.

```
echo "You searched for: {$xml->Body->LibrarySearchResponse->RequestInfo->
     keyword}<br>";
```

```
echo "Here are your {$xml->Body->LibrarySearchResponse->ResponseInfo->ResultCount}
     results<br>";
foreach($xml->Body->LibrarySearchResponse->ResponseInfo->Item AS &$item)
{
   echo "{$item->Title} by {$item->Author}<br>";
}
```

This will generate identical output as the REST request shown earlier. Note the different syntax used to acquire the search keyword. It isn't an attribute this time, so access is different.

Parsing the Response with NuSOAP

Accessing the object provided by NuSOAP is a little different from the methods used with SimpleXML, but the internal data structure is quite similar. Modifying the code to work with the NuSOAP object only takes a few moments.

```
echo "You searched for: " .
  $xml['Body']['LibrarySearchResponse']['RequestInfo']['keyword'] . "<br>";
echo "Here are your
  {$xml['Body']['LibrarySearchResponse']['ResponseInfo']['ResultCount']}
  results<br>";
foreach($xml['Body']['LibrarySearchResponse']['ResponseInfo']['Item'] AS &$item)
{
  echo "{$item['Title']} by {$item['Author']}<br>";
}
```

With NuSOAP, the internal data is accessed much the same way as an associative array, so rather than the OO method of using -> to access child elements, further array information is included. This element will output identically to the previous example.

SOAP is an effective method of querying APIs when the additional overhead is permissible. The encapsulation of all elements allows for easy reading, and variable scope within the request. Creating SOAP requests can be as easy as writing them out once, then just replacing key variables. Alternatively, it can also be accomplished by using a tool such as NuSOAP. Accessing the SOAP response can be accomplished in much the same manner as the REST response when the request has been completed manually. In the case of requests completed with NuSOAP, the access method is structurally identical, with only a few minor changes to the syntax used.

Summary

This chapter introduced Web APIs, and discussed the differences between APIs and feeds. At this point you should understand the following:

- The basics of interacting with Web APIs using REST and SOAP
- How to generate web service requests both manually and by utilizing a number of tools that can help generate dynamic requests
- How to handle and parse the server responses utilizing SimpleXML or MiniXML

The next few chapters take an in-depth look at several of the most popular and most useful APIs on the Web today. The knowledge and familiarity gained in this chapter should prove useful when examining that code.

6

Interacting with the Google API

Google's name has become ubiquitous with searching the Internet, and in a continuing effort to provide its users with effective search solutions, Google provides a direct link to its powerful search engine via its API.

The search API can be used to accomplish the same set of tasks Google's search accomplishes via its website. However, by wrapping these functions within your own software, you can provide more advanced and customized solutions. Examples might include simple tasks such as creating custom search result pages that appear identical to your overall website. Or you might consider a more advanced cross-domain search or even a keyword monitor (watching your ranking on important words or phrases). By using the Google API, you are able to leverage the #1 search engine on the planet for your own needs, and to better your user's experience. This chapter's key topics include the following:

- Examining a raw request in depth
- Presenting a simple search interface
- Enhancing a search page
- Monitoring search usage
- Fudging results to help users find what they need
- Monitoring keywords
- Multiple domain search

Introducing the API

Google launched its search API in 2002 to allow developers to directly access search results in an organized and manageable manner. Prior to that launch, many developers had been "scraping" Google search result pages (in violation of its Terms of Service (TOS)) to obtain information on rankings and perform more advanced search types. The API gives developers full access to the breadth of Google's search engine in an easier to manage format all without violating the TOS.

As with most commercial APIs, registration is required before use. If you already have an account for one of Google's services (not including GMail), you can use that account, otherwise the registration is pretty standard. You can find the registration page as well as documentation for the API at `www.google.com/apis/index.html`.

Registration will provide you with your own license key, which must be included with all queries against the API. Your license key will entitle you to 1,000 queries per day. However, if you anticipate using more than that, or even close to that number, it would be a good idea to contact Google and explain what you are planning to do with the API. They may be willing to increase your maximum query limit for you.

Once you have completed your registration, download the developer's kit from that same page; it contains documentation for the API, XML examples, a license, and so forth. The code examples are unfortunately (unless, for example, you want to write a book) not in PHP. However, all is not lost—the package includes a WSDL (Web Services Description Language) file called `GoogleSearch.wsdl`, which describes the functionality of the service in full. The soap-samples directory is also of particular interest because it contains sample transactions showing both the request and response in the appropriate format.

Beta Limitations

Google's entire API system is still considered (by Google, that is) to be in its Beta stages. As such, Google has clearly reserved the right to make major changes to the system in the future. These could range from simple protocol modifications to major licensing requirements or even a switch to a completely fee-based service. I have some belief in the theory that Google doesn't move a service out of the Beta stages until it can determine how to receive revenue from it. Knowing that there may be changes required to realize that revenue, Google retains the "Beta" tag until the possible revenue stream is fully understood. Regardless of the reasoning, keep your eyes open for news on how the service might change. That said, Google may simply decide to continue generously offering free access to its API in perpetuity. Just keep its restrictions and possible changes in mind when developing.

Sample Transaction

All transactions examined in this book make use of HTTP (which should be somewhat familiar, because it is the protocol on which the World Wide Web is used). Understanding what a SOAP transaction looks like in its most basic form (the raw HTTP transactions) will come in useful when trying to diagnose problems later. The following sample transaction performs a search for "paul reinheimer" and requests only the first two results.

Request Headers

The purpose of the request headers in this context is to declare where the request itself is being sent, and indicate what is being asked for. Though indicating where the request is being sent may seem redundant because that sort of information is also included when addressing the TCP/IP packets, remember that multiple sites can be hosted on the same machine. This information, present in the HTTP request, allows the server to determine which site should receive the request.

```
POST /search/beta2 HTTP/1.0
Host: api.google.com
Connection: close
Accept: */*
Content-Length: 992
SOAPAction: "urn:GoogleSearchAction"
Content-Type: text/xml; charset="utf-8"
```

As you can see, the request header itself is rather brief. This brevity is due in part to it being manually generated. The headers created by a web browser are much longer, because they include lots of optional information. The rest of this section goes through this line by line.

```
POST /search/beta2 HTTP/1.0
```

A `POST` request is being made against the script on the server located at `/search/beta2`, and this request will follow the HTTP 1.0 protocol. `POST` (and its companion `GET`) should be familiar from form processing; the encoding is similar, only the content changes.

This is one of those cases where my tendency to leave a trailing slash on all URLs actually managed to bite me back. Performing a `POST` *against /search/beta2/ will fail; Google returns that the script at that location does not accept* `POST` *requests.*

```
Host: api.google.com
```

This line defines the `Host` that the request is being directed to. The inclusion of the `Host` line in the `HTTP` headers allows a single server to easily handle requests directed to multiple domains on the same IP; it also allows certain network devices to route requests to different servers to assist in load balancing. Note that the information from both the `Host` and `POST` lines can be combined to give the overall URL for the resource, which is `http://api.google.com/search/beta2`. You can split a URL down to its component parts with the `parse_url()` function.

```
Connection: close
```

This line states that the connection will close immediately after this request is completed, as opposed to a persistent request, where several transactions could occur successively. Persistent requests are useful when requesting an item such as an HTML document, where embedded images will likely need to be downloaded from the same server once the HTML has been received and parsed. That isn't the case here, so the `close` method makes far more sense. Note that this line *does not* close the connection; it merely sets the connection type.

```
Accept: */*
```

The `Accept` header indicates which content types are acceptable, in order of preference. In this case you are willing to accept any content that Google would care to return to you. You do, however, know what Google will return because the specification for the API indicates that you will always be sent `application/xml`.

```
Content-Length: 992
```

The `Content-Length` header warns the server as to the length of the body of the message in bytes. The `strlen()` function will prove to be invaluable when populating this element.

```
SOAPAction: "urn:GoogleSearchAction"
```

This is a custom header under the SOAP protocol. The Google API defines this header and its contents.

```
Content-Type: text/xml; charset="utf-8"
```

This `Content-Type` header defines what the body of the message will contain — text, formatted in XML. The character set used will be UTF-8. Google requires all transactions to be performed in UTF-8. This is clearly defined in its specification, and included in a note in the WSDL file.

Request Body

The body of the request contains the actual SOAP request for the server. The information required here is defined by Google. SOAP requests are presented in XML (a quick crash course in XML was presented in Chapter 3); this allows you to generate requests quickly and allows Google to parse that request in a similar quick and easy fashion.

```
<?xml version="1.0" encoding="UTF-8" standalone="no"?>
<SOAP-ENV:Envelope
  xmlns:SOAP-ENV="http://schemas.xmlsoap.org/soap/envelope/"
  xmlns:typens="urn:GoogleSearch"
  xmlns:xsd="http://www.w3.org/2001/XMLSchema"
  xmlns:soap="http://schemas.xmlsoap.org/wsdl/soap/"
  xmlns:xsi="http://www.w3.org/2001/XMLSchema-instance">
  <SOAP-ENV:Body>
    <mns:doGoogleSearch xmlns:mns="urn:GoogleSearch" SOAP-
ENV:encodingStyle="http://schemas.xmlsoap.org/soap/encoding/">
    <key xsi:type="xsd:string">u6U/r39QFHK18Qcjz/XdWSbptVaj9k1t</key>
    <q xsi:type="xsd:string">paul reinheimer</q>
    <start xsi:type="xsd:int">0</start>
    <maxResults xsi:type="xsd:int">2</maxResults>
    <filter xsi:type="xsd:boolean">1</filter>
    <restrict xsi:type="xsd:string"></restrict>
    <safeSearch xsi:type="xsd:boolean">1</safeSearch>
    <lr xsi:type="xsd:string"></lr>
    <ie xsi:type="xsd:string"></ie>
    <oe xsi:type="xsd:string"></oe>
    </mns:doGoogleSearch>
  </SOAP-ENV:Body>
</SOAP-ENV:Envelope>
```

As mentioned previously, each SOAP request includes both the `Envelope` and the `Body`. The envelope defines the namespaces used in the request and encapsulates the body, which contains the API call itself. Each section of the request body is examined in detail here.

```
<?xml version="1.0" encoding="UTF-8" standalone="no"?>
<SOAP-ENV:Envelope
  xmlns:SOAP-ENV="http://schemas.xmlsoap.org/soap/envelope/"
  xmlns:typens="urn:GoogleSearch"
  xmlns:xsd="http://www.w3.org/2001/XMLSchema"
  xmlns:soap="http://schemas.xmlsoap.org/wsdl/soap/"
  xmlns:xsi="http://www.w3.org/2001/XMLSchema-instance"
>
```

These lines declare the document to be written as XML version 1.0, with UTF-8 encoding. Then begin the `SOAP-ENV` root element (the SOAP envelope) and declare the appropriate namespaces.

```
<SOAP-ENV:Body>
    <mns:doGoogleSearch xmlns:mns="urn:GoogleSearch"
      SOAP-ENV:encodingStyle="http://schemas.xmlsoap.org/soap/encoding/">
```

Here the SOAP `Body` element begins, ready to encapsulate the request itself; the second line adds additional namespaces to the `Body` element.

```
<key xsi:type="xsd:string">u6U/r39QFHK18Qcjz/XdWSbptVaj9k1t</key>
```

The `key` element must be included with every request you send to Google. This is the API key issued to you when you register for the Google API (covered earlier in this chapter). The `xsi:type="xsd:string"` portion of the element defines the type of data being sent, in this case, a string. More information on the types can be found at the URLs listed when the namespaces were defined in the `Envelope` element.

```
<q xsi:type="xsd:string">paul reinheimer</q>
```

The `q` represents the query that will be sent to Google; again, a string is being sent.

Google only cares about the first 10 terms (or words) sent in a query, something to keep in mind when using the service.

```
<start xsi:type="xsd:int">0</start>
<maxResults xsi:type="xsd:int">2</maxResults>
```

The `start` element defines the first index of the first element to be returned; Google counts just like arrays, starting at 0. `maxResults` defines how many results you wish to receive, in this case 2. Google will not return more than 10 results at a time—if you require more results, use multiple requests. With each successive request increment the `start` element. Note the type for both elements is `int` (integer).

```
<filter xsi:type="xsd:boolean">1</filter>
<restrict xsi:type="xsd:string"></restrict>
```

The `filter` element when enabled (set to 1) filters results in two ways: First, nearly duplicate content is removed from the result set, and second, if many results are located on the same domain, only the first two are returned. These filters are on by default when using the standard Google web front end, but can be turned off here by sending a 0 rather than a 1. The `restrict` element can be used to restrict results to pages from a particular country or topic. For example, you use `unclesam` in the `restrict` element to limit results to U.S. Government topics. For a full listing of topic and country restrictions available, see the `APIs_Reference.html` document that came in your GoogleAPI download.

```
<safeSearch xsi:type="xsd:boolean">1</safeSearch>
```

Turning `safeSearch` on (by setting it to 1) instructs Google to remove adult sites from the search results. Keep in mind that no filter is perfect, so you may still see some adult sites in the result set.

```
<lr xsi:type="xsd:string"></lr>
<ie xsi:type="xsd:string"></ie>
<oe xsi:type="xsd:string"></oe>
```

The `lr` element allows you to restrict results by the language in which they are written. `lang_en`, for example, restricts results to pages in the English language. For a full listing of available language restrictions, see the `APIs_Reference.html` file that came with the API documentation download. `ie` and `oe` are both required elements that represent input encoding and output encoding, respectively. However, these values are both ignored and all input is expected to be UTF-8, and all output will be UTF-8 as well.

```
    </mns:doGoogleSearch>
  </SOAP-ENV:Body>
</SOAP-ENV:Envelope>
```

The message namespace, body, and envelope are closed in turn.

Response Header

The response header is quite similar to the request header generated earlier. It serves many of the same purposes. The information here helps the client machine understand what type of information it is about to receive, and what occurrence on the server generated that information.

```
HTTP/1.0 200 OK
Content-Type: text/xml; charset=utf-8
Cache-control: private
Date: Sun, 16 Jan 2005 21:06:04 GMT
Server: GFE/1.3
Connection: Close
```

The HTTP response header returned after performing the request looks quite similar to the original request header, so only new elements are examined here.

```
HTTP/1.0 200 OK
```

Quite similar to the request header, this defines the response as being `HTTP` version `1.0`. It also gives the HTTP response code of `200` and a short description of that status code, `OK`. The most commonly known HTTP response code would probably be `404: Not found`. If you happen to receive that response while attempting to access an API, you have the wrong URL.

```
Cache-control: private
Date: Sun, 16 Jan 2005 21:06:04 GMT
Server: GFE/1.3
```

The `Cache-control: private` declaration states that the content may be cached, but not in any sort of a shared cache. For the purposes of the applications here, this element will be ignored. However, servers between your applications and the Google server will note this header, and (hopefully) not attempt to cache any of the transactions. The `Date` header is relatively self-explanatory; note that it will always contain a time in GMT. The `Server` line is an optional header declaring the name and version of the server software used.

Response Body

The response body contains the server's response to your SOAP request. The response returned is quite long, even though you requested only the first two search results. As such, it has been broken into more manageable chunks here. Also note that white space has also been modified to allow for easy reading. After the segmented form has been covered, the entire process will be reexamined in greater detail.

```
<?xml version='1.0' encoding='UTF-8'?>
<SOAP-ENV:Envelope xmlns:SOAP-ENV="http://schemas.xmlsoap.org/soap/envelope/"
xmlns:xsi="http://www.w3.org/1999/XMLSchema-instance"
xmlns:xsd="http://www.w3.org/1999/XMLSchema">
 <SOAP-ENV:Body>
 <ns1:doGoogleSearchResponse xmlns:ns1="urn:GoogleSearch"
   SOAP-ENV:encodingStyle="http://schemas.xmlsoap.org/soap/encoding/">
  <return xsi:type="ns1:GoogleSearchResult">
   <directoryCategories xmlns:ns2="http://schemas.xmlsoap.org/soap/encoding/"
     xsi:type="ns2:Array" ns2:arrayType="ns1:DirectoryCategory[0]">
   </directoryCategories>
   <documentFiltering xsi:type="xsd:boolean">false</documentFiltering>
   <endIndex xsi:type="xsd:int">2</endIndex>
   <estimateIsExact xsi:type="xsd:boolean">false</estimateIsExact>
   <estimatedTotalResultsCount xsi:type="xsd:int">2070</estimatedTotalResultsCount>
```

This top section first takes care of defining the namespaces that will be used throughout the document, then follows the body of the response and declaration of the response namespaces. Here the response begins in earnest with information regarding what Google found in response to your query.

```
<resultElements xmlns:ns3="http://schemas.xmlsoap.org/soap/encoding/"
  xsi:type="ns3:Array" ns3:arrayType="ns1:ResultElement[2]">
 <item xsi:type="ns1:ResultElement">
  <URL xsi:type="xsd:string">http://www.preinheimer.com/</URL>
  <cachedSize xsi:type="xsd:string">60k</cachedSize>
  <directoryCategory xsi:type="ns1:DirectoryCategory">
   <fullViewableName xsi:type="xsd:string"></fullViewableName>
   <specialEncoding xsi:type="xsd:string"></specialEncoding>
  </directoryCategory>
  <directoryTitle xsi:type="xsd:string"></directoryTitle>
  <hostName xsi:type="xsd:string"></hostName>
  <relatedInformationPresent
    xsi:type="xsd:boolean">true</relatedInformationPresent>
  <snippet xsi:type="xsd:string">&lt;b&gt;...&lt;/b&gt; Posted by
    &lt;b&gt;Paul&lt;/b&gt; &lt;b&gt;Reinheimer&lt;/b&gt; in Computing at 20:57 |
    Comments (0) | Trackbacks (0). &lt;b&gt;...&lt;/b&gt;&lt;br&gt; thanks
    &lt;b&gt;paul&lt;/b&gt;. Posted by &lt;b&gt;Paul&lt;/b&gt;
    &lt;b&gt;Reinheimer&lt;/b&gt; at 22:45 | Comments (2) | Trackbacks (0).
    &lt;b&gt;...&lt;/b&gt;  </snippet>
  <summary xsi:type="xsd:string"></summary>
  <title xsi:type="xsd:string">preinheimer.com</title>
 </item>

 <item xsi:type="ns1:ResultElement">
  <URL xsi:type="xsd:string">
    http://p2p.wrox.com/blogs_bio.asp?AUTHOR_ID=22424</URL>
  <cachedSize xsi:type="xsd:string">17k</cachedSize>
  <directoryCategory xsi:type="ns1:DirectoryCategory">
```

```
      <fullViewableName xsi:type="xsd:string"></fullViewableName>
      <specialEncoding xsi:type="xsd:string"></specialEncoding>
    </directoryCategory>
    <directoryTitle xsi:type="xsd:string"></directoryTitle>
    <hostName xsi:type="xsd:string"></hostName>
    <relatedInformationPresent
      xsi:type="xsd:boolean">true</relatedInformationPresent>
    <snippet xsi:type="xsd:string">&lt;b&gt;...&lt;/b&gt; p2p.wrox.com Forums, Blogs
      &amp;gt; &lt;b&gt;Paul&lt;/b&gt; &lt;b&gt;Reinheimer&amp;#39;s&lt;/b&gt; Bio.
      Wrox Blogs. Archive RSS&lt;br&gt; Feed, &lt;b&gt;Paul&lt;/b&gt;
      &lt;b&gt;Reinheimer&lt;/b&gt;. Homepage: http://www.preinheimer.com.
      &lt;b&gt;...&lt;/b&gt;  </snippet>
    <summary xsi:type="xsd:string"></summary>
    <title xsi:type="xsd:string">p2p.wrox.com Forums</title>
  </item>
</resultElements>
```

Here you have the two search results you requested. Note that the returned elements are encapsulated with then `resultElements` element, then each result is an `item` in itself. Also note that appropriate text has been HTML-encoded — `<` instead of < and such.

```
<searchComments xsi:type="xsd:string"></searchComments>
<searchQuery xsi:type="xsd:string">paul reinheimer</searchQuery>
<searchTime xsi:type="xsd:double">0.05788</searchTime>
<searchTips xsi:type="xsd:string"></searchTips>
<startIndex xsi:type="xsd:int">1</startIndex>
</return>
</ns1:doGoogleSearchResponse>
</SOAP-ENV:Body>
</SOAP-ENV:Envelope>
```

Finally, a few last pieces of information about your request, and closure of the request namespace, the `Body`, and finally the `Envelope`.

In Depth

```
<?xml version='1.0' encoding='UTF-8'?>
<SOAP-ENV:Envelope xmlns:SOAP-ENV="http://schemas.xmlsoap.org/soap/envelope/"
xmlns:xsi="http://www.w3.org/1999/XMLSchema-instance"
xmlns:xsd="http://www.w3.org/1999/XMLSchema">
 <SOAP-ENV:Body>
```

These initial lines are very similar to the ones used in the request: The document is declared as `XML`, the `SOAP Envelope` begins, some namespaces are declared, and the `SOAP Body` begins.

```
 <ns1:doGoogleSearchResponse xmlns:ns1="urn:GoogleSearch"
   SOAP-ENV:encodingStyle="http://schemas.xmlsoap.org/soap/encoding/">
  <return xsi:type="ns1:GoogleSearchResult">
```

Here the response namespace beings, and similar to the request, you see the `encodingStyle` namespace added. The return element will encapsulate all the information related to your search, not just the search results themselves.

```
<directoryCategories xmlns:ns2="http://schemas.xmlsoap.org/soap/encoding/"
  xsi:type="ns2:Array" ns2:arrayType="ns1:DirectoryCategory[0]">
</directoryCategories>
```

The `directoryCategories` element will contain an array listing all of the categories the search matched in the Open Directory Project (dmoz.org) when available. This search didn't match any, so none were returned.

```
<documentFiltering xsi:type="xsd:boolean">false</documentFiltering>
<endIndex xsi:type="xsd:int">2</endIndex>
```

The `documentFiltering` element indicates whether any filtering was performed on the search results. It would only be true if the request indicated that filtering was desired `AND` filtering was accomplished. In this case filtering was requested, but none was required. `endIndex` indicates the index of the last search result returned in this set; note that `endIndex` is a 1-based count (start counting at 1 rather than 0).

```
<estimateIsExact xsi:type="xsd:boolean">false</estimateIsExact>
<estimatedTotalResultsCount xsi:type="xsd:int">2070</estimatedTotalResultsCount>
```

The `estimateIsExact` element indicates whether the following `estimatedTotalResultsCount` is actually an exact value. You will likely only see true when performing a search that has very few results.

```
<resultElements xmlns:ns3="http://schemas.xmlsoap.org/soap/encoding/"
  xsi:type="ns3:Array" ns3:arrayType="ns1:ResultElement[2]">
```

The `resultElements` element is of significant interest. It contains all available results, each within its own `item` element.

```
<item xsi:type="ns1:ResultElement">
  <URL xsi:type="xsd:string">http://www.preinheimer.com/</URL>
  <cachedSize xsi:type="xsd:string">60k</cachedSize>
```

The `item` element declares itself to be a `ResultElement`, and as such you can expect it to contain all of the information regarding this particular search result. The `URL` element declares the URL for this search result, and `cachedSize` indicates the size (in kilobytes) of Google's cache of this page.

```
<directoryCategory xsi:type="ns1:DirectoryCategory">
 <fullViewableName xsi:type="xsd:string"></fullViewableName>
 <specialEncoding xsi:type="xsd:string"></specialEncoding>
</directoryCategory>
<directoryTitle xsi:type="xsd:string"></directoryTitle>
```

These directory-based items indicate in which categories the Open Directory Project classifies this particular result. My website is apparently unclassifiable (or, alternatively, not worth classifying). The `directoryTitle` element would indicate the title of the page according to the ODP. Generally, I have found little use for these elements; they haven't been populated with enough frequency to make it worth the effort to code around them.

```
<hostName xsi:type="xsd:string"></hostName>
```

The `hostName` element is used only when a filter was turned on in the request and many results were found in the same domain. In that case, the second result (remember when a filter is on, only the first two results from any domain are returned) will have the `hostName` value set. In this case you may want to run a second search, adding `site: <hostname>` to the query to obtain further results from that specific domain.

```
<relatedInformationPresent
  xsi:type="xsd:boolean">true</relatedInformationPresent>
```

When the `relatedInformationPresent` value is set to true, Google knows of other pages similar to this result. To obtain them, perform another query in the form `related: <URL>`. Note that the `related` query cannot be combined with any other query.

```
<snippet xsi:type="xsd:string">&lt;b&gt;...&lt;/b&gt; Posted by
  &lt;b&gt;Paul&lt;/b&gt; &lt;b&gt;Reinheimer&lt;/b&gt; in Computing at 20:57 |
  Comments (0) | Trackbacks (0). &lt;b&gt;...&lt;/b&gt;&lt;br&gt; thanks
  &lt;b&gt;paul&lt;/b&gt;. Posted by &lt;b&gt;Paul&lt;/b&gt;
  &lt;b&gt;Reinheimer&lt;/b&gt; at 22:45 | Comments (2) | Trackbacks (0).
  &lt;b&gt;...&lt;/b&gt;  </snippet>
```

This is a snippet from the result; note that all appropriate characters are HTML-encoded. You may want to run `html_entity_decode()` on the snippet if you are displaying it to users (be careful what you allow through because this is foreign data).

```
 <summary xsi:type="xsd:string"></summary>
 <title xsi:type="xsd:string">preinheimer.com</title>
</item>
```

Finally, the `summary` element is only populated if the page has an entry in the ODP. The `title` comes from the page in question (in HTML this would be the `<title></title>` value; in other page types such as PDF it comes from their equivalent), and the item is closed.

For the sake of brevity I have skipped the second item element.

```
<searchComments xsi:type="xsd:string"></searchComments>
<searchQuery xsi:type="xsd:string">paul reinheimer</searchQuery>
<searchTime xsi:type="xsd:double">0.05788</searchTime>
<searchTips xsi:type="xsd:string"></searchTips>
<startIndex xsi:type="xsd:int">1</startIndex>
```

The `searchComments` element may be populated with a textual message for the end user. It may contain information that certain common words were removed from the search query (for example, *The following words are very common and were not included in your search: as a*). `searchQuery` will contain the search that was completed (the `q` from the request), and `searchTime` will contain the amount of time it took Google to complete the request. `searchTips` will contain textual tips for the end user on how to better use Google, and `startIndex` will contain the index of the first result (1-based).

```
</return>
</ns1:doGoogleSearchResponse>
</SOAP-ENV:Body>
</SOAP-ENV:Envelope>
```

Finally, all of the open tags are closed, and so ends the response header.

NuSOAP

For all SOAP's popularity, the last example probably succeeded in making some aspects of its use rather complicated. Fortunately, this isn't the case. Several existing SOAP classes are available that will save you dealing with all the details. Notable PHP classes include NuSOAP, PEAR:SOAP, PHP SOAP, exSOAP, and Krysalis. I have selected NuSOAP for these examples for a few reasons: namely, ease of install for non-root users, decent compatibility with tested servers, ease of use, and finally, compatibility with both PHP4 and 5.

Here is a brief example using NuSOAP that performs roughly the same action as the previous example:

```
<?php
require('../lib/nusoap.php');
$client = new soapclient("http://example.org/googleapi/GoogleSearch.wsdl", true);
```

In this example, you require the NuSOAP library, and create the client object. When creating the `soapclient` object, you can do it one of two ways: You can specify the location of the `wsdl` file that describes the service, or you can specify the target for the URL for the service. If you use the first method (as shown in the preceding code), the second parameter must be set to true; if you use the second method, it must be false.

```
$client->soap_defencoding = 'UTF-8';
$query = array(
  'key'=>'u6U/r39QFHK18Qcjz/XdWSbptVaj9klt',
  'q'=>'paul reinheimer',
  'start'=>0,
  'maxResults'=>2,
  'filter'=>true,
  'restrict'=>'',
  'safeSearch'=>true,
  'lr'=>'',
  'ie'=>'',
  'oe'=>''
);
```

Here you see the default encoding set to UTF-8 (remember that Google only accepts UTF-8 in its API, and will only send UTF-8 as a response), and generation of the query object. The names of the various elements should be familiar from the previous example.

```
$result = $client->call("doGoogleSearch", $query, "urn:GoogleSearch",
  "urn:GoogleSearch");
echo '<pre>';
print_r($result);
echo '</pre>';
?>
```

Finally, the `$result` object is created to contain the results of the query itself, and the results are printed to the screen.

```
Array
(
  [directoryCategories] =>
```

```
    [documentFiltering] => 1
    [endIndex] => 2
    [estimateIsExact] =>
    [estimatedTotalResultsCount] => 2110
    [resultElements] => Array
    (
      [0] => Array
      (
        [URL] => http://www.preinheimer.com/
        [cachedSize] => 60k
        [directoryCategory] => Array
            (
                [fullViewableName] =>
                [specialEncoding] =>
            )
        [directoryTitle] =>
        [hostName] =>
        [relatedInformationPresent] => 1
        [snippet] => <b>...</b> Posted by <b>Paul</b> <b>Reinheimer</b> in Computing
  at 20:57 | Comments (0) | Trackbacks (0). <b>...</b><br> thanks <b>paul</b>. Posted
  by <b>Paul</b> <b>Reinheimer</b> at 22:45 | Comments (2) | Trackbacks (0).
  <b>...</b>
        [summary] =>
        [title] => preinheimer.com
      )
      [1] => Array
      (
        [URL] => http://p2p.wrox.com/blogs_bio.asp?AUTHOR_ID=22424
        [cachedSize] => 17k
        [directoryCategory] => Array
            (
                [fullViewableName] =>
                [specialEncoding] =>
            )
        [directoryTitle] =>
        [hostName] =>
        [relatedInformationPresent] => 1
        [snippet] => <b>...</b> p2p.wrox.com Forums, Blogs &gt; <b>Paul</b>
  <b>Reinheimer&#39;s</b> Bio. Wrox Blogs. Archive RSS<br> Feed, <b>Paul</b>
  <b>Reinheimer</b>. Homepage: http://www.preinheimer.com. <b>...</b>
        [summary] =>
        [title] => p2p.wrox.com Forums
      )
    )
    [searchComments] =>
    [searchQuery] => paul reinheimer
    [searchTime] => 0.035023
    [searchTips] =>
    [startIndex] => 1
  )
```

Visually, the output of this script is quite similar to the outputs of SimpleXML objects that were examined in Chapter 3. Accessing the information provided is just as easy. For example, replacing the output portion of the last script with the following:

```
echo "<b>Search Query</b>: <i>" . $result['searchQuery'] . "</i><br>";
$x = $result['startIndex'];
$y = $result['endIndex'];

if ($result['estimateIsExact'])
{
  echo "Displaying results $x to $y, out of " .
$result['estimatedTotalResultsCount'] . " results<br>";
}else
{
  echo "Displaying results $x to $y, out of an estimated " .
$result['estimatedTotalResultsCount'] . " results<br>";
}
$queryResults = $result['resultElements'];
foreach($queryResults as $item)
{
  echo "<a href=\"{$item['URL']}\">{$item['title']}</a><br>";
  echo $item['snippet'] . "<br><br>";
}
```

gives a more user-friendly output, as shown in Figure 6-1.

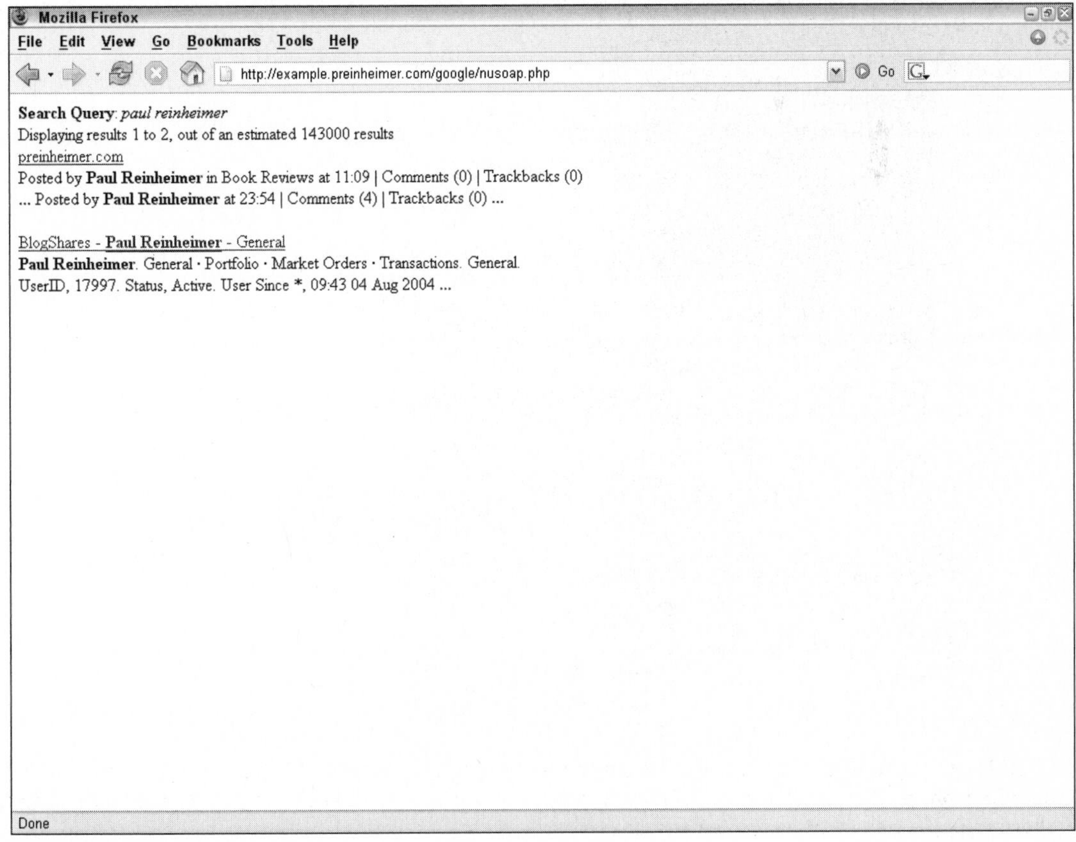

Figure 6-1

Simple Search Interface

Presenting a simple search interface requires only a small amount of code, and it turns the previous hard-coded example into your own personal Google. To simplify this (and future) examples, the process of constructing a query has been moved into its own function:

```
function runGoogleSearch($client, $searchQuery, $start)
{
   $query = array(
       'key'=>'u6U/r39QFHK18Qcjz/XdWSbptVaj9k1t',
       'q'=>$searchQuery,
       'start'=>$start,
       'maxResults'=>10,
       'filter'=>true,
       'restrict'=>'',
       'safeSearch'=>true,
       'lr'=>'',
       'ie'=>'',
       'oe'=>''
  );

  $result = $client->call("doGoogleSearch", $query, "urn:GoogleSearch",
"urn:GoogleSearch");
  return $result;
}
```

This function performs the same basic search as shown in the previous example; really nothing new to see here. I haven't included any of the other attributes in the parameter list for this function to keep things simple. If you need them, feel free to add them. The two places you will most often see the Google API at work are templated search results for a small corporate website, and an automated process to monitor keywords. In the first case you generally want to present as few options as possible (to reduce confusion, and save on screen real estate), and in the second, all of the required options are generally known ahead of time.

```
<html>
<head>
<title>Simple Search Interface</title>
</head>
<body>
<form action="" method="get">
<input type="hidden" name="start" value="0">
<input type="text" name="query" value="">
<input type="submit">
</form>
<br>
<?php
```

This is just your basic HTML form — the hidden variable will be sent to Google to indicate the desired first result. It doesn't do anything here, but when you request the second set of results it will be incremented. I have used a GET variable (rather than POST) here for two main reasons: It is the same method Google uses on its search page, and it will assist in easy transfer from one page to another when paging through the results.

```
if (isset($_GET['query']))
{
```

The code to execute the API call will only be executed if you do in fact have a query to run. This is something to keep in mind because you are only given 1,000 queries per day to play with.

```
  require('../lib/nusoap.php');
  $searchQuery = $_GET['query'];
  $start = $_GET['start'];
```

The information from the two GET variables passed from the form are assigned to their own variables. Though no actual filtering is performed here, it is good practice to never use $_GET or $_POST in a function call not directly related to filtering the data. Data filtering is implemented in the next example.

```
  $client = new soapclient("http://example.org/googleapi/GoogleSearch.wsdl", true);
  if ($client->getError())
  {
    echo "Error creating client <pre>" . $client->getError() . "</pre>";
    exit;
  }
  $client->soap_defencoding = 'UTF-8';
```

Here you check to ensure that the client object was created successfully. You might hit errors at this point if the WSDL file specified in the creation of the object is invalid or unreachable. It is far better to catch things like this now, gracefully, than later when other elements start breaking.

```
  $result = runGoogleSearch(&$client, $searchQuery, $start);
```

The results are obtained from the new function declared previously. Notice the use of the ampersand before $client; this is to ensure the object is passed by reference rather than by value. This way if the $client object raises an error, you will be able to check for it later.

```
  if ($client->fault)
  {
    echo 'Client Fault<pre>';
    print_r($result);
    echo '</pre>';
```

The promised error checking is performed. A client fault is an error handled in the SOAP protocol. There are four acceptable fault codes:

- Server — Something bad happened on the side of the server. It isn't your fault, and generally if you wait, this will resolve itself (this occurred during writing, and it resolved itself in a few hours).
- Client — For some reason the server didn't understand your request. Check your code again and try again.

- VersionMismatch — This happens when the version of SOAP declared in the envelope doesn't match something the server can understand or provide (allows for graceful failures with newer versions).

- MustUnderstand — These errors occur when a header entry includes a MustUnderstand=1 attribute, but the server does not in fact understand the entry. Check the specification for the feed and try again.

```
} else {
  if ($client->getError())
 {
  echo 'Error<pre>' . $client->getError() . '</pre>';
```

A client error encountered here is an error of a different sort. Something went wrong in interpreting the results (for example, if Google returned a malformed SOAP response body) and the appropriate response object couldn't be created.

```
    } else
    {
      echo "<b>Search Query</b>: <i>" . $result['searchQuery'] . "</i><br>";
      $x = $result['startIndex'];
      $y = $result['endIndex'];
      if ($result['estimateIsExact'])
      {
        echo "Displaying results $x to $y, out of " .
          $result['estimatedTotalResultsCount'] . " results<br>";
      }else
      {
        echo "Displaying results $x to $y, out of an estimated " .
          $result['estimatedTotalResultsCount'] . " results<br>";
      }
      $queryResults = $result['resultElements'];
      foreach($queryResults as $item)
      {
        echo "<a href=\"{$item['URL']}\">{$item['title']}</a><br>";
        echo $item['snippet'] . "<br><br>";
      }
      $nextStart = $result['endIndex'];
      echo "<br><br>";
      echo "<a href=\"./nusoap.simple.php?query=$searchQuery&start=$nextStart\">Next
        10 Results</a>";
    }
  }
}
</body></html>
```

Finally, the results are printed out in some semblance of an attractive manner. Notice the last two echo statements near the end — they produce a link to allow the user to select the next 10 results. Performing a simple search for my name with this interface gives you something like that shown in Figure 6-2.

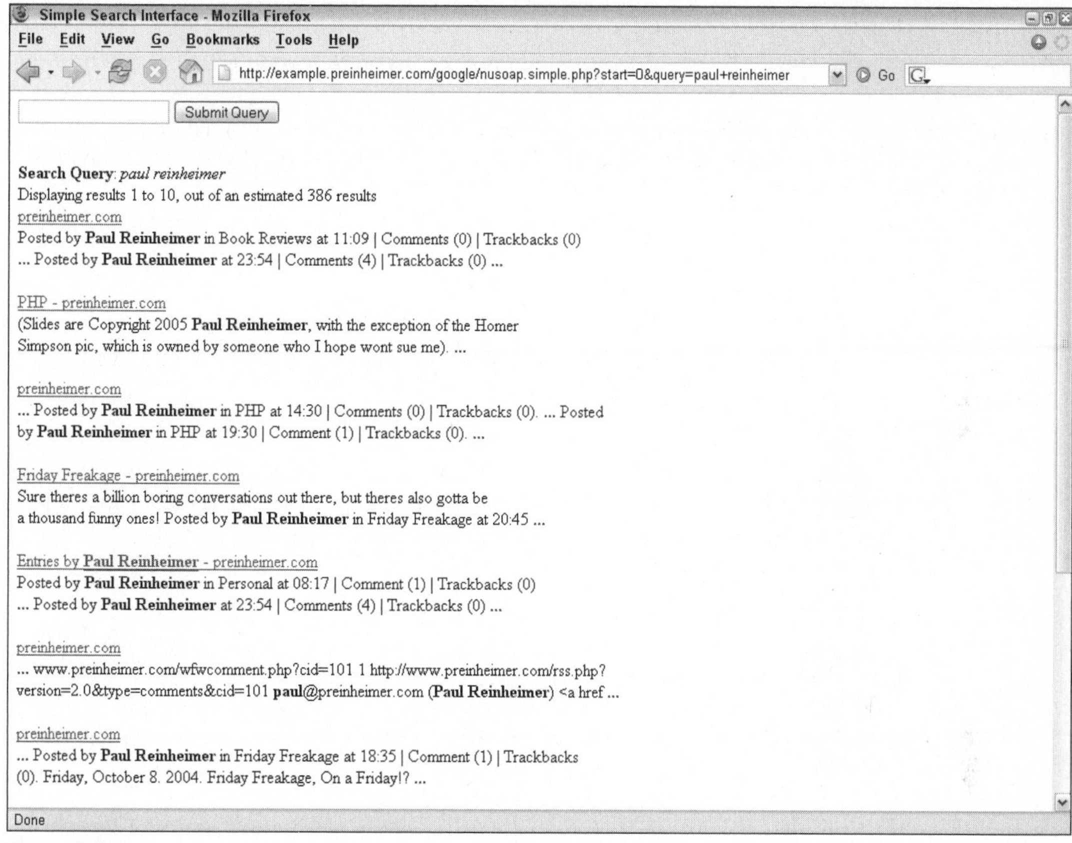

Figure 6-2

Enhancing Results

Although the preceding example works rather well for testing, and begins to show just how easy it can be to perform searches through the API, graphically it is far from pleasing. The next example conceptually presents several of the concepts necessary in integrating Google search results within your own website. Keep in mind that every page (or template) is different, and the steps and effort required will vary based on the complexity of the template and your familiarity with it:

1. Create a development copy.

   View the source of the target page, then copy and paste it into your development program. Take a quick look through for relative links (try searching for `="/` or `="`), and change them to the absolute location. CSS (Cascading Style Sheets) in particular are important ones to fix.

2. Examine the development copy.

   Take a look at the development copy in your web browser; it should look identical to the original. If not, check again for relative links. It isn't imperative that everything is perfect; as long as the overall flow of the page remains the same, you can continue. Take a look at the major block elements of the page (table cells or major DIV/SPAN blocks). Using a Mozilla web browser with the Web Developer extension can make this trivial, because it can outline these elements under the Outline drop-down list. Consider where the search box and results will be displayed, and which current page elements they should be styled after.

3. Remove unneeded content from development copy.

   Unless the target page was rather empty to begin with, the search results will be displacing content previously on the page. Remove the unneeded content from the page; be careful to avoid removing structural data. At this point, the page layout may break. If this happens, one of two things has occurred. First, it is possible that the height of the content area was an integral part of the design, and removing it caused other elements to be sized improperly. If this happened, insert some meaningless text and check again. In the complete example, the search results will take up that space. Second, it is possible that there were some structural elements mixed in with the content that was just removed (for example, if each story on a news page was contained in its own table cell). Undo your changes and examine the code more closely.

4. Insert the search code from the previous example into the development copy.

   Take the search code from the previous example and insert it into the development copy. Place the code in the hole created by removing content. If the content contained a few essential structural elements, try splitting the results up among them, with the search result information (keywords, result count, and so) in one, the results in the next, and the link for the next page in the last. If the content contained many structural elements, echo the appropriate HTML code within the `foreach` loop that iterates through the results.

5. View the resultant page in your web browser.

   Take a look at the page in your web browser. It should look relatively in tune with the original. Run a few searches to see how things work. Make sure you run at least one search designed to have only a few or no results to ensure the page still works structurally.

6. Tweak the document to use appropriate stylistic elements.

   Now that the document works structurally and is able to properly display both large and small result sets, start adding the appropriate style elements noted in Step 2. It is a good idea to check your progress frequently, because errors placed within the `foreach` loop can drastically affect output and can make the document more difficult to diagnose later.

7. Make a small code change to ensure that Google only searches your site.

   There isn't much point in giving people a standard Google search box on your site. Everyone knows where Google is already, and what good would it do you if someone did a search and the number one result was one of your competitors!? Making a small change to the code will ensure that only results from your domain are returned.

```
'q'=>"site:preinheimer.com " . $searchQuery,
```

8. Putting that in place of the previous query line will instruct Google to only return search results from the target domain. Note a few things, however. First, you can only specify one site at a

time (a workaround is presented later in this chapter). Second, notice that there is no space between the colon and the beginning of the domain name — that is important. Finally, notice that there is a space after the domain name and before the query. I performed this addition to the query here, rather than elsewhere, so that the addition would be invisible to the end user. Their original query will still be displayed.

9. Reexamine the original page for nonstatic content.

   If the source document was a static document, your work is/would be done. However, this is rarely the case with modern sites. Check the source document for nonstatic content that will need to be added to the search page (dynamic side bars, footers, and so on), and integrate those elements into the search page, replacing their static counterparts. Alternatively, save the code used to present the search results as its own file, and include it into the document in the appropriate location with whatever means are provided on the site.

By following this series of steps, I was able to turn the previous simplistic search page into an integrated page, shown in Figure 6-3.

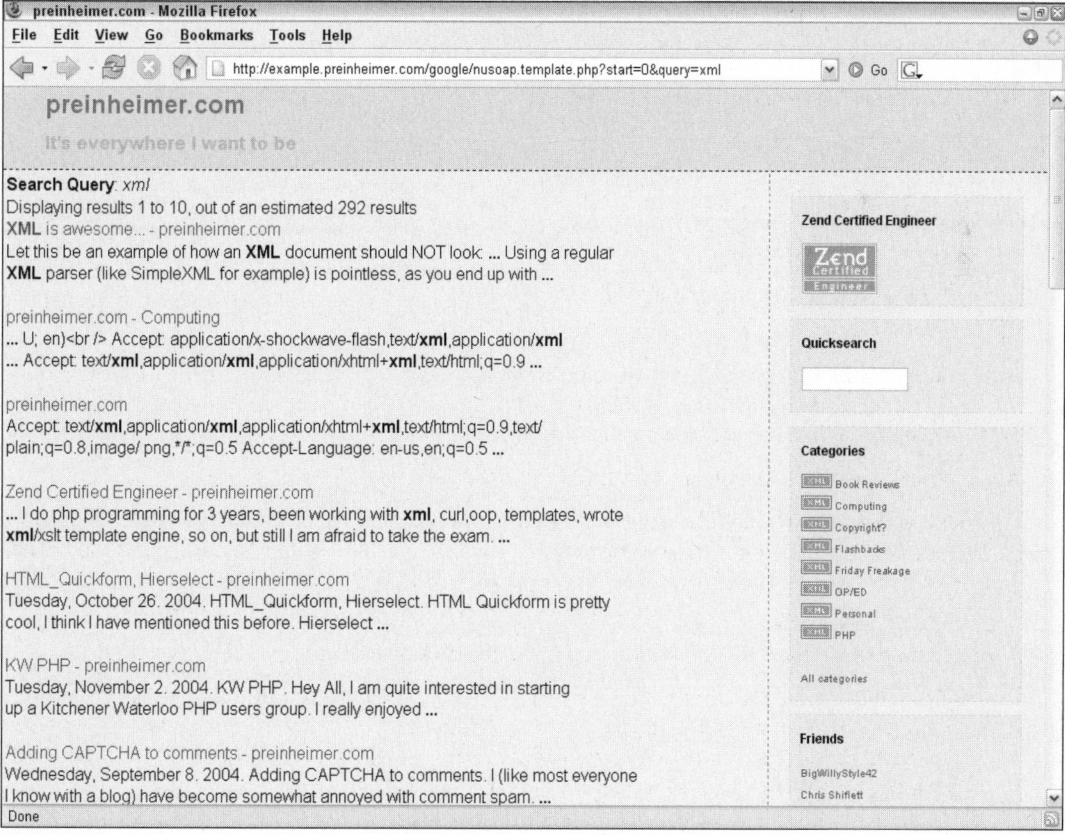

Figure 6-3

Caching Results

Google's limit of 1,000 queries per day might seem a little short, but much can be done to ensure you get the most out of your query limit. Many users of your search system will likely be searching for the same things, and by caching the results, you can minimize the number of queries performed and likely speed results to the end user. Examining frequently queried terms can also prove to be a valuable resource to your web development team. If the same items are sought time and time again, perhaps the site design should be modified to make the searched-for items easier to find.

This caching function was designed to be a layer sitting between the calling function and the actual API calling function. This way the same saved results can be used across different pages, different templates, and so on. An easier (though more limited) method to accomplish this task would be to make use of the uniqueness of the URL (since the search parameters are on there) and just save the whole page to disk. Then, when a request comes in, check for an existing page. If it exists, serve it; if not, capture output with output buffering and save a copy to disk for next time.

```
function getGoogleResults(&$client, $searchQuery, $start)
{
  $key = md5($start . $searchQuery);
  $query = "SELECT * FROM 06_google_cache_meta WHERE `key` = '$key' AND
    ((NOW() - `time`) < 84600)";
  $results = getAssoc($query);
```

The function takes the `$client` object as a parameter, even though it isn't actually needed by the function itself. This is done so the object can be passed off to the `runGoogleSearch` function if required (I avoid global variables like the plague). First, `$key` is generated—this is the primary key within the database, simply a hash of the `$start` offset and the search query itself (this is discussed in greater detail shortly). A query is generated to check for cached data matching the current request. The `getAssoc()` function will return an associative array of the results. The full code listing for the `getAssoc()` function is available in Appendix A.

```
  if (count($results) > 0)
  {
    //echo "Using cached data";
    $result = array();
    $result['estimateIsExact'] = $results['estimateIsExact'];
    $result['estimatedTotalResultsCount'] = $results['estimatedTotalResultsCount'];
    $result['startIndex'] = $start + 1;
    $searchResultQuery = "SELECT * FROM 06_google_cache WHERE `query` =
'$searchQuery' AND `start`= '$start'";
    $searchResults = getAssoc($searchResultQuery);
    $result['endIndex'] = $start + count($searchResults);
    $result['resultElements'] = $searchResults;
    return $result;
  }else
```

If results are found to the query, cached data exists, and it is recent enough to be of use. A `$request` object is created and populated with information from the initial query. Then, a second query is performed to obtain the actual search results. Because the `getAssoc()` function returns an array (and the names of the appropriate rows are identical to those returned by the Google API), it may be directly added to the `$request` object. Some basic math is performed to obtain the values for `startIndex` and `endIndex` to save on space in the database.

```
    {
      //echo "Ran query against API";
      $result = runGoogleSearch(&$client, $searchQuery, $start);
      if ($client->fault)
      {
            return $result;
      } else {

            if ($client->getError())
            {
            return $result;
```

Because the database did not contain relevant cached items, the Google API will need to be called to obtain the requested search results. In the event of an error, return the generated `$result` object to the calling function. It can be dealt with there, just as it would be if you were not caching results.

```
          } else
          {
            $linkID = db_connect();
            $key = md5($start . $searchQuery);
            $query = mysql_escape_string($searchQuery);
            $insertQuery = "REPLACE INTO 06_google_cache_meta
              (`key`, `query`, `start`, `estimateIsExact`,
                `estimatedTotalResultsCount`, `time`)
              VALUES ('$key', '$query', '$start', '{$result['estimateIsExact']}',
                '{$result['estimatedTotalResultsCount']}', null)";
            insertQuery($insertQuery);
```

Here the results begin to be cached. First the meta-information about the query is cached, namely the query, the start index, and information on the estimated total result count. The key that is generated is used so that MySQL's handy `REPLACE INTO` syntax can be used, which will replace a row if it exists already, or just insert a new one if not (but it requires a primary key to run). The MD5 (Message-Digest Algorithm 5) hashing algorithm is handy to generate these keys because it is of predictable length.

```
            $queryResults = $result['resultElements'];
            $index = 0;
            if (count($queryResults) > 1)
            {
```

The search result element is copied out of the `$result` element so it can be iterated through via the upcoming `foreach()` loop. An index is created so you can note which result in particular is being worked on, so results are printed in order when the cached copy is used. The check to ensure that the total result count is higher than 0 is needed to avoid errors with running a `foreach()` on an empty element.

```
              foreach($queryResults as $item)
              {
                $url = mysql_escape_string($item['URL']);
                $snippet = mysql_escape_string($item['snippet']);
                $title = mysql_escape_string($item['title']);
                $key = md5($start . $index . $query);
```

Because the data is being saved to the database, it must be escaped. It is always preferable to use the database-specific escape function because it will escape all required characters, rather than a few common ones. Again the `md5()` function is used to generate a unique key.

```
                $insertQuery = "REPLACE INTO 06_google_cache
                  (`key`, `index`, `query`, `start`, `snippet`, `title`, `url`)
                 VALUES
                  ('$key', '$index', '$query', '$start', '$snippet', '$title',
                  '$url')";
                replaceQuery($insertQuery, $linkID);
                $index++;
            }
        }
        return $result;
      }
    }
  }
}
```

Finally, the information is replaced into the database and the index value is incremented. The original `$result` object returned by the API call is returned to the calling function to be used.

> *Note that the use of the* `md5()` *function here could conceivably cause some issues. Although the MD5 hashing algorithm itself is more than secure enough for this purpose, the inputs used are subject to collision. A search for "paul" with a start index of 11, and a search for "1paul" and a start index of 1 would both provide the* `md5()` *function with identical input, and as such an identical key would be returned. To resolve this, ensure all inputs are* `trim()`*'d before entry, and add a space into the* `md5()` *call.*

The `06_google_cache` table:

```
CREATE TABLE `06_google_cache` (
  `key` varchar(32) NOT NULL default '',
  `index` int(11) NOT NULL default '0',
  `query` varchar(255) NOT NULL default '',
  `start` int(11) NOT NULL default '0',
  `snippet` text NOT NULL,
  `title` varchar(75) NOT NULL default '',
  `url` varchar(255) NOT NULL default '',
  PRIMARY KEY  (`key`)
) TYPE=MyISAM;
```

The values used are relatively arbitrary, with the exception of the key value. The result of `md5()` is always the same length.

The `06_google_cache_meta` table:

```
CREATE TABLE `06_google_cache_meta` (
  `key` varchar(32) NOT NULL default '',
  `query` varchar(255) NOT NULL default '',
  `start` int(11) NOT NULL default '0',
  `estimateIsExact` set('1','') NOT NULL default '',
  `estimatedTotalResultsCount` int(11) NOT NULL default '0',
  `time` timestamp(14) NOT NULL,
  PRIMARY KEY  (`key`)
) TYPE=MyISAM;
```

Monitoring Search Usage

Adding a customized search interface to your website can be a great boon to both you and your users. However, by simply providing the interface without monitoring, you are only receiving a portion of the available benefit. Keeping an eye on which words are searched for most often, and what links users select when performing those searches, can give you critical suggestions on which parts of your website are used most often or are hardest to find. Monitoring searches should be trivial, and you have a few options:

1. Dump the cache database on a regular basis.

   Watch for reccurring searches over a period of time.

2. Use your website stats to monitor searches.

   Because all search requests are performed with GET requests, they should prompt as unique URLs within your server logs.

3. Modify the caching function to increment a separate database each time a query is run.

This will provide you with the most detailed set of results on which queries were performed most often. Rather than record simple totals, you may want to record the IP of the visitor with each query, and tabulate totals on a regular basis. This additional information will allow you to determine if users are performing multiple queries in search of a single piece of information.

Using the Search Data

An important item to note would be if a single search commonly had multiple pages of requested results. This shows not only that the item has proven difficult to locate on your site, but also that users are having a hard time selecting appropriate search terms to locate the result. You may want to reevaluate the position of that item within your site to make it more prominent, or use the fudging example shown later in the chapter to provide users with an easier method to access the desired information. Do not be alarmed when first presented with tabulated search information; research has shown that over half of Internet users are search-dominant. Search-dominant (see *Designing Web Usability: The Practice of Simplicity*, Jakob Nielsen, Publisher: New Riders; 1999) users are task oriented, and usually go straight for the search function on any site they visit (rather than attempting to use whatever navigational aids you have provided). So you will likely see a large number of searches for items that you had thought were easy to find. This is normal, and not generally cause for alarm.

Finding Which Search Results Are Useful

Knowing which searches are performed is useful, but only half the battle. Knowing which results users are selecting further enhances the picture of how the search function is being used. Tracking this usage has two key steps. First, rewriting the link provided in the search results, and second, creating an intermediate page for users to be sent to that redirects them to the appropriate search result.

Editing the link should be trivial:

```
foreach($queryResults as $item)
{
```

```
        echo "<a href=\"http://example.org/jump.php?
          q={$searchQuery}&t={$item['URL']}\">{$item['title']}</a><br>";
        echo $item['snippet'] . "<br><br>";
    }
```

The target URL for the link is simply rewritten to point to the intermediate page. `t` & `q` are selected for the GET variable names rather than something more understandable (such as target and query, respectively) in an effort to keep the URL as short as possible. To shorten the URL further, name your script with a single character name ("j" for example, no extension), and instruct your web server to interpret that page as a PHP script.

Creating the intermediate page isn't much more difficult:

```
<?php
require("../common_db.php");
$linkID = db_connect();
$DIRTYtarget = $_GET['t'];
$query = mysql_real_escape_string($_GET['q'], $linkID);
$target = mysql_real_escape_string($DIRTYtarget, $linkID);
$ip = $_SERVER['REMOTE_ADDR'];
$query = "INSERT INTO 06_google_cache_clicked (time, query, url, ip)
  VALUES(null, '$query', '$target', '$ip')";
insertQuery($query);
header("Location: $DIRTYtarget");
?>
```

The code is pretty unremarkable; I choose to save the IP of the user in an attempt to get some handle on when users need to click on multiple links to find the data they are looking for. If your site requires a login, and as such additional data is available (generally either from a cookie or session data), you may want to store that instead. Conversely, you may want to store the MD5 of the user's IP in an effort to protect their privacy (this shouldn't be considered secure, however, because a brute force attack to determine which IP corresponds with a given hash is possible).

Fudging Google Results

Although Google is an excellent tool for searching the Net at large, there may be instances where you disagree with Google's ranking of certain items within your own domain, or even across the Net at large. By using the previous caching example, fudging results couldn't be easier. Just edit the database!

For example, doing a search (restricted to my domain) for "MetaMachine" (a previous employer) yields the following results:

```
1) mysql_connect() [function.mysql-connect]: Can&#39;t connect to MySQL server...
2) I am a big fan of ?distributed? downloads (as I should be, being a past...
3) or use: forgot your password? or send a check or money order for $20 US...
```

The first result is obviously a big embarrassment—it points to a broken page. You can definitely do better than that for a past employer. You could just fix the page, but it would probably be easier just to fudge the results a little bit.

First, pick the target page. In this case, I have chosen the homepage of one of MetaMachine's software programs, eDonkey. Finally, update the record in the database to contain the fudged information:

```
INSERT INTO `06_google_cache` VALUES ('95b63f2c42287a18a4552f061acac3ed', 0,
'MetaMachine', 0, 'MetaMachine are the authors of the eDonkey file sharing program,
fast error-free downloads every time!', 'eDonkey', 'http://www.edonkey.com/');
```

Next update the meta table, because it contains the timestamp:

```
UPDATE 06_google_cache_meta SET time = '20090118215927' WHERE query = 'metamachine'
```

Now that result set will not expire until 2009. I think it is safe to assume that this code will be long gone by then.

Generally, when I want to fudge results, it is to insert a particularly relevant result that Google has either missed or ranked more poorly; however, the opposite is also possible. If there is a result that you do not want to appear, but do not have a suggested replacement (other than the next relevant result), simply delete the row and increment the other results. You may either leave only nine results on that page, or duplicate the last result from the next page of results.

Imitating Google Adwords

Though the previous methods of fudging examples work, they either necessitate freezing a result set or taking a more complicated approach. There is a simple replacement: copying the design of Google Adwords. While Google accepts paid advertisements, it does not allow these advertisements to produce search results (unlike several competing search engines). Paid advertisements are placed on the same page as the results, but are clearly identified, as shown in Figure 6-4.

When trying to determine how to best handle a search-related situation, just ask yourself WWGD? (What Would Google Do?)

Advertiser (or "sponsor") links are highlighted in Figure 6-4.

Although fudged results likely don't constitute sponsors, a change in terminology to *suggested* will suit the situation perfectly. Creating a suggested word table and using it when presenting results gives the advantages of fudged results, because the preferred results are clearly presented without locking result sets.

```
function getSuggested($query)
{
  $suggestions = array();
  $query = explode(" ", $query);
```

`Explode` is a terrific function. It will turn the query string supplied by the user into an array, with each element in the array consisting of one of the words from the query string. Each word can then be iterated through quite easily. If you want (or need) to include phrases rather than just individual words, the code will need to get a bit more complex. Rather than iterate through the query words, you will need to iterate through the possible phrases, and see if the phrases exist within the query with something like `strripos()`.

```
  foreach($query AS $word)
  {
    $word = mysql_real_escape_string($word, $linkID);
```

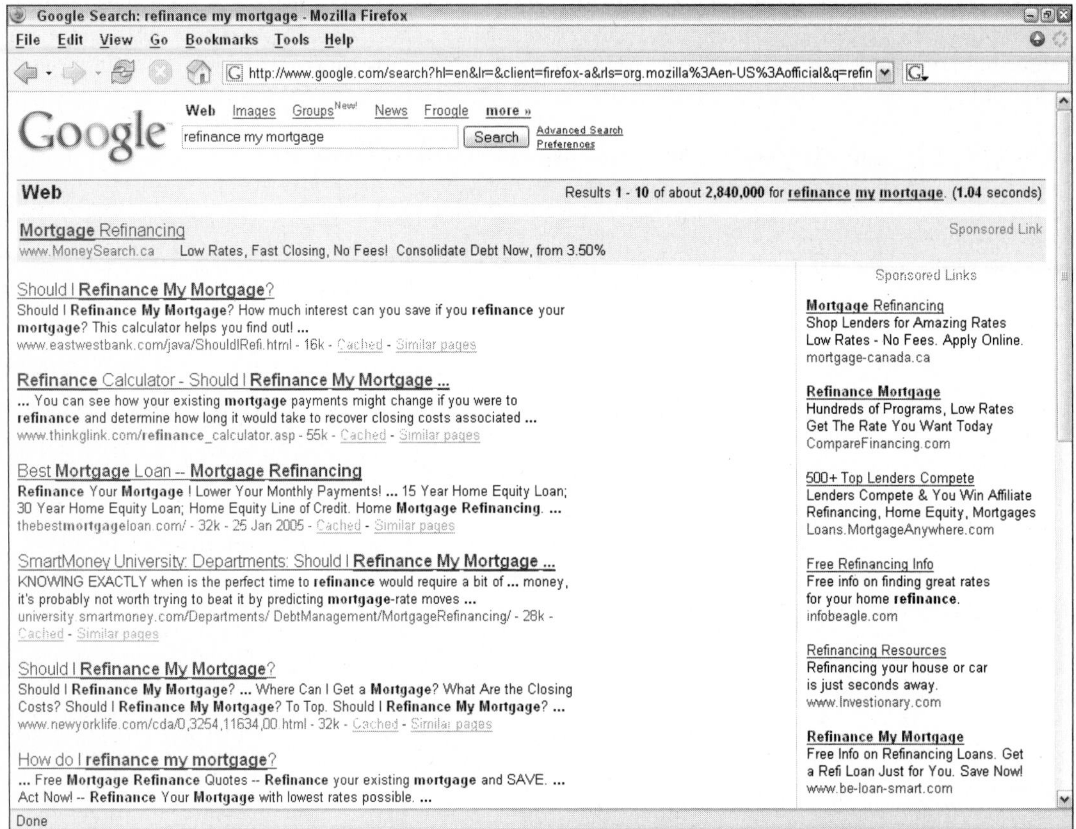

Figure 6-4

It is very easy to forget to escape short strings like this, especially when running a lookup query. Train yourself to always escape before a query, always.

```
      $query = "SELECT * FROM 06_google_suggest WHERE `word` = '$word'";
      $suggest  = getAssoc($query, 2);
```

The second parameter sent to `getAssoc` specifies that you want an array of results in return, so should there be only a single result, it can be iterated through once, rather than accidentally iterating through the result itself. The full code for the function is available in Appendix A.

```
      if (count($suggest) > 0)
      {
        foreach ($suggest as $suggestion)
        {
          $suggestions[] = $suggestion;
        }
      }
    }
    return $suggestions;
  }
```

Finally, if there are any suggestions, they are added to the `suggestions` array, and the results (if any) are returned to the calling function. With this information in hand, the calling function can present the information independently of the real search results, in whatever manner best suits the page template overall.

You can see the suggested and regular results displayed clearly in Figure 6-5.

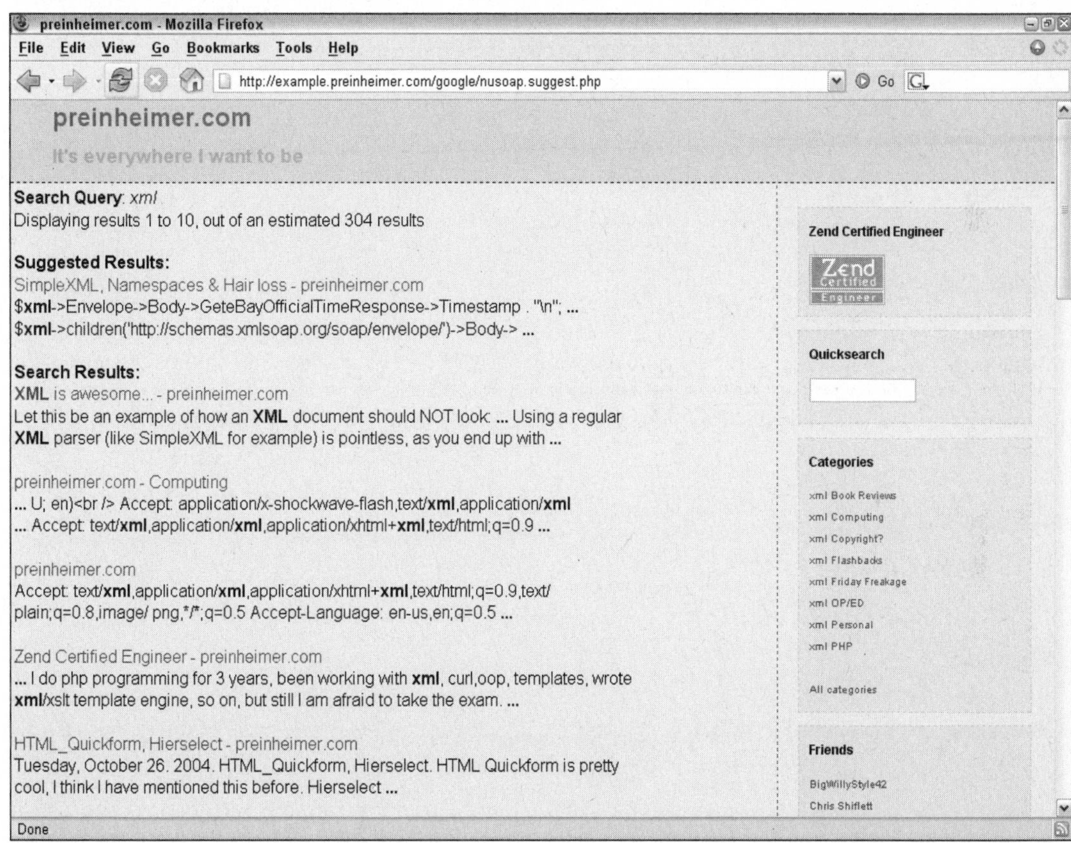

Figure 6-5

Case Study: Monitoring Keywords

With the increasing popularity of the Internet, and Internet-driven sales in that manner, high ranking for common keywords has become an integral part of business. An entire industry, SEO (Search Engine Optimization), has evolved to offer complex solutions to customers in an attempt to increase search engine visibility. Whether or not you can afford these services, monitoring your placement within Google for keyword searches is likely of great interest and value to you.

Using the search function discussed earlier in this chapter, monitoring keywords could not be easier. Conceptually, the monitoring system is a lot of nested loops. First, you will need to loop through all of the query terms that should be checked. Inside that you need to loop through API calls until you receive a result set that contains the result you are looking for (this is necessary because you may be monitoring keywords that do not fall in the first 10 results provided by Google). Inside that you loop through the current result set looking for the appropriate result. If that result is found, the placement of that result is recorded, and the loop is broken to ensure duplicate matches are not recorded (often the same domain will offer several results on the same page). After each query term is found, a check is made to determine whether the Google ranking has risen or fallen further than the specified "allowance." If so, a message is generated to be sent to the appropriate party.

Two database tables will be required: the first to contain the Google queries that will be monitored and the second for the results from those searches.

First, the table containing the queries to be monitored:

```
CREATE TABLE `06_google_monitor` (
  `query` varchar(25) NOT NULL default '',
  `allowance` int(11) NOT NULL default '0'
) TYPE=MyISAM;
```

The `query` field holds the terms that will be checked on a regular basis. The maximum length of 25 characters is an arbitrary choice, but reasonable given its use. The `allowance` field contains the maximum variance between one check of the term and the next. It can be set to 0 to be informed of any change, or a higher value to allow some flexibility between scans. Note that allowing any flexibility would allow for drastic changes over time.

Second, the table containing the placement of those queries:

```
CREATE TABLE `06_google_monitor_results` (
  `query` varchar(25) NOT NULL default '',
  `placement` int(11) NOT NULL default '0',
  `timestamp` timestamp(14) NOT NULL
) TYPE=MyISAM;
```

The `query` field holds the term that was searched, `placement` holds the number of the search result, and `timestamp` holds the timestamp at which the search was performed.

The check to determine whether a given search result has risen or fallen more than the allowance indicated will be performed by the `checkResults` function.

```
function checkResults($searchQuery, $allowance)
{
  $query = "SELECT placement FROM 06_google_monitor_results
  WHERE `query` = '$searchQuery' ORDER BY timestamp DESC LIMIT 2";
  $recentResults = getAssoc($query, 2);
  $thisRun = $recentResults[0]['placement'];
  $lastRun = $recentResults[1]['placement'];
```

The query to be examined as well as the allowance is handed to the function. The query will select the two most recent keyword checks, and the `getAssoc()` function will hand back an array of the results. The `$thisRun` and `$lastRun` variables are created merely for clarity, and to ensure things fit on one line.

```
  if (($thisRun - $lastRun) > $allowance)
  {
```

```
      return "Ranking for $searchQuery has dropped from $lastRun to $thisRun\n";
    }else if (($lastRun - $thisRun) > $allowance)
    {
      return "Ranking for $searchQuery has increased from $lastRun to $thisRun\n";
    }else
    {
      return "";
    }
  }
```

Checks are done to determine whether there has been a large enough change in the ranking to warrant a message. If so, it is generated and returned.

The rest of the program will follow. Note that the error checking presented in previous examples has been omitted for the sake of brevity; it is, however, present in the version you can download from the Wrox website.

```
  require("../common_db.php");
  require('../lib/nusoap.php');
  $client = new soapclient("http://example.org/googleapi/GoogleSearch.wsdl", true);
```

The required files are included, and the SOAP object is initialized.

```
  $desiredURL = "http://www.example.com";
  $length = strlen($desiredURL);
  $message = "";
```

The `$desiredURL` should point to your domain. This program will compare each result to this URL seeking to match the desired domain. The length of the URL is used later in combination with `substr()` to perform that check. Finally, `$message` will contain any messages relating to a change in placement in any of the result sets.

```
  $query = "SELECT * FROM 06_google_monitor";
  $searchTerms = getAssoc($query);
  foreach($searchTerms as $term)
  {
```

All of the query terms are retrieved from the database and stored in the `$searchTerms` object to be iterated through. This allows you to easily add more terms later; just add them to the database.

```
    $placement = 1;
    $start = 0;
    $found = 0;
    $searchQuery = $term['query'];
    $allowance = $term['allowance'];
```

This code contains a lot of variable assignments. `$placement` will be incremented with each result, so the position of a result within the set can be accurately determined. This is needed because the Google API does not return the results placement with the information. `$start` will be used as usual, to indicate the desired offset when requesting results from the API. `$found` will indicate whether the specified domain has been found, to break out of the upcoming `while` loop. `$searchQuery` and `$allowance` indicate the query and allowance for the current item; they exist only for clarity.

```
while ($found == 0 && $start < 50)
{
  $result = runGoogleSearch(&$client, $searchQuery, $start);
  $queryResults = $result['resultElements'];
  foreach($queryResults as $item)
  {
```

This `while` loop is required in the event that the desired result isn't in the first 10 results. The second conditional (`$start < 50`) is used to avoid creating an endless loop looking for a search result that isn't there; 50 seems appropriate because if you aren't on the first five pages of search results, it's unlikely users will find you, so tracking seems meaningless. Next, the API call is made (note this call is made directly, rather than using the caching functions introduced earlier), and as usual the results to the query are identified and iterated through.

```
    if(substr($item['URL'], 0, $length) == $desiredURL)
    {
      $query = "INSERT INTO 06_google_monitor_results (`query`, `placement`,
        `timestamp`)
      VALUES ('$searchQuery', '$placement', null)";
      insertQuery($query);
      $found = 1;
      break;
    }
    $placement++;
```

Here a check is made to determine if this result matches the desired URL. When this occurs, the location of the result, as well as the time it was located, are saved to the database. `$found` is set to 1 to break from the `while` loop, and the `break` statement is used to exit the `foreach` loop. This allows the code to continue with the next query term, if applicable. If this wasn't the desired result, the `$placement` value is incremented.

I know the `break;` *statement in there looks ugly and seems unnecessary, but it is needed. Without the* `break` *statement, the same check would be performed on the remaining results in this set. Should the desired URL show up again, it will be recorded again. Then, when the check is made to determine if a change was made in ranking, it will compare the two results from this scan, and report that you moved up in ranking, every time. Structurally it is possible to write around that and remove the break, but this method seems the most clear.*

```
    }
    $start = $start + 10;
  }
  if ($found == 0)
  {
    $query = "INSERT INTO 06_google_monitor_results (`query`, `placement`,
`timestamp`)
       VALUES ('$searchQuery', '999', null)";
  }
  $message .= checkResults($searchQuery, $allowance);

}
```

The `start` value is incremented to allow the next API call to deal with the next set of results. If after scanning multiple sets of results the desired URL was never found, record a suitable high value as a placeholder to the database. Finally, regardless of whether or not a result was found, make the call to `checkResults()` to report on the activity for the result in question.

This example hasn't included any code showing what to do with the `$message` variable; it is really up to you. If this code is executed as part of a script that mails results to an administrator, you could merely echo them. Alternatively (and more attractively), email them to someone in marketing who gets paid to worry about this sort of thing.

Because all results are saved over time, it would be easy to either generate a graph with PHP or export the data to another program to generate one for you. Showing the movement of key query terms over time can present interesting information.

Possible Changes to This Code

This code has been structured in such a way as to allow a lot of changes. Here are a couple good ideas on how to use it differently.

Monitor Page Placement, Rather Than Domain Placement

Add an additional field to the monitor table for the specific URL you want to monitor, and use it to populate the `$desiredURL` variable on each iteration through the query set. This has the added benefit of being able to track pages from multiple domains.

Rather than track movement, warn if results fall below a certain threshold.

Treat the allowance field as a minimum, and only examine the most recent result. If it is below the specified minimum value, email the appropriate parties informing them of the broken threshold.

Example Application: Multiple Domain Search

One of the limitations of a Google search is that you can only restrict your search to one domain at a time. This isn't usually a problem, but there are several instances where this isn't ideal. For example, you may want to allow users to search both the corporate pages and the community forums at the same time; this could pose a significant problem if the corporate pages were hosted at example.com, while the community forums were held at communityexample.com. The site restriction would not allow you to complete that search. To take another example, say you wanted users to search www.example.com and forums.example.com, but not beta.example.com or people.example.com — again the restrictions of the search do not allow for this functionality.

There are a couple options when dealing with the multiple result sets that will be generated when performing searches like these. Unfortunately, Google does not provide a match percentage with results, so the attractive option of mixing results as indicated by their percentage isn't available. An alternative would be to fold the results together, one from one set, one from the other, and so on. The approach taken for this example, however, is to present the results from the primary domain first, then in a graphically identifiable manner, and the results from the community forums second, so they are available, but distinct.

Overall, this code does not introduce many new features, but it does present a complete, ready-to-use example showing how the Google API can be used. I have removed the templating code, because it is quite site specific.

Features:

- Errors are reported to an administrator, rather than the end user
- Queries are cached to save on keyword use
- Results are fully templated for integration into the overall site
- Results are sent through a jump page for monitoring
- Jump page uses `md5()` to screen IP address

`search.php`:

```
<?php
require ("../common_db.php");
$admin = "$adminJoe@example.org";

if (isset($_GET['query']))
{
  require('../lib/nusoap.php');
  $searchQuery = html_entity_decode($_GET['query']);
  $start = $_GET['start'];
  //$client = new soapclient("http://api.google.com/search/beta2", false);
  $client = new
soapclient("http://example.preinheimer.com/google/googleapi/GoogleSearch.wsdl",
true);
  if ($client->getError())
  {
    $error =  "Error creating client " . $client->getError() . "\n";
    echo "An error was encountered while trying to fulfill your request, please try
again later.";
    mail($admin, "Error creating client object", "$error");
    exit;
  }
  $client->soap_defencoding = 'UTF-8';

  $mainResult = getGoogleResults(&$client, "site:www.example.com " . $searchQuery,
$start);
  $forumResult = getGoogleResults(&$client, "site:forum.example.com " .
$searchQuery, $start);
  $suggestions = getSuggested($searchQuery);


  if ($client->fault)
  {
    echo "An error was encountered while trying to fulfill your request, please try
again later.";

    ob_start();
    print_r($result);
    $error = ob_get_clean();
    mail($admin, "Client Fault", "$error");
```

```
  } else {

    if ($client->getError())
    {

                echo "An error was encountered while trying to fulfill your
request, please try again later.";
          mail($admin, "Client Fault", $client->getError());
        } else
        {

                $searchQuery = htmlentities($searchQuery);
        echo "<b>Search Query</b>: <i>" . $searchQuery . "</i><br>";
      $x = $mainResult['startIndex'];
      $y = $mainResult['endIndex'];

      $queryResults = $mainResult['resultElements'];
      if (count($queryResults) > 1)
      {
        foreach($queryResults as $item)
        {
          echo "<a href=\"{$item['URL']}\">{$item['title']}</a><br>\n";
          echo $item['snippet'] . "<br><br>\n";
        }
      }else
      {
        echo "No results to display";
      }

      echo "Search results from our community forum, note that example.com is not
      responsible for the content provided in the community forums<br><br>";

      $x = $forumResult['startIndex'];
      $y = $forumResult['endIndex'];

      $queryResults = $forumResult['resultElements'];
      if (count($queryResults) > 1)
      {
        foreach($queryResults as $item)
        {
          echo "<a href=\"{$item['URL']}\">{$item['title']}</a><br>\n";
          echo $item['snippet'] . "<br><br>\n";
        }
      }else
      {
        echo "No results to display";
      }

      $nextStart = $mainResult['endIndex'];
      echo "<br><br>";

      echo "<a
href=\"./nusoap.simple.php?query={$searchQuery}&start=$nextStart\">Next 10
Results</a>";
    }
  }
```

```
}

function runGoogleSearch($client, $searchQuery, $start)
{
   $query = array(
         'key'=>'u6U/r39QFHK18Qcjz/XdWSbptVaj9k1t',
         'q'=> $searchQuery,
         'start'=>$start,
         'maxResults'=>10,
         'filter'=>true,
         'restrict'=>'',
         'safeSearch'=>true,
         'lr'=>'',
         'ie'=>'',
         'oe'=>''
   );

  $result = $client->call("doGoogleSearch", $query, "urn:GoogleSearch",
"urn:GoogleSearch");
  return $result;
}

function getGoogleResults($client, $searchQuery, $start)
{
  $key = md5($start . $searchQuery);
  // Check for recent items
  $query = "SELECT * FROM 06_google_cache_meta WHERE `key` = '$key' AND ((NOW() -
`time`) < 84600)";
  $results = getAssoc($query);

  print_r($results);
  if (count($results) > 0)
  {
    echo "Using Cached Data";
    //Cache exists and is recent, Create object to return
    $result = array();
    $result['estimateIsExact'] = $results['estimateIsExact'];
    $result['estimatedTotalResultsCount'] = $results['estimatedTotalResultsCount'];
    $result['startIndex'] = $start + 1;

    $searchResultQuery = "SELECT * FROM 06_google_cache WHERE `query` =
'$searchQuery' AND `start`= '$start'";
    $searchResults = getAssoc($searchResultQuery);
    $result['endIndex'] = $start + count($searchResults);
    $result['resultElements'] = $searchResults;
    return $result;
  }else
  {
    //Save results
    $result = runGoogleSearch(&$client, $searchQuery, $start);

    if ($client->fault)
    {
         return $result;
    } else {

         if ($client->getError())
```

```
        {
                return $result;
        } else
        {
          $linkID = db_connect();
                $queryResults = $result['resultElements'];
                $query = mysql_escape_string($searchQuery);
                $index = 0;

                $insertQuery = "REPLACE INTO 06_google_cache_meta
                 (`key`, `query`, `start`, `estimateIsExact`,
`estimatedTotalResultsCount`, `time`)
                VALUES
                 ('$key', '$query', '$start', '{$result['estimateIsExact']}',
'{$result['estimatedTotalResultsCount']}', null)";
                insertQuery($insertQuery);

                if (count($queryResults) > 1)
                {
          foreach($queryResults as $item)
          {

            $url = mysql_escape_string($item['URL']);
            $snippet = mysql_escape_string($item['snippet']);
            $title = mysql_escape_string($item['title']);
            $key = md5($start . $index . $query);

            $insertQuery = "REPLACE INTO 06_google_cache
            (`key`, `index`, `query`, `start`, `snippet`, `title`, `url`)
            VALUES
            ('$key', '$index', '$query', '$start', '$snippet', '$title', '$url')";
            replaceQuery($insertQuery, $linkID);
            $index++;
          }
        }
        return $result;
      }
    }
  }

}

function getSuggested($query)
{
  $suggestions = array();
  $query = explode(" ", $query);
  $linkID = db_connect();
  foreach($query AS $word)
  {
    $word = mysql_real_escape_string($word, $linkID);
    $query = "SELECT * FROM 06_google_suggest WHERE `word` = '$word'";
    $suggest  = getAssoc($query, 2);
    if (count($suggest) > 0)
    {
      foreach ($suggest as $suggestion)
      {
```

```
            $suggestions[] = $suggestion;
            echo "Added a suggestion";
        }
      }
    }
    return $suggestions;
  }

  ?>
```

jump.php:

```
<?php
require("../common_db.php");
$linkID = db_connect();
$DIRTYtarget = $_GET['t'];
$query = mysql_real_escape_string($_GET['q'], $linkID);
$target = mysql_real_escape_string($DIRTYtarget, $linkID);
$ip = md5($_SERVER['REMOTE_ADDR']);
$query = "INSERT INTO 06_google_cache_clicked (time, query, url, ip)
  VALUES(null, '$query', '$target', '$ip')";
insertQuery($query);
header("Location: $DIRTYtarget");
?>
```

The resulting output, matched to your site's overall design, will easily allow you to present consistent results from multiple domains either internal or external to your firm. By combining these results in one location overall, you're presenting a very powerful tool, and thanks to Google's help you're doing it without a lot of code.

Summary

This chapter introduced the SOAP messaging protocol, with a quick look at the HTTP protocol that carries it from client to server. It also took a detailed look at the Google SOAP format and its element parts. This information was used to manually generate an API request and examine Google's response. Once the nitty-gritty portion of the protocol was discussed, the NuSOAP tool was introduced, which made dealing with requests considerably easier. At first a simple search interface was presented, using NuSOAP, rather than your own manual requests. Gradually this example was added to, to present a full-featured search engine, matching that of an example site. Other topics such as fudging or suggesting alternate results, monitoring search usage, or caching results to save on queries were also discussed. Finally, the search framework was used to monitor key queries over time, and warn if placement changed, and again to present search results from multiple domains at once. Overall, the main goals of this chapter were as follows:

- A good understanding of the transaction behind a SOAP request to Google
- Using NuSOAP to handle the request
- Presenting a search interface
- Caching results and monitoring usage

- Fudging results and presenting suggested topics
- Monitoring keywords over time

A few security-related topics were also discussed, the overall lesson being, always, always, filter incoming data, especially when it is destined for a database. The SOAP information obtained in this chapter will be useful when looking at the Amazon API in the next chapter, which allows developers access through both SOAP and REST.

7

Interacting with the Amazon API

Amazon, while serving as little more than a website and virtual warehouse, has built itself into one of the most recognized names in e-business. With an original product catalog consisting entirely of dead trees, it (with the assistance of partners) has now expanded to sell nearly everything imaginable, from shoes to blenders, diamond rings to dishwashers. Amazon's API offers great flexibility and a possible revenue stream for a site owner. By enrolling in the Associates program, you can earn a percentage of sales generated through your website. This allows site owners to not only present their visitors with relevant products and cross promotions, but also to receive some money for their troubles.

Amazon also offers localized websites from around the globe: Canada, United Kingdom, Germany, Japan, France, and China. Until recently, only a few of these sites offered APIs; however, Amazon launched its API service for all sites in January 2005. Keep in mind, however, that each API offers its own functionality, and not all features are available in all areas. The examples presented in this book are run against the U.S. server, utilizing the WSDL (Web Services Description Language) file for the U.S. as well.

Amazon's API allows for a tremendous variety of different queries, but unfortunately only a few variants can be examined here. The full documentation for the newest version of the API is 457 pages long, which can seem overwhelming at first, but many of the queries are very similar, requiring only a few minor changes to be used.

This chapter examines the following:

- A simple REST call
- A simple SOAP call
- Searching by author or keyword with SOAP
- Monitoring prices or sales ranks over time
- Creating a personal storefront

Introducing the Amazon API

Amazon's API presents two different methods of interaction: REST (Representational State Transfer) and SOAP (Simple Object Access Protocol). The majority of the examples within this chapter utilize the SOAP method; I will, however, initially present an interaction using REST for completeness. I have selected SOAP for use within the chapter because of the relatively clean level of abstraction that can be obtained by using a SOAP class such as NuSOAP, and to offer a counterpoint to Amazon's own examples, which are almost exclusively REST. This chapter covers a few common methods of interacting with Amazon's API; a full listing of available interfaces is presented in Appendix C.

Registering for the Amazon API

You can register for the Amazon API by visiting the root page (`www.amazon.[com/jp/ca/co.uk/`, and so on]) for the desired version of Amazon. Scroll to the bottom of the page and click the Join Associates link. This will bring you to the previously unseen Make Money tab. From there, click the Web Services link underneath the tab bar, and then click Register for AWS on the left side. This will provide you with a `developer` tag, which will allow you to begin running queries against the API; however, you can't earn any referral fees yet. In order to earn any referral fees, you need to register as an Associate. To register as an Associate, return to the Make Money tab, select the Associates subtab, and click the Join Now button on the left. Registering as an Amazon Associate will provide you with an `associate` id. This id will be passed with your requests, and the resulting URLs will have that id coded in, to allow Amazon to track which customers you send its way.

Limitations of the Amazon API

The Google API was quite restrictive in the number of queries you could run per day — only 1,000 (which is really only like 40 requests per hour). However, the Amazon API is much more giving, allowing *one request per second*. This likely stems from the fact that results presented with the Google API represent a loss in revenue (because API results do not include advertisements, one of Google's primary revenue streams), whereas results presented from Amazon's API represent potential revenue for Amazon and *you*.

Possibilities with the Amazon API

Amazon allows a tremendous variety of different requests to be run against its service. Items can be searched for by a multitude of criteria (keyword being only one of them), shopping carts can be created and loaded to the brim (50 unique items), and Amazon's lists can be accessed. All of this gives you a variety of ways to determine which products to display to your visitor, and a variety of ways to make revenue from those referrals.

Utilizing the Amazon API

Developer tag in hand, you are now ready to start working with Amazon's API. The big choice that you're going to need to make early on is whether you want to work with it via its REST interface or the SOAP interface. Both provide similar functionality; the difference is going to be how you access it. While researching this book, I encountered countless examples utilizing the REST interface, and very few demonstrating the SOAP interface. To get the most out of this chapter, I've decided to take the opposite stance — this chapter concentrates on SOAP with only a brief introduction to REST.

Sample REST Search

Performing any API call over REST, especially during testing, should be quite easy. First, create a simple web form pointing to the appropriate URL, and set the form to use the GET method. Create hidden form variables for any required elements, and use a text box for any user-specified elements. For example, using the following page and entering a search for `paul reinheimer` will constitute a valid, and useful, REST request:

```
<html>
<head>
<title>Rest Sample</title>
</head>
<body>
<form method="get" action="http://webservices.amazon.com/onca/xml">
<input type="hidden" name="t" value="preinheimerco-20">
<input type="hidden" name="Service" value="AWSECommerceService">
<input type="hidden" name="SubscriptionId" value="1PHH5VTRY7D300H7JTR2">
<input type="hidden" name="Operation" value="ItemSearch">
<input type="hidden" name="SearchIndex" value="Books">
<input type="text" name="Keywords" value="Books">
<input type="submit" name="submit" value="post">
</form>
</body>
</html>
```

Most of the parameters there are self-explanatory, but a few could do with some explanation. The parameter named `t` with a value of `preinheimerco-20` contains my *associate ID* (from joining the Amazon Associates program), which will allow the API to encode resultant URLs with my ID for revenue tracking. The `SubscriptionID` and value represent my *developer key*, necessary for all requests. `Operation` indicates what type of request I am performing this time—an `ItemSearch`—and `SearchIndex` indicates that I want to search only Amazon's book inventory this time. Finally, the text input field allows users to enter their own search `Keywords`.

The result from Amazon is quite verbose, but still readable. First some basic information about the request is returned, followed by the actual result items. Each item contains an ASIN (Amazon Standard Identification Number), the URL for the item, a title, and other basic information. In the following request, the authors of the book are returned.

```
<?xml version="1.0" encoding="UTF-8"?>
<ItemSearchResponse
xmlns="http://webservices.amazon.com/AWSECommerceService/2005-01-19">
<OperationRequest>
 <HTTPHeaders>
  <Header Name="UserAgent" Value="Mozilla/5.0 (Windows; U; Windows NT 5.1;
    rv:1.7.3) Gecko/20041001 Firefox/0.10.1"></Header>
 </HTTPHeaders>
 <RequestId>0JQ4GT363KKWN5RBNS6X</RequestId>
 <Arguments>
  <Argument Name="Service" Value="AWSECommerceService"></Argument>
  <Argument Name="submit" Value="post"></Argument>
  <Argument Name="SearchIndex" Value="Books"></Argument>
  <Argument Name="t" Value="preinheimerco-20"></Argument>
  <Argument Name="SubscriptionId" Value="1PHH5VTRY7D300H7JTR2"></Argument>
```

```
      <Argument Name="Keywords" Value="paul reinheimer"></Argument>
      <Argument Name="Operation" Value="ItemSearch"></Argument>
    </Arguments>
    <RequestProcessingTime>0.0342471599578857</RequestProcessingTime>
  </OperationRequest>
  <Items>
    <Request>
      <IsValid>True</IsValid>
      <ItemSearchRequest>
        <Keywords>paul reinheimer</Keywords>
        <SearchIndex>Books</SearchIndex>
      </ItemSearchRequest>
    </Request>
    <TotalResults>1</TotalResults>
    <TotalPages>1</TotalPages>
    <Item>
      <ASIN>0764589547</ASIN>
      <DetailPageURL>http://www.amazon.com/exec/obidos/redirect?tag=ws%26link_code=xm2
      %26camp=2025%26creative=165953%26path=http://www.amazon.com/gp/redirect.html%253f
      ASIN=0764589547%2526location=/o/ASIN/0764589547%25253FSubscriptionId=1PHH5VTRY7
      D300H7JTR2</DetailPageURL>
      <ItemAttributes>
        <Author>Paul  Reinheimer</Author>
        <Author>Chris  Shiflett</Author>
        <ProductGroup>Book</ProductGroup>
        <Title>Professional Web APIs with PHP: eBay, Google, Paypal, Amazon, FedEx plus
          Web Feeds</Title>
      </ItemAttributes>
    </Item>
  </Items>
</ItemSearchResponse>
```

This request only returned a single result (`item`). Had there been more results, the `item` tag would have repeated.

As you can see, the elements required to perform a transaction using `REST` are relatively straightforward. It would have been trivial to retrieve the result document with `file_get_contents()` (or any of a number of similar constructs) and parse the XML with a tool like SimpleXML or MiniXML. You would then be able to present results to the user in an attractive manner. Alternatively, you could use an XSLT stylesheet to directly translate the result set into a user-accessible document.

The remainder of this chapter concentrates on the SOAP interface to the Amazon API. The REST services are quite well documented, and there is an abundance of sample code already available. My hope is that by providing samples for SOAP, which presently seem to be lacking, you will be better able to use the API in whatever manner you wish.

Performing Searches with SOAP

Amazon breaks the mold set by most major APIs in presenting access to its database through both SOAP and REST. Both request types allow access to essentially the same internal functions, the key difference being the structure of the request.

When exploring complicated APIs, it is often very useful to be presented with an easy-to-read list of available queries. To that end I would recommend taking a look at the Generic Soap Client available at `http://soapclient.com/SoapTest.html`. Give it the URL to any `.wsdl` file, and it will display the different available requests and the parameters for each request. It also goes the additional step of allowing you to actually make the query, in which case it will display either the request or response depending on your selection.

A Simple Search Request

Performing the same search as used in the REST request using SOAP requires a slightly different approach:

```
<?php
require('../lib/nusoap.php');
$client =
new soapclient("http://soap.amazon.com/schemas2/AmazonWebServices.wsdl", true);
```

The NuSOAP libraries are included and the `$client` object is created. The `.wsdl` file here is for the U.S. version of the API. Different `.wsdl` documents are used for the regional sites.

```
$query = array(
            'keyword'    => 'paul reinheimer',
            'page'        => 1,
            'mode'        => 'books',
            'tag'         => 'preinheimerco-20',
            'type'        => 'lite',
            'devtag'      => '1PHH5VTRY7D300H7JTR2'
);
```

The query itself is generated. The same search is being performed as in the REST request. Notice the additional element `type`, set to `lite`. The same request performed with the `heavy` tag instead of the `lite` tag is presented shortly.

```
$namespace = 'http://soap.amazon.com';
$action = 'http://soap.amazon.com';
$method = "KeywordSearchRequest";
$result = $client->call($method,
  array('KeywordSearchRequest' => $query),
  $namespace, $action);

print_r($result);
?>
```

Finally the namespace, action, and method are defined and the query is run against the API server. The results are printed, and shown here:

```
Array
(
  [TotalResults] => 1
  [TotalPages] => 1
  [Details] => Array
```

```
  (
    [0] => Array
    (
      [Url] => http://www.amazon.com/exec/obidos/ASIN/0764589547/
        preinheimerco-20?dev-t=1PHH5VTRY7D300H7JTR2%26camp=2025%26link_code=sp1
      [Asin] => 0764589547
      [ProductName] => Professional Web APIs with PHP: eBay, Google, Paypal,
        Amazon, FedEx plus Web Feeds
      [Catalog] => Book
      [Authors] => Array
      (
        [0] => Paul  Reinheimer
        [1] => Chris  Shiflett
      }
      [ReleaseDate] => 18 July, 2005
      [Manufacturer] => John Wiley & Sons
      [ImageUrlSmall] =>
        http://images.amazon.com/images/P/0764589547.01.THUMBZZZ.jpg
      [ImageUrlMedium] =>
        http://images.amazon.com/images/P/0764589547.01.MZZZZZZZ.jpg
      [ImageUrlLarge] =>
        http://images.amazon.com/images/P/0764589547.01.LZZZZZZZ.jpg
      [Availability] => This item is currently not available.
    )
  )
)
```

The results returned are very similar to what you saw with the REST request. Note that the SOAP request isn't prepended with your original request.

> *I have used my name as an example for a search to ensure the result listing is brief; however, because the book isn't actually available yet, you may have noticed some fields are missing, namely the price. Available products will contain a* `ListPrice` *element. Note that this is indeed the list price, which is likely higher than Amazon's actual selling price. Amazon's selling price is available via a heavy request.*

Using the previous code, but replacing the `lite type` tag with `heavy`, gives the following:

```
Array
(
  [TotalResults] => 1
  [TotalPages] => 1
  [Details] => Array
  (
    [0] => Array
    (
      [Url] => http://www.amazon.com/exec/obidos/ASIN/0764589547/
        preinheimerco-20?dev-t=1PHH5VTRY7D300H7JTR2%26camp=2025%26link_code=sp1
      [Asin] => 0764589547
      [ProductName] => Professional Web APIs with PHP: eBay, Google, Paypal,
        Amazon, FedEx plus Web Feeds
      [Catalog] => Book
```

```
            [Authors] => Array
            (
              [0] => Paul  Reinheimer
              [1] => Chris  Shiflett
            )
            [ReleaseDate] => 18 July, 2005
            [Manufacturer] => John Wiley & Sons
            [ImageUrlSmall] =>
              http://images.amazon.com/images/P/0764589547.01.THUMBZZZ.jpg
            [ImageUrlMedium] =>
              http://images.amazon.com/images/P/0764589547.01.MZZZZZZZ.jpg
            [ImageUrlLarge] =>
              http://images.amazon.com/images/P/0764589547.01.LZZZZZZZ.jpg
            [BrowseList] => Array
            (
              [0] => Array
              (
                  [BrowseName] => Computer Programming
              )

              [1] => Array
              (
                  [BrowseName] => Computers / Programming / General
              )
            )
            [Media] => Paperback
            [Isbn] => 0764589547
            [Availability] => This item is currently not available.
          )
        )
    )
```

More information is returned, such as the ISBN and Amazon's categorization of the item. The information returned in this request is rather slim because the book hasn't been released yet. When available, a heavy request will include information like similar products, user comments, and an array of applicable browse listings.

Presenting Results

Presenting the results from a given search in a usable manner isn't much more difficult. The query against the API will be performed as before (though with different criteria), but this time, rather than using `print_r()` to view the results, the results will be iterated through, and outputted with accompanying HTML:

```
<?php
require('../lib/nusoap.php');
$client =
new soapclient("http://soap.amazon.com/schemas2/AmazonWebServices.wsdl", true);
$params = array(
            'keyword'    => 'elements of style',
```

```
                'page'          => 1,
                'mode'          => 'books',
                'tag'           => 'preinheimerco-20',
                'type'          => 'heavy',
                'devtag'        => '1PHH5VTRY7D300H7JTR2'
);
$namespace = 'http://soap.amazon.com';
$action = 'http://soap.amazon.com';
$method = "KeywordSearchRequest";
$result = $client->call($method,
  array('KeywordSearchRequest' => $params),
  $namespace, $action);
$resultItems = $result['Details'];
foreach ($resultItems AS $item)
{
  $title = $item['ProductName'];
  $url = $item['Url'];
  $image = $item['ImageUrlSmall'];
  $authorList = implode($item['Authors'], ", ");
  $price = $item['ListPrice'];
  echo "<img src=\"$image\" align=\"left\">";
  echo "<a href=\"$url\" title=\"Learn More at Amazon.com\">$title<a><br>";
  echo "Author(s): " . $authorList . "<br>";
  echo "List Price: " . $price;
  echo "<hr>";
}
?>
```

Here a basic `foreach()` loop iterates through each of the result items, and variables are created for each of the desired result elements. This is done mainly for clarity and compatibility with the size of this printed page; generally I would use something more like this:

```
echo "<a href=\"{$item['Url']}\" title=\"Learn More at
Amazon.com\">{$item['ProductName']}<a><br>";
```

This is a little harder to read, but it saves on a variable assignment. The `implode()` function is very useful here, quickly turning the array of authors into a comma-delimited string. The output of this function shows the results of a search for "elements of style," shown in Figure 7-1.

Usable Search Page

Previous examples worked well and began to explore some of the functionality that the Amazon API presents; however, they did not include any error checking, and used hard-coded search terms and criteria. As already mentioned, it is always best not to trust any external content just in case—you never know what you are going to get.

Accordingly, the following program allows an end user to search for products. Functionally, the program will have three main components: presenting the search form and validating passed data, performing the query, and presenting the results.

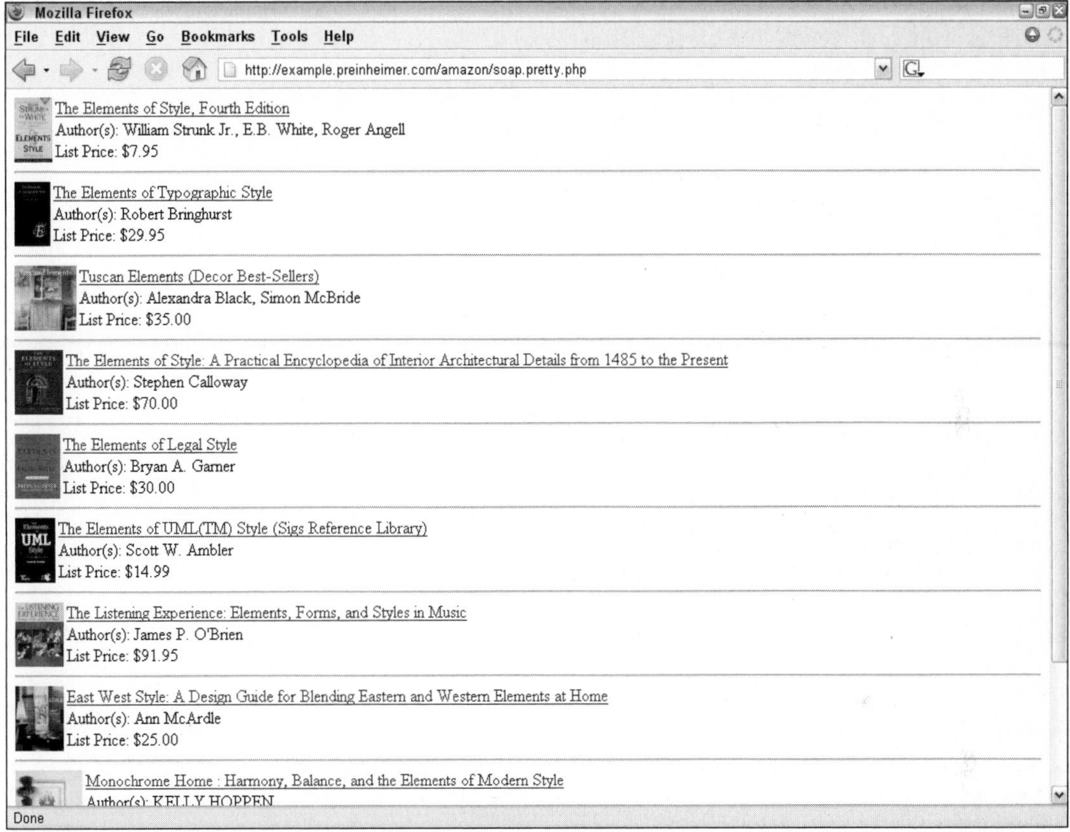

Figure 7-1

Different product types contain different information — books have authors, movies have stars, and music has artists. As such, results will be passed to one of three different functions, one each for the different search types presented.

```
function displayBook($resultItems)
{
  foreach ($resultItems AS $item)
  {
    $title = $item['ProductName'];
    $url = $item['Url'];
    $image = $item['ImageUrlSmall'];
    $authorList = implode($item['Authors'], ", ");
    $price = $item['ListPrice'];
    if ($url != "") echo "<img src=\"$image\" align=\"left\">";
    echo "<a href=\"$url\" title=\"Learn More at Amazon.com\">$title<a><br>";
    echo "Author(s): " . $authorList . "<br>";
```

```
        echo "List Price: " . $price;
        echo "<hr>";
    }
}
```

The `displayBook()` function is identical (except for the function wrapping) to the code shown in the previous example.

```
function displayDVD($resultItems)
{
    foreach ($resultItems AS $item)
    {
        $title = $item['ProductName'];
        $url = $item['Url'];
        $image = $item['ImageUrlSmall'];
        $stars = @implode($item['Starring'], ", ");
        $price = $item['ListPrice'];
        if ($url != "") echo "<img src=\"$image\" align=\"left\">";
        echo "<a href=\"$url\" title=\"Learn More at Amazon.com\">$title<a><br>";
        if ($stars != "") echo "Starring: " . $stars . "<br>";
        echo "List Price: " . $price . "<br><br>";
        echo "<hr>";
    }
}
```

For DVDs, the `Starring` value is imploded to be displayed.

```
function displayCD($resultItems)
{
    foreach ($resultItems AS $item)
    {
        $title = $item['ProductName'];
        $url = $item['Url'];
        $image = $item['ImageUrlSmall'];
        $artists = implode($item['Artists'], ", ");
        $price = $item['ListPrice'];
        if ($url != "") echo "<img src=\"$image\" align=\"left\">";
        echo "<a href=\"$url\" title=\"Learn More at Amazon.com\">$title<a><br>";
        echo "Artist(s): " . $artists . "<br>";
        echo "List Price: " . $price;
        echo "<hr>";
    }
}
```

For CDs, the artist's value is again imploded for display.

Although the differences presented here are not too significant, using different functions for different object types does allow a lot of flexibility. Displaying Director in the DVD function would be trivial, as would choosing to display the label for music or the publisher for books. It's important not to feel constrained to displaying the data common across all types when working with the API, because there is such a great variety. That being said, further examples in this chapter concentrate on books; the code for other result types tends to be repetitive.

```
function runSearchQuery($client, $keywords, $page, $mode, $type = 'lite')
{
  $params = array(
    'keyword'     => $keywords,
    'page'         => $page,
    'mode'         => $mode,
    'tag'          => 'preinheimerco-20',
    'type'         => $type,
    'devtag'       => '1PHH5VTRY7D300H7JTR2'
  );

  $namespace = 'http://soap.amazon.com';
  $action = 'http://soap.amazon.com';
  $method = "KeywordSearchRequest";
  $result = $client->call($method,
  array('KeywordSearchRequest' => $params),
  $namespace, $action);

  return $result;
}
```

Running the query against the Amazon API uses code very similar to the previous example. The hard-coded variables for keyword, page, mode, and type have been replaced with variables. The encapsulation of this code into its own function should help keep things clear, and will save on overhead later.

Finally, here is the body of the code itself:

```
<html>
<head>
<title>Amazon.com Search Interface</title>
</head>
<body>
<form action="./soap.search.php" method="get">
<input type="text" name="query">
<input type="hidden" name="page" value="1">
<select name="mode">
```

Here a basic form is started to allow users to enter their search criteria. The `page` variable is used to allow users to navigate through multiple pages of search results.

```
<?php
$modes = array();
$modes[] = "books";
$modes[] = "dvd";
$modes[] = "cd";
foreach ($modes as $mode)
{
  echo "<option value=\"$mode\">$mode</option>";
}
?>
</select>
```

```
<input type="submit">
</form>
```

An array is created to contain each type of request the program is capable of performing. Structuring your code in this manner allows you to add other search types easily later on, and will come in handy when it comes time to validate the user's input.

```
<?php
if (!isset($_GET['query']))
{
  exit;
}else
{
  $query = $_GET['query'];
}
```

If a query has not been received, there is no point in continuing. This is most likely the case when a user visits the page for the first time.

```
if (in_array($_GET['mode'], $modes))
{
  $mode = $_GET['mode'];
}else
{
  echo "Invalid mode selected was " . $_GET['mode'];
  exit;
}
```

Here the array originally used to populate the select box is used to validate the data. Looking at the form, it may seem impossible to receive any other value, but remember that the request is passed in the address bar, and requests can be created by other parties manually.

```
if (is_numeric($_GET['page']))
{
  $page = $_GET['page'];
}else
{
  echo "Invalid page requested, was: " . $_GET['page'];
  exit;
}
```

Finally, the `page` variable is populated if the passed variable is numeric.

```
require('../lib/nusoap.php');
$client =
new soapclient("http://soap.amazon.com/schemas2/AmazonWebServices.wsdl", true);
$error = $client->getError();
if ($error) {
```

```
        echo 'Error creating search client, please try again later';
        // It would be a great idea to email $error to an administrator
        exit;
    }
```

The NuSOAP library is included into the program at this point rather than earlier to save on overhead when it isn't needed (which is the case for the first request). The SOAP client is created, and is checked for errors. If an error is encountered at this point, it is likely that the `.wsdl` file was either inaccessible or invalid. It would be a great idea to do something with errors like this when you encounter them.

```
    $result = runSearchQuery($client, $query, $page, $mode, 'heavy');
    $error = $client->getError();
    if ($client->fault || $error)
    {
      echo "I wasn't able to retrieve your search results, please try again later";
      //It would be a great idea to email $client->fault to an admin
      exit;
    }
```

Next the query is run, and again errors are checked for. A client fault is different from an error, so both are checked for at this point. Again, don't just check for errors, do something about them.

```
    $resultItems = $result['Details'];

    switch ($mode)
    {
      case "dvd":
        displayDVD($resultItems);
        break;
      case "books":
        displayBook($resultItems);
        break;
      case "cd":
        displayCD($resultItems);
        break;
    }

    if ($result['TotalPages'] > $page)
    {
      $page++;
      echo "<a href=\"soap.search.php?query=$query&mode=$mode&page=$page\">Next 10
    Results</a>";
    }
```

Finally, the `resultItems` variable is created to contain all of the result items, and the appropriate display function is called. If the current page is less than the total number of pages available (as indicated by Amazon), it displays a link to the next page.

And that's it; users can now perform searches for books, DVDs, or CDs, page through the results, and click on a link to be taken directly to that item on Amazon. Hopefully they make a purchase, because the inclusion of my tag with the query will ensure I make a percentage of any referred sale! A search for a DVD is shown in Figure 7-2, and a search for a music CD is shown in Figure 7-3.

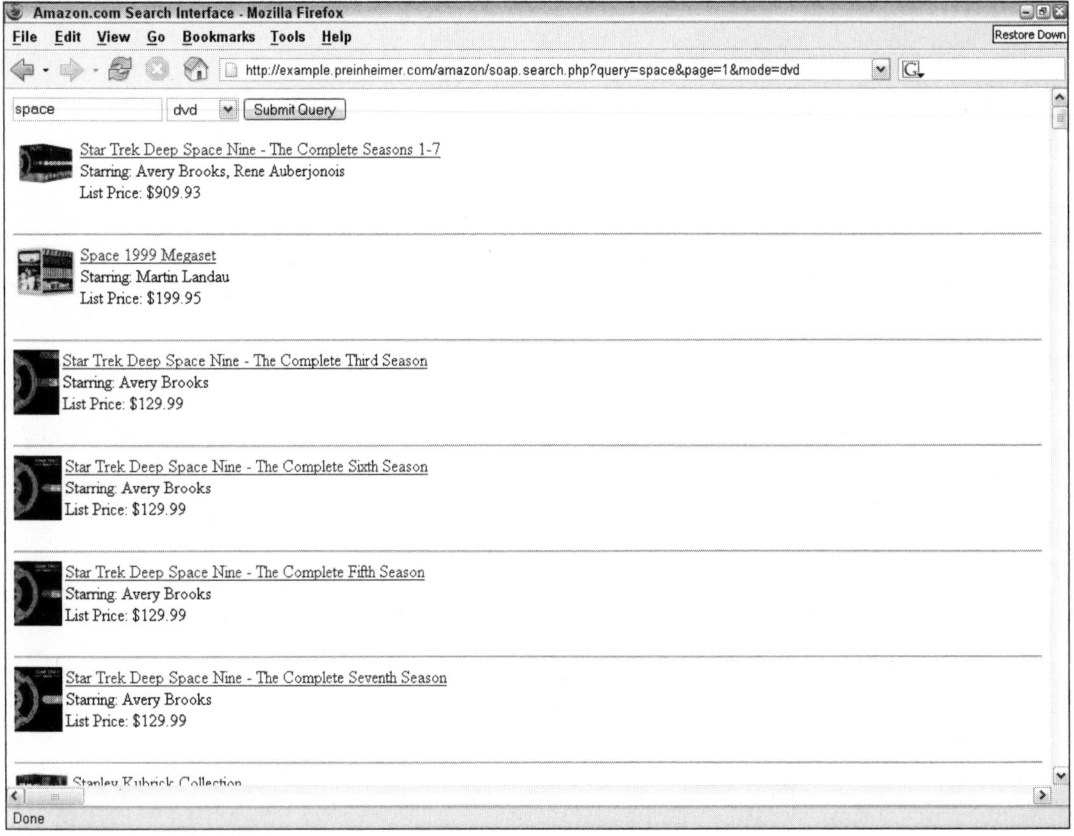

Figure 7-2

Searching by Author

In a previous example I searched for my name, which managed to return exactly what I was looking for in that case. However, that search included both the title of books and the author when examining records, which may have undesired results. For example, a search for "Winston Churchill" will result in books by and about him. In order to perform a search specifically by author, a separate function is called.

> *Though I am only presenting the search for Author here, similar search functions are available to search for Actors, Directors, or Artist.*

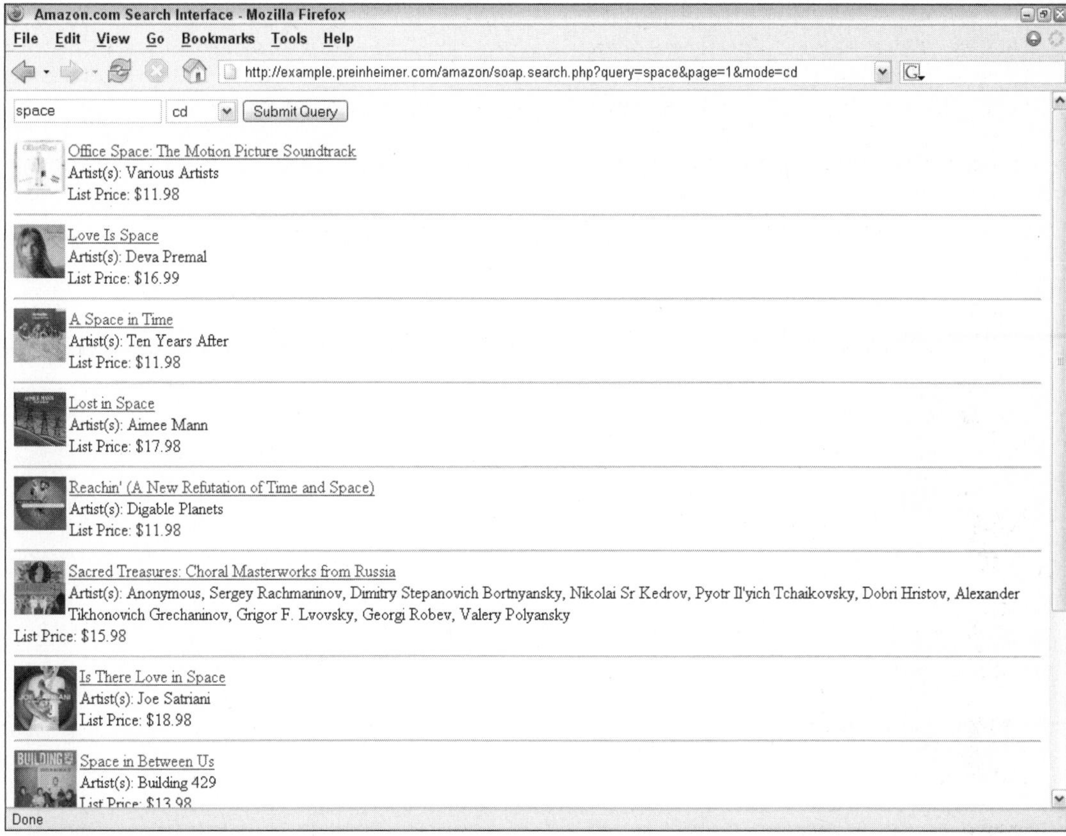

Figure 7-3

This function performs in a similar manner to the earlier search example. However, the main difference is the fact that it calls `AuthorSearchRequest` rather than `KeywordSearchRequest`:

```
function runAuthorSearchQuery($client, $author, $page, $mode, $type = 'lite')
{
  $params = array(
    'author'    => $author,
    'page'       => $page,
    'mode'       => $mode,
    'tag'        => 'preinheimerco-20',
    'type'       => $type,
    'devtag'     => '1PHH5VTRY7D300H7JTR2'
  );

  $namespace = 'http://soap.amazon.com';
  $action = 'http://soap.amazon.com';
```

```
    $method = "AuthorSearchRequest";
    $result = $client->call($method,
    array('AuthorSearchRequest' => $params),
    $namespace, $action);

    return $result;
  }
```

As mentioned, this function is quite similar to the earlier keyword search function. The two differences are the call to `AuthorSearchRequest` rather than `KeywordSearchRequest`, and the keyword parameter is replaced with `author`.

```
  <?php
  if (!isset($_GET['author']))
  {
    echo "no author";
    exit;
  }else
  {
    $author = $_GET['author'];
  }
  if (is_numeric($_GET['page']))
  {
    $page = $_GET['page'];
  }else
  {
    $page = 1;
  }
  require('../lib/nusoap.php');
  $client =
  new soapclient("http://soap.amazon.com/schemas2/AmazonWebServices.wsdl", true);
  $result = runAuthorSearchQuery($client, $author, $page, 'books', 'heavy');
  $error = $client->getError();
  if ($error) {
    echo "<pre>";
    print_r($error);
    echo "</pre>";
    exit;
  }
  $resultItems = $result['Details'];
  displayBook($resultItems);
  if ($result['TotalPages'] > $page)
  {
    $page++;
    echo "<a href=\"soap.author.php?author=$author&page=$page\">Next 10 Results</a>";
  }
```

Much of the code here is identical to the last example. `$_GET['AUTHOR']` is confirmed to exist rather than the query used in the last example. A change is also made to the handling of the page variable. This page will be linked to in future examples, and it will be easier not to require the page variable set in the URL.

Figure 7-4 shows a search for "Dan Brown."

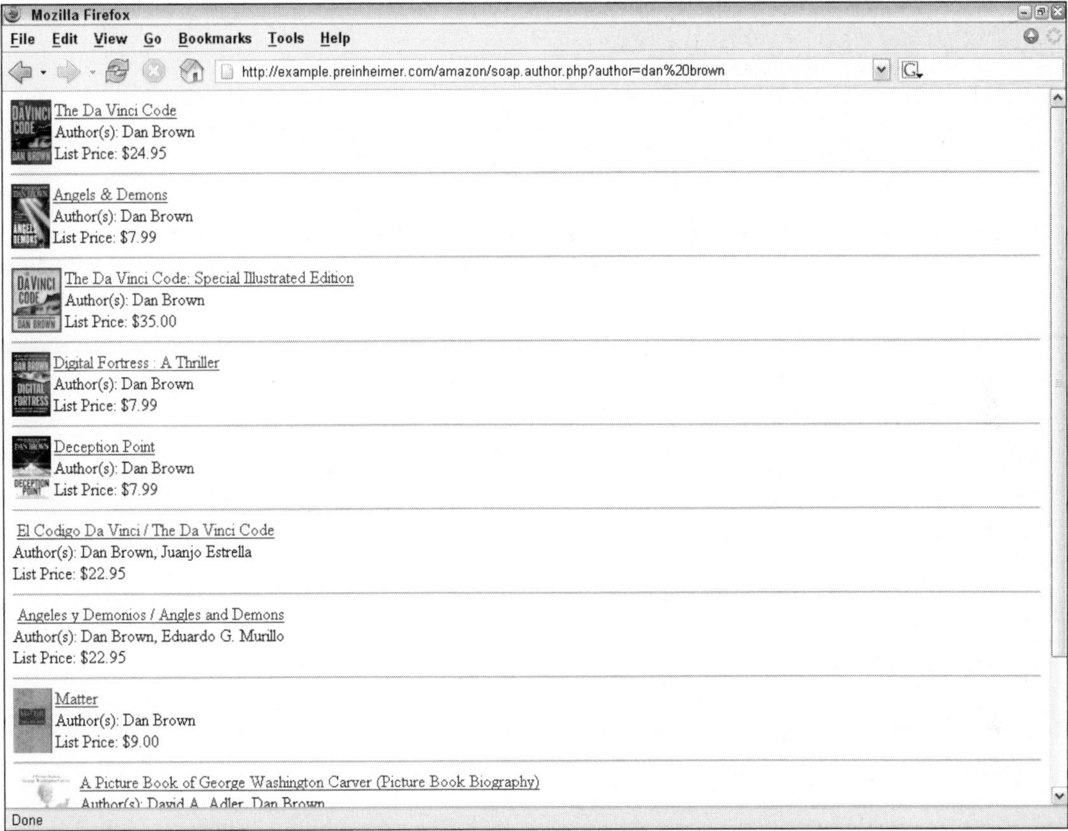

Figure 7-4

Examining a Product in Depth

Using Amazon's search function returns information on a large set of items. However, frequently you will only need the information for one specific product, or only want to display a single product to the end user. You can retrieve that information using the API's `AsinSearchRequest` method.

Conceptually, this script isn't too different from earlier examples, though a few extra functions have been created to make the page more interactive.

```
function runASINQuery($client, $asin, $type = 'heavy')
{
  $params = array(
                    'asin'        => $asin,
                    'type'        => $type,
                    'tag'         => 'preinheimerco-20',
                    'devtag'      => '1PHH5VTRY7D300H7JTR2'
  );
  $namespace = 'http://soap.amazon.com';
  $action = 'http://soap.amazon.com';
```

```
    $method = "AsinSearchRequest";
    $result = $client->call($method,
    array('AsinSearchRequest' => $params),
    $namespace, $action);
    return $result;
  }
```

Here the actual call to the API is made. Notice the lack of parameters used previously, such as mode, which are irrelevant because the ASIN points to a specific item within Amazon's catalog. All previous query functions defaulted to requesting the `lite` result set; this one defaults to `heavy`. Because only a single item is being displayed, you can make use of the additional data returned. This will require you to implement a few more functions as follows:

```
  function getAuthorList($authors)
  {
    $authorList = "";
    foreach($authors as $item)
    {
      $a = urlencode($item);
      $authorList .= "<a href=\"./soap.author.php?author=$a\"
        title=\"More from $item\">$item</a>, ";
    }
    return $authorList;
  }
```

This is the first function used to aid in the display of data. Here the list of authors of the book is parsed, and each author is presented as a link. This links to the previous script, so users can find books from the same author quickly. Note the use of `urlencode()`; this is important because author names will frequently contain spaces, which should be encoded before being presented in a link.

```
  function getCategoryList($browseList)
  {
    $categoryList = "";
    foreach ($browseList as $item)
    {
      $categoryList .= $item['BrowseName'] . ", ";
    }
    return $categoryList;
  }
```

You will also present a list of categories to which the book belongs. This information is nested twice, so a `foreach()` loop is used rather than a simple `implode()` call.

Finally, here is the main portion of the code:

```
  <?php

  if (!isset($_GET['asin']))
  {
    exit;
  }else
```

```
{
  $asin = $_GET['asin'];
}
require('../lib/nusoap.php');
$client =
new soapclient("http://soap.amazon.com/schemas2/AmazonWebServices.wsdl", true);
$result = runASINQuery($client, $asin, 'heavy');
$error = $client->getError();
if ($error) {
  echo "<pre>";
  print_r($error);
  echo "</pre>";
  exit;
}
$result = $result['Details']['0'];
```

As usual, the passed parameter is checked first, before any other files are included. Results to an ASIN query are presented in the same manner as search results, within `Details`, then an array is presented (which has a single element). To make accessing that data easier, the `$result` variable is set to that smaller scope.

```
$image = $result['ImageUrlMedium'];
$url = $result['Url'];
$productName = $result['ProductName'];
$authors = getAuthorList($result['Authors']);
$listPrice = $result['ListPrice'];
$amazonPrice = $result['OurPrice'];
$categories = getCategoryList($result['BrowseList']);
$availability = $result['Availability'];
$rating = $result['Reviews']['AvgCustomerRating'];

echo "<img src=\"$image\" align=\"left\">";
echo "<b>Title</b>: <a href=\"$url\"
   title=\"Buy at Amazon!\">$productName</a><br>";
echo "<b>Authors</b>: $authors<br>";
echo "<b>List Price</b>: $listPrice, <b>Amazon's Price</b>: $amazonPrice<br>";
if ($categories) echo "<b>Categories</b>: $categories<br>";
echo "<b>Availability</b>: $availability<br>";
echo "<b>Average Customer Rating</b>: $rating<br><br>";

$customerReviews = $result['Reviews']['CustomerReviews'];
foreach ($customerReviews AS $review)
{
  echo "<b>Rating</b>: {$review['Rating']}<br>";
  echo "<b>Summary</b>: {$review['Summary']}<br>";
  echo "<b>Comment</b>: {$review['Comment']}<br><br>";
}
```

Finally, the results are echo'd to the end user. Notice that the medium-sized image was used in this case, rather than the small image used in search results. Both the list price and Amazon's price are displayed. Also notice that a full category listing, linked author names, and a listing of customer reviews are also provided. Figure 7-5 shows detailed information on "The Elements of Style."

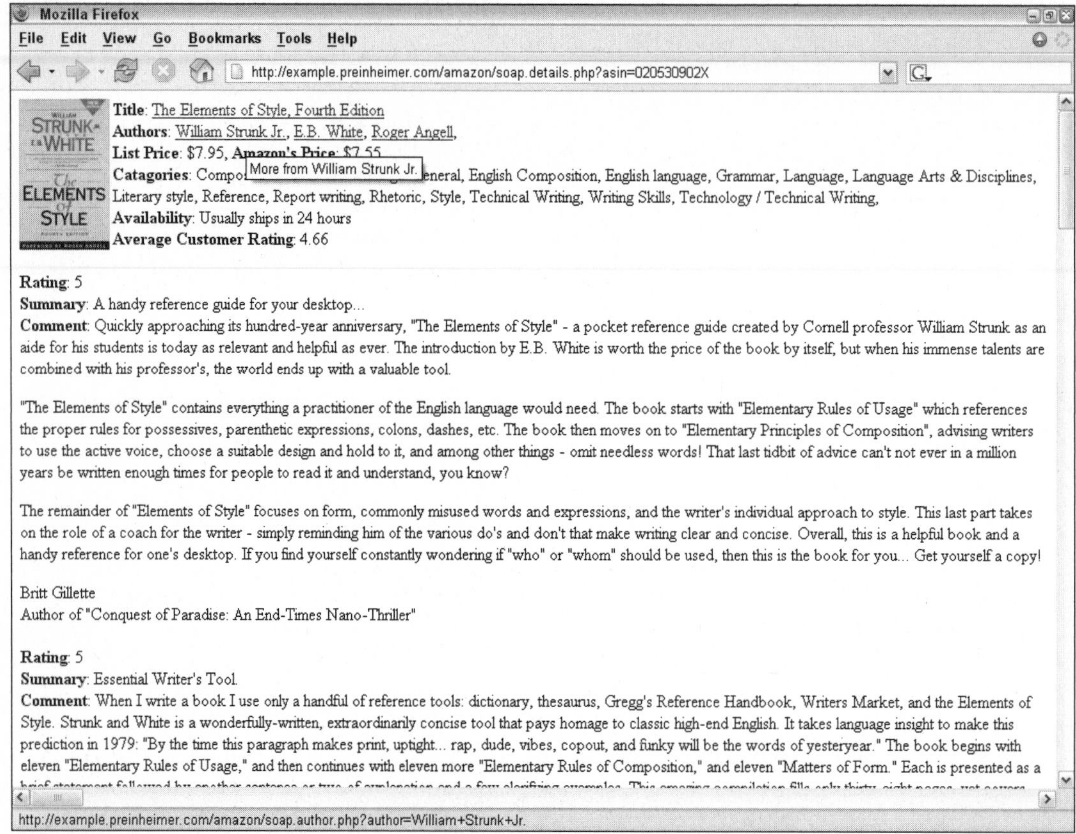

Figure 7-5

This details page works best when linked to from other result pages. For example, change the destination in both the Keyword search and Author search programs to point to this page. Users will then see a larger cover image and more detailed pricing information.

Monitoring Prices

Amazon offers a wide selection and competitive pricing, but you may encounter products priced a little higher than you would like. Both businesses and individuals take a keen interest in pricing, and may want to be informed if the price on any particular item they are interested in changes. With the code presented here, you can save those products and have your script periodically check for lowered prices.

```
require('../common_db.php');
require('../lib/nusoap.php');

$client =
new soapclient("http://soap.amazon.com/schemas2/AmazonWebServices.wsdl", true);

$query = "SELECT * FROM `07_amazon_monitor_price_list`";
$results = getAssoc($query);
foreach($results AS $item)
{
```

```
    $result = runASINQuery($client, $item['asin']);
    $result = $result['Details']['0'];
    $listPrice = $result['ListPrice'];
    $amazonPrice = $result['OurPrice'];
    $query = "INSERT INTO 07_amazon_monitor_price_results
      (`asin`, `listPrice`, `amazonPrice`, `timestamp`)
      VALUES ('{$item['asin']}', '$listPrice', '$amazonPrice', null)";
    insertQuery($query);
  }
```

I have removed the error checking to keep this example light, but the concept should be clear. A list of desired ASINs to watch is retrieved from the database, each item is checked in turn, and both its list price and Amazon's price are recorded, along with the timestamp.

What you do with this information is entirely up to you. You could graph prices of books over time, send a message when the price drops, or anything else, for that matter. The two tables used are shown here:

```
CREATE TABLE `07_amazon_monitor_price_results` (
  `asin` varchar(10) NOT NULL default '',
  `listPrice` varchar(10) NOT NULL default '0',
  `amazonPrice` varchar(10) NOT NULL default '0',
  `timestamp` timestamp(14) NOT NULL
) TYPE=MyISAM;
CREATE TABLE `07_amazon_monitor_price_list` (
  `asin` varchar(10) NOT NULL default '',
  PRIMARY KEY  (`asin`)
) TYPE=MyISAM;

INSERT INTO `07_amazon_monitor_price_list` VALUES ('059600656X');
INSERT INTO `07_amazon_monitor_price_list` VALUES ('0672324547');
INSERT INTO `07_amazon_monitor_price_list` VALUES ('0764589547');
INSERT INTO `07_amazon_monitor_price_list` VALUES ('1565926811');
```

In both tables, a length of 10 is specified for the length of the ASIN — ASINs are always 10 characters long.

Monitoring Amazon Sales Rank

Another useful piece of information Amazon makes available is the sales rank for all its products. This is of particular interest if you (for example) wrote a book and are curious as to how it is performing. This code fits into the same framework as the previous example.

```
$query = "SELECT * FROM `07_amazon_monitor_rank_list`";
$results = getAssoc($query);
foreach($results AS $item)
{
  $result = runASINQuery($client, $item['asin']);
  $result = $result['Details']['0'];
  $salesRank = $result['SalesRank'];
  $query = "INSERT INTO 07_amazon_monitor_rank_results
    (`asin`, `rank`, `timestamp`)
    VALUES ('{$item['asin']}', '$salesRank', null)";
  insertQuery($query);
}
```

Again, all of the error checking code has been removed to save on space. The two tables used are shown here:

```
CREATE TABLE `07_amazon_monitor_rank_results` (
  `asin` varchar(10) NOT NULL default '',
  `rank` int(11) NOT NULL default '0',
  `timestamp` timestamp(14) NOT NULL
) TYPE=MyISAM;\
CREATE TABLE `07_amazon_monitor_rank_list` (
  `asin` varchar(10) NOT NULL default '',
  PRIMARY KEY  (`asin`)
) TYPE=MyISAM;

INSERT INTO `07_amazon_monitor_rank_list` VALUES ('059600656X');
INSERT INTO `07_amazon_monitor_rank_list` VALUES ('0672324547');
INSERT INTO `07_amazon_monitor_rank_list` VALUES ('0764589547');
INSERT INTO `07_amazon_monitor_rank_list` VALUES ('1565926811');
```

Using the information gleaned in this example, as well as the sales data obtained from the previous example, can yield interesting information. Does the sales rank increase when price drops, how does the sales rank change as time passes since the book's release increases, and so on.

Personal Store

Amazon's wide range of products and high brand recognition combined with revenue potential has prompted many individuals and firms to advertise selected Amazon products through their own websites. Although the examples presented earlier allow users to search through Amazon's entire catalog, that may not be what you are looking for. By creating a miniature "personal store," you can present selected items to your visitors, and still earn a percentage of any sales generated.

There are four methods of choosing products to display to your visitors that are programmatically significant (by that, I mean four ways to select the products from Amazon's catalog, not four ways for you to choose which products to display). First, you could maintain a list of desired ASIN numbers in a local database, then retrieve all or a portion of that list, populate the information from Amazon, and display it to the end user. Second, you could select products from Amazon based on some common criteria that Amazon allows you to search by, and query the database in that manner. Third, you could create a list (*Listmania* is the terminology used on Amazon's site) via Amazon's regular interface. Finally, you could select products indiscriminately based on keywords associated with your site.

Maintaining a list of desired ASINs in a local database is a rather simple but elegant solution. The values are sought and recorded locally. These items are then displayed (generally a random selection of the elements is displayed) to the end user, possibly depending on which page in particular they are visiting within a site. Implementing this solution should be simple using the code discussed earlier in the chapter; as such, the code is not presented here (it is available online with the code from this book).

There are two things to keep in mind with this approach. First, you may want to retrieve more ASIN values from the database than you will actually need, so products that are not available (either the result is returned and the `Availability` value is set to `not available`, or you are unable to get a result for that item) can be skipped. Second, caching will likely be really tempting, but make sure you read the Amazon web services Terms of Service carefully. There are requirements on how long you can hold information that has been removed from Amazon's database.

The method of selecting products via common criteria should also be rather easy programmatically based on earlier examples; as such, the code is available online if needed. The author search example can be easily modified to find all products by a given manufacturer or publisher, both of which have custom search functions on Amazon. Individual products may then be selected for display; you may want to use price or availability as a criterion in this selection.

The method of creating a list of items on Amazon is both attractive and programmatically interesting. I find this approach appealing because it allows me to move the job of selecting which products to display to a third party, which is presumably not a programmer but someone who is better suited to the job. They can then use the Amazon interface that they are already (if I may presume) familiar with to create and maintain a list of desirable products. This is a great zero-maintenance solution for programs to be given to third parties, because they can keep their lists fresh and you don't need to intervene or educate new users on how to add new items to the list. This approach is discussed in depth later in the chapter.

Selecting random products via some keywords is an attractive approach for sites that garner a significant number of visitors. With a large number of visitors, you must select a lot of products in order for the offerings to remain fresh — there is little point in offering four of the same ten products to visitors 50 times. If they didn't click the first time, they won't click the next 20 times. This method is also discussed in depth later.

Using Amazon's List to Populate a Personal Store

Before there is any confusion on the issue, the list discussed here is not a wish list, but instead a list usually shown under *Listmania*! Selections made from wish lists are by default shipped to the creator of the list, then removed from the list itself, neither of which are the desired action in this case. What you are trying to do is present products that you feel the buyer would like for themselves, so they should be shipped to the user, and should remain on the list for other visitors to see.

Creating a list on Amazon for the first time might be a bit tricky. First, the user selecting the items will need an account (this does not need to be attached in any way to the developer account or associate account), which should be easy (go to amazon.com, click on Your Account, and register). The next step is the tricky one, the option to create a list under *Listmania*! doesn't appear anywhere under the *Your Account* menu. Browse on Amazon product, then scroll down. *Listmania*! should either appear on the left sidebar or in the central column; if not, choose another product.

Once you have found the *Listmania*! listing, click on a list, and at that point you will have the opportunity to create your own list (there should be a link in the top-right corner of the screen). Re-enter your password and select some privacy options, and you can begin working on your list. You will need a title and the ASINs for the items in question. The ASIN for a product should be listed under Product Details, near the bottom of that list. You can also enter a description of each item added to the list.

Note the List ID. You can determine this by looking at the URL shown when you examine the list itself:

```
http://www.amazon.com/exec/obidos/tg/listmania/list-browse/-/3OI5ZK8PHO3WG/103-
3019150-3420664
```

The List ID is the 13-character string shown after `/list-browse/-/`, which is `3OI5ZK8PHO3WG` in this example. All other information can be ignored; Amazon likes to keep lots of information in their URLs.

Next, plug that ID into a new query function:

```
function runListManiaQuery($client, $type = 'lite')
{
  $params = array(
                    'lm_id'        => '3OI5ZK8PHO3WG',
                    'type'         => $type,
                    'page'         => $page,
                    'tag'          => 'preinheimerco-20',
                    'devtag'       => '1PHH5VTRY7D300H7JTR2'
  );
  $namespace = 'http://soap.amazon.com';
  $action = 'http://soap.amazon.com';
  $method = "ListManiaSearchRequest";
  $result = $client->call($method,
  array('ListManiaSearchRequest' => $params),
  $namespace, $action);
  return $result;
}
```

This function is again very similar to the ones presented earlier, but it does allow you to select exactly which items are returned. Using that function, and with a little effort to make the results attractive, you can end up with My Amazon List shown as a sidebar for my blog in Figure 7-6.

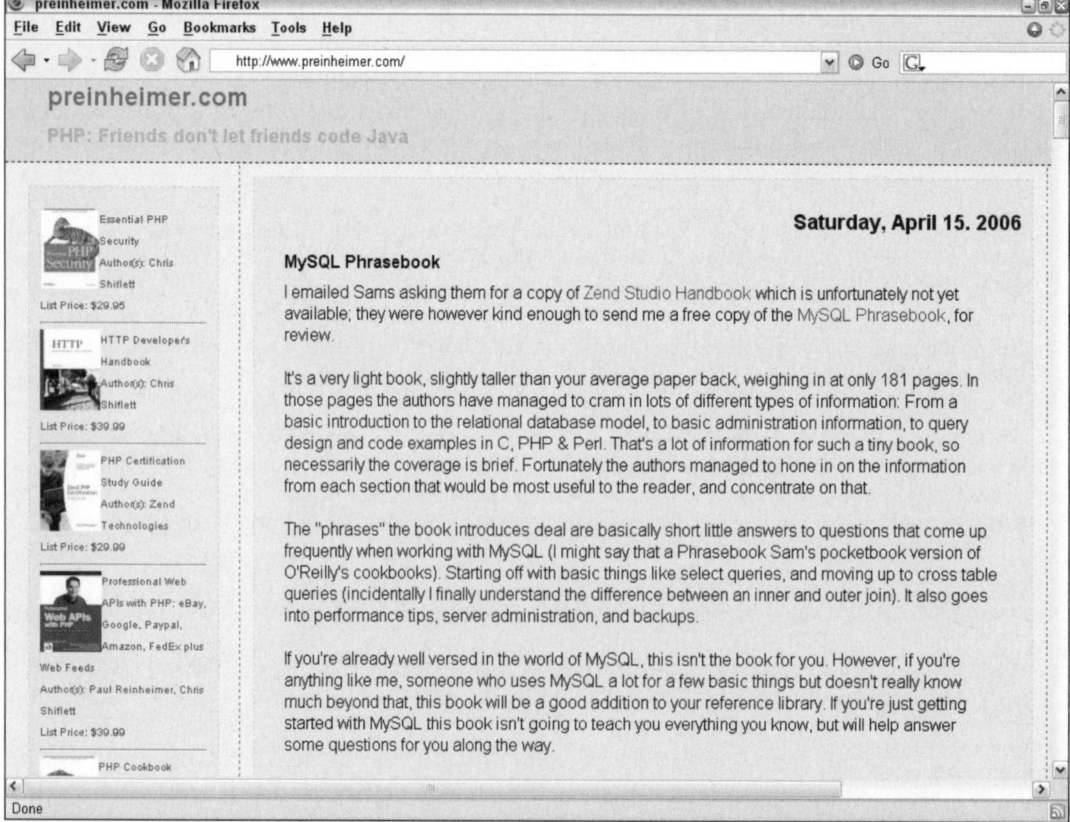

Figure 7-6

Using Keywords to Populate Your Personal Store

Using keywords relevant to your site to select random products to display to your visitors is an easy way to ensure that users are constantly presented with fresh, relevant content. You can reuse the `runSearchQuery()` function presented toward the beginning of the chapter, and with a small addition, present random products to your users. Basically, what I'm suggesting is that you determine a series of keywords relating to your site. For example, a community site for people who knit might use keywords like knitting, yarn, and patterns.

Conceptually, the code to select the random elements is pretty simple. First, select a keyword from the hard-coded array and run the query. Next, select and output the required number of elements. I have used some rather fun code to avoid checking for duplication or manually generating random numbers. I have left out the error checking code (it's identical to other examples) for the sake of brevity.

```
<?php

$keywords = array();
$keywords[] = "php";
$keywords[] = "mysql";
$keywords[] = "apache";
$keywords[] = "linux";
$keyword = $keywords[array_rand($keywords)];
```

Here the desired keywords are defined, and one is selected at random. Using PHP's built-in array functions rather than manually generating a random number based on the length of the array helps keep your code short and fast. Note that `array_rand()` returns the index of the selected element, not the element itself, which is why it is encapsulated in `$keywords[]`.

```
require('../lib/nusoap.php');
$client =
new soapclient("http://soap.amazon.com/schemas2/AmazonWebServices.wsdl", true);

$result = runSearchQuery($client, $keyword, '1', 'books', 'lite');
$error = $client->getError();

$resultItems = $result['Details'];
```

This code should look quite familiar by now.

```
for ($i = 0; $i < 4; $i++)
{
    $selection = array_rand($resultItems);
    $item = $resultItems[$selection];
    array_splice($resultItems, $selection, 1);
```

Again the `array_rand()` function is used to select an element from the array. This time, however, you can't directly access that element, because you need to know which one was selected. Using that selection value and `array_splice()`, you remove the element from the array to ensure it is not selected in a future run.

```
        $title = $item['ProductName'];
        $url = $item['Url'];
        $image = $item['ImageUrlSmall'];
        $authorList = @implode($item['Authors'], ", ");
        $price = $item['ListPrice'];
        if ($url != "") echo "<img src=\"$image\" align=\"left\">";
        echo "<a href=\"$url\" title=\"Learn More at Amazon.com\">$title<a><br>";
        echo "Author(s): " . $authorList . "<br>";
        echo "List Price: " . $price;
        echo "<hr>";
    }
    ?>
```

This code was stolen from the `displayBooks()` function presented earlier.

Figure 7-7 shows random results from using the keyword PHP on the first run. Figure 7-8 shows random results from using the keyword PHP on the second run.

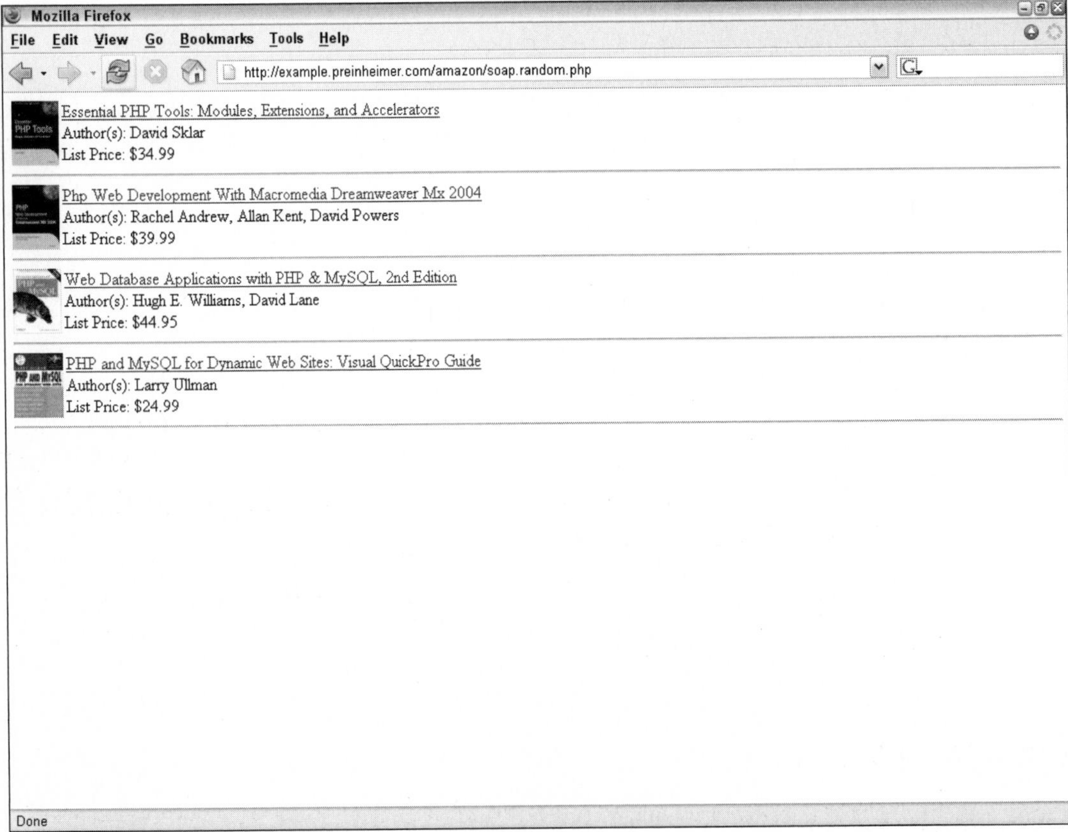

Figure 7-7

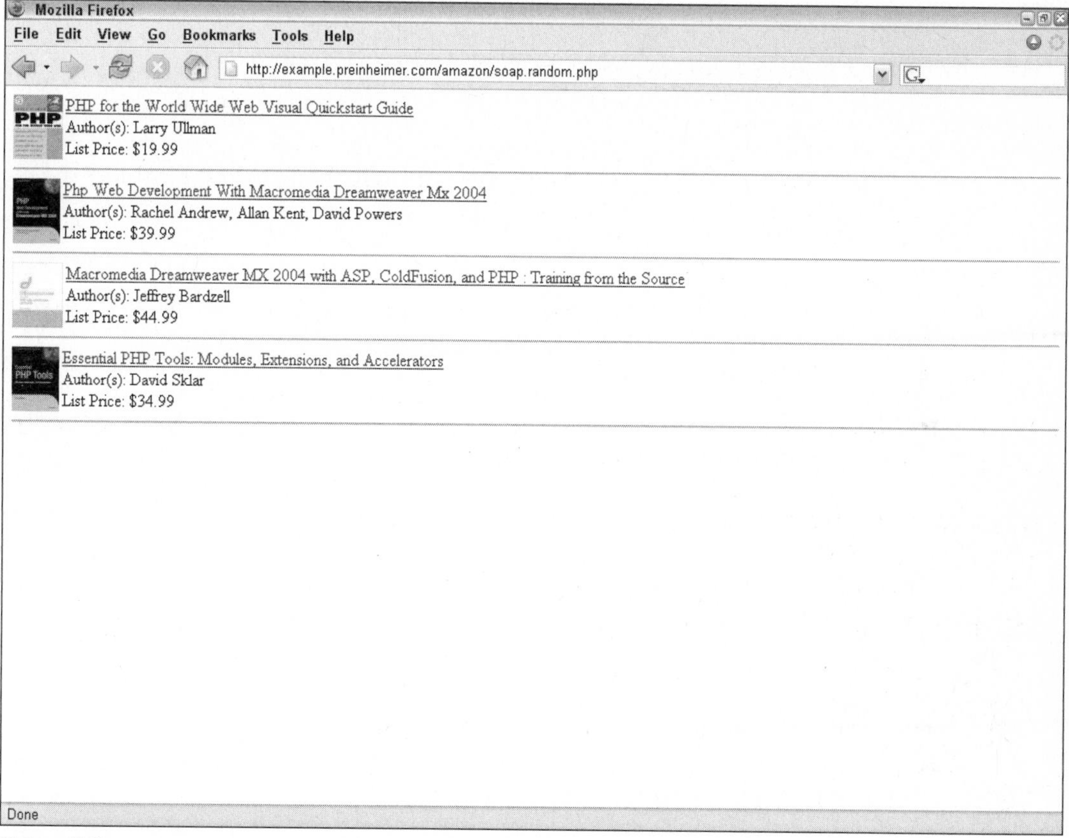

Figure 7-8

As you can see, this code effectively selects random items, using random keywords to keep the displays shown to your users fresh. To get an even wider variety of results, you may want to consider replacing the hard-coded value for page with a random number. Just be careful to ensure that the number is low enough to be valid for all search terms (or simply use a multidimensional array for the search terms, the first element being the term, the second being the number of pages available).

Presenting a list of Amazon products on your site may seem a little odd. However, it can be quite profitable. Many technical authors I know have commented that they make just as much money from Amazon selling their books from their website as they do in royalties from actually writing it!

Summary

This chapter explored Amazon API, initially using both the REST and SOAP protocols, then concentrating on the SOAP protocol for the more detailed examples. Several different methods of exploring the Amazon API were introduced: searching by Keyword, Author, and finally the ASIN. A few different uses for the information were explored, such as to allow tracking of prices and sales rank over time. Finally, the concept of a personal store was introduced, allowing you to present selected items to your users on an ongoing basis. Key elements of this chapter included the following:

- An introduction to the API itself
- Presentation of a sample REST request
- Introducing several different SOAP search formats
- Examples demonstrating different uses of the API

You now have the information you need to incorporate the Amazon API into your site. By presenting products available from Amazon to your customers (you could, for example, link product reviews to the appropriate Amazon item), you not only give your visitors an easy way to order the product, but you also open up a valuable revenue stream for your site. The next chapter introduces the FedEx API, to allow you to automatically view cost shipments, generate shipping labels, track packages, and accept returns.

8

Interacting with the FedEx API

Federal Express (FedEx) is an international brand name in express shipping. By accessing its API you can not only save time and effort when it comes to shipping products to your customers, but you can also give your customers more information. You can provide information on the various shipment methods available to them, as well as detailed tracking information on their orders after they have been shipped. Finally, in the unfortunate case that a customer needs to return a product, FedEx (and thus the API) also eases that process.

This chapter covers several of the most useful API calls:

- Registering your account number to obtain a meter number
- Determining which FedEx delivery services are available between given addresses
- Obtaining rate information for a given service
- Shipping a package
- Canceling a shipment
- Tracking a package
- Accepting returns

Registering to Use the API

Unfortunately, the steps involved in accessing the API differ internationally. The rules in the United States seem to be quite simple — simply open a business shipping account and request access. You will then be provided with an account number. In other countries, however (Canada, for example), the process can be a bit more involved, and may require signing a nondisclosure agreement. This chapter covers the process from the U.S. perspective, but if you live elsewhere, I recommend speaking to FedEx representatives on the phone. I found that once I actually reached someone on the phone directly, things moved a lot more smoothly.

First, obtain a commercial FedEx account. This is as simple as filling out the appropriate forms on the website (`www.fedex.com`). You will need a major credit card. If you have any problems, I recommend calling the toll-free number, because whoever answers the phone is a lot more helpful and lenient with requirements than the website is.

Second, request access to the API. You're going to need to send an email to `websupport@fedex.com` (or your regional office) and request access to the API, as well as the URL for the test server. The URL isn't published anywhere (and to respect that, it isn't in this book either), and you might as well save yourself an email and get it at the same time.

Third, use the account number you've received to execute a subscription request. This will give you a meter number. You must include both your account number and this meter number with all your requests. You only need to make the request once, but save the meter number forever.

A Few Notes about the Testing Environment

The FedEx test API seems to have been developed as a very basic test bed for you to check the formatting of requests, and nothing more. When a shipment is created, the API returns the requisite data, and that's all. It does not add fake tracking information or delivery confirmation, nor does any checking appear to be done when canceling a shipment request (any tracking number is accepted).

I would suggest testing your applications with the testing API as far as possible and using the sample XML responses provided in the documentation for the calls (like tracking) that return little. Then, after you get certified (and after changing the endpoint URL in your code), test a little more exhaustively.

Getting Certified to Go Live

The certification process isn't too difficult; the key requirement is mailing FedEx a sample shipping label to be examined to ensure it meets all of their requirements. The shipping label is discussed in greater detail a little later once the shipping request is presented, and is discussed at great length within the API documentation.

Your First Call

Your first call against the API is special in two ways: It's the first call, and you should only execute it once. While you have an account number, you will also need a meter number in order to use the API. A `FDXSubscriptionRequest` call will give you that number.

The FedEx API provides only a basic XML interface; it uses neither SOAP nor REST. As such, requests are generated manually, then sent using cURL (pronounced see-URL), which provides HTTPS support. You then parse the response with SimpleXML. Support for cURL is provided through the `libcurl` library, which is not compiled by default. Appendix C has additional information on the configuration of the development box. The following function handles the basics of the request:

```
function callFedEx($request)
{
  global $endpoint;
  $ch = curl_init();
  curl_setopt($ch, CURLOPT_URL, $endpoint);
  curl_setopt($ch, CURLOPT_POST, TRUE);
  curl_setopt($ch, CURLOPT_POSTFIELDS, $request);
  curl_setopt($ch, CURLOPT_RETURNTRANSFER, TRUE);
  $response = curl_exec($ch);
  if (curl_error($ch))
  {
    echo "<br>\n";
    echo "Errors were encountered:";
    echo curl_errno($ch);
    echo curl_error($ch);
    curl_close($ch);
    return NULL;
  }else
  {
    curl_close($ch);
    $xml = simplexml_load_string($response);
    return $xml;
  }
}
```

After pulling the `endpoint` out of the `Global` scope, it sets up and executes the request. Should an error be encountered by cURL (this will likely only happen if your server can't contact FedEx), it will be returned. Otherwise, the response is parsed into a SimpleXML object and returned.

The request you need to execute should look something like this:

```
$request = <<< XMLREQUEST
<?xml version="1.0" encoding="UTF-8" ?>
<FDXSubscriptionRequest xmlns:api="http://www.fedex.com/fsmapi"
  xmlns:xsi="http://www.w3.org/2001/XMLSchema-instance"
  xsi:noNamespaceSchemaLocation="FDXSubscriptionRequest.xsd">
  <RequestHeader>
    <CustomerTransactionIdentifier>Test String</CustomerTransactionIdentifier>
    <AccountNumber>1234567890</AccountNumber>
  </RequestHeader>
  <Contact>
    <PersonName>Paul Reinheimer</PersonName>
    <CompanyName>Wrox</CompanyName>
    <Department>IT</Department>
    <PhoneNumber>5191234567</PhoneNumber>
    <E-MailAddress>paul@example.com</E-MailAddress>
  </Contact>
  <Address>
    <Line1>123 Main Street</Line1>
    <City>Example Ville</City>
    <StateOrProvinceCode>NY</StateOrProvinceCode>
    <PostalCode>10011</PostalCode>
    <CountryCode>US</CountryCode>
  </Address>
</FDXSubscriptionRequest>
XMLREQUEST;
```

The format is pretty basic, and set by FedEx, but there are two elements I want to bring to your attention:

- `CustomerTransactionIdentifier` — This is an element that can contain any string you want up to a maximum of 40 characters. The string will be returned to you in the response.
- `AccountNumber` — This is the commercial account number that was added to the test server at your request.

Finally, here is the code to execute the request and obtain your meter number:

```
$endpoint = '';
echo "<pre>";
echo htmlentities($request);
echo "</pre>";
$response = callFedEx($request);
echo "Your meter number is: {$response->MeterNumber}, write that down\n";
echo "<pre>";
print_r($response);
echo "</pre>";
```

You should see the meter number output as shown in Figure 8-1.

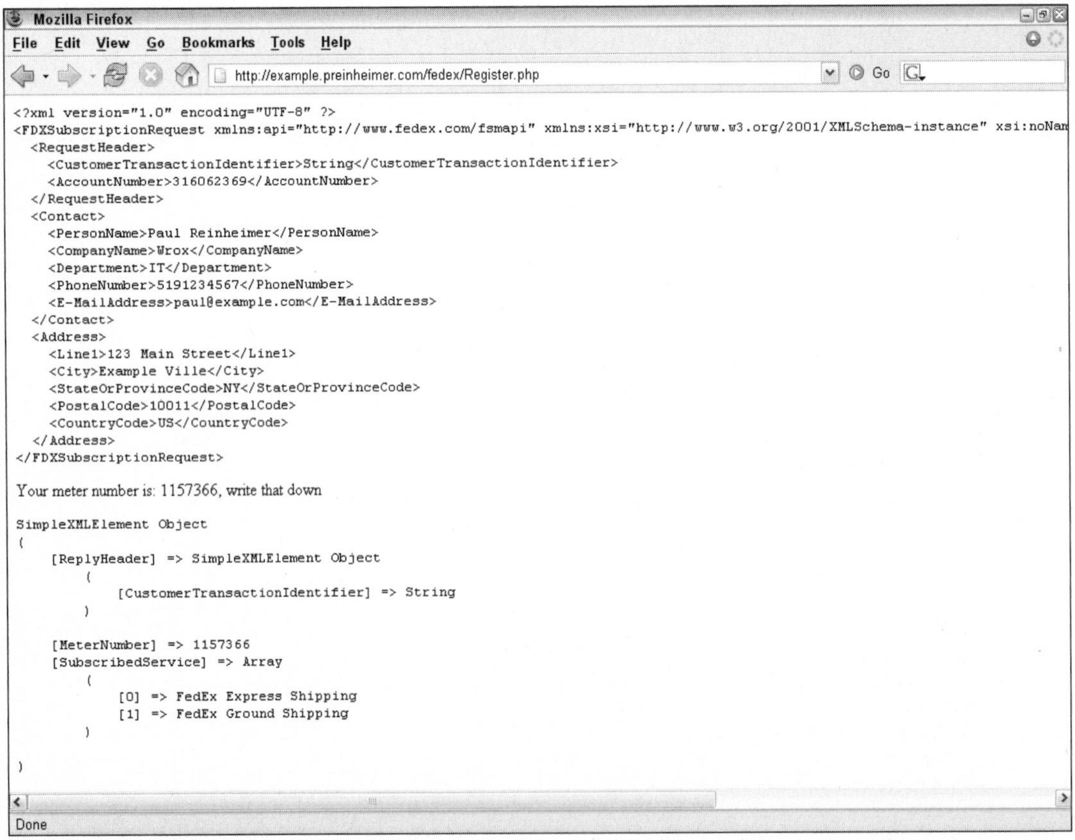

```
Mozilla Firefox
File Edit View Go Bookmarks Tools Help
http://example.preinheimer.com/fedex/Register.php        Go

<?xml version="1.0" encoding="UTF-8" ?>
<FDXSubscriptionRequest xmlns:api="http://www.fedex.com/fsmapi" xmlns:xsi="http://www.w3.org/2001/XMLSchema-instance" xsi:noNam
  <RequestHeader>
    <CustomerTransactionIdentifier>String</CustomerTransactionIdentifier>
    <AccountNumber>316062369</AccountNumber>
  </RequestHeader>
  <Contact>
    <PersonName>Paul Reinheimer</PersonName>
    <CompanyName>Wrox</CompanyName>
    <Department>IT</Department>
    <PhoneNumber>5191234567</PhoneNumber>
    <E-MailAddress>paul@example.com</E-MailAddress>
  </Contact>
  <Address>
    <Line1>123 Main Street</Line1>
    <City>Example Ville</City>
    <StateOrProvinceCode>NY</StateOrProvinceCode>
    <PostalCode>10011</PostalCode>
    <CountryCode>US</CountryCode>
  </Address>
</FDXSubscriptionRequest>

Your meter number is: 1157366, write that down

SimpleXMLElement Object
(
    [ReplyHeader] => SimpleXMLElement Object
        (
            [CustomerTransactionIdentifier] => String
        )

    [MeterNumber] => 1157366
    [SubscribedService] => Array
        (
            [0] => FedEx Express Shipping
            [1] => FedEx Ground Shipping
        )

)

Done
```

Figure 8-1

Determining Which Services Are Available

FedEx offers a number of shipping services with different delivery guarantees and targeted distances (domestic, international, and so on). To determine which services are available for a given shipment, and the associated costs and delivery dates, you use the `FDXRateAvailableServicesRequest` call.

Before actually making the call, an array is set up containing a visually attractive version of all FedEx's shipping services:

```
$serviceOptions = array();
$serviceOptions['PRIORITYOVERNIGHT'] = "Priority Overnight";
$serviceOptions['STANDARDOVERNIGHT'] = "Standard Overnight";
$serviceOptions['FIRSTOVERNIGHT'] = "First Overnight";
$serviceOptions['FEDEX2DAY'] = "Two Day";
$serviceOptions['FEDEXEXPRESSSAVER'] = "Express Saver";
$serviceOptions['INTERNATIONALPRIORITY'] = "International Priority";
$serviceOptions['INTERNATIONALECONOMY'] = "International Economy";
$serviceOptions['INTERNATIONALFIRST'] = "International First";
$serviceOptions['FEDEX1DAYFREIGHT'] = "One Day Freight";
$serviceOptions['FEDEX2DAYFREIGHT'] = "Two Day Freight";
$serviceOptions['FEDEX3DAYFREIGHT'] = "Three Day Freight";
$serviceOptions['FEDEXGROUND'] = "Ground";
$serviceOptions['GROUNDHOMEDELIVERY'] = "Ground Home Delivery";
$serviceOptions['INTERNATIONALPRIORITY FREIGHT'] = "International Priority
  Freight";
$serviceOptions['INTERNATIONALECONOMY FREIGHT'] = "International Economy Freight";
$serviceOptions['EUROPEFIRSTINTERNATIONALPRIORITY'] = "Europe First International
  Priority";
```

This will be used to convert the response into data that can be shown to an end user.

The call will look something like this:

```
$request = <<< XMLREQUEST
<?xml version="1.0" encoding="UTF-8" ?>
  <FDXRateAvailableServicesRequest xmlns:api="http://www.fedex.com/fsmapi"
  xmlns:xsi="http://www.w3.org/2001/XMLSchema-instance"
  xsi:noNamespaceSchemaLocation="FDXRateRequest.xsd">
  <RequestHeader>
    <CustomerTransactionIdentifier>1</CustomerTransactionIdentifier>
    <AccountNumber>$accountNumber</AccountNumber>
    <MeterNumber>$meterNumber</MeterNumber>
    <CarrierCode>$carrier</CarrierCode>
  </RequestHeader>
  <ShipDate>2006-04-17</ShipDate>
  <DropoffType>REGULARPICKUP</DropoffType>
  <Packaging>FEDEXBOX</Packaging>
  <WeightUnits>LBS</WeightUnits>
  <Weight>10.0</Weight>
  <ListRate>1</ListRate>
  <OriginAddress>
    <StateOrProvinceCode>DC</StateOrProvinceCode>
    <PostalCode>20500</PostalCode>
    <CountryCode>US</CountryCode>
```

```
    </OriginAddress>
    <DestinationAddress>
      <StateOrProvinceCode>DC</StateOrProvinceCode>
      <PostalCode>20310-6605</PostalCode>
      <CountryCode>US</CountryCode>
    </DestinationAddress>
    <Payment>
      <PayorType>SENDER</PayorType>
    </Payment>
    <PackageCount>1</PackageCount>
  </FDXRateAvailableServicesRequest>
  XMLREQUEST;
```

The `CarrierCode` element allows you to indicate whether FedEx Express (FDXE) or FedEx Ground (FDXG) will be used to handle the shipment. The examples in this chapter all deal with FedEx Express. The main difference programmatically (apart from the `CarrierCode`) is that while Express shipments are accepted and processed individually automatically, Ground shipments must be closed (with a separate call) before being considered complete, and cannot be canceled or deleted once that close call is made.

`DropOffType` indicates how FedEx will obtain the package. Valid tokens are as follows:

- `REGULARPICKUP`—FedEx will pick up the package during a regularly scheduled pickup (most businesses schedule a regular pickup time).
- `REQUESTCOURIER`—A courier will be dispatched to pick up the package on the requested day.
- `DROPBOX`—The item will be deposited in a FedEx drop box.
- `BUSINESSSERVICECENTER`—The item will be dropped off at a service center.
- `STATION`—The item will be dropped off at a FedEx station.

`Packaging` indicates what type of package will be used for shipping. FedEx provides its shipping materials free of charge to business customers, so it's a good option. If you use your own packaging, you must instead include the package's dimensions. All of FedEx's shipping materials are clearly labeled with a name that should match one of the items on the list. Order a few of everything to get an idea of what works for your products. Valid tokens are as follows:

- `FEDEXENVELOPE`—8.5×11-inch envelope, holds up to 30 pages
- `FEDEXPAK`—Tear- and water-resistant oversized envelope for larger documents
- `FEDEXBOX`—One of FedEx's three standard box sizes
- `FEDEXTUBE`—Blueprint or poster tube
- `FEDEX10KBOX`—Larger corrugated cardboard box (brown)
- `FEDEX25KBOX`—Even larger corrugated cardboard box (also brown)
- `YOURPACKAGING`—Anything not provided by FedEx

To ship with your own packaging, change the `Packaging` line to `YOURPACKAGING` and include the dimensions of your package:

```
<Dimensions>
  <Length>10</Length>
  <Width>4</Width>
  <Height>2</Height>
  <Units>IN</Units>
</Dimensions>
```

The `Units` element can either be `IN` for inches or `CM` for centimeters. U.S. Domestic Express requests must be in inches. Use whole numbers only for both units.

`WeightUnits` can either be `LBS` or `KGS`. Again, U.S. Domestic Express requests require the imperial value, `LBS`. The `Weight` value can contain up to one decimal place.

`ListRate` requests FedEx to return the list rate for the shipment in addition to the discounted rate. In my experience, most stores charge the list rate, and pocket the difference.

Commercial customers doing large volumes of shipping earn discounts on each package they ship, and by default, the API only returns the discounted value. When `ListRate` is set to 1 (or TRUE), the API will also return the list rate for the shipment.

To execute the call, the response just needs to be passed to the function introduced earlier; in this case, the response is parsed and displayed:

```
echo "<h3>Request</h3>\n";
echo "<pre>\n";
print_r(simplexml_load_string($request));
echo "</pre>\n";
echo "<h3>Response</h3>\n";
$response = callFedEx($request);
foreach ($response->Entry AS $service)
{
  echo "It would cost \${$service->EstimatedCharges->DiscountedCharges->NetCharge}
    to mail the package with " . $serviceOptions["{$service->Service}"] . ' ';
  echo "Which has an estimated delivery date of " . date('l dS \of F',
    strtotime($service->DeliveryDate)) . "<br>";
}
echo "<pre>";
print_r($response);
echo "</pre>";
```

The XML response from the API looks like this:

```
<?xml version="1.0" encoding="UTF-8"?>
<FDXRateAvailableServicesReply
  xmlns:xsi="http://www.w3.org/2001/XMLSchema-instance">
<ReplyHeader>
  <CustomerTransactionIdentifier>1</CustomerTransactionIdentifier>
</ReplyHeader>
<entry>
  <Service>PRIORITYOVERNIGHT</Service>
  <Packaging>FEDEXBOX</Packaging>
```

```
    <DeliveryDate>2006-04-18</DeliveryDate>
    <DeliveryDay>TUE</DeliveryDay>
    <DestinationStationID>IAD</DestinationStationID>
    <EstimatedCharges>
      <DimWeightUsed>false</DimWeightUsed>
      <RateScale>01486</RateScale>
      <RateZone>2</RateZone>
      <CurrencyCode>USD</CurrencyCode>
      <BilledWeight>10.0</BilledWeight>
      <DimWeight>0.0</DimWeight>
      <DiscountedCharges>
        <BaseCharge>26.05</BaseCharge>
        <TotalDiscount>0.00</TotalDiscount>
        <TotalSurcharge>3.00</TotalSurcharge>
        <NetCharge>29.05</NetCharge>
        <TotalRebate>0.00</TotalRebate>
      </DiscountedCharges>
      <ListCharges>
        <BaseCharge>26.05</BaseCharge>
        <TotalDiscount>0.00</TotalDiscount>
        <TotalSurcharge>3.00</TotalSurcharge>
        <NetCharge>29.05</NetCharge>
        <TotalRebate>0.00</TotalRebate>
      </ListCharges>
      <EffectiveNetDiscount>0.00</EffectiveNetDiscount>
    </EstimatedCharges>
    <SignatureOption>NONE</SignatureOption>
  </entry>
  <Entry>
    <Service>FEDEX2DAY</Service>
    <Packaging>FEDEXBOX</Packaging>
    <DeliveryDate>2006-04-19</DeliveryDate>
    <DeliveryDay>WED</DeliveryDay>
    <DestinationStationID>IAD</DestinationStationID>
    <EstimatedCharges>
      <DimWeightUsed>false</DimWeightUsed>
      <RateScale>05980</RateScale>
      <RateZone>2</RateZone>
      <CurrencyCode>USD</CurrencyCode>
      <BilledWeight>10.0</BilledWeight>
      <DimWeight>0.0</DimWeight>
      <DiscountedCharges>
        <BaseCharge>11.80</BaseCharge>
        <TotalDiscount>0.00</TotalDiscount>
        <TotalSurcharge>1.36</TotalSurcharge>
        <NetCharge>13.16</NetCharge>
        <TotalRebate>0.00</TotalRebate>
      </DiscountedCharges>
      <ListCharges>
        <BaseCharge>11.80</BaseCharge>
        <TotalDiscount>0.00</TotalDiscount>
        <TotalSurcharge>1.36</TotalSurcharge>
        <NetCharge>13.16</NetCharge>
        <TotalRebate>0.00</TotalRebate>
```

```
      </ListCharges>
      <EffectiveNetDiscount>0.00</EffectiveNetDiscount>
    </EstimatedCharges>
    <SignatureOption>NONE</SignatureOption>
  </Entry>
  <Entry>
    <Service>STANDARDOVERNIGHT</Service>
    <Packaging>FEDEXBOX</Packaging>
    <DeliveryDate>2006-04-18</DeliveryDate>
    <DeliveryDay>TUE</DeliveryDay>
    <DestinationStationID>IAD</DestinationStationID>
    <EstimatedCharges>
      <DimWeightUsed>false</DimWeightUsed>
      <RateScale>01283</RateScale>
      <RateZone>2</RateZone>
      <CurrencyCode>USD</CurrencyCode>
      <BilledWeight>10.0</BilledWeight>
      <DimWeight>0.0</DimWeight>
      <DiscountedCharges>
        <BaseCharge>21.80</BaseCharge>
        <TotalDiscount>0.00</TotalDiscount>
        <TotalSurcharge>2.51</TotalSurcharge>
        <NetCharge>24.31</NetCharge>
        <TotalRebate>0.00</TotalRebate>
      </DiscountedCharges>
      <ListCharges>
        <BaseCharge>21.80</BaseCharge>
        <TotalDiscount>0.00</TotalDiscount>
        <TotalSurcharge>2.51</TotalSurcharge>
        <NetCharge>24.31</NetCharge>
        <TotalRebate>0.00</TotalRebate>
      </ListCharges>
      <EffectiveNetDiscount>0.00</EffectiveNetDiscount>
    </EstimatedCharges>
    <SignatureOption>NONE</SignatureOption>
  </entry>
  </FDXRateAvailableServicesReply>
```

As you can see, after returning the `CustomerTransactionIdentifier`, the response includes an `Entry` for each available service type. Each `Entry` includes the name of the service, delivery date, and both discounted and list charges applicable to the shipment. In this case, because I don't ship that much, no discount is applicable. The applicable output of this script should look something like this:

```
It would cost $29.05 to mail the package with Priority Overnight which has an
    estimated delivery date of Tuesday 18th of April
It would cost $13.16 to mail the package with Two Day which has an estimated
    delivery date of Wednesday 19th of April
It would cost $24.31 to mail the package with Standard Overnight which has an
    estimated delivery date of Tuesday 18th of April
```

This tells me that it would cost $29.05 to ship a 10-pound box from the White House to the Pentagon with Priority Overnight shipping (those are the zip codes used in the original request).

Making a Rate Request

In many circumstances, you may want to check the rate for a single shipping type, rather than the rates for all available types by making a `FDXRateRequest` request. The format and required information is similar to the previous call.

The request will take a format similar to this:

```
<?xml version="1.0" encoding="UTF-8" ?>
  <FDXRateRequest xmlns:api="http://www.fedex.com/fsmapi"
    xmlns:xsi="http://www.w3.org/2001/XMLSchema-instance"
    xsi:noNamespaceSchemaLocation="FDXRateRequest.xsd">
  <RequestHeader>
    <CustomerTransactionIdentifier>1</CustomerTransactionIdentifier>
    <AccountNumber>$accountNumber</AccountNumber>
    <MeterNumber>$meterNumber</MeterNumber>
    <CarrierCode>$carrier</CarrierCode>
  </RequestHeader>
  <ShipDate>2006-04-17</ShipDate>
  <DropoffType>REGULARPICKUP</DropoffType>
  <Service>PRIORITYOVERNIGHT</Service>
  <Packaging>FEDEXBOX</Packaging>
  <WeightUnits>LBS</WeightUnits>
  <Weight>10.0</Weight>
  <ListRate>1</ListRate>
  <OriginAddress>
    <StateOrProvinceCode>DC</StateOrProvinceCode>
    <PostalCode>20500</PostalCode>
    <CountryCode>US</CountryCode>
  </OriginAddress>
  <DestinationAddress>
    <StateOrProvinceCode>DC</StateOrProvinceCode>
    <PostalCode>20310-6605</PostalCode>
    <CountryCode>US</CountryCode>
  </DestinationAddress>
  <Payment>
    <PayorType>SENDER</PayorType>
  </Payment>
  <PackageCount>1</PackageCount>
</FDXRateRequest>
XMLREQUEST;
```

The main change here is the addition of the `Service` element (which can optionally be included with the `FDXRateAvailableServicesRequest` request shown previously, making it very similar to this request), and allowing you to select the service type you would like a quote for.

The code to execute the request and show the result of the request looks like this:

```
echo "<h3>Request</h3>\n";
echo "<pre>\n";
print_r(simplexml_load_string($request));
```

```
echo "</pre>\n";

echo "<h3>Response</h3>\n";
$response = callFedEx($request);
echo "It would cost \${$response->EstimatedCharges->DiscountedCharges->NetCharge}
    to mail the package";
echo "<pre>";
print_r(callFedEx($request));
echo "</pre>";
```

And the raw response looks like this:


```
<?xml version="1.0" encoding="UTF-8"?>
<FDXRateReply xmlns:xsi="http://www.w3.org/2001/XMLSchema-instance">
  <ReplyHeader>
    <CustomerTransactionIdentifier>1</CustomerTransactionIdentifier>
  </ReplyHeader>
  <EstimatedCharges>
    <RateScale>01486</RateScale>
    <RateZone>2</RateZone>
    <CurrencyCode>USD</CurrencyCode>
    <BilledWeight>10.0</BilledWeight>
    <DiscountedCharges>
      <BaseCharge>26.05</BaseCharge>
      <TotalDiscount>0.00</TotalDiscount>
      <Surcharges>
      <Fuel>3.00</Fuel>
      <Other>0.00</Other>
      </Surcharges>
      <TotalSurcharge>3.00</TotalSurcharge>
      <NetCharge>29.05</NetCharge>
      <TotalRebate>0.00</TotalRebate>
    </DiscountedCharges>
    <ListCharges>
      <BaseCharge>26.05</BaseCharge>
      <TotalDiscount>0.00</TotalDiscount>
      <Surcharges>
      <Fuel>3.00</Fuel>
      <Other>0.00</Other>
      </Surcharges>
      <TotalSurcharge>3.00</TotalSurcharge>
      <NetCharge>29.05</NetCharge>
      <TotalRebate>0.00</TotalRebate>
    </ListCharges>
    <EffectiveNetDiscount>0.00</EffectiveNetDiscount>
  </EstimatedCharges>
  <SignatureOption>NONE</SignatureOption>
</FDXRateReply>
```


As you can see, the response here is very similar to the previous request, the key difference being that you receive a quote for a single service type. The relevant output would simply be this:

```
It would cost $29.05 to mail the package
```

Shipping a Package

So you've displayed estimated shipping costs to your customer, they've selected an option, confirmed their order, and completed payment. Now it's time to actually ship the package. This call requires a little more detail than the rate requests (a full address is required, including contact information), but other than that, they look quite similar:

```
$request = <<< XMLREQUEST
<?xml version="1.0" encoding="UTF-8" ?>
  <FDXShipRequest xmlns:api="http://www.fedex.com/fsmapi"
  xmlns:xsi="http://www.w3.org/2001/XMLSchema-instance"
  xsi:noNamespaceSchemaLocation="FDXShipRequest.xsd">
  <RequestHeader>
    <CustomerTransactionIdentifier>1</CustomerTransactionIdentifier>
    <AccountNumber>$accountNumber</AccountNumber>
    <MeterNumber>$meterNumber</MeterNumber>
    <CarrierCode>$carrier</CarrierCode>
  </RequestHeader>
  <DropoffType>REGULARPICKUP</DropoffType>
  <Service>PRIORITYOVERNIGHT</Service>
  <Packaging>FEDEXBOX</Packaging>
  <WeightUnits>LBS</WeightUnits>
  <Weight>4.0</Weight>
  <Origin>
    <Contact>
      <PersonName>Paul Reinheimer</PersonName>
      <CompanyName>Wrox</CompanyName>
      <PhoneNumber>5191234567</PhoneNumber>
      <E-MailAddress>paul@preinheimer.com</E-MailAddress>
    </Contact>
    <Address>
      <Line1>564 Elm Street</Line1>
      <Line2>Little Nook under the stairs</Line2>
      <City>NowhereVille</City>
      <StateOrProvinceCode>TN</StateOrProvinceCode>
      <PostalCode>38017</PostalCode>
      <CountryCode>US</CountryCode>
    </Address>
  </Origin>
  <Destination>
    <Contact>
      <PersonName>Chris Shiflett</PersonName>
      <CompanyName>Wrox</CompanyName>
      <PhoneNumber>6121234567</PhoneNumber>
      <E-MailAddress>chriss@preinheimer.com</E-MailAddress>
    </Contact>
    <Address>
      <Line1>37 East 14th St</Line1>
      <Line2>Suite 204</Line2>
      <City>New York</City>
      <StateOrProvinceCode>NY</StateOrProvinceCode>
      <PostalCode>10011</PostalCode>
      <CountryCode>US</CountryCode>
    </Address>
  </Destination>
```

```
    <SpecialServices>
      <EMailNotification>
        <Shipper>
          <ShipAlert>1</ShipAlert>
          <DeliveryNotification>1</DeliveryNotification>
          <LanguageCode>EN</LanguageCode>
        </Shipper>
        <Recipient>
          <ShipAlert>1</ShipAlert>
          <DeliveryNotification>1</DeliveryNotification>
          <LanguageCode>EN</LanguageCode>
        </Recipient>
      </EMailNotification>
    </SpecialServices>
    <Payment>
      <PayorType>SENDER</PayorType>
    </Payment>
    <ReferenceInfo>
      <CustomerReference>Order 6541325</CustomerReference>
    </ReferenceInfo>
    <Label>
      <Type>2DCOMMON</Type>
      <ImageType>PNG</ImageType>
    </Label>
  </FDXShipRequest>
XMLREQUEST;
```

Apart from the familiar elements, and the ones with obvious use (the address information), there are a few new elements here worthy of note:

- `SpecialServices - EMailNotification`—Here you can specify up to four parties to be notified by email when the package is shipped and delivered. The first two shown in this example, the sender and receiver, have already had their email addresses set in the `Contact` portion of the request. If a `Broker` is also included with the request (for international shipments requiring a customs broker, when you have chosen to use a broker other than FedEx), they can also be included here for email notification. Finally, you can also add an `Other` tree, with the same elements as shown in the preceding code (`ShipAlert`, `DeliveryNotification`, `LanguageCode`) as well as `E-MailAddress`.
- `SpecialServices - Other`—FedEx provides the ability to include a large number of special services with your shipment such as dry ice, hazardous materials shipment, alcohol shipment, and so on. Please see the API's documentation for more information on these options.
- `ReferenceInfo`—This allows you to specify an extra piece of information that will be printed on the shipping label. The customer's order number would be a great choice.
- `Label`—This allows you to specify how FedEx should return label information to you. Your options are 2DCOMMON and PNG as shown here, which are to be used with a laser printer (inkjets or deskjets are not acceptable) or one of several thermal printer options. For more information on the thermal printing options, please see the API's documentation.

The response will look like this:

```
<?xml version="1.0" encoding="UTF-8"?>
```

```
<FDXShipReply xmlns:xsi="http://www.w3.org/2001/XMLSchema-instance"
xsi:noNamespaceSchemaLocation="FDXShipReply.xsd">
  <ReplyHeader>
    <CustomerTransactionIdentifier>1</CustomerTransactionIdentifier>
  </ReplyHeader>
  <Tracking>
    <TrackingNumber>470034028693</TrackingNumber>
    <FormID>0201</FormID>
    <CodReturnTrackingNumber></CodReturnTrackingNumber>
  </Tracking>
  <ServiceTypeDescription>PRIORITY OVERNIGHT</ServiceTypeDescription>
  <PackagingDescription>BOX</PackagingDescription>
  <EstimatedCharges>
    <DimWeightUsed>false</DimWeightUsed>
    <RateScale>01552</RateScale>
    <RateZone>5</RateZone>
    <CurrencyCode>USD</CurrencyCode>
    <BilledWeight>4.0</BilledWeight>
    <DimWeight>0.0</DimWeight>
    <DiscountedCharges>
      <BaseCharge>38.20</BaseCharge>
      <TotalDiscount>0.00</TotalDiscount>
      <Surcharges>
       <Fuel>4.39</Fuel>
      </Surcharges>
      <TotalSurcharge>4.39</TotalSurcharge>
      <NetCharge>42.59</NetCharge>
      <TotalRebate>0.00</TotalRebate>
    </DiscountedCharges>
    <ListCharges>
     <Surcharges/>
    </ListCharges>
  </EstimatedCharges>
  <Routing>
  <UrsaRoutingCode>XAKLLA</UrsaRoutingCode>
  <ServiceCommitment>A1</ServiceCommitment>
  <DeliveryDay>TUE</DeliveryDay>
  <DestinationStationID>EWR</DestinationStationID>
  <DeliveryDate>14FEB06</DeliveryDate>
  <UrsaPrefixCode>XA</UrsaPrefixCode>
  </Routing>
  <Labels>
    <OutboundLabel>XXXX</OutboundLabel>
  </Labels>
  <SignatureOption>NONE</SignatureOption>
</FDXShipReply>
```

Particular items to note here include the `TrackingNumber`, `DeliveryDate`, and `OutboundLabel`. The tracking number is the useful little number customers can enter into the FedEx website to obtain information on the current status of their package. `DeliveryDate` is the estimated delivery date for the package. Finally, `OutboundLabel` includes a Base64-encoded `.png` image of the shipping label that needs to be printed off (this is covered shortly) and attached to the package (likely in a FedEx-provided pouch).

Here is the code used to execute the request and save the shipping label:

```
echo "<h3>Request</h3>\n";
echo "<pre>\n";
print_r(simplexml_load_string($request));
echo "</pre>\n";
echo "<h3>Response</h3>\n";
$response = callFedEx($request);
echo "Shipment Confirmed, your tracking number is: " .
    $response->Tracking->TrackingNumber;
echo "<pre>";
print_r($response);
$label = base64_decode($response->Labels->OutboundLabel);
file_put_contents("/str/label/{$response->Tracking->TrackingNumber}.png", $label);
echo "</pre>";
```

As you can see, extracting the shipping label is as easy as using the `base64_decode()` function, then saving the output to a file. I've used the tracking number from the order as a filename; you may wish to use the customer's order number or the like instead. The shipping label itself should look somewhat similar to Figure 8-2.

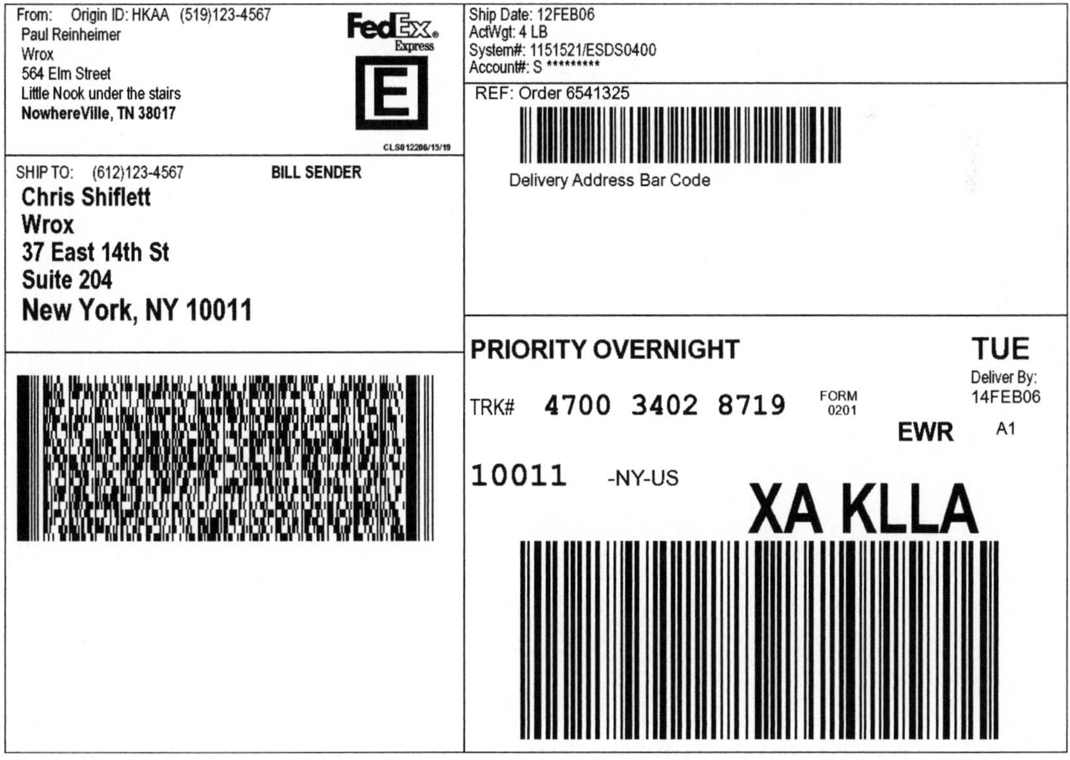

Figure 8-2

Both your address and the address of the recipient are clearly shown, and on the right-hand side of the label you can also see the contents of the `CustomerReference` field. The API documentation includes a 13-page document specifying exactly how labels are to be printed. In short, this `.png` file is going to be printed on a standard 8.5-×-11-inch piece of paper (portrait mode) so that the resulting image is 7 × 4.5 inches (that's a 3/4-inch margin on each side of the paper). This works out perfectly for the page to be folded in half and then placed inside the document pouch attached to the package.

Canceling a Shipment

The situation may arise where you need to cancel a shipment to a customer. This cancellation must be made before the end of business on the day the request was placed. The request and response for this operation are very short:

```
$request = <<< XMLREQUEST
<?xml version="1.0" encoding="UTF-8" ?>
 <FDXShipDeleteRequest xmlns:api="http://www.fedex.com/fsmapi"
xmlns:xsi="http://www.w3.org/2001/XMLSchema-instance"
xsi:noNamespaceSchemaLocation="FDXShipDeleteRequest.xsd">
  <RequestHeader>
    <CustomerTransactionIdentifier>Test Delete</CustomerTransactionIdentifier>
    <AccountNumber>$accountNumber</AccountNumber>
    <MeterNumber>$meterNumber</MeterNumber>
    <CarrierCode>$carrier</CarrierCode>
  </RequestHeader>
 <TrackingNumber>470034028693</TrackingNumber>
</FDXShipDeleteRequest>
XMLREQUEST;
```

The `TrackingNumber` is of course the tracking number you received when you scheduled the item to be shipped. The response is brief to say the least:

```
<?xml version="1.0" encoding="UTF-8"?>
<FDXShipDeleteReply xmlns:xsi="http://www.w3.org/2001/XMLSchema-instance"
xsi:noNamespaceSchemaLocation="FDXShipDeleteReply.xsd">
  <ReplyHeader>
    <CustomerTransactionIdentifier>Test Delete</CustomerTransactionIdentifier>
  </ReplyHeader>
</FDXShipDeleteReply>
```

Had a `CustomerTransactionIdentifier` not been present, the response would have been practically non-existent. The code required to submit the request remains very similar to previous examples:

```
echo "<h3>Request</h3>\n";
echo "<pre>\n";
print_r(simplexml_load_string($request));
echo "</pre>\n";
echo "<h3>Response</h3>\n";
$response = callFedEx($request);
if (isset($response->Error->Code))
{
  echo "There was a problem canceling that request";
```

```
}else
{
  echo "Shipment Cancelled";
}
echo "<pre>";
print_r($response);
echo "</pre>";
```

I've added a check for the error condition here just as an example to show how it would be done. As mentioned at the beginning of the chapter, the test API contains only very basic functionality, which doesn't appear to check for existence or even validity of the tracking number provided in the request. This makes it very difficult to test for an error condition (there is a sample response showing an error in the xml transaction guide provided by FedEx).

Tracking a Package

Most online stores offer the ability to track purchased items from within the store's website. This functionality can be achieved with a `FDXTrackRequest` request. The request will look something like this:

```
$request = <<< XMLREQUEST
<?xml version="1.0" encoding="UTF-8" ?>
  <FDXTrackRequest xmlns:api="http://www.fedex.com/fsmapi"
    xmlns:xsi="http://www.w3.org/2001/XMLSchema-instance"
    xsi:noNamespaceSchemaLocation="FDXShipRequest.xsd">
  <RequestHeader>
    <AccountNumber>$accountNumber</AccountNumber>
    <MeterNumber>$meterNumber</MeterNumber>
    <CarrierCode>$carrier</CarrierCode>
  </RequestHeader>
  <PackageIdentifier>
    <Value>470034028693</Value>
    <Type>TRACKING_NUMBER_OR_DOORTAG</Type>
  </PackageIdentifier>
  <DestinationCountryCode>US</DestinationCountryCode>
  <DetailScans>1</DetailScans>
</FDXTrackRequest>
XMLREQUEST;
```

Apart from the tracking number, the interesting piece of information here is `DetailScans`. A value of 1 indicates that all scans for the package should be returned (being picked up, arriving at the sorting facility, leaving the sorting facility, and so on) rather than just the most recent scan (which would be a value of 0).

Absent from the sample request are `ShipDateRangeBegin` and `ShipDateRangeEnd` or `ShipDate`. These elements give the API server more information on when the shipment was made to make its job of finding the tracking information easier. They are not required, but are recommended. If your application stores this information, it would be a good idea to include it in tracking requests (you only need the start and end of a range, or the exact [+– 5] ship date, not both). The dates follow the same format of other dates with this API, YYYY-MM-DD.

Also absent is the `PagingToken` value, which should always be empty for an initial request. If the higher detail level has been requested, and the shipment has a *lot* of scan points, it may exceed the maximum length of the response document, in which case not all scans will be reported in the initial request. In that case, a `PagingToken` value will be returned with the truncated request. That same value should be passed on in a subsequent `FDXTrackRequest` request to obtain further values.

The response should look something like this (this sample response is unrelated to the previous examples):


```
<?xml version="1.0" encoding="UTF-8"?>
<FDXTrackReply xmlns:xsi="http://www.w3.org/2001/XMLSchema-instance"
xsi:noNamespaceSchemaLocation="FDXTrackReply.xsd">
<ReplyHeader>
  <CustomerTransactionIdentifier>FDXTrack</CustomerTransactionIdentifier>
</ReplyHeader>
<MoreData>false</MoreData>
<TrackProfile>
  <TrackingNumber>643133236401</TrackingNumber>
  <CarrierCode>FDXE</CarrierCode>
  <ShipDate>2006-01-21</ShipDate>
  <DestinationAddress>
    <City>DETROIT</City>
    <StateOrProvinceCode>MI</StateOrProvinceCode>
    <PostalCode>48243</PostalCode>
    <CountryCode>US</CountryCode>
  </DestinationAddress>
  <DeliveredDate>2006-01-22</DeliveredDate>
  <DeliveredTime>09:53</DeliveredTime>
  <SignedForBy>R.Smith</SignedForBy>
  <DeliveredLocationCode>1</DeliveredLocationCode>
  <DeliveredLocationDescription>Front Desk</DeliveredLocationDescription>
  <Service>Priority Pak</Service>
  <Weight>4.0</Weight>
  <WeightUnits>LBS</WeightUnits>
<FedExURL>http://fedex.com/cgibin/tracking?action=track&amp;language=english&amp;cn
    try_code=us&amp;initial=x&amp;tracknumbers=123456789123456</FedExURL>
  <ScanCount>5</ScanCount>
  <Scan>
    <Date>2006-01-11</Date>
    <Time>09:56</Time>
    <ScanType>20</ScanType>
    <ScanDescription>Delivered</ScanDescription>
    <City>DETROIT</City>
    <StateOrProvinceCode>MI</StateOrProvinceCode>
    <CountryCode>US</CountryCode>
  </Scan>
  <Scan>
    <Date>2006-01-11</Date>
    <Time>07:26</Time>
    <ScanType>11</ScanType>
    <ScanDescription>On FedEx vehicle for delivery</ScanDescription>
    <City>DETROIT</City>
    <StateOrProvinceCode>MI</StateOrProvinceCode>
    <CountryCode>US</CountryCode>
  </Scan>
  <Scan>
    <Date>2006-01-11</Date>
    <Time>05:49</Time>
```

```
      <ScanType>02</ScanType>
      <ScanDescription>Arrived at FedEx Destination Location</ScanDescription>
      <City>DETROIT</City>
      <StateOrProvinceCode>MI</StateOrProvinceCode>
      <CountryCode>US</CountryCode>
    </Scan>
    <Scan>
      <Date>2006-01-11</Date>
      <Time>01:39</Time>
      <ScanType>10</ScanType>
      <ScanDescription>Left FedEx Sort Facility</ScanDescription>
      <City>MEMPHIS</City>
      <StateOrProvinceCode>TN</StateOrProvinceCode>
      <CountryCode>US</CountryCode>
    </Scan>
    <Scan>
      <Date>2006-01-10</Date>
      <Time>15:44</Time>
      <ScanType>08</ScanType>
      <ScanDescription>Picked up by FedEx</ScanDescription>
      <City>MEMPHIS</City>
      <StateOrProvinceCode>TN</StateOrProvinceCode>
      <CountryCode>US</CountryCode>
    </Scan>
  </TrackProfile>
  </FDXTrackReply>
```

As you can see, even with domestic shipments there can be quite a lot of scans for a single package. Parsed and nicely formatted output is much more useful:

```
2006-01-11,09:53 - Delivered in DETROIT, MI
2006-01-11,07:34 - On FedEx vehicle for delivery in DETROIT, MI
2006-01-11,06:39 - Arrived at FedEx Destination Location in DETROIT, MI
2006-01-11,03:41 - Left FedEx Sort Facility in MEMPHIS, TN
2006-01-10,18:44 - Picked up by FedEx in MEMPHIS, TN
```

Additionally, recognize that FedEx returns scan information with the most recent information at the top, rather than chronologically. I generally find it more convenient to reverse this, so I can read details in chronological order. The opposing viewpoint (presumably FedEx's) is that by presenting information in this order one can more quickly obtain the latest information.

The code to send the request and give the output is as follows:

```
echo "<h3>Request</h3>\n";
echo "<pre>\n";
print_r(simplexml_load_string($request));
echo "</pre>\n";
echo "<h3>Response</h3>\n";
$response = callFedEx($request);
if (!isset($response->TrackProfile->SoftError))
{
  foreach ($response->TrackProfile->Scan AS $scanPoint)
  {
    echo "{$scanPoint->Date},{$scanPoint->Time} - {$scanPoint->ScanDescription} in
```

```
        {$scanPoint->City}, {$scanPoint->StateOrProvinceCode}<br>";
    }
  }else
  {
    echo "Tracking information not yet available";
  }
  echo "<pre>";
  print_r($response);
  echo "</pre>";
```

Accepting Returns

Unfortunately, situations may arise where you need to accept a return from a customer at your own expense. To facilitate this, FedEx provides the `FDXExpressTagRequest` call. This call will instruct FedEx to print a shipping label, send an agent to the sender's address (your customer) with the shipping label, and accept the package for shipment with the label they printed. The request is similar to that of a regular shipment, but note that the `Origin` should be your customer's address, and the `Destination` should be your address.

This type of shipment isn't added to accounts by default. You will need to speak to your account manager to request access to this type of shipment; you will also need to email the API support team to get access to this request type via the API.

```
$request = <<< XMLREQUEST
<?xml version="1.0" encoding="UTF-8" ?>
<FDXExpressTagRequest xmlns:xsi="http://www.w3.org/2001/XMLSchemainstance"
xsi:noNamespaceSchemaLocation="FDXExpressTagRequest.xsd">
  <RequestHeader>
      <AccountNumber>$accountNumber</AccountNumber>
      <MeterNumber>$meterNumber</MeterNumber>
      <CarrierCode>$carrier</CarrierCode>
    </RequestHeader>
  <DispatchDate>2006-02-22</DispatchDate>
  <LatestPickupTime>16:00:00</LatestPickupTime >
  <ReadyTime>12:00:00</ReadyTime>
    <Origin>
      <Contact>
        <PersonName>Chris Shiflett</PersonName>
        <CompanyName>Wrox</CompanyName>
        <PhoneNumber>6121234567</PhoneNumber>
        <E-MailAddress>chriss@preinheimer.com</E-MailAddress>
      </Contact>
      <Address>
        <Line1>37 East 14th St</Line1>
        <Line2>Suite 204</Line2>
        <City>New York</City>
        <StateOrProvinceCode>NY</StateOrProvinceCode>
        <PostalCode>10011</PostalCode>
        <CountryCode>US</CountryCode>
      </Address>
    </Origin>
    <Destination>
```

```
          <Contact>
            <PersonName>Paul Reinheimer</PersonName>
            <CompanyName>Wrox</CompanyName>
            <PhoneNumber>5191234567</PhoneNumber>
            <E-MailAddress>paul@preinheimer.com</E-MailAddress>
          </Contact>
          <Address>
            <Line1>564 Elm Street</Line1>
            <Line2>Little Nook under the stairs</Line2>
            <City>NowhereVille</City>
            <StateOrProvinceCode>TN</StateOrProvinceCode>
            <PostalCode>38017</PostalCode>
            <CountryCode>US</CountryCode>
          </Address>
        </Destination>
        <Payment>
          <PayorType>RECIPIENT</PayorType>
          <AccountNumber>$accountNumber</AccountNumber>
        </Payment>
      <RMA>
        <Number>1234567</Number>
      </RMA>
      <CourierInstructions>Please knock loudly, bell broken</CourierInstructions>
      <CustomerReference>Manuscript Return</CustomerReference>
      <CurrencyCode>USD</CurrencyCode>
      <Service>STANDARDOVERNIGHT</Service>
      <Packaging>FEDEXBOX</Packaging>
      <WeightUnits>LBS</WeightUnits>
      <Weight>4</Weight>
      <DeclaredValue>13</DeclaredValue>
      <PackageCount>1</PackageCount>
    </FDXExpressTagRequest>
    XMLREQUEST;
```

Apart from the address reversal, I've included a few new tags in this request. `DispatchDate` replaces `ShipDate` from earlier requests, indicating when FedEx should dispatch a driver to obtain the package. `ReadyTime` and `LatestPickupTime` indicate the earliest and latest times the package will be available.

The response is succinct:

```
<?xml version="1.0" encoding="UTF-8" ?>
<FDXExpressTagReply xmlns:xsi="http://www.w3.org/2001/XMLSchema-instance">
  <ReplyHeader>
   <CustomerTransactionIdentifier>Express Tag Test</CustomerTransactionIdentifier>
  </ReplyHeader>
  <DispatchConfirmationNumber>00001</DispatchConfirmationNumber>
  <Location>HKAA</Location>
  <AccessTime>02:00:00</AccessTime>
  <CutoffTime>21:00:00</CutoffTime>
  <DeliveryCommitmentDate>2004-10-13</DeliveryCommitmentDate>
  <DeliveryCommitmentTime>15:00:00</DeliveryCommitmentTime>
  <TrackingNumber>301000658338</TrackingNumber>
</FDXExpressTagReply>
```

Apart from the `TrackingNumber` (which, just like the tracking number for a regular shipment, can be used to track the package with the `FDXTrackRequest` call), the response includes information on when FedEx needs the package to be available for pickup. Depending on the pickup location, the times may differ from those specified in your request.

Summary

This chapter introduced the Federal Express API and the various calls likely to be required during the operation of an online store. Though I personally experienced many problems initially with this API (due mainly to my location in Canada), overall I would say that this API was a pleasure to work with. The documentation is very good, and perhaps most impressively, the API support team answers email promptly and is accessible by phone most of the day. Having completed this chapter, you are now prepared to integrate shipping into an online store, supporting the following:

- Estimating shipping costs for different shipping methods
- Shipping a package
- Canceling a shipment
- Tracking that package while en route
- Accepting returns

This information is useful on its own, but also combines well with the next two APIs presented: eBay and PayPal. By integrating code from these three chapters, you could create a very robust online presence with a minimum of direct interaction on your part.

9

Interacting with the eBay API

eBay, being one of the few survivors of the dot-com crash, has become the world's largest online auction house, with thousands of items for sale in many categories from users around the world. The API eBay offers is by far the most complex discussed in this book, offering more than 100 different calls. Obviously, only a small fraction of these can be discussed here. Simply signing up and obtaining all the information required to make your first API call with eBay can be more difficult than some of the applications discussed in other chapters.

eBay offers both a REST and a SOAP interface for its API. The REST API is quite limited, offering only a basic search interface, with limited information included in the response. Meanwhile, the SOAP API is expansive, offering not only a huge variety of calls, but also a variety of detail levels associated with those calls, which can allow you to fine-tune the information returned to your specific needs.

This chapter walks you through interacting with the eBay API, showing you the following:

- How to register yourself as an eBay developer
- Using the REST API with eBay
- Getting started with eBay's SOAP API
- Searching eBay items with the SOAP API
- Adding auction items to eBay using the API

Registering to Use the API

Getting everything set up to start using the eBay API can be a bit complex. The process has numerous steps and requires at least two separate accounts (one for the development sandbox, and a regular eBay account). I don't usually like to outline the registration process in too much detail because things change, but I have made an exception in this case because I (as well as a few associates I had try the process) ran into some difficulties.

Understanding What Is Required

Developing for the API with an individual (free) account requires at least four separate accounts:

- A regular eBay.com account that will be associated with your development account
- A development account, which is a free account required to access the API
- At least one sandbox user account to act as a seller for auctions you create during testing
- At least one sandbox user account to act as a buyer for auctions you create during testing

The sandbox user accounts (discussed later) can all come from the same pool (for example, during different tests various accounts can be used for bidding or selling), but you will need at least two accounts; you can't bid on your own items. The first account (the regular eBay account) is only required when you select the Individual (or free) tier. If you have selected another tier (at print time, the cheapest commercial tier is US $500), you will not be required to associate your account with a regular eBay account.

Registering with eBay.com

If you don't already have an eBay account (and you intend to use the Individual tier for API registration), you will need to register for one first. You can do this through the normal `www.ebay.com` interface, and the steps are self-explanatory. You must use a real email address because there are validation steps.

Creating Your Development Account

Head over to `http://developer.ebay.com/join` and click the rather prominently displayed Join Now button.

Membership Tiers

The eBay API offers several membership tiers, and these tiers offer you varying levels of support and query limits. The Individual tier is free, and offers you 5,000 queries per month. Unless you are going to require eBay's support while developing your application, I would recommend starting at this level and upgrading if your situation warrants it. If you do need help while developing your application, there are already numerous online communities with forums and mailing lists.

Username

Your development username must be different than your regular eBay username, and must contain at least one letter and at least one number (I ended up appending a 1 to my username).

Other Fields

The rest of the form is pretty standard; as usual, choose a secure password.

Password Safe is a great tool to store all of your various login information. You can get it at `http://sourceforge.net/passwordsafe`.

License Agreement

After entering your information, you will be presented with some details regarding the membership tier you selected, as well as the opportunity to create a regular (nondeveloper) eBay account. Scroll down, read the license agreement (in the unnecessarily small box), and if you agree, check the box and continue. If not, you can skip the rest of this chapter.

Check Your Email

You should promptly receive an email from eBay, welcoming you to the developer program. This kind of email is often ignored, but in this case, don't ignore it. The email, though given a welcoming subject, is your email verification notice and is absolutely necessary. Click the link in the email, log into the developer sandbox (with your developer credentials), and on the new form enter your regular user credentials and the confirmation code from the email. You will then be provided with three key/value pairs that should look something like this:

```
DevID = C481VH1E49RGK2J21C5H96R143H641
AppID = WROXP91H134FC2I9R276TB6J6945CT
CertID = P76S15991C6$HFI91JM21-Y7F7V7RD
```

Save those values in a safe place. You will need them to acquire request tokens later, and they can also be a pain to recover.

Create a Sandbox Account

This is where the fun really starts. There are two facets to accessing the API, the first being your development account (which you have already created) and the second being a nondevelopment account to which the requests will be attributed (in this case this will be a sandbox account, but the process for using a regular account is identical). Generally (when you develop an application and allow others to use it to perform actions under their own account), you will provide users with a link to a page hosted at eBay, as well as the three tokens you just received. By doing things in this manner, the users' credentials are never presented to you, and users require your tokens in order to access the API (remember that there are query limits associated with your account, so you don't want nonclients running up the total).

You need to head over to `www.sandbox.ebay.com/` and register a user account, preferably two (one to act as a buyer, and the other as a seller) to test your applications fully.

Alternatively, you can use eBay's Sandbox User Registration Tool to quickly generate accounts without jumping through all the hoops normally associated with creating an account; you can access this tool at `http://developer.ebay.com/DevZone/sandboxuser.asp`. Using this tool also lets you pre-set the account's feedback score and back-date the user's creation.

Generating Authentication Tokens

The fun of generating all your credentials has just gotten started. Next, head over to `http://developer.ebay.com/tokentool/` and enter the three values you received while creating your development account. In this case you will want to generate your tokens for the sandbox; also make sure you check the box to generate REST keys. Once you have entered your three values, you will need to enter your

User Sandbox Account information. You should then be provided with two tokens, along with the presentation of your username:

```
User: wroxuser
Token:
AgAAAA**AQAAAA**aAAAAA**S0XcQg**nY+sHZ2PrBmdj6wVnY+sEZ2PrA2dj6wJnY+lCpaDpQ+dj6x9nY+
seQ**WVQAAA**AAMAAA**mVU/W1cVxRscpy4SAd3Ou9urcp9z08pOzBXIdf2KlOThmHVKptfdyftAk4Us1d
CDt2J4xT5Jpm+ZjTnMZX32EWA45oMxTJZxFTgQ4D7QQyCYJ0f2QHipmxdnDYF6r92yfMflF8YTrTNUSN8Dc
yJcN6GlHU8jsoZyn93v7KVhy9NMNIs6WO60qXOxg8ZpwuliQWo745ZBrVGCtg9lxDFfFQr+anSPoLSPkSKU
QOZ7W6zSkpD/fQ8iZewjCz571lBfMfoN+1u++nLURmHq9PfqXAlVbWMtWz5st6GNVcJDvRQ1ETk+zaFEBft
zwBeG0gcUXLUrrX5/P+13Iq4lFYI80lFHX9xiR5S16ayT7csnryIPKIuS6BkKDLyVC0CRWEkwsdmSt9+VmI
Jk/kw7HbqLD5DPkzsab1ifn2yKUxcn7/Jcqs+x/PqCXpOPs8+aTy6cAifeOskwZ/Y2iZJGqt/U+K88HJy8s
5QLpDfnkNheQykS6cTiQ4/fAqPmwolFYnqshvZ3bbA6C0erg2ejIB/sVo1Wucov1Z18CdroQWwb19QaTP6U
pFYfjEhaWx7W1T6fP9oRfJu5XKa7uOEHKdQbYnKNR+bSeuZhfK1GaGwp6ECZnt9bCsSX3dJRd65AKDUPU4F
GTb4baSsBH/bwz66PiQIbOVNHtrWK4fh6o64/ymFDJjVFPYFINC758SupZs7Q7G6FxXs2ViVv3nFEOa8b6M
lEr0wq9v2Hs+GFcwSkpecAESdQykuXAkQIYylVd0iS
REST Token: oVAr7OhSbdw%3D**%2Bs1d4ta8quAac9G3rvTuhs8IPvg%3D
```

The REST token is obviously used with REST requests (where the request size is limited), and the regular token is used with SOAP requests. Store them both in a safe place.

Congratulations! You've created two or three accounts with secure passwords, and received five tokens. You're either well on your way to making your first eBay API call, or a you're on your way to a headache.

Basic REST Request

The eBay API offers both REST and SOAP interfaces for its API. The REST portion, however, only offers search access.

The following code will make a hard-coded request against the eBay Sandbox API, and display the results to the screen, `restExample.php`:

```
<?php
  header("Content-Type: application/xml");
  $endPoint = "http://rest.api.sandbox.ebay.com/restapi";
  $requestToken    = "oVAr7OhSbdw%3D**%2Bs1d4ta8quAac9G3rvTuhs8IPvg%3D";
  $requestUserId   = "wroxuser";
  $searchTerms     = "boat";
  $fullEndPoint = $endPoint . "?RequestToken={$requestToken}&RequestUserId=
    {$requestUserId}&Query={$searchTerms}&CallName=GetSearchResults";
  $results =  file_get_contents($fullEndPoint);
  echo $results;
?>
```

The first line sets the `Content-Type` for the output. Because the code will print the resulting XML directly to the screen, not only is this the right thing to do, but it will help ensure that it is displayed attractively. The next three lines define constants for the request. The `requestToken` is the token you received when you logged in with your Sandbox user account, and the `requestUserId` is simply the username associated with that account. `searchTerms` are the keywords you want to search for (remember to URL-encode anything you enter, structured, the request is made, and the results a

The endpoint the program retrieves is as follo

```
http://rest.api.sandbox.ebay.com/re
ac9G3rvTuhs8IPvg%3D&RequestUserId=w
```

And the server returns the following respons

```
<?xml version="1.0" encoding="utf-8
<eBay>
  <EBayTime>2005-07-19 18:07:48</E
  <Search>
    <Items>
      <Item>
        <Id>4503294022</Id>
        <Title><![CDATA[Boat Capta
          </Title>
        <SubtitleText><![CDATA[]]>
        <CurrencyId>1</CurrencyId>
        <Link><![CDATA[http://cgi.ebay.com/ws/eBayISAPI.dll?ViewItem&item=
          4503294022&category=20563]]></Link>
        <CurrentPrice>9.99</CurrentPrice>
        <LocalizedCurrentPrice>$9.99</LocalizedCurrentPrice>
        <BINPrice>US $0.00</BINPrice>
        <BidCount>0</BidCount>
        <StartTime>2005-07-14 19:43:26</StartTime>
        <EndTime>2005-07-21 19:43:26</EndTime>
        <BillPointRegistered>0</BillPointRegistered>
        <ItemProperties>
          <BoldTitle>0</BoldTitle>
          <Featured>0</Featured>
          <Gallery>1</Gallery>
          <GalleryFeatured>0</GalleryFeatured>
          <GalleryURL><![CDATA[http://thumbs.ebay.com//pict/4503294022.jpg]]>
            </GalleryURL>
          <Picture>1</Picture>
          <Highlight>0</Highlight>
          <Border>0</Border>
          <New>0</New>
          <BuyItNow>0</BuyItNow>
          <IsFixedPrice>0</IsFixedPrice>
          <Type>1</Type>
          <Gift>0</Gift>
          <CharityListing>0</CharityListing>
          <MotorsGermanySearchable>0</MotorsGermanySearchable>
        </ItemProperties>
      </Item>
      <Item>
        <Id>4503294023</Id>
        <Title><![CDATA[Sailboat Boat Nautical Canvas Accent  Bed Throw
          Pillow]]></Title>
        <SubtitleText><![CDATA[]]></SubtitleText>
```

```
yId>
://cgi.ebay.com/ws/eBayISAPI.dll?ViewItem&item=
gory=20563]]></Link>
.99</CurrentPrice>
entPrice>$9.99</LocalizedCurrentPrice>
$0.00</BINPrice>
0</BidCount>
me>2005-07-14 19:43:26</StartTime>
me>2005-07-21 19:43:26</EndTime>
lPointRegistered>0</BillPointRegistered>
temProperties>
    <BoldTitle>0</BoldTitle>
    <Featured>0</Featured>
    <Gallery>1</Gallery>
    <GalleryFeatured>0</GalleryFeatured>
    <GalleryURL><![CDATA[http://thumbs.ebay.com//pict/4503294023.jpg]]>
      </GalleryURL>
    <Picture>1</Picture>
    <Highlight>0</Highlight>
    <Border>0</Border>
    <New>0</New>
    <BuyItNow>0</BuyItNow>
    <IsFixedPrice>0</IsFixedPrice>
    <Type>1</Type>
    <Gift>0</Gift>
    <CharityListing>0</CharityListing>
    <MotorsGermanySearchable>0</MotorsGermanySearchable>
  </ItemProperties>
</Item>
</Items>
<Count>2</Count>
<HasMoreItems>0</HasMoreItems>
<PageNumber>1</PageNumber>
<GrandTotal>2</GrandTotal>
</Search>
</eBay>
```

The response, while verbose, does have a pretty basic structure, and the key information should be pretty easy to pick out. Within the `Search` branch, the `Items` branch holds all of the relevant search results within `Item`. Most of the values within that branch are self-explanatory, but a few are explained in more detail shortly. After the `Items` branch concludes, `Count` indicates the number of items returned in this response. `HasMoreItems` is a binary value indicating if there are more results available on another page. `PageNumber` indicates the page of this result, and `GrandTotal` indicates the total number of results available from all pages.

Some of the elements contained in each `Item` include the following:

- `Id`—A unique identifier for the item within the eBay system.
- `CurrencyID`—An integer that represents the native currency for the auction. The integers and the currency they represent include the following:
    - 1—US Dollar ($)
    - 2—Canadian Dollar (C $)

- 3—UK Pound Sterling (GBP)
- 5—Australian Dollar (AU $)
- 7—Euro (EUR)
- 13—Swiss Franc (CHF)
- 41—Taiwanese Dollar (NT $)

- `LocalizedCurrentPrice`—Returns the highest bid on the item, taking into account the currency of the item as well as the current location of the requestor (which can be specified in a more complex query). So, an item up for sale within the United States (and under the U.S. currency) viewed from someone with another location (say Canada) would have a localized price of US $20.00, whereas a client within the United States would simply see $20.00.
- `BINPrice`—This is the Buy It Now price. A bidder willing to pay the full Buy It Now price may end the auction immediately.
- `BillPointRegistered`—Bill Point is a payment system eBay used to offer. It is no longer used, so the value will always be zero.
- `IsFixedPrice`—A binary value. A 1 indicates that the item is for sale at a set price and a 0 indicates a regular auction.
- `Type`—An integer that indicates the type of auction that is being run. eBay offers several auction types beyond the normal. The integer and type of auctions are as follows:
    - 0—Unknown auction type
    - 1—Chinese auction
    - This is the standard auction type that you likely already associate with eBay. A single item is offered for sale, and a time frame is set. Bids are placed competitively during that time frame; at the end, the individual that has placed the highest bid is awarded the item at the highest bid price.
    - 2—Dutch auction
    - In a Dutch auction, two or more items are placed up for sale, in which bidders can place a bid not only for an amount per item, but also the number of items desired (for example, you could place a bid for $100, and state that you desire 3 items [at $100 each]). At the end of the auction, items are awarded to the highest bidder, then the second highest, and so on, at the individual bidder's price.
    - 5—Live auction
    - Similar to a Chinese auction, except the auction takes place both on eBay and in a live setting where non-eBay members may also bid on the item.
    - 6—Ad Type auction
    - An advertisement for a real estate listing designed to generate leads rather than bids. This is a nonpurchase listing.
    - 7—eBay Stores Inventory (fixed-price items).
    - Similar to fixed-price items, except items are listed only within the seller's store, not within a general eBay category.

- 8 — Personal Offer auction
- A special type of listing where the seller offers a specific item at a set price to another eBay user. This is a Second Chance offer, used by the seller to offer an item to a nonwinning bidder when the winning bidder didn't complete the transaction.
- 9 — Fixed-Price item (combined with Buy It Now)
- One or more items are offered for sale at a fixed price — there is no progressive bidding. Buyers may purchase an item or several items at a set price and complete the transaction immediately. The listing ends either when the duration is exhausted or when all of the available items are sold.

- `CharityListing` — Depreciated. A binary value, with a 1 indicating that the seller has chosen to donate a percentage of the proceeds of the sale to a selected nonprofit organization, and a 0 of course indicating that the full purchase price will be kept by the seller.
- `MotorsGermanySearchable` — A depreciated value, used to indicate that the item was dual listed with `mobile.de`.

As you have seen, it takes very little code to make a simple search query against the server, and the results returned are quite verbose (and only two items returned with the preceding code; most searches I tried returned 0 or the maximum of 100).

The eBay Sandbox is populated entirely by people testing their applications; it is not automatically populated with anything. As such, you can't rely on anything being present you if you didn't create it yourself.

A Useful REST Request

The preceding request works, but doesn't actually deal with any of the data returned or allow users to perform searches on their own. This example will. First, because auctions are very time sensitive, you will need a function to turn seconds into a nice, human-readable format:

```
function prettyTimeRemaining($timestamp)
{
  $timeRemaining = "";
  $weeks = floor($timestamp / 604800);
  $timestamp = $timestamp -  ($weeks * 604800);
  if ($weeks > 0)
  {
    $timeRemaining .= "$weeks Week(s) ";
  }
  $days = floor($timestamp / 86400);
  $timestamp = $timestamp - ($days * 86400);
  if ($days > 0)
  {
    $timeRemaining .= "$days Day(s) ";
  }
  $hours = floor($timestamp / 3600);
  $timestamp = $timestamp - ($hours * 3600);
  if ($hours > 0)
```

```
    {
      $timeRemaining .= "$hours Hour(s) ";
    }
    $minutes = floor($timestamp / 60);
    $timestamp = $timestamp - ($minutes * 60);
    if ($minutes > 0)
    {
      $timeRemaining .= "$minutes Minute(s) ";
    }
    $seconds = $timestamp;
    $timeRemaining .= "$seconds Second(s)";
    return $timeRemaining;
  }
```

The function is pretty basic — it will turn a value like `297143` into `3 Day(s) 10 Hour(s) 32 Minute(s)`. The mechanics are pretty simple; the values used for division are merely the number of seconds in that time period. `Floor` rounds any number down to the nearest whole number (1.8 becomes 1).

With that function out of the way, here is `quickSearch.php`:

```
<html>
<head>
<title>eBay Quick Search REST API</title>
</head>
<body>
<form method="get">
  Search Terms: <input type="text" name="search"><br>
  <input type="submit">
</form>
<pre>
```

To allow users to enter whatever query they would like, a form will be needed; returning that HTML code before starting the script saves escaping.

```
<?php

$endPoint = "http://rest.api.sandbox.ebay.com/restapi";
$requestToken    = "oVAr7OhSbdw%3D**%2Bs1d4ta8quAac9G3rvTuhs8IPvg%3D";
$requestUserId   = "wroxuser";
$resultsPerPage = 10;
```

A few basic variables are set, the basic endpoint is set, as well as the number of results shown per page.

```
if (isset($_GET['search']))
{
   if (isset($_GET['page']) && ctype_digit($_GET['page']))
   {
      $page = $_GET['page'];
   }else
   {
      $page = 0;
   }
```

If the script has not received a value for the search parameter, this is likely the first run and there's no point in accessing the API. A page parameter is also allowed; if it is present and is only digits (you don't want a nefarious user sneaking something else in there), it is used, otherwise it is set to zero.

```
$skip = $page * $resultsPerPage;
$searchTerms = urlencode($_GET['search']);
$fullEndPoint = $endPoint . "?RequestToken={$requestToken}&RequestUserId=
  {$requestUserId}&Query={$searchTerms}&CallName=GetSearchResults&MaxResults=
  $resultsPerPage&Skip={$skip}";
$results =  file_get_contents($fullEndPoint);
$xml = simplexml_load_string($results);
echo "Your search for <b>$searchTerms</b> yielded a total of <b>
 {$xml->Search->GrandTotal}</b> results<br>";
echo "These are results <b>" . ($page * $resultsPerPage + 1) . "</b> to <b>" .
 ((1 + $page) * $resultsPerPage) . "</b><br><br>";
```

The API allows you to specify how many results you would like to be skipped. That value is calculated using the number of results displayed per page as well as the page value calculated earlier. The `file_get_contents` function is used to make the request and obtain results, which are then dropped into a `SimpleXML` object. Using that `SimpleXML` object, some basic information regarding the search is presented.

```
foreach($xml->Search->Items->Item AS $item)
{
 $link = $item->Link;
 $link = str_replace("http://cgi.ebay.com/", "http://cgi.sandbox.ebay.com/",
   $link);
 echo "<a href=\"$link\">{$item->Title}</a><br>";
 echo "Current Price: <b>{$item->LocalizedCurrentPrice}</b> \t Bids: <b>
   {$item->BidCount}</b><br>";
```

Each of the items returned by the search is iterated through to print the basic item information. For reasons I don't quite understand, the sandbox returns a link pointing at the live site, where the items returned no longer exist. This link is replaced with a working one pointing at the sandbox. The `LocalizedCurrentPrice` is used to ensure the user gets a clear idea of the price of the item.

```
 if ($item->ItemProperties->BuyItNow == 1)
 {
   echo "Buy it Now Price: <b>{$item->BINPrice}</b><br>";
 }
```

If the item has a `BuyItNow` price, it is displayed to the user.

```
 echo "Auction Start: <b>{$item->StartTime}</b> \t Auction End: <b>
   {$item->EndTime}</b><br>";
 $endTime = strtotime($item->EndTime);
 $timeRemaining = $endTime - time();
 echo "Time Remaining: <b>" . prettyTimeRemaining($timeRemaining) ."</b><br>";
 echo "<br><br>";
}
```

The timing information is displayed, along with a clear representation of the amount of time remaining before the auction ends.

```
    if (trim($xml->Search->HasMoreItems) == 1)
    {
      echo "<a href=\"?search={$searchTerms}&page=" . ($page + 1) . "\">
         Next Page</a><br>";
    }
}
?>
</pre>
</body>
</html>
```

Finally, if there are more search results available, they are displayed, and the HTML code is nicely concluded. Figure 9-1 shows the resultant page output `quickSearch.php` output.

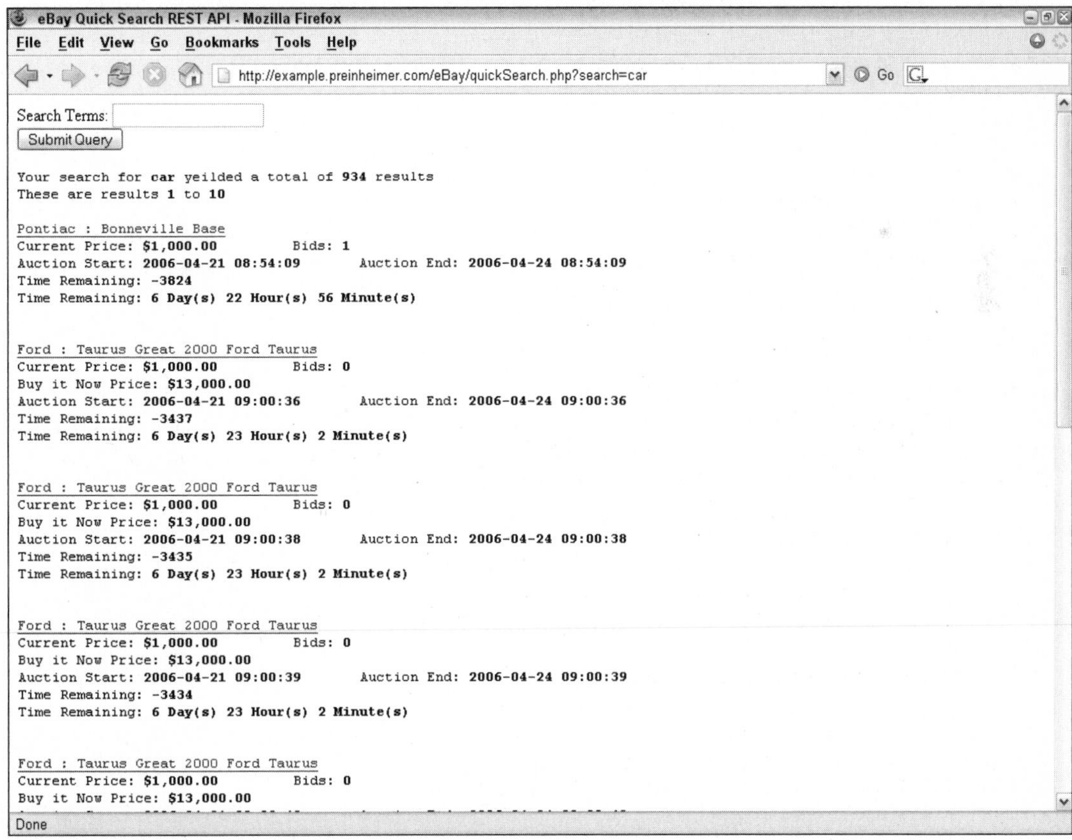

Figure 9-1

SOAP

eBay's SOAP interface is simply massive. The WSDL document alone weighs in at a hefty 1.4MB, and the documentation PDF weighs in at a terrifying 1,209 pages! It's a lot to get your head around. Luckily, the requests examined here are not too complex, and should serve as a great foundation for your applications. Unfortunately, eBay and NuSOAP do not presently work well together (beyond the HTTPS requirements), so requests will be generated manually, rather than using the NuSOAP framework.

Unlike the majority of SOAP APIs, eBay requires information to be sent in the HTTP header as well as within the request itself. The presence of these headers allows eBay to route requests internally to different servers depending on the type of request.

Hello World

The eBay SOAP equivalent of the Hello World program is obtaining official eBay time. This request isn't entirely trivial because all SOAP requests are sent over HTTPS, and as such, cURL will need to be used to perform the request. Additionally, there are a number of required HTTP headers for eBay SOAP requests.

General SOAP Caller

```
function calleBay($callName, $request, $returnRAW = FALSE)
{
  global $appID, $version, $endPoint;
  $requestURL = "$endPoint?callname=$callName&appid=$appID
    &version=$version&routing=default";
  $length = strlen($request);
  $headers = array();
  $headers[] = 'SOAPAction: ""';
  $headers[] = "Content-Type: text/xml";
  $headers[] = "Content-Length: $length";
```

As mentioned earlier, several of the request parameters will be passed in the GET line, and the endpoint for the request is generated, including the name request being made and some specifics about the application making the request.

```
  $ch = curl_init();
  curl_setopt($ch, CURLOPT_URL, $requestURL);
  curl_setopt($ch, CURLOPT_HEADER, false);
  curl_setopt($ch, CURLOPT_HTTPHEADER, $headers);
  curl_setopt($ch, CURLOPT_POST, true);
  curl_setopt($ch, CURLOPT_POSTFIELDS, $request);
  curl_setopt($ch, CURLOPT_RETURNTRANSFER, true);
  curl_setopt($ch, CURLOPT_SSL_VERIFYHOST, false);
  curl_setopt($ch, CURLOPT_SSL_VERIFYPEER, false);
  $data = curl_exec($ch);
  curl_close($ch);
  if ($returnRAW == TRUE)
  {
    return $data;
  }else
```

```
    {
      $xml = simplexml_load_string($data);
      $newXML = $xml->children('http://schemas.xmlsoap.org/soap/envelope/')->
        children('urn:ebay:apis:eBLBaseComponents');
      return $newXML;
    }
  }
```

The function will optionally return the raw response in plain text (very useful when making a new call for the first time) or the relevant portion of the response as a SimpleXML object (the namespaces are discussed in the next section).

The `cURL` options used in the request are as follows:

- `CURLOPT_URL` — This sets the endpoint for the call.
- `CURLOPT_HEADER` — Binary value, indicating you want the headers from the response returned (true), or indicating you do not (false).
- `CURLOPT_HTTPHEADER` — Allows specific HTTP headers to be set using an array.
- `CURLOPT_POST` — Binary value, indicating whether POST values will be sent (true) or will not be present (false).
- `CURLOPT_POSTFEILDS` — Allows the POST string to be set.
- `CURLOPT_RETURNTRANSFER` — Binary value, indicating whether the response should be returned (true) or sent directly to the browser (false).
- `CURLOPT_SSL_VERIFYHOST` — Instructs `libcurl` not to verify the host.
- `CURLOPT_SSL_VERIFYPEER` — Instructs `libcurl` not to verify the certificate's authentication chain.

Hard-Coded getTime Request

A lot was introduced with the generic caller, so in an attempt to keep this "simple" example simple, a hard-coded request will be used:

```
function getSimpleTime()
{
  global $version, $devID, $appID, $cert, $token;
  $call = "GeteBayOfficialTime";
  $message = <<< XMLBLOCK
<?xml version="1.0" encoding="utf-8"?>
<soapenv:Envelope xmlns:soapenv="http://schemas.xmlsoap.org/soap/envelope/"
    xmlns:xsd="http://www.w3.org/2001/XMLSchema"
    xmlns:xsi="http://www.w3.org/2001/XMLSchema-instance">
  <soapenv:Header>
    <RequesterCredentials soapenv:mustUnderstand="0"
         xmlns="urn:ebay:apis:eBLBaseComponents">
       <eBayAuthToken>$token</eBayAuthToken>
       <ns:Credentials xmlns:ns="urn:ebay:apis:eBLBaseComponents">
        <ns:DevId>$devID</ns:DevId>
```

```
        <ns:AppId>$appID</ns:AppId>
        <ns:AuthCert>$cert</ns:AuthCert>
       </ns:Credentials>
    </RequesterCredentials>
  </soapenv:Header>
  <soapenv:Body>
  <GeteBayOfficialTimeRequest xmlns="urn:ebay:apis:eBLBaseComponents">
  <ns1:Version xmlns:ns1="urn:ebay:apis:eBLBaseComponents">$version</ns1:Version>
  </GeteBayOfficialTimeRequest>
  </soapenv:Body>
</soapenv:Envelope>
XMLBLOCK;
  $RAWxml = calleBay($call, $message, TRUE);
  $xml = simplexml_load_string($RAWxml);

  print_r($xml);
  echo "Time: " . $xml->children('http://schemas.xmlsoap.org/soap/envelope/')
    ->children('urn:ebay:apis:eBLBaseComponents')->GeteBayOfficialTimeResponse
    ->Timestamp . "\n";
}
```

The output should look something like this:

```
<soapenv:Envelope xmlns:soapenv="http://schemas.xmlsoap.org/soap/envelope/"
  xmlns:xsd="http://www.w3.org/2001/XMLSchema"
  xmlns:xsi="http://www.w3.org/2001/XMLSchema-instance">
 <soapenv:Body>
  <GeteBayOfficialTimeResponse xmlns="urn:ebay:apis:eBLBaseComponents">
   <Timestamp>2005-11-02T03:57:39.309Z</Timestamp>
   <Ack>Success</Ack>
   <Version>429</Version>
   <Build>e429_intl_Bundled_1949355_R1</Build>
  </GeteBayOfficialTimeResponse>
 </soapenv:Body>
</soapenv:Envelope>

SimpleXMLElement Object
(
  [Body] => SimpleXMLElement Object
  (
    [GeteBayOfficialTimeResponse] => SimpleXMLElement Object
    (
      [Timestamp] => 2005-11-02T03:54:05.481Z
      [Ack] => Success
      [Version] => 429
      [Build] => e429_intl_Bundled_1949355_R1
    )
  )
)
Time: 2005-11-02T03:54:05.481Z
```

I've decided to list all three versions of the output here (raw, `SimpleXML`, and desired) to point out that namespaces is one of those places where `SimpleXML` turns out to be not quite so simple. The basic

`SimpleXML` tree shown matches the raw XML rather nicely (ignoring the namespaces), but once it becomes time to access those elements, you need to start worrying about those namespaces again. It's important to remember that when dealing with namespaces, `SimpleXML` needs the URI for the namespace, not the name used.

Simplifying Requests

A pair of basic functions can be used to automate request generation and save you the problems of manually coding each new request. Generating the body of the request separately from the envelope portion is done for two reasons: simplicity, and to allow for manual generation of either should the situation warrant it.

Generating the Body of a Request

```
function generateBody($callName, $attributes)
{
  $body = "<soapenv:Body>\n";
  $body .= "<{$callName}Request xmlns=\"urn:ebay:apis:eBLBaseComponents\">\n";
  foreach ($attributes AS $key => $value)
  {
    $body .= "<ns1:$key xmlns:ns1=\"urn:ebay:apis:eBLBaseComponents\">
      $value</ns1:$key>\n";
  }
  $body .= "</{$callName}Request>\n";
  $body .= "</soapenv:Body>";
  return $body;
}
```

The name of the call is suffixed with `Request` to satisfy the formatting requirements of the SOAP document. The suffix is added here rather than simply being required in the `$callName` variable to allow the same variable to be used here and as a `GET` parameter. `Attributes` is an associative array containing all of the parameters the request requires; it is iterated through and added to the body of the request.

Completing the Request

```
function generateRequest($body)
{
  global $version, $endPoint, $devID, $appID, $cert, $token;
   $request = <<< XMLBLOCK
<?xml version="1.0" encoding="utf-8"?>
<soapenv:Envelope xmlns:soapenv="http://schemas.xmlsoap.org/soap/envelope/"
  xmlns:xsd="http://www.w3.org/2001/XMLSchema"
  xmlns:xsi="http://www.w3.org/2001/XMLSchema-instance">
  <soapenv:Header>
    <RequesterCredentials soapenv:mustUnderstand="0"
      xmlns="urn:ebay:apis:eBLBaseComponents">
      <eBayAuthToken>$token</eBayAuthToken>
        <ns:Credentials xmlns:ns="urn:ebay:apis:eBLBaseComponents">
        <ns:DevId>$devID</ns:DevId>
        <ns:AppId>$appID</ns:AppId>
        <ns:AuthCert>$cert</ns:AuthCert>
      </ns:Credentials>
    </RequesterCredentials>
```

```
    </soapenv:Header>
    $body
  </soapenv:Envelope>
  XMLBLOCK;
    return $request;
  }
```

Simplified getTime Request

Using the newly created functions, you can now request the time from eBay very easily:

```
function newGetTime()
{
  $call = "GeteBayOfficialTime";
  $queryInfo = array();
  $queryInfo["Version"] = 425;
  $myRequest = generateBody($call, $queryInfo);
  $message = generateRequest($myRequest);
  $xml =  calleBay($call, $message, FALSE);
  echo "Time: " . $xml->GeteBayOfficialTimeResponse->Timestamp . "\n";
}
```

Browsing the eBay Categories

For easy browsing, eBay's extensive auctions are divided into numerous categories and subcategories, and sub-subcategories to the nth degree. This makes things really easy when using the regular eBay websites, but it can make things a bit more difficult when interacting with the API. In order to properly access the eBay category listings, a few more options for the API need to be introduced.

Category Organization

Categories are organized in a basic tree; there are a few root elements (such as Antiques or Cars) that can contain any number of subcategories (which can contain subcategories of their own, and so on). When retrieving a record for a specific category, you receive only a limited amount of information:

```
<Category>
 <AutoPayEnabled>true</AutoPayEnabled>
 <CategoryID>63561</CategoryID>
 <CategoryLevel>3</CategoryLevel>
 <CategoryName>Cabinets, Armoires, Cupboards</CategoryName>
 <CategoryParentID>20091</CategoryParentID>
 <Expired>false</Expired>
 <IntlAutosFixedCat>false</IntlAutosFixedCat>
 <LeafCategory>false</LeafCategory>
 <Virtual>false</Virtual>
 <LSD>false</LSD>
 <ORPA>false</ORPA>
 <BestOfferEnabled>true</BestOfferEnabled>
</Category>
```

In terms of organization, there are five relevant fields: `CategoryID`, `CategoryLevel`, `CategoryParentID`, and `LeafCategory`. `CategoryID` , and `CategoryName` are the unique identifiers for the category, and every category has one. `CategoryLevel` indicates the depth of the category in the tree. `CategoryParentID` is (surprisingly enough) the ID of the category's parent. Finally, `LeafCategory` is a boolean value indicating whether this category is a leaf (leafs have no children).

When making a `getCategory` request, you can optionally specify the maximum depth (`LevelLimit`) you want to retrieve categories from. This is always relative to the root of the hierarchy, not the category you are requesting information for.

> *For categories with a Level of 1,* `CategoryID` *will equal* `CategoryParentID`. *The root level is not considered a parent.*

Detail Level

Many eBay requests allow you to specify a detail level with the request. This value can be used to either request all available information pertaining to your request, or only a limited subset of that information. This is quite useful when (for example) attempting to determine if the local cached copy of eBay's category hierarchy is up to date. By specifying a low detail level (or specifying no detail level at all) in the request, eBay will return only basic version information about the current category hierarchy. If that information matches the local cache, it can be used safely. If not, the same request will be repeated, changing only the detail level to request all available information.

This may sound silly; just keep in mind how massive some of the responses eBay may return are. The full detail response to a request for the full category hierarchy is (at print time) 8.7MB. Requesting that much information on every page load as a user navigates eBay's categories is not only a horrible waste, but a huge performance hit.

Site ID

This refers to a specific site within the eBay network. This information is only required when making a request applicable to a site other than the one the request is actually being made against. For example, if you are using the US API endpoint, and want the category information for the Canadian site, you would need to specify a site ID.

Your options are as follows:

- 0–US
- 2–Canada
- 3–United Kingdom
- 15–Australia
- 16–Austria
- 71–France
- 77–Germany
- 101–Italy
- 104–Japan

- 146–Netherlands
- 193–Switzerland
- 196–Taiwan
- 123–Belgium NL
- 23–Belgium FR

Retrieving the Categories

Retrieving the categories using the code presented previously is pretty easy; however, because the full response for the `getCategories` request is so long, some caching will need to be implemented. The function will optionally accept a single parameter indicating the category for which the children should be retrieved, or just the root of the listings. The `getCategories` request returns by default only basic information about the hierarchy. You need to include a `DetailLevel` attribute in your request (with a value such as `ReturnAll`) to obtain the desired information.

```
function getCategories($parent = -1)
{
  $call = "GetCategories";
  $attributes = array();
  $attributes['Version'] = 425;
  $attributes['CategorySiteID'] = 0;

  if ($parent != -1)
  {
    $attributes['CategoryParent'] = $parent;
  }else
  {
    $attributes['LevelLimit'] = 1;
  }
```

If a specific category was requested, the `CategoryParent` element is added to the request; otherwise, `LevelLimit` is capped at 1 to keep the request size down. Notice that for all other categories the full depth will be returned.

```
  $myRequest = generateBody($call, $attributes);
  $message = generateRequest($myRequest);
  $breifXML = simplexml_load_string(calleBay($call, $message, TRUE));
  $lastUpdated = $parent . "." . $breifXML->
    children('http://schemas.xmlsoap.org/soap/envelope/')->
    children('urn:ebay:apis:eBLBaseComponents')->GetCategoriesResponse->
    UpdateTime . ".xml";
```

A request is made without specifying a detail level, so eBay returns only very basic information about the current category hierarchy (version, timestamp for last update). This timestamp is used to generate a filename for caching purposes.

```
  if (file_exists("/eBayCatCache/$lastUpdated"))
  {
    echo "<!-- CACHE -->\n";
    $xml = simplexml_load_file("/tmp/$lastUpdated");
```

If the file exists, load it into a `SimpleXML` object and continue.

```
    }else
    {
      echo "<!-- NEW -->\n";
      $attributes['DetailLevel'] = 'ReturnAll';
      $myRequest = generateBody($call, $attributes);
      $message = generateRequest($myRequest);
      $xml = calleBay($call, $message, TRUE);
      file_put_contents("/tmp/$lastUpdated", $xml);
      $xml = simplexml_load_string($xml);
    }
```

Otherwise, add the `DetailLevel` attribute to the request to obtain full category information. Note that the `calleBay()` function is called requesting raw output (a string containing the response, rather than a `SimpleXML` object). This is done so that the entire request may be saved to disk.

```
    $xml = $xml->children('http://schemas.xmlsoap.org/soap/envelope/')-
  >children('urn:ebay:apis:eBLBaseComponents');
    return $xml;
  }
```

Finally, the relevant portion of the `SimpleXML` object is returned. The object returned when passed 37903 as parent is shown here:

```
SimpleXMLElement Object
(
  [Timestamp] => 2005-11-07T04:26:24.166Z
  [Ack] => Success
  [Version] => 429
  [Build] => e429_intl_Bundled_1949355_R1
  [CategoryArray] => SimpleXMLElement Object
  (
    [Category] => Array
    (
      [0] => SimpleXMLElement Object
      (
        [AutoPayEnabled] => true
        [CategoryID] => 37903
        [CategoryLevel] => 2
        [CategoryName] => Antiquities (Classical, Amer.)
        [CategoryParentID] => 20081
        [Expired] => false
        [IntlAutosFixedCat] => false
        [LeafCategory] => false
        [Virtual] => false
        [LSD] => false
        [ORPA] => false
        [BestOfferEnabled] => true
      )
      ...
```

```
        [5] => SimpleXMLElement Object
        (
          [AutoPayEnabled] => true
          [CategoryID] => 73464
          [CategoryLevel] => 3
          [CategoryName] => Other
          [CategoryParentID] => 37903
          [Expired] => false
          [IntlAutosFixedCat] => false
          [LeafCategory] => true
          [Virtual] => false
          [LSD] => false
          [ORPA] => false
          [BestOfferEnabled] => true
        )
      )
    )
    [CategoryCount] => 6
    [UpdateTime] => 2005-10-11T02:59:22.000Z
    [CategoryVersion] => 56
    [ReservePriceInclusive] => false
    [MinimumReservePrice] => 0.0
    [ReduceReserveInclusive] => true
)
```

Notice that category `37903` is included in the response; eBay includes the category you request along with its children as part of the response.

Displaying the Categories

Using the previous function, the categories can be displayed to the screen in an easily navigated format:

```
function displayCategoryListings($parent = -1)
{
 $xml = getCategories($parent);
 foreach($xml->GetCategoriesResponse->CategoryArray->Category AS $category)
 {
   if ($category->CategoryID == $parent)
   {
     if ($category->CategoryLevel == 1)
     {
      echo "<h3>{$category->CategoryName}</h3>";
      echo "(<a href=\"?\">Return to parent</a>)\n\n";
     }else
     {
       echo "<h3>{$category->CategoryName}</h3>";
       echo "(<a href=\"?loadCat={$category->CategoryParentID}\">Return to parent
         </a>)\n";
     }
```

After obtaining the relevant XML using the `getCategories()` function presented earlier, the resulting categories are iterated through. Because the response includes the category in question, it must be treated as a special case. If this category is a top-tier category, the link to return to the parent will not specify a parent (to obtain the root level items); otherwise the link will go to the specified parent.

```
      }else
      {
        if ($category->CategoryParentID == $parent || $parent == -1)
        {
          if ($category->LeafCategory == "true")
          {
            echo "<span class=\"catTitle\">{$category->CategoryName}</span>
              (<a href=\"?listCategory={$category->CategoryID}\"
              class=\"viewItems\">view items</a>)\n";
          }else
          {
            echo "<a href=\"?loadCat={$category->CategoryID}\" class=\"catTitle\">
           {$category->CategoryName}</a> (<a href=\"?listCategory=
           {$category->CategoryID}\" class=\"viewItems\">view items</a>) \n";
          }
        }
      }
    }
  }
```

For the remaining categories, there are two options: either the category is a leaf (has no children), in which case it will not be presented as a link, or a link is provided to view that category's children. In either case, a link is provided to view listings in that category (the code for which is presented next).

Figure 9-2 shows Category listings for eBay.

Retrieving Items for Sale in a Category

Unlike the category hierarchy, the items for sale in a specific category are constantly changing, more so on the live system than the sandbox, but while it's a large amount of data, it's not a good candidate for caching. As such, a second function to handle caching isn't needed, there's enough. abstraction with the functions that are needed already.

```
function getCategoryListings($category)
{
  $call = "GetCategoryListings";
  $attributes = array();
  $attributes['Version'] = 425;
  $attributes['CategoryID'] = $category;
  $myRequest = generateBody($call, $attributes);
  $message = generateRequest($myRequest);
  $xml = calleBay($call, $message, FALSE);
  echo "<h3>Listings in {$xml->GetCategoryListingsResponse->Category->
    CategoryName}</h3>\n";
  $parentID = getCategoryID($xml->GetCategoryListingsResponse->Category->
    CategoryID);
  echo "Return to <a href=\"?loadCat={$parentID}\">Categories</a> Listing\n";
```

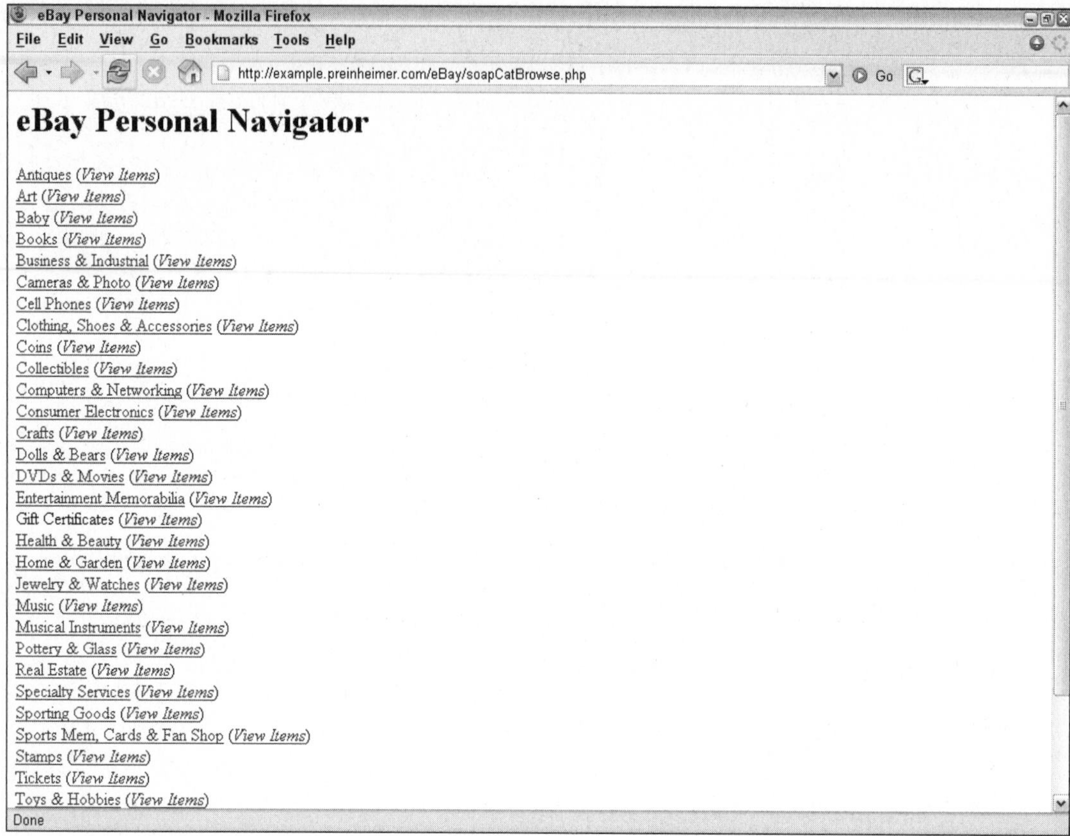

Figure 9-2

Generate the request and print the basic category information.

```
if (isset($xml->GetCategoryListingsResponse->ItemArray->Item))
{
  foreach($xml->GetCategoryListingsResponse->ItemArray->Item AS $item)
  {
    echo "<a href=\"?{$item->ItemID}\">{$item->Title}</a> currently has a high
      bid of $ {$item->SellingStatus->CurrentPrice} after a total of {$item->
      SellingStatus->BidCount} bids\n";
  }
}else
{
  echo "No listings, Sorry\n";
}
```

Some items (particularly in the sandbox environment) don't have any listings, so this is handled gracefully. Otherwise the items available are iterated through with basic information.

```
    if (isset($xml->GetCategoryListingsResponse->SubCategories->Category))
    {
      echo "<h3>Sub-Categories</h3>";
      foreach($xml->GetCategoryListingsResponse->SubCategories->Category AS
        $category)
      {
         echo "<a href=\"?listCategory={$category->CategoryID}\">{$category->
         CategoryName}</a> has {$category->NumOfItems} items listed\n";
      }
    }
  }
```

Finally, with the `GetCategoryListings` call, subcategories are returned with basic information about the listings available within. If these subcategories are present within the response, they are iterated through, with links provided. Figure 9-3 shows Listings within a category.

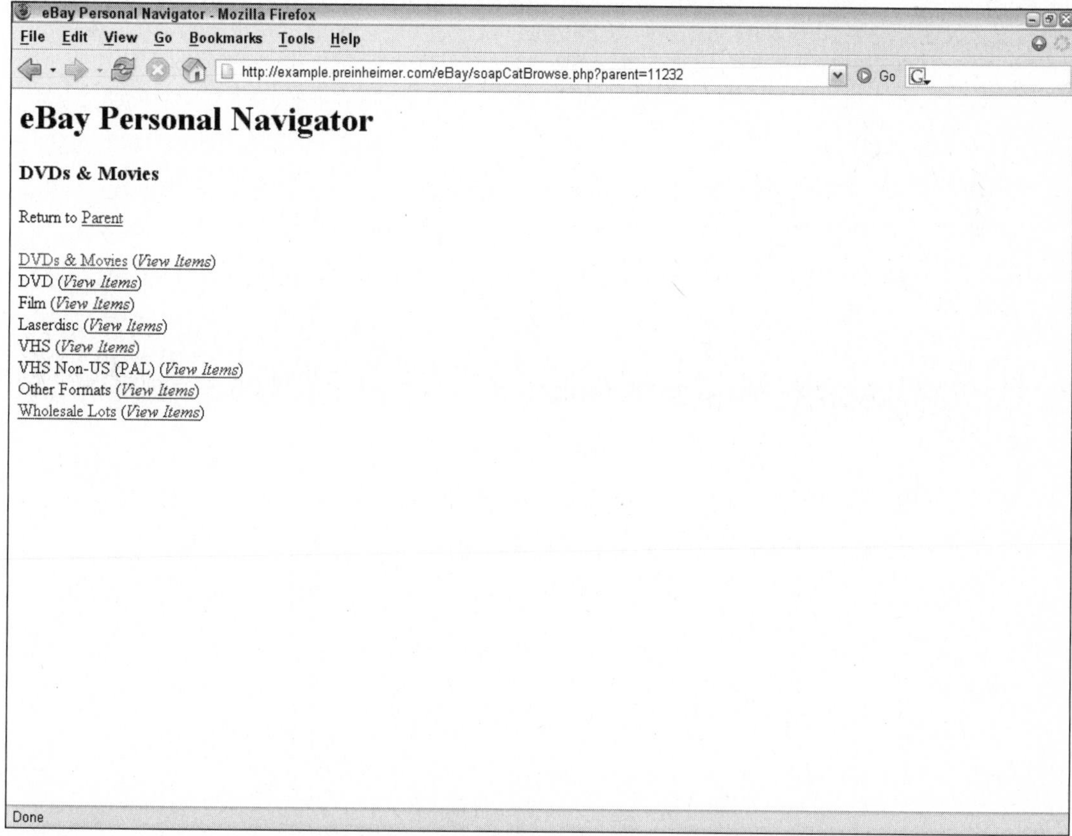

Figure 9-3

Searching eBay

Browsing categories is all well and good, but with the depth of categories and sheer number of listings on the live sites, searching will likely become a necessity.

Basic Search

Using the basic query interface with the functions already defined is a simple matter of substitution:

```
function doBasicSearch($query)
{
  $call = "GetSearchResults";
  $attributes = array();
  $attributes['Version'] = 425;
  $attributes['Query'] = $query;
  $myRequest = generateBody($call, $attributes);
  $message = generateRequest($myRequest);
  $xml = calleBay($call, $message, FALSE);
```

Here the basics of the call are set up, and the call itself is generated. As you can see, the name of the call is `GetSearchResults`, and it requires a single attribute `Query` specifying the user's search query.

```
  echo "<div class=\"resultHeading\">";
  echo "<span class=\"resultHeader\">Search Results for: $query</span>";
  echo "</div>";
  if ($xml->GetSearchResultsResponse->PaginationResult->TotalNumberOfEntries == 0)
  {
    echo "Sorry, there are no results to display";
  }else
  {
```

The heading information is displayed, and the zero result case is handled.

```
    foreach($xml->GetSearchResultsResponse->SearchResultItemArray->SearchResultItem
    AS $searchResult)
    {
      $results = array();
      foreach($xml->GetSearchResultsResponse->SearchResultItemArray->
        SearchResultItem AS $searchResult)
      {
        $results[] = $searchResult->Item;
      }
      displayItems($results);
    }
  }
}
```

Unfortunately, things don't go quite as smoothly here as one might hope. The problem is how eBay encapsulates its return information for different calls. When you perform a `GetCategoryListings` request, the items are available in `$xml->GetCategoryListingsResponse->ItemArray->Item`, which is easy to handle. However, the `GetSearchResults` request presents the array at `$xml->GetSearchResultsResponse->SearchResultItemArray->SearchResultItem`, and each item is then stored within an `Item` element. This leaves two choices: Either the display function must be written to handle a variety of inputs, or a temporary variable needs to be used (in this case, `GetCategoryListings` is fine) to present information to the display function in a consistent manner. I've chosen the latter, because it allows me to keep the display functions cleaner, hopefully allowing for a cleaner separation of business and presentation logic.

Figure 9-4 shows a Basic Search for DVD.

Searching Within a Category

From a coding standpoint, searching within a category is trivial; you merely add an additional parameter to the request, and display results in much the same manner. The difficulty stems from presenting this to the user in a coherent manner. Simply presenting a drop-down containing all available categories to the user and asking them to select one would be pointless, because there's simply too many for that to be useful. The obvious method, which is the method presented here and is similar to the one used on eBay itself, is to allow users to search within a category once they have navigated there via the category listings. Though this is slightly less powerful than some alternatives, it is very user friendly.

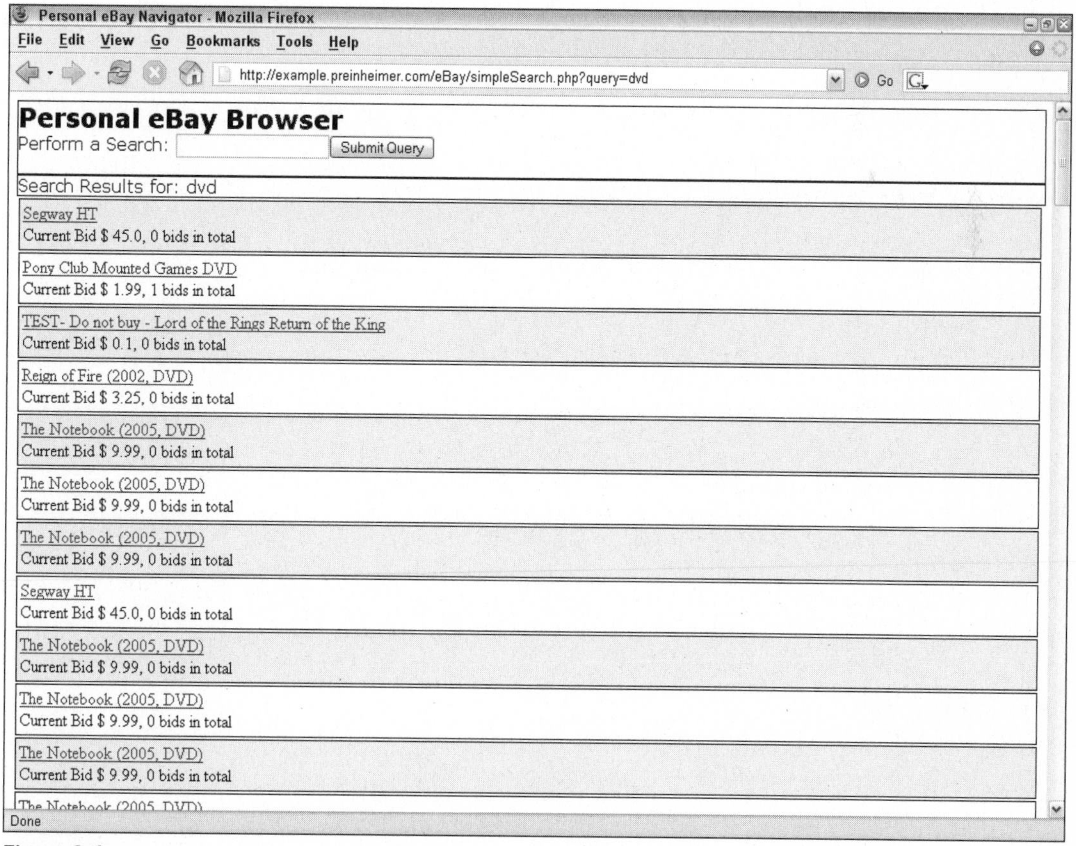

Figure 9-4

In order to implement this searching method, a small addition must be made to the Category listing function to allow the user to enter a search query:

```
function displayCategoryListings($parent = -1)
{
 $xml = getCategories($parent);
 if ($parent != -1)
 {
   echo "<div class=\"resultHeading\">";
   echo '<span class=\"resultHeader\">Search this Category: <form method="get">
     <input type="hidden" name="categoryname" value=""><input type="text"
     name="query"><input type="submit"></span>';
   echo "</div>";
 }
 foreach($xml->GetCategoriesResponse->CategoryArray->Category AS $category)
 {
```

This is just a basic form. The comparison to `$parent` is done to avoid displaying this limited search while the user is viewing the root category listings (which would be redundant and confusing).

The search function itself is quite similar to the function seen previously:

```
function doCategorySearch($query, $category)
{
  $call = "GetSearchResults";
  $attributes = array();
  $attributes['Version'] = 425;
  $attributes['Query'] = $query;
  $attributes['CategoryID'] = $category;
  $myRequest = generateBody($call, $attributes);
  $message = generateRequest($myRequest);
  $xml =  calleBay($call, $message, FALSE);
  echo "<div class=\"resultHeading\">";
  echo "<span class=\"resultHeader\">Search Results for: $query</span>";
  echo "</div>";
  if ($xml->GetSearchResultsResponse->PaginationResult->TotalNumberOfEntries == 0)
  {
    echo "Sorry, there are no results to display, <a href=\"?query=$query\">Search
      all of eBay</a>";
  }else
  {
    $results = array();
    foreach($xml->GetSearchResultsResponse->SearchResultItemArray->SearchResultItem
      AS $searchResult)
    {
      $results[] = $searchResult->Item;
    }
    displayItems($results);
  }
}
```

As you can see, the only changes are the addition of the `CategoryID` attribute and the addition of the user-friendly option to extend the search when no results are obtained.

Figure 9-5 shows a category search with results.

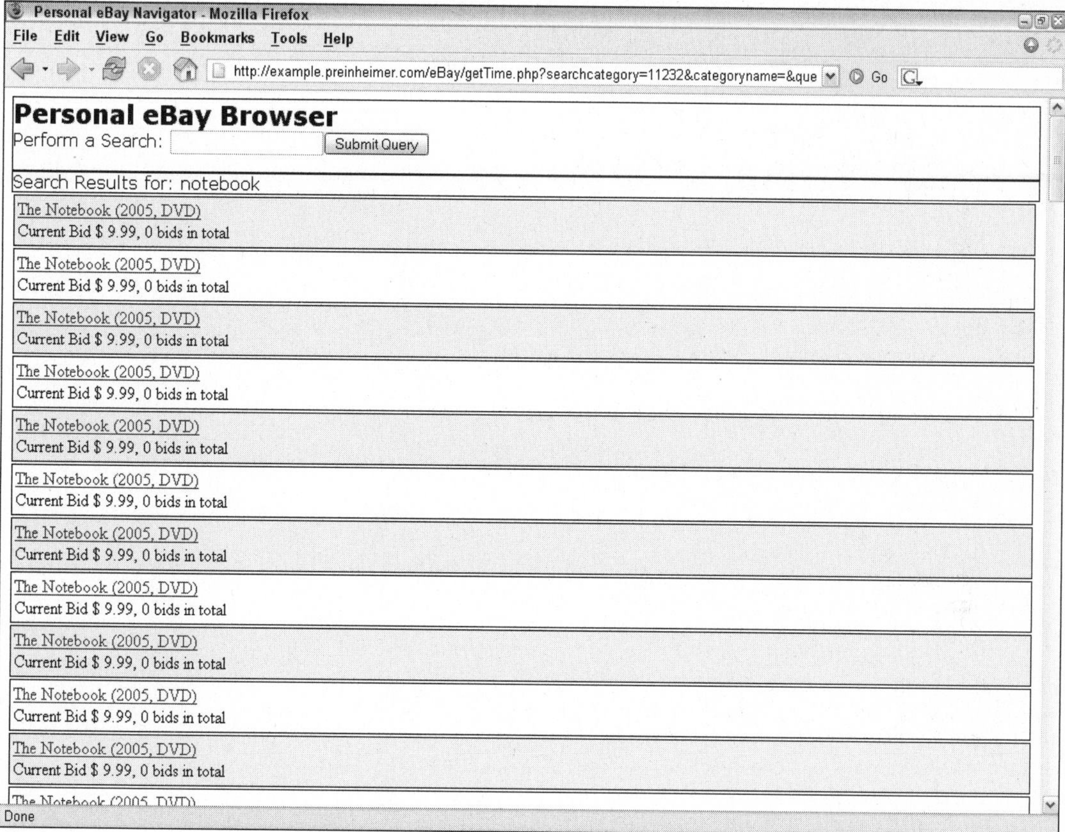

Figure 9-5

Figure 9-6 shows a category search with zero results.

Putting Items up for Auction

Listing items on eBay requires making a call more complex than the ones introduced thus far; multiple levels of nested elements are required to make even the most basic listing. As such, `generateBody()` will finally receive some improvements. Also, remember that you must use a Sellers account when listing items; otherwise the API will return an error.

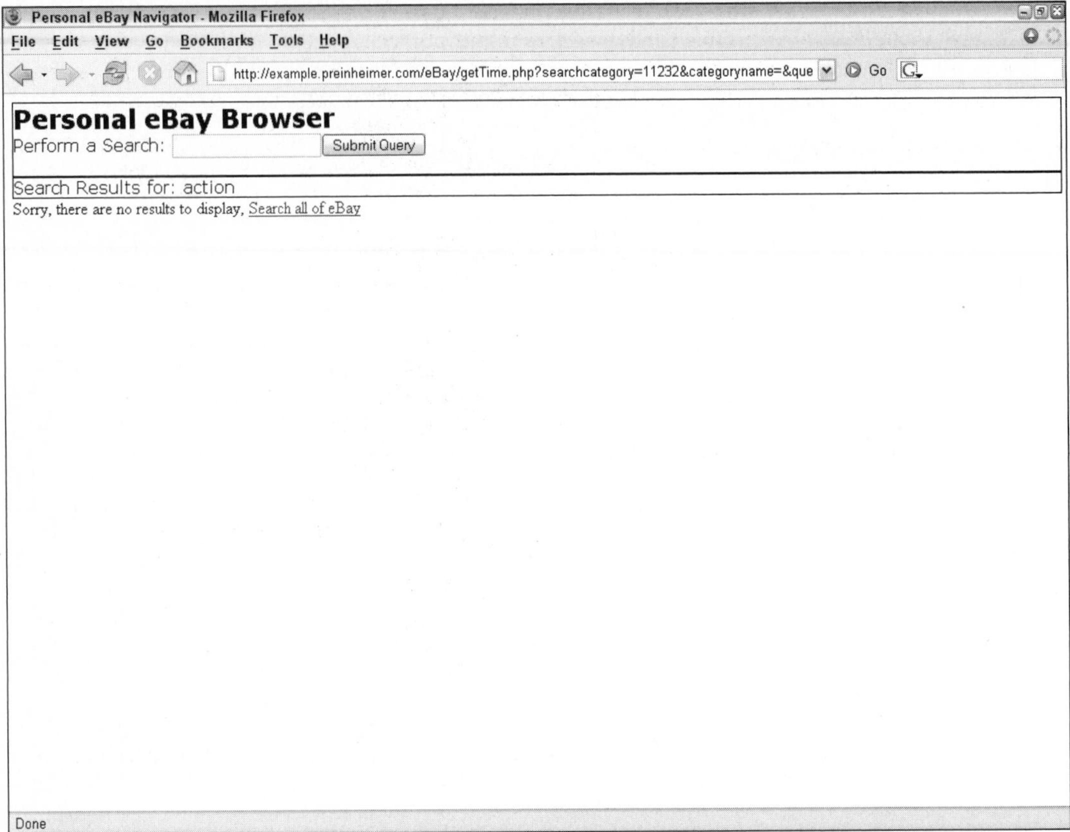

Figure 9-6

Improving generateBody()

To handle nested elements, the function will need to be refactored to function recursively.

In order to pass elements that will need to be nested, the calling function will declare them, something like this:

```
$queryInfo = array();
$queryInfo["Version"] = 425;
$queryInfo["Item"] = array();
$queryInfo["Item"]["Country"] = "CA";
$queryInfo["Item"]["PrimaryCategory"] = array();
$queryInfo["Item"]["PrimaryCategory"]["CategoryID"] = "23";
$queryInfo["Item"]["Quantity"] = 1;
```

As you can see, upper-level elements are still defined as normal. When nesting must occur, the item is declared as an array, and elements are added. This example demonstrates several levels of nesting.

For the function itself, I've introduced an additional parameter, `$depth`. This serves two purposes: First, it allows the function to determine if it is generating the outermost portions of the request (and encapsulate accordingly), and second, it allows the code to indent the request properly. The function also adds an `is_array()` check to the loop, making the recursive call when an array is located.

```
function advGenerateBody($callName, $attributes, $depth = 0)
{
  $body = "";
  $prefix = str_repeat("\t", $depth);
  if ($depth == 0)
  {
    $body .= "<soapenv:Body>\n";
    $body .= "<{$callName}Request xmlns=\"urn:ebay:apis:eBLBaseComponents\">\n";
  }
  foreach ($attributes AS $key => $value)
  {
    if (is_array($value))
    {
      $body .=$prefix."<ns1:$key xmlns:ns1=\"urn:ebay:apis:eBLBaseComponents\">\n";
      $body .= $prefix . advGenerateBody($callName, $value, ($depth + 1));
      $body .= $prefix . "</ns1:$key>\n";
```

When an array element is located, it indicates nesting, and the recursive call is made. Depth is incremented both to avoid duplicating the outer elements and to ensure proper indentation.

```
    }else
    {
      $body .=$prefix."<ns1:$key xmlns:ns1=\"urn:ebay:apis:eBLBaseComponents\">
        $value</ns1:$key>\n";
    }
  }
  if ($depth == 0)
  {
    $body .= "</{$callName}Request>\n";
    $body .= "</soapenv:Body>";
  }
  return $body;
}
```

For reference, the output of the example elements referred to in the preceding code would be as follows:

```
<soapenv:Body>
<AddItemRequest xmlns="urn:ebay:apis:eBLBaseComponents">
<ns1:Version xmlns:ns1="urn:ebay:apis:eBLBaseComponents">425</ns1:Version>
<ns1:Item xmlns:ns1="urn:ebay:apis:eBLBaseComponents">
  <ns1:Country xmlns:ns1="urn:ebay:apis:eBLBaseComponents">CA</ns1:Country>
  <ns1:PrimaryCategory xmlns:ns1="urn:ebay:apis:eBLBaseComponents">
    <ns1:CategoryID xmlns:ns1="urn:ebay:apis:eBLBaseComponents">23</ns1:CategoryID>
  </ns1:PrimaryCategory>
  <ns1:Quantity xmlns:ns1="urn:ebay:apis:eBLBaseComponents">1</ns1:Quantity>
</ns1:Item>
</AddItemRequest>
</soapenv:Body>
```

With this improved function in hand, you're able to make an `addItem` request.

Adding Your First Item

As mentioned previously, listing an item with eBay requires quite a few parameters to be passed along. This is a bare-bones request, containing just enough information to list the item. This call will be hard-coded; subsequent ones will make use of user input. The following table lists the parameters being sent with this request. For more information on specific elements, please see the API documentation.

Name	Format	Description
Version	int	Version of the API being referenced.
Item	Container	Contains all information regarding the item being listed.
Country	String	Two-letter ISO 3166 country code for the current location of the item.
Currency	String	Three-letter representation of the currency of the auction. For example, USD and CAD (US Dollar and Canadian Dollar, respectively).
Title	String	Title of the listing as it will appear in search results and at the top of the listing. Plain text.
Description	String	A detailed description of the item. If you wish to use HTML, encapsulate the content within CDATA.
`ListingDuration`	Token	One of the following: Days_1, Days_3, Days_5, Days_7, Days_10, Days_21, Days_30, Days_60, Days_90, Days_120, GTC. A seller must have a positive feedback of 10 or higher to make a 1-day listing.
Location	String	Indicates the current location of the item, including country. Maximum length 45 characters.
`PaymentMethods`	Token	A token indicating accepted payment methods. Acceptable values include PayPal, AmEx, VisaMC.
`PayPalEmailAddress`	String	Email address of the seller's PayPal account (required if PayPal is an accepted payment type).
`PrimaryCategory`	Container	Container for the `CategoryID`.
`CategoryID`	Int	Contained by `PrimaryCategory`, indicates the primary category for the listing.
Quantity	Int	The number of items being sold.
`StartPrice`	Double	The minimum starting bid for the item.

With that information in mind, the call can actually be made:

```
$call = "AddItem";
$queryInfo = array();
$queryInfo["Version"] = 425;
$queryInfo["Item"] = array();
$queryInfo["Item"]["Country"] = "CA";
$queryInfo["Item"]["Currency"] = "USD";
$queryInfo["Item"]["Title"] = "Simple Test Auction";
$queryInfo["Item"]["Description"] = "Professional Web APIs, The Movie!";
$queryInfo["Item"]["ListingDuration"] = "Days_3";
$queryInfo["Item"]["Location"] = "Windsor, Ontario, Canada";
$queryInfo["Item"]["PaymentMethods"] = "PayPal";
$queryInfo["Item"]["PayPalEmailAddress"] = "reinhei@uwindsor.ca";
$queryInfo["Item"]["PrimaryCategory"] = array();
$queryInfo["Item"]["PrimaryCategory"]["CategoryID"] = "617";
$queryInfo["Item"]["Quantity"] = 1;
$queryInfo["Item"]["StartPrice"] = "9.99";
$myRequest = advGenerateBody($call, $queryInfo);
$message = generateRequest($myRequest);
$xml =  calleBay($call, $message,TRUE);
```

The full request for this call as sent to eBay is (token trimmed):

```
<?xml version="1.0" encoding="utf-8"?>
<soapenv:Envelope xmlns:soapenv="http://schemas.xmlsoap.org/soap/envelope/"
  xmlns:xsd="http://www.w3.org/2001/XMLSchema"
  xmlns:xsi="http://www.w3.org/2001/XMLSchema-instance">
 <soapenv:Header>
   <RequesterCredentials soapenv:mustUnderstand="0"
        xmlns="urn:ebay:apis:eBLBaseComponents">
      <eBayAuthToken>...</eBayAuthToken>
      <ns:Credentials xmlns:ns="urn:ebay:apis:eBLBaseComponents">
       <ns:DevId>C481VH1E49RGK2J21C5H96R143H641</ns:DevId>
       <ns:AppId>WROXP91H134FC2I9R276TB6J6945CT</ns:AppId>
       <ns:AuthCert>P76S15991C6$HFI91JM21-Y7F7V7RD</ns:AuthCert>
      </ns:Credentials>
   </RequesterCredentials>
 </soapenv:Header>
 <soapenv:Body>
<AddItemRequest xmlns="urn:ebay:apis:eBLBaseComponents">
<ns1:Version xmlns:ns1="urn:ebay:apis:eBLBaseComponents">425</ns1:Version>
<ns1:Item xmlns:ns1="urn:ebay:apis:eBLBaseComponents">
 <ns1:Country xmlns:ns1="urn:ebay:apis:eBLBaseComponents">CA</ns1:Country>
 <ns1:Currency xmlns:ns1="urn:ebay:apis:eBLBaseComponents">USD</ns1:Currency>
 <ns1:Title xmlns:ns1="urn:ebay:apis:eBLBaseComponents">Simple Test
  Auction</ns1:Title>
 <ns1:Description xmlns:ns1="urn:ebay:apis:eBLBaseComponents"> Professional Web
  APIs, The Movie!</ns1:Description>
 <ns1:ListingDuration
  xmlns:ns1="urn:ebay:apis:eBLBaseComponents">Days_3</ns1:ListingDuration>
 <ns1:Location xmlns:ns1="urn:ebay:apis:eBLBaseComponents">Windsor, Ontario,
  Canada</ns1:Location>
 <ns1:PaymentMethods
```

```
   xmlns:ns1="urn:ebay:apis:eBLBaseComponents">PayPal</ns1:PaymentMethods>
  <ns1:PayPalEmailAddress xmlns:ns1="urn:ebay:apis:eBLBaseComponents">
   example@example.com</ns1:PayPalEmailAddress>
  <ns1:PrimaryCategory xmlns:ns1="urn:ebay:apis:eBLBaseComponents">
    <ns1:CategoryID
xmlns:ns1="urn:ebay:apis:eBLBaseComponents">617</ns1:CategoryID>
  </ns1:PrimaryCategory>
  <ns1:Quantity xmlns:ns1="urn:ebay:apis:eBLBaseComponents">1</ns1:Quantity>
  <ns1:StartPrice xmlns:ns1="urn:ebay:apis:eBLBaseComponents">9.99</ns1:StartPrice>
</ns1:Item>
</AddItemRequest>
</soapenv:Body>
</soapenv:Envelope>
```

The associated response is quite lengthy:

```
<?xml version="1.0" encoding="UTF-8"?>
<soapenv:Envelope xmlns:soapenv="http://schemas.xmlsoap.org/soap/envelope/"
xmlns:xsd="http://www.w3.org/2001/XMLSchema"
xmlns:xsi="http://www.w3.org/2001/XMLSchema-instance">
 <soapenv:Body>
  <AddItemResponse xmlns="urn:ebay:apis:eBLBaseComponents">
   <Timestamp>2006-01-11T05:10:04.066Z</Timestamp>
   <Ack>Success</Ack>
   <Version>439</Version>
   <Build>e439_intl_Bundled_2267338_R1</Build>
   <ItemID>4504419255</ItemID>
   <StartTime>2006-01-11T05:10:02.644Z</StartTime>
   <EndTime>2006-01-14T05:10:02.644Z</EndTime>
   <Fees>
    <Fee>
     <Name>AuctionLengthFee</Name>
     <Fee currencyID="USD">0.0</Fee>
    </Fee>
    <Fee>
     <Name>BoldFee</Name>
     <Fee currencyID="USD">0.0</Fee>
    </Fee>
    <Fee>
     <Name>BuyItNowFee</Name>
     <Fee currencyID="USD">0.0</Fee>
    </Fee>
    <Fee>
     <Name>CategoryFeaturedFee</Name>
     <Fee currencyID="USD">0.0</Fee>
    </Fee>
    <Fee>
     <Name>FeaturedFee</Name>
     <Fee currencyID="USD">0.0</Fee>
    </Fee>
    <Fee>
     <Name>FeaturedGalleryFee</Name>
     <Fee currencyID="USD">0.0</Fee>
```

```
  </Fee>
  <Fee>
   <Name>FixedPriceDurationFee</Name>
   <Fee currencyID="USD">0.0</Fee>
  </Fee>
  <Fee>
   <Name>GalleryFee</Name>
   <Fee currencyID="USD">0.0</Fee>
  </Fee>
  <Fee>
   <Name>GiftIconFee</Name>
   <Fee currencyID="USD">0.0</Fee>
  </Fee>
  <Fee>
   <Name>HighLightFee</Name>
   <Fee currencyID="USD">0.0</Fee>
  </Fee>
  <Fee>
   <Name>InsertionFee</Name>
   <Fee currencyID="USD">0.35</Fee>
  </Fee>
  <Fee>
   <Name>InternationalInsertionFee</Name>
   <Fee currencyID="USD">0.0</Fee>
  </Fee>
  <Fee>
   <Name>ListingDesignerFee</Name>
   <Fee currencyID="USD">0.0</Fee>
  </Fee>
  <Fee>
   <Name>ListingFee</Name>
   <Fee currencyID="USD">0.35</Fee>
  </Fee>
  <Fee>
   <Name>PhotoDisplayFee</Name>
   <Fee currencyID="USD">0.0</Fee>
  </Fee>
  <Fee>
   <Name>PhotoFee</Name>
   <Fee currencyID="USD">0.0</Fee>
  </Fee>
  <Fee>
   <Name>ReserveFee</Name>
   <Fee currencyID="USD">0.0</Fee>
  </Fee>
  <Fee>
   <Name>SchedulingFee</Name>
   <Fee currencyID="USD">0.0</Fee>
  </Fee>
  <Fee>
   <Name>SubtitleFee</Name>
   <Fee currencyID="USD">0.0</Fee>
  </Fee>
  <Fee>
```

```
        <Name>BorderFee</Name>
        <Fee currencyID="USD">0.0</Fee>
      </Fee>
      <Fee>
        <Name>ProPackBundleFee</Name>
        <Fee currencyID="USD">0.0</Fee>
      </Fee>
    </Fees>
  </AddItemResponse>
 </soapenv:Body>
</soapenv:Envelope>
```

The key pieces of information in that response are the `ACK`, `ItemID`, `StartTime`, `EndTime`, and the non-zero fees. The `ACK` is important because it identifies that the listing was successful, and the item has been listed with eBay with an ID of `ItemID`. `StartTime` and `EndTime` should likely be presented to the users for their records. Finally, the fees — first, it's important to note that these are not the final fees associated with listing an item; eBay charges a fee in relation to the final selling price of the item, which can't be determined at list time. Second, because of how many different fees there are, I would recommend simply iterating through them, and presenting the end users with an itemized (and totaled) list of the fees associated with their listing.

If you want to present the user with estimated listing fees before actually listing the item, a `VerifyAddItem` call can be made instead of an `AddItem` call. The parameters are identical (in the case of this sample code, just change the first line to `$call = "VerifyAddItem"`), but the item is not listed, just checked for validity and estimated costs are returned.

Note that there is a delay between submitting an item and it being available on the site via a keyword search, or via category browsing. In my experience, this delay runs anywhere between 15 and 60 seconds. The item is, however, immediately visible by doing a search for its listing ID.

Adding an Image to the Item Description

eBay doesn't provide a mechanism within its API to upload pictures to its servers, and as such, the eBay Picture Services system is unavailable to us (developers using the Java SDK or the Windows SDK, however, can hit those services). As such, to include an image with an eBay listing, it must first be hosted on a web server. The mechanisms involved in allowing a user to upload an image are rather trivial, and as such, are not covered here, but keep in mind a few considerations:

- Restrict the types of files users can upload to images; don't rely on form-side checking; repeat it all server side. You can use local image libraries to ensure it is in fact an image.
- If you generally do referrer checking to avoid problems with hot-linking, lax the rules for the appropriate folders. Images will likely also be downloaded via email clients (when people email descriptions to each other) or other API-based clients.
- Watermarking images with the item number or seller's name can be a good idea; many eBayers have in the past reported problems with other users "stealing" their images for their own sales. PHP's image libraries make this an easy value-add for your customers.

Including an HTML image tag in the item description is easy and quick once you have the image on your server. The previous example could be modified to include an image like this:

```
$queryInfo["Item"]["Description"] = '<![CDATA[Professional Web APIs, The Movie!
<img src="http://www.example.com/images/dvd_cover.jpg">]]>';
```

Simply adding the image to the item description will have the desired effect of showing the image to the customer; it will not, however, activate the small camera icon used in search result or category listings to indicate that the listing has a picture. Because the API has no specific method to add the icon to the listing, it must be approached in a backwards manner. The API will add the icon whenever a valid image is present URL is presented in one of the Picture branches. That knowledge, combined with a specified null image URL, will allow you to toggle the camera icon when images are included in the description:

```
$queryInfo["Item"]["VendorHostedPicture"] = array();
$queryInfo["Item"]["VendorHostedPicture"]["SelfHostedURL"] =
  "http://pics.ebay.com/aw/pics/dot_clear.gif";
```

Other Options of Note

Although the main options associated with creating a new listing have already been discussed, that is far from the end of the matter. eBay offers an extensive list of additional options in an attempt to cater to different listing types and different sellers. Many additional request parameters carry additional charges for some or all auctions, so it's important to present accurate listing fees when additional parameters are included.

Setting a Reserve Price

eBay allows sellers to set a reserve price above of the item's starting bid. This will, for example, allow a seller to start the bidding on a new iPod at $0.99 with a reserve price of $80.00. This is designed to generate a lot of interest, and hopefully bids, while still ensuring a minimum price for the item. The reserve price is not revealed to bidders during the auction process; if the winning bid of the item is below the item's reserve price, the seller is under no obligation to sell the item. An additional fee is associated with listing an item with a reserve price; however, it is refunded if the item is sold successfully.

Continuing with the previous example, the following code will set a reserve price of $14.99:

```
$queryInfo["Item"]["ReservePrice"] = "14.99";
```

Setting a Secondary Category

eBay has many, many, many categories, and in some circumstances an item may belong in several categories. The video example used thus far could (if shipped along with the book) be listed under both the DVD & Movies ➪ DVD and Books ➪ Textbooks, Education categories like this:

```
$queryInfo["Item"]["PrimaryCategory"] = array();
$queryInfo["Item"]["PrimaryCategory"]["CategoryID"] = "617";
$queryInfo["Item"]["SecondaryCategory "] = array();
$queryInfo["Item"]["SecondaryCategory "]["CategoryID"] = "2228";
```

Enhancing the Listing

eBay is a very competitive marketplace, and it offers sellers a few methods to draw attention to their listings to differentiate themselves from other sellers, at a cost. The enhancements available (as they would appear in the API call) are as follows:

- `Border` — Places a border around the listing in search and category listings
- `BoldTitle` — The title appears in bold in search and category listings
- `Featured` — Listing appears as a Featured Plus item
- `Highlight` — Listing is highlighted in a different color in listings
- `HomePageFeatured` — Listing is featured on the eBay homepage
- `ProPackBundle` — Includes Bold, Border, Featured, and Highlight

The code to accomplish one of these listings is quite easy:

```
$queryInfo["Item"]["ListingEnhancements"] = "BoldTitle";
```

Adding Application Data

The API gives you the opportunity to tie a piece of information to a specific listing that eBay isn't going to use anywhere on its own. It will, however, return the information if you request data about the specific listing. This is most frequently used to match a listing to a specific record in a local database (think primary key). Adding the attribute is as easy as ever:

```
$queryInfo["Item"]["ApplicationData"] = "23113131231";
```

Summary

The eBay API is a large and complex interface. This chapter walked you through a number of things to help you get started working with the eBay API, including the following:

- Signing up for the API
- Performing your first REST call
- Performing a series of SOAP calls

The initial `GetTime` request allowed the development of a few functions that made generating further calls rather easy. Navigating the category hierarchy and searching eBay built on those generic functions to allow building of a few sample applications. Finally, listing an item with eBay required some basic improvements to those generic functions to handle the more advanced call types. Keep in mind that this chapter just scratched the surface of eBay's SOAP API — there's a lot more to it, so if developing for eBay is a priority for you, I strongly recommend reading through eBay's SOAP WSDL documentation.

The last few chapters have covered some of the major websites and their APIs. The next chapter and Chapter 11 looks at a few other interesting web APIs available to you before you move on to create your own.

10

Interacting with the PayPal API

PayPal is an international payment gateway allowing businesses and individuals to transfer funds in a secure manner over the Internet. Using PayPal to accept payments has several advantages for online merchants: It is a recognized brand when it comes to Business to Consumer (B2C) transactions, creating a business account with PayPal is easier (and faster) than opening the merchant account required to accept credit card payments directly, and finally, because PayPal lends its name to the transaction, customers may feel more comfortable entering into a transaction with a previously unknown merchant. That being said, however, PayPal's transaction dispute system requires a tracking number from a shipped package to respond to a customer dispute. If the product is purely electronic (a download or access to a site, for example), your response to disputes will be quite limited.

Several of the API examples shown in this chapter make use of the `cURL` and `OpenSSL` libraries, which are not compiled into PHP by default. Please see Appendix C for more information on how the development box was configured to include these libraries.

This chapter covers the following:

- An overview of the PayPal API
- PayPal's development sandbox
- How to accept payment via PayPal with a payment badge
- Encrypting the transaction
- Instant Payment Notification

- ❑ How to search and retrieve transaction details
- ❑ How to issue refunds
- ❑ How to use the MassPay feature

API Usage Overview

Using the PayPal API is a little different from most of the other APIs discussed in this book. The majority of the time, one of PayPal's servers will initiate the process by contacting your server. This is an "Instant Payment Notification," which is sent whenever money is transferred into your account by another user. Your server will then contact PayPal to confirm the transaction before any further actions are taken. Generally speaking, the only time in which your server will initiate new transactions with PayPal is to issue refunds. A few other functions are available, but are beyond the scope of this brief introduction. See Figure 10-1.

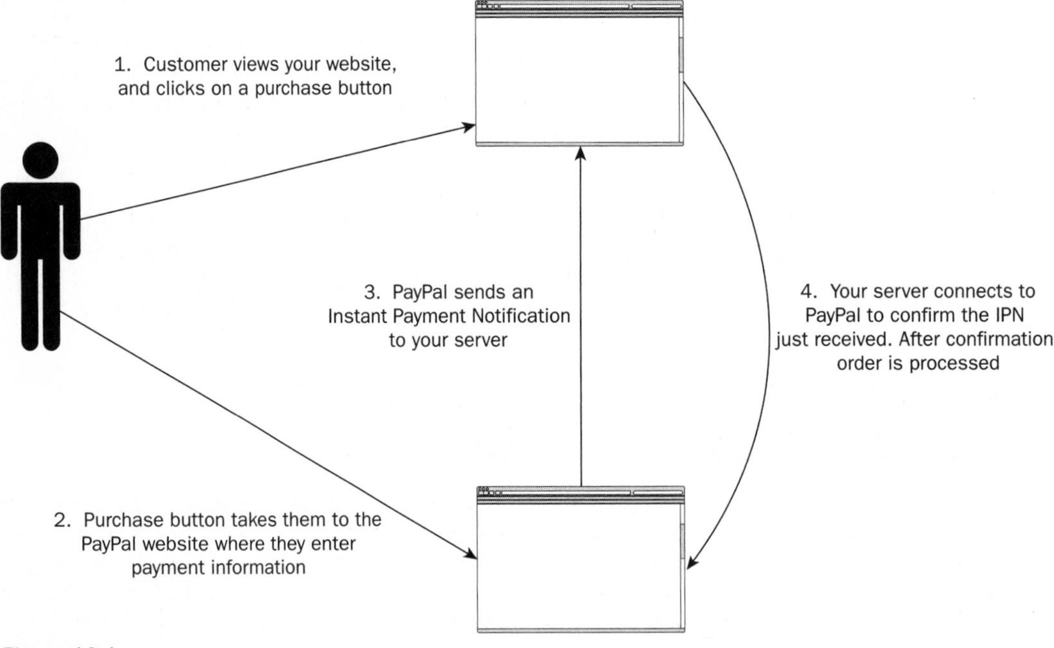
1. Customer views your website, and clicks on a purchase button
2. Purchase button takes them to the PayPal website where they enter payment information
3. PayPal sends an Instant Payment Notification to your server
4. Your server connects to PayPal to confirm the IPN just received. After confirmation order is processed

Figure 10-1

Developer Sandbox

The PayPal developer sandbox is quite impressive. Not only does it allow testing and exploration of the different account types as well as the API, but it also allows you to create any number of PayPal accounts with relative ease. When creating an account in the development system, fake billing information may be used, and the checking of account and credit card numbers is turned off.

Although most of the validation code is turned off or relaxed for accounts created within the developer system, the password rules have remained the same. Because you will be creating several accounts to test payments, refunds, and the like, you will need to manage all of those new accounts. While traditional methods like writing it all down on a sticky note work fine, I would heartily recommend Password Safe (http://`passwordsafe.sourceforge.net/`*). Password Safe stores all of your usernames and passwords in a secure file, reducing the number of passwords you must memorize from some large number (I have 43) to one. Storing the program and database on a USB memory key allows for greater portability and an additional layer of security.*

Within the development sandbox, you are going to need to create at least two separate accounts. First, you will need an account to represent you or your business. This will be the account to which most payments will be sent. Second, you will need a number of accounts that you will use to send money to the first account. I would recommend creating at least a few test accounts to send money with; try creating a few with two-line addresses, foreign countries, both short and long zip codes, and so on. Keep in mind that PayPal's restrictions on usernames may be far less restrictive than yours, and try to test multiple names in different character sets with your application before going live.

One particularly useful feature of the development sandbox is the ability to clear or fail any pending (or uncleared) payment on demand. This allows for immediate testing of pending payment and failed payment code. I would strongly recommend testing all IPN applications with all three major payment states (completed, pending, and failed). To manually affect a payment's status, select the details of the payment from within the PayPal Account Overview. On the Payment Details screen, there should be two links toward the bottom of the page, one for each option.

One problem you may encounter while using the sandbox is the inability to be logged into several different accounts at once. Once you have logged into the second account, all of your cookies get overwritten and all windows now belong to the most recently logged-in account. I've worked around that problem by using multiple web browsers concurrently, keeping one account open in Mozilla Firefox and another in Internet Explorer.

Creating a Payment Badge

The easiest way to allow customers to purchase an item from your site is to simply place a PayPal image or "badge" on your site, linking to the PayPal payment page (the link is quite complex, because it passes quite a bit of information). The users complete the purchase by either entering their user information or simply entering their credit card information (a PayPal account is not required). Once the transaction is complete, PayPal will notify you of the transaction via its Instant Payment Notification system.

To create a payment badge, log in to the development sandbox and into the business account you created and select the Merchant Tools tab. From within that tab, select the Buy Now Buttons link under the Accepting Website Payments heading in the main column. Here you have several options to describe the product or service being sold. This information will be returned to your server when a purchase is made via the Instant Payment Notification system. For this example I have entered "Professional Web APIs with PHP" as the Item Name/Service, 0764589547 as the Item ID/Number, and $49.99 as the price. I have left currency as U.S. Dollars, and allowed the buyers to choose their own country. Finally, I have selected the default button, and chosen not to encrypt the payment button. The button creation interface is visible in Figure 10-2.

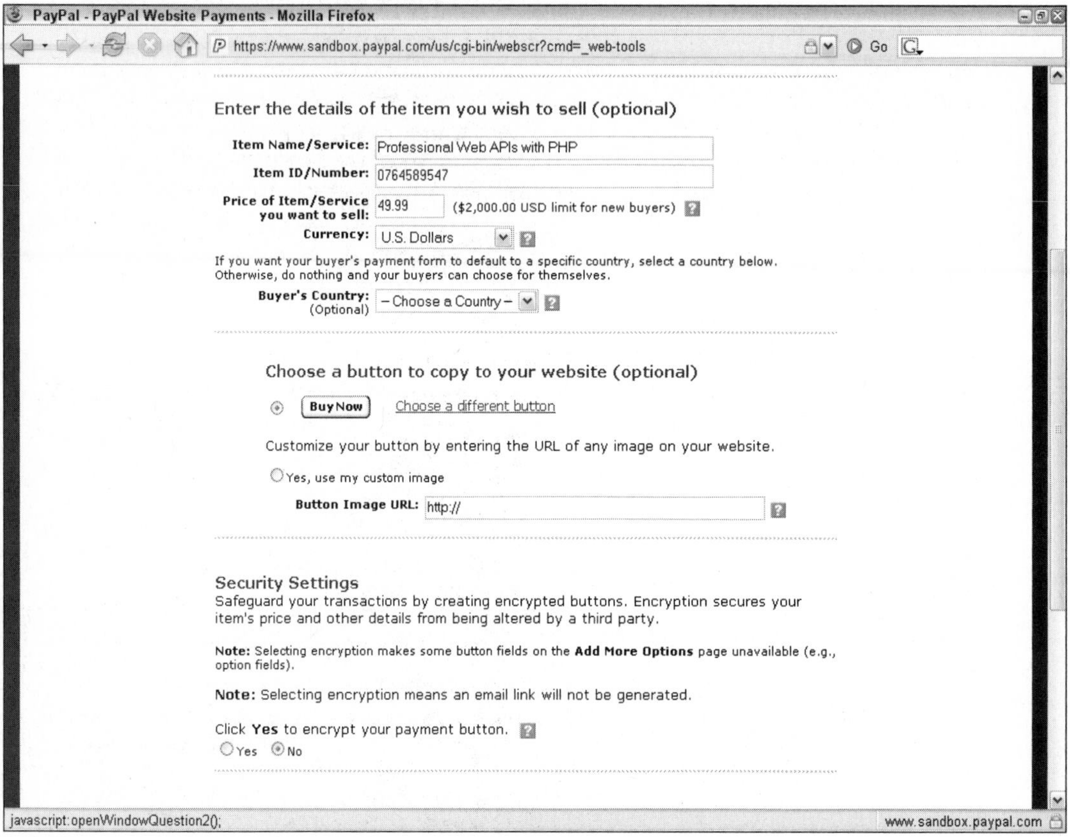

Figure 10-2

Clicking on Create Button gives me the following code:

```
<form action="https://www.sandbox.paypal.com/cgi-bin/webscr" method="post">
<input type="hidden" name="cmd" value="_xclick">
<input type="hidden" name="business" value="stb@preinheimer.com">
<input type="hidden" name="item_name" value="Professional Web APIs with PHP">
<input type="hidden" name="item_number" value="0764589547">
<input type="hidden" name="amount" value="49.99">
<input type="hidden" name="no_note" value="1">
<input type="hidden" name="currency_code" value="USD">
<input type="image" src="https://www.sandbox.paypal.com/en_US/i/btn/x-click-
but23.gif" border="0" name="submit" alt="Make payments with PayPal - it's fast,free
and secure!">
</form>
```

Most of the information placed in the form comes straight from the information entered when the button was created. The value for `business` is simply the account name I chose when I created this test account. The `no_note` value instructs PayPal not to allow purchasers to enter a note while paying. Also notice that both the destination URL and the image URL are for the sandbox; you will need a sandbox account to send payments (real PayPal accounts will not work).

Speaking directly from personal experience, you do not want customers to enter a note when they order a product or service. The customer's expectation when entering a note is that the note is read either before or at the same time as the order is processed, and as such, they feel it appropriate to include any and all manner of special instructions, clarifications, questions, restrictions, and so on in that note field. Because the entire point of the IPN system is to automate the process, it is quite likely that the note will not be read until long after the order is processed (because it likely takes just seconds), if ever. I would recommend replacing this opportunity for customer contact with two separate systems: First, make it easy for customers to contact you with questions before they place an order; a prominent link or button should do the trick. Second, once an order is received, email the users confirming receipt, and indicate in that email what their customer service contact options are (email, phone, web support, and so on).

To Encrypt or Not to Encrypt

Had the option to encrypt the button been selected, the resulting code would have looked like this:

```
<form action="https://www.sandbox.paypal.com/cgi-bin/webscr" method="post">
<input type="hidden" name="cmd" value="_s-xclick">
<input type="image" src="https://www.sandbox.paypal.com/en_US/i/btn/x-click-
but23.gif" border="0" name="submit" alt="Make payments with PayPal - it's fast,
free and secure!">
<input type="hidden" name="encrypted" value="-----BEGIN PKCS7-----
MIIHeQYJKoZIhvcNAQcEoIIHajCCB2YCAQExggE6MIIBNgIBADCBnjCBmDELMAkGA1UEBhMCVVMxEzARBgN
VBAgTCkNhbGlmb3JuaWExETAPBgNVBAcTCFNhbiBKb3NlMRUwEwYDVQQKEwxQYXlQYWwsIEluYy4xFjAUBg
NVBAsUDXNhbmRib3hfY2VydHMxFDASBgNVBAMUC3NhbmRib3hfYXBpMRwwGgYJKoZIhvcNAQkBFg1yZUBwY
XlwYWwuY29tAgEAMA0GCSqGSIb3DQEBAQUABIGApKLZV1cHVPGwkBI6Y1WR7ggpr5/bQjJ6A8pRvRgOHt9Q
8Uu16fTpMG0wbT9pBZq+s82r4SRakQoKvJSnbH8tiHnP7S35sgxTMp2+0a1uC/WL8qL1qS1hIg+X8TfS1ei
hmHmjE8zP2scLWtU1cGkp7OaF7g5z5X912aCuCfNYKUgxCzAJBgUrDgMCGgUAMIHEBgkqhkiG9w0BBwEwFA
YIKoZIhvcNAwcECIbH67fnTf+dgIGgyOd3skXL0ghwzex7F/lPVHMdjcIPWh4ihA6hW9/Ei9eGf8ApE/U+T
Mb3cu80Lx+ws6icj1i/gO8ssmLNXCRymc+r7Bk7p5rvMB+IJz3hYMUMUr6EsJyyuEN+2nFpVcSHnbzcROXb
guIXENtdgIc69eSQNjYOstJSCNd1+wYMOKddvMhGHbfdTv3mLsSmzNod3xy0qQLj+qVweQVKlhqqZKCCA6U
wggOhMIIDCqADAgECAgEAMA0GCSqGSIb3DQEBBQUAMIGYMQswCQYDVQQGEwJVUzETMBEGA1UECBMKQ2FsaW
Zvcm5pYTERMA8GA1UEBxMIU2FuIEpvc2UxFTATBgNVBAoTDFBheVBhbCwgSW5jLjEWMBQGA1UECxQNc2FuZ
GJveF9jZXJ0czEUMBIGA1UEAxQLc2FuZGJveF9hcGkxHDAaBgkqhkiG9w0BCQEWDXJlQHBheXBhbC5jb20w
HhcNMDQwNDE5MDcwMjU0WhcNMzUwNDE5MDcwMjU0WjCBmDELMAkGA1UEBhMCVVMxEzARBgNVBAgTCkNhbGl
mb3JuaWExETAPBgNVBAcTCFNhbiBKb3NlMRUwEwYDVQQKEwxQYXlQYWwsIEluYy4xFjAUBgNVBAsUDXNhbm
Rib3hfY2VydHMxFDASBgNVBAMUC3NhbmRib3hfYXBpMRwwGgYJKoZIhvcNAQkBFg1yZUBwYXlwYWwuY29tM
IGfMA0GCSqGSIb3DQEBAQUAA4GNADCBiQKBgQC3luO//Q3So3dOIEv7X4v8SOk7WN6o9okLV8OL5wLq3q1N
tDnk53imhPzGNLM0flLjyId1mHQLsSp8TUw8JzZygmoJKkOrGY6s771BeyMdYCfHqxvp+gcemw+btaBDJSY
Ow3BNZPc4ZHf3wRGYHPNygvmjB/fMFKlE/Q2VNaic8wIDAQABo4H4MIH1MB0GA1UdDgQWBBSDLiLZqyqILW
unkyzzUPHyd9Wp0jCBxQYDVR0jBIG9MIG6gBSDLiLZqyqILWunkyzzUPHyd9Wp0qGBnqSBmzCBmDELMAkGA
1UEBhMCVVMxEzARBgNVBAgTCkNhbGlmb3JuaWExETAPBgNVBAcTCFNhbiBKb3NlMRUwEwYDVQQKEwxQYXlQ
YWwsIEluYy4xFjAUBgNVBAsUDXNhbmRib3hfY2VydHMxFDASBgNVBAMUC3NhbmRib3hfYXBpMRwwGgYJKoZ
IhvcNAQkBFg1yZUBwYXlwYWwuY29tggEAMAwGA1UdEwQFMAMBAf8wDQYJKoZIhvcNAQEFBQADgYEAVzbzwN
gZf4Zfb5Y/93B1fB+Jx/6uUb7RX0YE8llgpklDTr1b9lGRS5YVD46l3bKE+md4Z7ObDdpTbbYIat0qE6sEl
FFymg7cWMceZdaSqBtCoNZ0btL7+XyfVB8M+n6OlQs6tycYRRjjUiaNklPKVslDVvk8EGMaI/Q+krjxx0Ux
ggGkMIIBoAIBATCBnjCBmDELMAkGA1UEBhMCVVMxEzARBgNVBAgTCkNhbGlmb3JuaWExETAPBgNVBAcTCFN
hbiBKb3NlMRUwEwYDVQQKEwxQYXlQYWwsIEluYy4xFjAUBgNVBAsUDXNhbmRib3hfY2VydHMxFDASBgNVBA
MUC3NhbmRib3hfYXBpMRwwGgYJKoZIhvcNAQkBFg1yZUBwYXlwYWwuY29tAgEAMAkGBSsOAwIaBQCgXTAYB
gkqhkiG9w0BCQMxCwYJKoZIhvcNAQcBMBwGCSqGSIb3DQEJBTEPFw0wNTA0MDcxNzM1MDlaMCMGCSqGSIb3
DQEJBDEWBBTsh8xXEk+Bzq7huQtBdVEInsWxQDANBgkqhkiG9w0BAQEFAASBgGeelyrgDIYDCQ0nzC3/Ibd
4O2DteTn5+gTSup72+kUrcDym4Eq5soY55vJGOyFBEp+aSQs9GcjjgpqnPN+XpfIvbD1ps1Wcp66iLM1HLN
Bjh4SsNc4LRqxqj4ORd3YT97EzoxbMNJso/va87LP/HwE4+VBiRD6JNcJTWhGLTmkl-----END PKCS7---
--
">
</form>
```

Obviously this is a little more unwieldy, but it does have some advantages. The code for the unencrypted form can be easily copied, then modified. For example, an "attacker" (and I use the loosest sense of the term in this case) could change the price from $49.95 to $1.00, save the page locally, and click the button. PayPal doesn't remember what buttons you have created, so everything will work fine, and the attacker will be able to have PayPal send your server an Instant Payment Notification for a purchase of item 0764589547 at a cost of $1.00.

Defending against this sort of attack is discussed in the "Instant Payment Notification" section.

Modifying the encrypted code is much more difficult, if not impossible. An attacker (with prior knowledge of the PayPal system) could still manually create a payment link of a different price, but would need to guess the correct values for the item's name and ID.

Though the unencrypted form can be easily faked by attackers, it can also be easily generated by your system. If you are selling multiple items, you can create payment buttons for each one automatically with a little bit of code, likely no more complicated than the code already being used to generate the pages themselves. Just change the `item_name`, `item_number`, and `amount` values as appropriate for each item in your inventory. This also grants you flexibility when you change prices, because these changes can be immediately reflected in your payment buttons.

If you have only a few products, with prices that change rarely, the encrypted buttons work really well and can provide an additional layer of protection. If you have a wide selection of products, changing prices, or require the additional functionality available, unencrypted buttons are probably the right choice.

Instant Payment Notification

Processing Instant Payment Notification is relatively easy, but it must be configured on PayPal's site before it can be used. Under the My Account tab, and Profile subtab, select Instant Payment Notification Preferences, which is under the Selling Preferences heading. Here you must enable IPN, and give it a URL to post to when a payment has been made.

Both portions of the IPN process (PayPal notifying your server and your server confirming the transaction with PayPal) can be performed over either HTTP or HTTPS. If the option is available to you, I would recommend taking advantage of this added layer of security. Although you will not be receiving payment information (such as credit card or bank account numbers), you will receive real names and addresses. Receiving the notification over HTTPS requires only that your server have a valid SSL certificate, and that the script be placed in a suitable location. Confirming the transaction with PayPal, however, requires that PHP was compiled with SSL support. To check your version of PHP, look at the output of the `phpinfo()` *command, specifically under Registered PHP Streams and Registered Stream Socket Transports. In order for PHP to initiate communications over HTTPS, you need HTTP in the former and SSL and TLS in the latter. Detailed information on the configuration of the development box is available in Appendix C.*

After IPN has been enabled, PayPal will start sending a POST request each and every time a transaction is made against your account as soon as the transaction is processed (this isn't a batch processing system). For example, the POST request generated after clicking the payment button shown earlier would look something like this:

Note that you will receive a post whenever a transaction is made against your account; this includes payments, refunds, charge backs, and so on. Be sure to code your applications to handle these different notifications.

```
[mc_gross] => 29.95
[address_status] => confirmed
[payer_id] => 7WPEM4M7HBDNW
[tax] => 0.00
[address_street] => 123 Sesame Street
[payment_date] => 10:30:15 Apr 07, 2005 PDT
[payment_status] => Completed
[address_zip] => N2K 1K9
[first_name] => Big
[mc_fee] => 1.47
[address_name] => Big Bird
[notify_version] => 1.6
[custom] =>
[payer_status] => verified
[business] => stb@preinheimer.com
[address_country] => Canada
[address_city] => CaringVille
[quantity] => 1
[payer_email] => bigbird@example.com
[verify_sign] => AXZRCbqawxfwAUFhW2J.g21PQqAiA0ONoj4WX-jxbANvyGgwXHThirqT
[txn_id] => 5NP73724H5715082L
[payment_type] => instant
[last_name] => Bird
[address_state] => Ontario
[receiver_email] => stb@preinheimer.com
[payment_fee] => 1.47
[receiver_id] => L3D7XTLLRU82J
[txn_type] => web_accept
[item_name] => Professional Web APIs with PHP
[mc_currency] => USD
[item_number] => 0764589547
[test_ipn] => 1
[payment_gross] => 29.95
```

The majority of the information presented in the post is self-explanatory. It contains the information from the purchaser (name, address, email, and so on), information about the selected product (name, item number, cost), and information about the transaction itself (fees, transaction IDs, and quantity). There are a couple things to note with this information: First, the `txn_id` (transaction id) value presented here is for PayPal's payment to you — it will not match any transaction id the purchaser was given. Second, the `mc_fee` and `payment_fee` values will only match each other when the transaction is completed in USD. The amount deposited into your account is equivalent to the `mc_gross` value minus the `mc_fee` value. Third, the `payment_status` value is critical. In this situation, the value is `Completed`, however it may also be set to `Pending`, in which case there will also be a `pending_reason` field, which will include more information as to why the payment is still pending.

Do *not* ship the product while payment is still pending because the payment itself can still fail for a variety of reasons. Once the payment is cleared, another IPN post will be made by PayPal.

When a transaction is received and payment is still pending, it would be a great idea to email the customer and let them know what is going on. The general expectation with online purchases is instant notification or (in the case of online products or services) instant receipt. Not informing the user that the payment has been noted, but not yet received, will likely result in a higher customer service workload, and canceled transactions or refund requests.

Processing the IPN

Processing an IPN has three essential steps: validating the post with PayPal, checking the purchase information against your own database (for product existence and price/product mismatch), and passing off the information to your ordering system. If you fail to validate the IPN with PayPal and confirm pricing information with your own local database, you open yourself up to abuse in two ways. First, malicious users can fake an IPN request to your server of an appropriate amount for a particular item, which your system will then treat as any other order and process accordingly. Second, users could send a token amount of money ($0.05) and order an expensive item. I've seen production systems vulnerable to either or both attacks.

Validating the IPN with PayPal

Validating the IPN is actually very easy, and quite well documented. You simply send the `$_POST` variable back to PayPal, adding one element of your own to indicate that this is a validation attempt. This is to ensure that the notification did in fact originate with PayPal, rather than an attacker attempting to mimic the notification.

The function has a few basic steps. First, it processes the received `$_POST` to generate a usable `POST` request of its own. Second, it creates the socket (returning an error if necessary). Third, it processes PayPal's response. Finally, based on that response, it returns `TRUE` for a valid IPN and `FALSE` for an invalid IPN.

```
function verifyIPN($data)
{
  $postdata = "";
  $response = array();

  foreach($data as $var=>$val)
  {
    $postdata .= $var . "=" . urlencode($val) . "&";
  }
  $postdata.="cmd=_notify-validate";
```

The required variables are declared and the received data is processed to be used for its own `POST` request. Though it does look tempting, `implode()` won't work with this associative array. An additional value, `cmd=_notify-validate`, is added to indicate that this is a validation attempt.

```
  $fp=@fsockopen("ssl://www.sandbox.paypal.com" ,"443",$errnum,$errstr,30);
```

Here the socket itself is opened. As indicated earlier, connections are being made over the Secure Sockets Layer (which uses port 443) to avoid any interception of customer data. Any error information will be saved in the indicated variables, and the script will wait 30 seconds before timing out.

```
    if(!$fp)
    {
      return "$errnum: $errstr";
    } else
    {
      fputs($fp, "POST /cgi-bin/webscr HTTP/1.1\r\n");
      fputs($fp, "Host: www.sandbox.paypal.com\r\n");
      fputs($fp, "Content-type: application/x-www-form-urlencoded\r\n");
      fputs($fp, "Content-length: ".strlen($postdata)."\r\n");
      fputs($fp, "Connection: close\r\n\r\n");
      fputs($fp, $postdata . "\r\n\r\n");
      while(!feof($fp)) { $response[]=@fgets($fp, 1024); }
      fclose($fp);
    }
```

First, the socket is checked to confirm a successful connection, and barring any problems, the `POST` request is sent. Notice the use of the `strlen()` function when sending `Content-Length`. This is the easiest way to get the right value. I prefer to generate that value during the connection, because generating it earlier has led to problems with code being introduced after the fact that changes the data (and hence the length).

```
    $response = implode("\n", $response);
    if(eregi("VERIFIED",$response))
    {
      return true;
    }else
    {
      return false;
    }
  }
```

The response is initially saved in an array; here it is imploded to exist within a flat string. The `eregi()` function is used to check for the specified text within the following text, and based on those results `TRUE` or `FALSE` is returned.

Confirming Product Information

The exact process required to confirm product information depends extensively on your needs, the way you store product information, and so on. That being said, here are a few tips:

- Remember the goal of this step: ensure that the amount received is correct for the product (and quantity) ordered.
- Double-check any shipping or tax amounts.
- Double-check currency if you accept payments in multiple currencies.
- If your site offers specials or discounts, remember to check those as well, including confirming the customer's eligibility for the unique price.
- Stress to the entire team that any price changes must be made in the appropriate places (like the database) rather than directly on the website in order for the system to work.

If the system is unable to match an incoming order with a product in the database, several actions should be taken. First, the customer should be notified that there was a problem with the order, that the problem isn't their fault, and that you will be looking into it shortly. Many customers will panic if they don't receive an email shortly after placing an order, so by contacting them and taking ownership of any problems, you can do a lot to allay their concerns. Second, the appropriate team should be notified of the issue. In this case it should probably be the customer service group, which should be able to determine if this is in fact a valid order (and process it accordingly), and if not, forward it on to the security team.

Here is a simple example of confirming an order against a database:

```
function confirmProduct($id, $name, $amount)
{
  if (!(ctype_digit($id) && is_numeric($amount)))
  {
    return false;
  }else
  {
    $name = mysql_escape_string($name);
  }
```

Confirming the order in this case only requires three variables: the ID of the product, the product's name, and the amount sent. The product ID should always be just digits, and the amount sent should be a numerical value. These checks can be confirmed before looking for the product in the database. This also ensures that both elements are safe to be put into a SQL query. If both values are appropriate, the product name is prepared for the SQL query.

```
  $query = "SELECT id FROM products WHERE `id` = '$id' AND `p_name` = '$name' AND
    `cost` = '$amount' LIMIT 1";
  if (rowCount($query) == 1)
  {
    return true;
  }else
  {
    return false;
  }
}
```

A simple query is done to check for the existence of the exact product within the database; the return value is based on that check.

As you can see, the process of checking every order against a local database of valid orders can be pretty simple, but is unfortunately often overlooked, leaving systems open to any number of fraudulent orders.

As mentioned earlier, I've personally seen payment systems (not always PayPal) vulnerable to either or both methods of attack mentioned here. It's critical that you validate every aspect of the incoming request to determine its validity.

Passing Off to the Regular Order System

How this section is handled is entirely dependent on the rest of your infrastructure. There are two things to consider here: First, remember that this script will be called with every order, and will hold onto the resources of your web server (and the TCP connection used for the request) until it exits. If the scripts used to process an order take anything more than a few moments to complete, you may end up leaving the web server crawling if many orders are placed at once. Second, the example script shown here has not yet done anything to the POST data received; it will need to be prepared appropriately before being used in any new database queries.

Putting It All Together

Combining all the code thus far, as well as a few minor additions, you have your Instant Payment Notification script, ipn.php:

```
<?php

  //Step 0. Record the transaction
    ob_start();
    echo date("D M j G:i:s T Y") . "\n";
    print_r($_SERVER);
    print_r($_POST);
    $body = ob_get_clean();
    file_put_contents("/logs/incomingPayments/IPN.txt", $body, FILE_APPEND);
```

Just in case things go awry, it is a good idea to get a record of the request before anything else happens.

```
  //Step 1. Verify IPN With PayPal
  $result=verifyIPN($_POST);
  if ($result == 0)
  {
    $subject = "FAKE IPN RECEIVED";
    $address = "security@example.com";
    $headers =
       "From: ipn_processor@example.com\r\n" .
       "Reply-To: donotreply@example.com\r\n" .
       "X-Mailer: PHP/" . phpversion();
    mail($address, $subject, $body, $headers);
    exit;
```

If the IPN is reported as being invalid by PayPal, notify the appropriate groups of the attempted transaction.

```
  }else if($result != 1)
  {
    $subject = "Unable to validate IPN";
    $body = "If this payment notification is valid it will need to be
        manually processed\n $result\n $body";
    $address = "support@example.com";
    $headers =
       "From: ipn_processor@example.com\r\n" .
       "Reply-To: donotreply@example.com\r\n" .
       "X-Mailer: PHP/" . phpversion();
    mail($address, $subject, $body, $headers);
    exit;
  }
```

This will occur if, for whatever reason, the script is unable to contact PayPal to confirm the transaction, and it will email the customer regarding the transaction. It will need to be confirmed (manually check to ensure it exists in PayPal's transaction database), then processed manually.

```
//Step 1.5 Check payment status
switch ($_POST['payment_status'])
{
  case "Completed":
    break;
  case "Pending":
    paymentPendingThankYou($_POST['payer_email']);
    break;
  default:
    $body = "Hi, an IPN was received that wasn't a completed payment or
      a pending payment. Please confirm this transaction against our records.";
    $body .= $post;
    $subject = "IPN Received";
    $address = "support@example.com";
    $headers =
      "From: ipn_processor@example.com\r\n" .
      "Reply-To: donotreply@example.com\r\n" .
      "X-Mailer: PHP/" . phpversion();
    mail($address, $subject, $body, $headers);
    exit;
  break;
}
```

If the payment is still `Pending`, the customer is emailed and informed of the status. Remember that several PayPal payment methods (such as eChecks) can take several business days to clear. The `paymentPendingThankYou()` function is presented shortly. If the payment status isn't `Pending` or `Completed`, it will likely be `Failed` (or something worse, like `Reversed`), in which case customer service is notified. In a case where a charge back was received, customer service may need to investigate or follow up with the customer.

```
//Step 2. Confirm Product Information
$result = confirmProduct($_POST['item_number'],
   $_POST['item_name'],$_POST['payment_gross']);
if ($result == false)
{
  $subject = "Product Name/ID/Price mis-match";
  $address = "support@example.com";
  $headers =
    "From: ipn_processor@example.com\r\n" .
    "Reply-To: donotreply@example.com\r\n" .
    "X-Mailer: PHP/" . phpversion();
  mail($address, $subject, $body, $headers);
  exit;
}
```

Here the order is checked against the available product database. If it turns out that the product and price point do not exist in the database, notify customer service. Depending on the response time of customer service (remember that orders may be received any time day or night, holidays and all), you may want to send the customer an email acknowledging the order and letting them know it will be processed manually.

```
    //Step 3. Process the order
    processOrder($_POST);
    exit;
```

Finally, the order is dispatched for processing.

```
function paymentPendingThankYou($address)
{
    $subject = "Order Received";
    $body = "Thanks for your order with Example.com!\n
      This message confirms that we have received notification from
      PayPal regarding your order. However, PayPal is still processing
      your payment at this time. Once PayPal confirms that they have completed
      processing your payment we will contact you again to confirm payment and
      include shipping details.\n\n
      If you have any questions please do not hesitate to contact us at
      support@example.com.\n\n
      We appreciate your business!";
    $headers =
        "From: OrderConfirmation@example.com\r\n" .
        "Reply-To: support@example.com\r\n" .
        "X-Mailer: PHP/" . phpversion();
    mail($address, $subject, $body, $headers);
    exit;
}
```

When a payment is received with `Pending` status, a quick email is sent to the client informing them of the status of their order.

```
function verifyIPN($data)
{
}

function confirmProduct($id, $name, $amount)
{
}
```

Code shown above, omitted for brevity.

```
function processOrder($data)
{
  // Your processing code goes here
}
```

This code is completely case specific, so you're on your own.

```
?>
```

As you can tell, PayPal's Instant Payment Notification system gives merchants an easy and secure manner to accept payments in an automated manner. While the implementation may seem backwards compared to other APIs presented (in that PayPal contacts you, rather than the other way around), this change presents few additional challenges.

Transaction Details Request

PayPal's API can be used to obtain additional information on previous transactions; I've found this feature to be most useful because you can use the transaction ID given to the merchant or to the client. As such, this system can be used to locate a payment based on the information a client has been given (as is usually the case for a customer service agent).

Remember for the average transaction where a customer purchases a product and pays PayPal via a credit card, three transaction IDs are issued: two to the client (one for the payment to the merchant, another for the transfer of funds from the credit card to the PayPal account), and one to the merchant (for the transfer of funds from the client). As the merchant, you only receive that one transaction ID, so to deal with a customer enquiry, you will need to search under a transaction ID they received, a function this interface provides. You will, however, need to ensure that the customers give you the transaction ID for the payment, not for the transfer of funds from their bank or credit card.

With this API, you return to the traditional method of your code contacting the server and parsing the response. However, unlike the majority of previous examples, NuSOAP will not be used. Unfortunately, NuSoap does not yet allow for the inclusion of a client certificate with a secure request. As such, cURL will be used. cURL is really the Swiss Army knife of Net transactions: It facilitates communications over `http`, `https`, `ftp`, `ftps`, `telnet`, `gopher`, and so on. Most importantly, it allows for the use of client-side certificates to authenticate when communicating over a secure protocol (which is what PayPal requires). CURL only provides the transport medium for the request; it is up to you to generate the request. Because the requests are pretty static (and have already ruled out NuSOAP), I have elected to generate the request by hand, and substitute the transaction ID as required.

This next function has two main steps. First, it generates the SOAP query to be sent to PayPal. Notice the use of the Heredoc syntax to encapsulate the SOAP request. This saves a lot of escaping, and still allows for variable replacement when it comes to the transaction ID. Next, the CURL object is initialized and configured to take care of the transaction itself.

Just in case you're not familiar with it, the Heredoc syntax allows you to quote a segment of text using your own string to start and end the quote. This allows you to quote a lot of other quotes without needing to worry about escaping anything. The format is shown below in the following code. It's basically three open braces followed by your own string, then after the quoted block, on its own line, the same variable again to close it. There is a big warning on the PHP documentation page that introduces the Heredoc syntax, but it's worth repeating. You absolutely cannot stick anything else on the line that ends the quoted block, particularly a tab character. The ending tag must be at the start of the line, and can be followed by a semicolon. That's it — no spaces, no tabs, no white space, nothing.

```
function transLookUp($transid)
{
  $username = "stb_api1.preinheimer.com";
  $password = "ZJXaRwTBoL8m";
```

```
$request = <<< End_Of_Quote
<SOAP-ENV:Envelope
  xmlns:xsi="http://www.w3.org/1999/XMLSchema-instance"
  xmlns:SOAP-ENC="http://schemas.xmlsoap.org/soap/encoding/"
  xmlns:SOAP-ENV="http://schemas.xmlsoap.org/soap/envelope/"
  xmlns:xsd="http://www.w3.org/1999/XMLSchema"
  SOAP-ENV:encodingStyle="http://schemas.xmlsoap.org/soap/encoding/">
  <SOAP-ENV:Header>
    <RequesterCredentials xmlns="urn:ebay:api:PayPalAPI"
      SOAP-ENV:mustUnderstand="1">
      <Credentials xmlns="urn:ebay:apis:eBLBaseComponents">
        <Username>$username</Username>
        <Password>$password</Password>
        <Subject/>
      </Credentials>
    </RequesterCredentials>
  </SOAP-ENV:Header>
```

Here the header for the SOAP request is defined. The `RequesterCredentials` section identifies the account the request is associated with, and the username and password are defined by PayPal and are different from your PayPal login account information. The `Subject` field is only needed if the transaction is being completed by one party on behalf of another (for example, if all of the PayPal API work was outsourced to another firm, they would log in with their credentials, not the account holders). The `Subject` line would indicate the account the transaction should be completed against. For more information, see the *Order Management Integration Guide* available within the PayPal development site.

```
  <SOAP-ENV:Body>
    <GetTransactionDetailsReq xmlns="urn:ebay:api:PayPalAPI">
      <GetTransactionDetailsRequest
        xsi:type="ns:GetTransactionDetailsRequestType">
        <Version xmlns="urn:ebay:apis:eBLBaseComponents"
          xsi:type="xsd:string">1.0</Version>
        <TransactionID xsi:type="ebl:TransactionId">$transid</TransactionID>
      </GetTransactionDetailsRequest>
    </GetTransactionDetailsReq>
  </SOAP-ENV:Body>
</SOAP-ENV:Envelope>
End_Of_Quote;
```

The body of the request contains the request itself. The structure here (and in the header) is explicitly defined by PayPal, and relatively easy to follow. The only two parameters being passed are the version of the API call (1.0 in this case) and the transaction ID being enquired about.

```
$ch = curl_init();
curl_setopt($ch, CURLOPT_URL, "https://api.sandbox.paypal.com/2.0/");
curl_setopt($ch, CURLOPT_SSLCERT, "../certs/cert_key_pem-1.txt");
curl_setopt($ch, CURLOPT_POST, TRUE);
curl_setopt($ch, CURLOPT_POSTFIELDS, $request);
curl_setopt($ch, CURLOPT_RETURNTRANSFER, TRUE);
```

The CURL object is created and configured. The `CURLOPT_URL` parameter defines the URL that the call should be made against. `CURLOPT_SSLCERT` declares the location on disk where the client certificate (provided by PayPal) is located. This client certificate is provided by PayPal and further authenticates you as an authorized user when making calls to the PayPal API. The certificate *must not* be stored within the document root. Not only does this allow anyone with some creativity and a web browser to crack half of the API security scheme, but it will also result in an army of security gnomes invading your house and forcing you to write "I will not store security certificates within the document root" on a blackboard 1,000 times. Just don't do it—store the certificate in a separate directory readable only by your web server. The `CURLOPT_POST` parameter defines this as a `POST` request, as opposed to a `GET` request. The `CURLOPT_POSTFIELDS` parameter sends along the SOAP request generated earlier. Finally, the `CURLOPT_RETURNTRANSFER` parameter instructs CURL to return the output of the request, rather than sending it directly to the end user.

```
    $response = curl_exec($ch);
    if (curl_error($ch))
   {
     file_put_contents("/tmp/curl_error_log.txt", curl_errno($ch) . ": " .
      curl_error($ch), "a+");
     curl_close($ch);
     return null;
   }else
   {
      curl_close($ch);
      $xml = simplexml_load_string($response);
      return $xml;
   }
  }
```

CURL sends all of its output directly to the browser, which isn't exactly what you are hoping for, so output buffering is started to record PayPal's response. The request itself is executed with the `cURL_exec()` call, and the response is stuck appropriately enough into the `$response` variable. If CURL encounters an error, null is returned, and the error is recorded to a log file for later examination. If all goes well, the connection is closed. The response is turned into a SimpleXML object, and returned for use.

PayPal's Response

Completely unlike the brief request, the response is quite expansive. I have trimmed the initial namespace declarations to save space, but other than that this is the full response:

```
<?xml version="1.0" encoding="UTF-8"?>
<SOAP-ENV:Envelope
 ..
 xmlns:ns="urn:ebay:api:PayPalAPI">
 <SOAP-ENV:Header>
  <Security xmlns="http://schemas.xmlsoap.org/ws/2002/12/secext"
    xsi:type="wsse:SecurityType"></Security>
  <RequesterCredentials xmlns="urn:ebay:api:PayPalAPI"
    xsi:type="ebl:CustomSecurityHeaderType">
   <Credentials xmlns="urn:ebay:apis:eBLBaseComponents"
    xsi:type="ebl:UserIdPasswordType">
   <Username xsi:type="xs:string"></Username>
   <Password xsi:type="xs:string"></Password>
```

```
    <Subject xsi:type="xs:string"></Subject></Credentials>
   </RequesterCredentials>
  </SOAP-ENV:Header>
  <SOAP-ENV:Body id="_0">
   <GetTransactionDetailsResponse xmlns="urn:ebay:api:PayPalAPI">
    <Timestamp xmlns="urn:ebay:apis:eBLBaseComponents">2005-04-15T02:53:24Z
     </Timestamp>
    <Ack xmlns="urn:ebay:apis:eBLBaseComponents">Success</Ack>
    <Version xmlns="urn:ebay:apis:eBLBaseComponents">1.000000</Version>
    <Build xmlns="urn:ebay:apis:eBLBaseComponents">1.0006</Build>
    <PaymentTransactionDetails xmlns="urn:ebay:apis:eBLBaseComponents"
     xsi:type="ebl:PaymentTransactionType">
     <ReceiverInfo xsi:type="ebl:ReceiverInfoType">
      <Business xsi:type="ebl:EmailAddressType">stb@preinheimer.com</Business>
      <Receiver xsi:type="ebl:EmailAddressType">stb@preinheimer.com</Receiver>
      <ReceiverID xsi:type="ebl:UserIDType">L3D7XTLLRU82J</ReceiverID>
     </ReceiverInfo>
     <PayerInfo xsi:type="ebl:PayerInfoType">
      <Payer xsi:type="ebl:EmailAddressType">bigbird@example.com</Payer>
      <PayerID xsi:type="ebl:UserIDType">JUVP4APFFAQZU</PayerID>
      <PayerStatus xsi:type="ebl:PayPalUserStatusCodeType">unverified
       </PayerStatus>
      <PayerName xsi:type="ebl:PersonNameType">
       <FirstName xmlns="urn:ebay:apis:eBLBaseComponents">Big</FirstName>
       <LastName xmlns="urn:ebay:apis:eBLBaseComponents">Bird</LastName>
      </PayerName>
      <PayerBusiness xsi:type="xs:string"></PayerBusiness>
      <Address xsi:type="ebl:AddressType">
       <Name xsi:type="xs:string">Big Bird</Name>
       <Street1 xsi:type="xs:string">123 Seasame St</Street1>
       <Street2 xsi:type="xs:string"></Street2>
       <CityName xsi:type="xs:string">CaringVille</CityName>
       <StateOrProvince xsi:type="xs:string">Ontario</StateOrProvince>
       <Country xsi:type="ebl:CountryCodeType">CA</Country>
       <CountryName>Canada</CountryName>
       <PostalCode xsi:type="xs:string">N1K 1K9</PostalCode>
       <AddressOwner xsi:type="ebl:AddressOwnerCodeType">PayPal</AddressOwner>
       <AddressStatus xsi:type="ebl:AddressStatusCodeType">Confirmed
         </AddressStatus>
      </Address>
     </PayerInfo>
     <PaymentInfo xsi:type="ebl:PaymentInfoType">
      <TransactionID>8N604562NC480291D</TransactionID>
      <ParentTransactionID xsi:type="ebl:TransactionId"></ParentTransactionID>
      <ReceiptID></ReceiptID>
      <TransactionType xsi:type="ebl:PaymentTransactionCodeType">web-accept
       </TransactionType>
      <PaymentType xsi:type="ebl:PaymentCodeType">instant</PaymentType>
      <PaymentDate xsi:type="xs:dateTime">2005-04-15T02:48:34Z</PaymentDate>
      <GrossAmount xsi:type="cc:BasicAmountType" currencyID="USD">29.95
       </GrossAmount>
      <FeeAmount xsi:type="cc:BasicAmountType" currencyID="USD">1.47</FeeAmount>
      <TaxAmount xsi:type="cc:BasicAmountType" currencyID="USD">0.00</TaxAmount>
      <ExchangeRate xsi:type="xs:string"></ExchangeRate>
```

```
      <PaymentStatus xsi:type="ebl:PaymentStatusCodeType">Completed
       </PaymentStatus>
      <PendingReason xsi:type="ebl:PendingStatusCodeType">none</PendingReason>
      <ReasonCode xsi:type="ebl:ReversalReasonCodeType">none</ReasonCode>
     </PaymentInfo>
     <PaymentItemInfo xsi:type="ebl:PaymentItemInfoType">
      <InvoiceID xsi:type="xs:string"></InvoiceID>
      <Custom xsi:type="xs:string"></Custom>
      <Memo xsi:type="xs:string"></Memo>
      <SalesTax xsi:type="xs:string">0.00</SalesTax>
      <PaymentItem xmlns="urn:ebay:apis:eBLBaseComponents"
       xsi:type="ebl:PaymentItemType">
       <Name xsi:type="xs:string">Professional Web APIs with PHP</Name>
       <Number xsi:type="xs:string">0764589547</Number>
       <Quantity xsi:type="xs:string">1</Quantity>
       <SalesTax xsi:type="xs:string"></SalesTax>
      </PaymentItem>
      <Subscription xsi:type="ebl:SubscriptionInfoType" recurring=""
       reattempt="">
       <SubscriptionID></SubscriptionID>
       <Username xsi:type="xs:string"></Username>
       <Password xsi:type="xs:string"></Password>
       <Recurrences xsi:type="xs:string"></Recurrences>
      </Subscription>
      <Auction xsi:type="ebl:AuctionInfoType" multiItem="">
       <BuyerID xsi:type="xs:string"></BuyerID>
      </Auction>
     </PaymentItemInfo>
    </PaymentTransactionDetails>
   </GetTransactionDetailsResponse>
  </SOAP-ENV:Body>
</SOAP-ENV:Envelope>
```

As you can tell, pretty much anything you need to know about the request, and a whole lot you don't, is available via the `GetTransactionDetails` API call. How you use the data available depends entirely on your implementation. Common uses would be to check on `PaymentStatus` following a customer enquiry, or using the full information to reprocess transactions that were lost due to an IPN failure.

The SimpleXML object returned contains the entire response. However, because of the namespacing used in SOAP responses, and the way SimpleXML handles those namespaces, accessing it can be a little bit tricky. The easiest way to access information nested within namespaced elements is to use SimpleXML's `xpath()` function:

```
$soapBody = $xml->xpath('/SOAP-ENV:Envelope/SOAP-ENV:Body');
```

`Xpath` searches the SimpleXML object for the specified tree, because depending on what type of search you run, multiple results are possible. The result is always given as an array, regardless of the number of results returned. Because only the data within the `GetTransactionDetailsResponse` tree are relevant for future processing, you can further trim the tree to contain only that information:

```
$body = $soapBody[0]->GetTransactionDetailsResponse;
```

Using this new body object, you can access all of the information within the response with relative ease:

```
$timestamp = $body->Timestamp;
$payerEmail = $body->PaymentTransactionDetails->PayerInfo->Payer;
$paymentStatus = $body->PaymentTransactionDetails->PaymentInfo->PaymentStatus;
```

Here the timestamp, payer's email, and payment status are copied into their own variables for possible use later. To access any particular element within the response, start with the name of the element you want on the right-hand side, and work toward the `GetTransactionDetailsResponse` branch, recording each parent you pass through along the way.

Sending a Refund

Unfortunately, at some point you are probably going to need to issue a refund to a customer for whatever reason. The code to send a refund is very similar to the previous example:

```
function refund($transid)
{
  $username = "stb_api1.preinheimer.com";
  $password = "ZJXaRwTBoL8m";
    $request = <<< End_Of_Quote
<SOAP-ENV:Envelope
  xmlns:xsi="http://www.w3.org/1999/XMLSchema-instance"
  xmlns:SOAP-ENC="http://schemas.xmlsoap.org/soap/encoding/"
  xmlns:SOAP-ENV="http://schemas.xmlsoap.org/soap/envelope/"
  xmlns:xsd="http://www.w3.org/1999/XMLSchema"
  SOAP-ENV:encodingStyle="http://schemas.xmlsoap.org/soap/encoding/">
  <SOAP-ENV:Header>
    <RequesterCredentials xmlns="urn:ebay:api:PayPalAPI"
      SOAP-ENV:mustUnderstand="1">
      <Credentials xmlns="urn:ebay:apis:eBLBaseComponents">
        <Username>$username</Username>
        <Password>$password</Password>
        <Subject/>
      </Credentials>
    </RequesterCredentials>
  </SOAP-ENV:Header>
  <SOAP-ENV:Body>
    <RefundTransactionReq xmlns="urn:ebay:api:PayPalAPI">
      <RefundTransactionRequest
        xsi:type="ns:RefundTransactionRequestType">
        <Version xmlns="urn:ebay:apis:eBLBaseComponents"
          xsi:type="xsd:string">1.0</Version>
        <TransactionID xsi:type="ebl:TransactionId">$transid</TransactionID>
        <RefundType>Full</RefundType>
      </RefundTransactionRequest>
    </RefundTransactionReq>
  </SOAP-ENV:Body>
</SOAP-ENV:Envelope>
End_Of_Quote;

  $ch = curl_init();
  curl_setopt($ch, CURLOPT_URL, "https://api.sandbox.paypal.com/2.0/");
  curl_setopt($ch, CURLOPT_SSLCERT, "./cert_key_pem-1.txt");
```

```
    curl_setopt($ch, CURLOPT_POST, TRUE);
    curl_setopt($ch, CURLOPT_POSTFIELDS, $request);

    ob_start();
    curl_exec($ch);
    $response = ob_get_clean();
     echo $response;
    if (curl_error($ch))
  .{
     file_put_contents("/tmp/curl_error_log.txt", curl_errno($ch) . ": " .
        curl_error($ch), "a+");
     curl_close($ch);
     return null;
   }else
   {
     curl_close($ch);
      $xml = simplexml_load_string($response);
      return $xml;
   }
  }
```

The body of the request differs because you are performing a different API call. However, the function itself, as well as the structure of the SOAP request, remains identical. Fortunately, the request for a refund transaction is much shorter (I have again cut out the namespace declarations for the sake of brevity):

```
<?xml version="1.0" encoding="UTF-8"?>
<SOAP-ENV:Envelope
  ...
  xmlns:ns="urn:ebay:api:PayPalAPI">
  <SOAP-ENV:Header>
    <Security xmlns="http://schemas.xmlsoap.org/ws/2002/12/secext"
      xsi:type="wsse:SecurityType"></Security>
    <RequesterCredentials xmlns="urn:ebay:api:PayPalAPI"
      xsi:type="ebl:CustomSecurityHeaderType">
      <Credentials xmlns="urn:ebay:apis:eBLBaseComponents"
        xsi:type="ebl:UserIdPasswordType">
        <Username xsi:type="xs:string"></Username>
        <Password xsi:type="xs:string"></Password>
        <Subject xsi:type="xs:string"></Subject>
      </Credentials>
    </RequesterCredentials>
  </SOAP-ENV:Header>
  <SOAP-ENV:Body id="_0">
    <RefundTransactionResponse xmlns="urn:ebay:api:PayPalAPI">
      <Timestamp xmlns="urn:ebay:apis:eBLBaseComponents">2005-04-15T04:05:17Z
        </Timestamp>
      <Ack xmlns="urn:ebay:apis:eBLBaseComponents">Success</Ack>
      <Version xmlns="urn:ebay:apis:eBLBaseComponents">1.000000</Version>
      <Build xmlns="urn:ebay:apis:eBLBaseComponents">1.0006</Build>
    </RefundTransactionResponse>
  </SOAP-ENV:Body>
</SOAP-ENV:Envelope>
```

The key element is the `Ack` element within the body, which reports the `Success` of the transaction. Using code similar to the previous example, you can access that element:

```
$soapBody = $xml->xpath('/SOAP-ENV:Envelope/SOAP-ENV:Body');
$body = $soapBody[0]->RefundTransactionResponse;
$success = $body->Ack;
```

Note that with PayPal, a merchant has 60 days to perform a refund on any transaction. During that time frame, PayPal only deducts the amount you actually received from your account, and refunds the transaction fee itself. If you need to issue a refund after the 60-day mark, you will instead need to issue a new payment for the full amount.

Improving the Code, a Modular Approach

The previous two examples were functionally identical, with only a few minor changes to a string to separate them. By examining the similarities and differences between the two SOAP calls, a modular function that can be used with both these API calls (and others to be covered later) can be written.

This function will take two parameters, the first being the name of the API call in question (to be inserted into the request body), and the second being an array of values containing the name, type, and value for all the required parameters, as in `paypal_api.php`:

```
function makeAPICall($specificAPIName, $APIParameters)
{
$username = "stb_api1.preinheimer.com";
$password = "ZJXaRwTBoL8m";
$parameterList = "";
foreach ($APIParameters as $parameter)
{
  $parameterList = "<{$parameter[0]} xsi:type=\"{$parameter[1]}\">{$parameter[2]}
    </{$parameter[0]}>\n";
}

$request = <<< End_Of_Quote
<SOAP-ENV:Envelope
  xmlns:xsi="http://www.w3.org/1999/XMLSchema-instance"
  xmlns:SOAP-ENC="http://schemas.xmlsoap.org/soap/encoding/"
  xmlns:SOAP-ENV="http://schemas.xmlsoap.org/soap/envelope/"
  xmlns:xsd="http://www.w3.org/1999/XMLSchema"
  SOAP-ENV:encodingStyle="http://schemas.xmlsoap.org/soap/encoding/">
  <SOAP-ENV:Header>
    <RequesterCredentials xmlns="urn:ebay:api:PayPalAPI"
      SOAP-ENV:mustUnderstand="1">
      <Credentials xmlns="urn:ebay:apis:eBLBaseComponents">
        <Username>$username</Username>
        <Password>$password</Password>
        <Subject/>
      </Credentials>
    </RequesterCredentials>
  </SOAP-ENV:Header>
```

```
    <SOAP-ENV:Body>
      <{$specificAPIName}Req xmlns="urn:ebay:api:PayPalAPI">
        <{$specificAPIName}Request xsi:type="ns:{$specificAPIName}RequestType">
          <Version xmlns="urn:ebay:apis:eBLBaseComponents"
            xsi:type="xsd:string">1.0</Version>
          $parameterList
        </{$specificAPIName}Request>
      </{$specificAPIName}Req>
    </SOAP-ENV:Body>
```

Every PayPal API call uses the same structure for its body: the name of the specific call being made, followed with a suffix depending on where it's being used. This allows for easy use throughout the body.

```
</SOAP-ENV:Envelope>
End_Of_Quote;

  $ch = curl_init();
  curl_setopt($ch, CURLOPT_URL, "https://api.sandbox.paypal.com/2.0/");
  curl_setopt($ch, CURLOPT_SSLCERT, "../certs/cert_key_pem-1.txt");
  curl_setopt($ch, CURLOPT_POST, TRUE);
  curl_setopt($ch, CURLOPT_POSTFIELDS, $request);
  curl_setopt($ch, CURLOPT_RETURNTRANSFER, TRUE);

  $response = curl_exec($ch);
  echo $response;
  if (curl_error($ch))
 {
   file_put_contents("/tmp/curl_error_log.txt", curl_errno($ch) . ": " .
curl_error($ch), "a+");
   curl_close($ch);
   return null;
 }else
 {
   curl_close($ch);
    $xml = simplexml_load_string($response);
    return $xml;
 }
}
```

This function, because it follows PayPal's general structure for all its API requests, should be able to complete any task you require of the API. The responses it gives will be identical to previous examples. To complete the details request shown earlier with this function, you would do this:

```
$parameters[] = array("TransactionID", "ebl:TransactionId", "8N604562NC480291D");
$xml = makeCall("GetTransactionDetails", $parameters);
```

To complete the refund, you would just need to add an additional parameter:

```
$parameters[] = array("RefundType", "ebl:token", "Full");
```

That's it.

Transaction Search Request

Using the new `makeAPICall()` function, additional requests can be coded and handled quickly. For example, the code necessary to search for a transaction by email address (which might be easily tied to a support system or a user look-up feature) would look like this:

```
function searchEmail($email)
{
  $parameters = array();
  $parameters[] = array("StartDate", "ebl:dateTime", "2000-01-29T12:00:01.00Z");
  $parameters[] = array("Payer", "ebl:string", "$email");
  $xml = makeAPICall("TransactionSearch", $parameters);
  return $xml;
}
```

`StartDate` is a required element in the request, so it is sent to an arbitrary date before any transactions are performed. `Payer` is used to search by the payer's email address, which is *very* useful because it will even find an email address if a user has changed his since payment. Unlike `TransactionDetailsSearch`, this will return multiple results matching your search criteria (which could include `EndDate`, `Payer`, `Receiver`, `ReceiptID`, `TransactionID`, `InvoiceID`, `PayerName`, or `AuctionItemNumber`). When called with

```
searchEmail("bigbird@example.com");
```

the results will look something like this:

```
<SOAP-ENV:Envelope xmlns:SOAP-ENV="http://schemas.xmlsoap.org/soap/envelope/"
  xmlns:ebl="urn:ebay:apis:eBLBaseComponents" xmlns:ns="urn:ebay:api:PayPalAPI">
 <SOAP-ENV:Header>
  ...
 </SOAP-ENV:Header>

 <SOAP-ENV:Body id="_0">
  <TransactionSearchResponse xmlns="urn:ebay:api:PayPalAPI">
  <Timestamp xmlns="urn:ebay:apis:eBLBaseComponents">2005-04-19T02:51:29Z
    </Timestamp>
  <Ack xmlns="urn:ebay:apis:eBLBaseComponents">Success</Ack>
  <Version xmlns="urn:ebay:apis:eBLBaseComponents">1.000000</Version>
  <Build xmlns="urn:ebay:apis:eBLBaseComponents">1.0006</Build>
  <PaymentTransactions xmlns="urn:ebay:apis:eBLBaseComponents"
    xsi:type="ebl:PaymentTransactionSearchResultType">
   <Timestamp xsi:type="xs:dateTime">2005-04-15T04:05:16Z</Timestamp>
   <Timezone xsi:type="xs:string">GMT</Timezone>
   <Type xsi:type="xs:string">Refund</Type>
   <Payer xsi:type="ebl:EmailAddressType">bigbird@example.com</Payer>
   <PayerDisplayName xsi:type="xs:string">Big Bird</PayerDisplayName>
   <TransactionID>0B816375MA2010907</TransactionID>
   <Status xsi:type="xs:string">Completed</Status>
   <GrossAmount xsi:type="cc:BasicAmountType" currencyID="USD">-29.95</GrossAmount>
   <FeeAmount xsi:type="cc:BasicAmountType" currencyID="USD">1.47</FeeAmount>
   <NetAmount xsi:type="cc:BasicAmountType" currencyID="USD">-28.48</NetAmount>
  </PaymentTransactions>
```

```
    <PaymentTransactions xmlns="urn:ebay:apis:eBLBaseComponents"
      xsi:type="ebl:PaymentTransactionSearchResultType">
     <Timestamp xsi:type="xs:dateTime">2005-04-15T02:48:34Z</Timestamp>
     <Timezone xsi:type="xs:string">GMT</Timezone>
     <Type xsi:type="xs:string">Payment</Type>
     <Payer xsi:type="ebl:EmailAddressType">bigbird@example.com</Payer>
     <PayerDisplayName xsi:type="xs:string">Big Bird</PayerDisplayName>
     <TransactionID>8N604562NC480291D</TransactionID>
     <Status xsi:type="xs:string">Refunded</Status>
     <GrossAmount xsi:type="cc:BasicAmountType" currencyID="USD">29.95</GrossAmount>
     <FeeAmount xsi:type="cc:BasicAmountType" currencyID="USD">-1.47</FeeAmount>
     <NetAmount xsi:type="cc:BasicAmountType" currencyID="USD">28.48</NetAmount>
    </PaymentTransactions>
   </SOAP-ENV:Body>
  </SOAP-ENV:Envelope>
```

As you can see, all of the transactions for this customer have been refunded — the amount refunded, as well as the fee (and finally the `NetAmount` that was deducted from your account).

MassPay

The MassPay API can greatly facilitate using PayPal to send automated payments to large numbers of individuals, providing you have a U.S.-based business account. This type of process could be used if employees are paid via PayPal, or you have a regular relationship with a supplier that requires regular payments. Unlike the majority of PayPal payments, the sender (you), not the receiver, is responsible for transaction fees. This means that more money will be deducted from your account than the mass payment totals. The processing fee is currently 2% of the payment, with a cap of USD $1.00 per item. You can send up to 250 payments in the same currency at a time with the MassPay API. More items than that, or different currencies, must be split into multiple transactions.

Using the MassPay API is a little more complex than previous examples, because there is an additional layer of nesting involved to allow for multiple payments, each with their own variables. A request looks something like this (continuing to trim the namespace declarations to save space):

```
<SOAP-ENV:Envelope
 SOAP-ENV:encodingStyle="http://schemas.xmlsoap.org/soap/encoding/">
 <SOAP-ENV:Header>
  <RequesterCredentials xmlns="urn:ebay:api:PayPalAPI"
   SOAP-ENV:mustUnderstand="1">
   <Credentials xmlns="urn:ebay:apis:eBLBaseComponents">
    <Username>stb_api1.preinheimer.com</Username>
    <Password>ZJXaRwTBoL8m</Password>
    <Subject/>
   </Credentials>
  </RequesterCredentials>
 </SOAP-ENV:Header>
 <SOAP-ENV:Body>
  <MassPayReq xmlns="urn:ebay:api:PayPalAPI">
   <MassPayRequest xsi:type="ns:MassPayRequestType">
```

```
    <Version xmlns="urn:ebay:apis:eBLBaseComponents"
     xsi:type="xsd:string">1.0</Version>
    <EmailSubject xsi:type="ebl:string">Work</EmailSubject>
    <MassPayItem xsi:type="ebl:MassPayItemType">
     <ReceiverEmail xsi:type="ebl:string">bigbird@example.com</ReceiverEmail>
     <Amount currencyID="USD" xsi:type="ebl:string">100.00</Amount>
     <Note xsi:type="ebl:string">Thanks</Note>
    </MassPayItem>
    <MassPayItem xsi:type="ebl:MassPayItemType">
     <ReceiverEmail xsi:type="ebl:string">oscar@example.com</ReceiverEmail>
     <Amount currencyID="USD" xsi:type="ebl:string">100.00</Amount>
     <Note xsi:type="ebl:string">Thanks</Note>
    </MassPayItem>
   </MassPayRequest>
  </MassPayReq>
 </SOAP-ENV:Body>
</SOAP-ENV:Envelope>
```

This additional depth of elements leaves three options: either the `MakeAPICall()` function presented earlier can be adapted to allow for this additional depth, the additional depth can be handled when making the call, or an entire new function can be written to handle just this type of call. I would rather leave the `makeAPICall()` function in its current state. It's pretty easy to read and relatively easy to debug if it comes to that. I would also rather not make an entire new function. If cURL changes need to be made down the line, or changes to the SOAP header, for example, it would increase upkeep, which leaves me with handling the depth when the call is made. Fortunately, the resulting code still looks pretty good:

```
function massPay($emails, $subject, $amount)
{
  $parameters = array();
  $parameters[] = array("EmailSubject", "ebl:string", "$subject");
  foreach($emails as $email)
  {
    $parameterList = "\t<ReceiverEmail xsi:type=\"ebl:string\">$email
      </ReceiverEmail>\n";
    $parameterList .= "\t<Amount currencyID=\"USD\" xsi:type=\"ebl:string\">$amount
      </Amount>\n";
    $parameterList .= "\t<Note xsi:type=\"ebl:string\">Thanks</Note>\n";
    $parameters[] = array("MassPayItem", "ebl:MassPayItemType", "$parameterList");
  }
  $xml = makeAPICall("MassPay", $parameters);
  return $xml;
}
```

Here a similar format is used as in earlier examples — the `parameters` array is populated with the optional and required elements for the call. In this case you "hide" the additional layer (or depth) of elements within the one `MassPayItem` element, allowing the `makeAPICall()` function to be used without any changes.

> *I debated how to handle this for quite a while. A more elegant solution might have been to introduce recursion within the* `makeAPICall()` *function to allow it to handle any required depth of parameters (and in fact this is the method that was used for the more complex eBay calls discussed in another chapter). In this case I sided with simplicity.*

PayPal doesn't return much when it comes to making a mass payment — merely success or failure of the payment. To get more details, you will need to perform a search (use the `TransactionSearch` call with the `TransactionClass` element set to `MassPay`).

```
<SOAP-ENV:Envelope xmlns:SOAP-ENV="http://schemas.xmlsoap.org/soap/envelope/"
  xmlns:ebl="urn:ebay:apis:eBLBaseComponents" xmlns:ns="urn:ebay:api:PayPalAPI">
  <SOAP-ENV:Header>
    <Security xmlns="http://schemas.xmlsoap.org/ws/2002/12/secext"
      xsi:type="wsse:SecurityType">
    </Security>
    <RequesterCredentials xmlns="urn:ebay:api:PayPalAPI"
      xsi:type="ebl:CustomSecurityHeaderType">
    <Credentials xmlns="urn:ebay:apis:eBLBaseComponents"
      xsi:type="ebl:UserIdPasswordType">
      <Username xsi:type="xs:string"></Username>
      <Password xsi:type="xs:string"></Password>
      <Subject xsi:type="xs:string"></Subject>
    </Credentials>
    </RequesterCredentials>
  </SOAP-ENV:Header>
  <SOAP-ENV:Body id="_0">
    <MassPayResponse xmlns="urn:ebay:api:PayPalAPI">
      <Timestamp xmlns="urn:ebay:apis:eBLBaseComponents">2005-04-19T03:48:25Z
        </Timestamp>
      <Ack xmlns="urn:ebay:apis:eBLBaseComponents">Success</Ack>
      <Version xmlns="urn:ebay:apis:eBLBaseComponents">1.000000</Version>
      <Build xmlns="urn:ebay:apis:eBLBaseComponents">1.0006</Build>
    </MassPayResponse>
  </SOAP-ENV:Body>
</SOAP-ENV:Envelope>
```

For this example, several of the values (the amount, for example) were restricted in a manner that the API does not require or enforce. If you want to send different amounts, or different notes to different recipients, the changes required should be quick.

Summary

Using PayPal's API introduces some new challenges with client-side certificates, and the inability of common tools to function in this manner. However, cURL's powerful connection libraries combined with PayPal's strong SOAP design (with minimal changes between requests) allow a single function to carry out all manner of requests.

Upon completing this chapter, you should be able to effectively use the PayPal API to do the following:

- Accept and process payments using PayPal notification features
- Request and search the details of a PayPal transaction
- Issue refunds with PayPal
- Use MassPay to send payments to a large number of people at once

Because transactions with PayPal involve real-world money rather than search results or product information, additional care should be taken. Client-side certificates must be kept outside the document root where they will be safer from the prying eyes of the curious user (or attacker). Programmers and maintainers must also be vigilant to ensure that proper authentication takes place before any of the calls are made, to ensure that unauthorized scripts or calls from the outside world cannot effect payments or refunds.

Even when payments are received from PayPal, care must be taken to ensure that the payment information received correctly matches an item within a local product database, because it is trivial for an attacker to modify simple identification items such as the product name or id.

These additional challenges are not without reward, however; using PayPal to process payments allows you to trade on PayPal's brand name in Internet payment processing. Speaking from experience, users are often far more willing to send a payment to an unknown website via PayPal than they are to give outside sources their credit card information. This is particularly useful when purchasing a digital-only product (such as access to a website or a download), because the option is available not to give a home address, which is generally required to authenticate credit card purchases.

This is the last full-chapter coverage of a single API. The next chapter introduces three different APIs in rapid succession, really just trying to help you hit the ground running when it comes to coding for their use.

11

Other Major APIs

This chapter seeks to introduce a few of the other APIs out there that have garnered some attention as of late. The coverage of each API is brief, but should allow you to hit the ground running if you decide to use any of these APIs in one of your projects. The three APIs introduced are the National Weather Service (NWS), which provides up-to-date weather information for locations (specified by longitude and latitude) within the U.S. only; Flickr, which is a photo publishing community site that allows you to share your photos with friends, with easy components to plug into blogs or other web spaces; and Del.icio.us (Delicious), which is a social bookmark manager that allows you to share your bookmarks with friends and people with similar interests, or pretty much everyone.

Overall, the goals of this chapter are as follows:

- Introduce you to a few different APIs with drastically different interface models
- Provide working code examples to get you up and running with three different APIs
- Start you thinking about different interface methods that could be used to develop your own API (this is discussed further in the next chapter)

National Weather Service

The U.S. NWS recently launched its own API, allowing users to request detailed weather information for any location within the contiguous United States. This information can be used to add a personal touch to websites (reporting either the weather at the site owner's location, or in combination with an IP lookup table, at the visitor's location), or be fully integrated with websites to complement other services (for example, travel websites). Unlike every other API discussed in this book, no authentication is required. The API is provided as a free service because the information gathered was provided at taxpayers' expense — no double charge.

The NWS provides access to two functions via its API: `NDFDGen` and `NDFDGenByDay` (NDFD stands for National Digital Forecast Database). `NDFDGen` provides weather forecasts in a granular manner over the specified period, whereas `NDFDGenByDay` provides only a summary of the data available. In these examples the `NDFDGenByDay` data is examined.

The NWS updates the data provided to the API once per hour, generally 45 minutes past the hour, so it is unnecessary and requested that you not request the data on page load. Your main options on how to handle this are (in decreasing order of preference): Cache the data that gets printed to the page and update that cache once an hour, cache the desired weather data and update that information once an hour, or cache the API's response and only update that cache once per hour.

In order to obtain weather information for a specific location, you will need the latitude and longitude. If you intend to display weather information for a static set of locations (you could, for example, display the weather at each of your company's offices), it should be simple just to calculate that information once (there are many websites that do zip code to latitude and longitude calculations for you) and store the results. If, on the other hand, you want to display a dynamic set of weather data (say, if you want to display the weather from a user's location), you will likely need to invest in an IP address to a physical location database. There are several commercial sources of this information. Remember that the United States is in the western hemisphere, so all longitude values will be negative.

SOAP Request

Requests against the NWS API are quite brief:

```
<?xml version="1.0" encoding="ISO-8859-1"?>
<SOAP-ENV:Envelope
  SOAP-ENV:encodingStyle="http://schemas.xmlsoap.org/soap/encoding/"
  xmlns:SOAP-ENV="http://schemas.xmlsoap.org/soap/envelope/"
  xmlns:xsd="http://www.w3.org/2001/XMLSchema"
  xmlns:xsi="http://www.w3.org/2001/XMLSchema-instance"
  xmlns:SOAP-ENC="http://schemas.xmlsoap.org/soap/encoding/"
  xmlns:si="http://soapinterop.org/xsd"
  xmlns:tns="http://weather.gov/forecasts/xml/DWMLgen/wsdl/ndfdXML.wsdl"
  xmlns:typens="http://weather.gov/forecasts/xml/DWMLgen/schema/ndfdXML.xsd">
  <SOAP-ENV:Body>
    <tns:NDFDgenByDay
      xmlns:tns="http://weather.gov/forecasts/xml/DWMLgen/wsdl/ndfdXML.wsdl">
      <latitude xsi:type="xsd:decimal">40.7409</latitude>
      <longitude xsi:type="xsd:decimal">-73.9997</longitude>
      <startDate xsi:type="xsd:date">2005-05-13</startDate>
      <numDays xsi:type="xsd:integer">5</numDays>
      <format xsi:type="typens:formatType">24 hourly</format>
    </tns:NDFDgenByDay>
  </SOAP-ENV:Body>
</SOAP-ENV:Envelope>
```

As usual, the SOAP `Envelope` contains a number of namespace declarations; these are dictated by the WSDL file provided by the NWS. The SOAP `Body` contains the essential portions of the request:

- `latitude` — The latitude for the location you are requesting information for. The latitude shown here is for southern Manhattan, New York City.

- `longitude` — The longitude for the location you are requesting information for. The longitude used is for southern Manhattan, New York City.
- `startDate` — The first day you want weather information for.
- `numDays` — The number of days you are requesting weather information for.
- `format` — There are two format options, `24 hourly` and `12 hourly`, returning data summarized in a 24- or 12-hour format, respectively.

SOAP Response

As also tends to be the case, the response is quite verbose:

```
<?xml version="1.0" encoding="ISO-8859-1"?>
<SOAP-ENV:Envelope
  SOAP-ENV:encodingStyle="http://schemas.xmlsoap.org/soap/encoding/"
  xmlns:SOAP-ENV="http://schemas.xmlsoap.org/soap/envelope/"
  xmlns:xsd="http://www.w3.org/2001/XMLSchema"
  xmlns:xsi="http://www.w3.org/2001/XMLSchema-instance"
  xmlns:SOAP-ENC="http://schemas.xmlsoap.org/soap/encoding/"
  xmlns:si="http://soapinterop.org/xsd">
  <SOAP-ENV:Body>
    <ns1:NDFDgenByDayResponse
      xmlns:ns1="http://weather.gov/forecasts/xml/DWMLgen/wsdl/ndfdXML.wsdl">
      <dwmlByDayOut xsi:type="xsd:string">
        <?xml version=;1.0; ?>
        <dwml version=;1.0; xmlns:xsd="http://www.w3.org/2001/XMLSchema"
        xmlns:xsi="http://www.w3.org/2001/XMLSchema-instance"
        xsi:noNamespaceSchemaLocation
      ="http://www.nws.noaa.gov/forecasts/xml/DWMLgen/schema/DWML.xsd">
        <head>
          <product concise-name="dwmlByDay" operational-mode="developmental">
            <title>NOAAs National Weather Service Forecast by 24 Hour period
              </title>
            <field>meteorological</field>
            <category>forecast</category>
            <creation-date refresh-frequency=;PT1H;>2005-05-13T16:06:09Z
              </creation-date>
          </product>
          <source>
            <more-information>http://www.nws.noaa.gov/forecasts/xml/
              </more-information>
            <production-center>Meteorological Development Laboratory
              <sub-center>Product Generation Branch</sub-center>
            </production-center>
            <disclaimer>http://www.nws.noaa.gov/disclaimer.html</disclaimer>
            <credit>http://weather.gov/</credit>
            <credit-logo>http://weather.gov/images/xml_logo.gif</credit-logo>
            <feedback>http://weather.gov/survey/nws-survey.php?code=xmlsoap
              </feedback>
          </source>
        </head>
        <data>
```

```
<location>
  <location-key>point1</location-key>
  <point latitude="40.7409" longitude="-73.9997" />
</location>
<time-layout time-coordinate="local" summarization="24hourly">
  <layout-key>k-p24h-n2-1</layout-key>
  <start-valid-time>2005-05-13T06:00:00-04:00</start-valid-time>
  <end-valid-time>2005-05-14T06:00:00-04:00</end-valid-time>
  <start-valid-time>2005-05-14T06:00:00-04:00</start-valid-time>
  <end-valid-time>2005-05-15T06:00:00-04:00</end-valid-time>
</time-layout>
<time-layout time-coordinate="local" summarization="12hourly">
  <layout-key>k-p12h-n4-2</layout-key>
  <start-valid-time>2005-05-13T06:00:00-04:00</start-valid-time>
  <end-valid-time>2005-05-13T18:00:00-04:00</end-valid-time>
  <start-valid-time>2005-05-13T18:00:00-04:00</start-valid-time>
  <end-valid-time>2005-05-14T06:00:00-04:00</end-valid-time>
  <start-valid-time>2005-05-14T06:00:00-04:00</start-valid-time>
  <end-valid-time>2005-05-14T18:00:00-04:00</end-valid-time>
  <start-valid-time>2005-05-14T18:00:00-04:00</start-valid-time>
  <end-valid-time>2005-05-15T06:00:00-04:00</end-valid-time>
</time-layout>
<parameters applicable-location="point1">
  <temperature type=;maximum; units="Fahrenheit" time-layout="k-p24h-n2-1">
    <name>Daily Maximum Temperature</name>
    <value>63</value>
    <value>69</value>
  </temperature>
  <temperature type=;minimum; units="Fahrenheit" time-layout="k-p24h-n2-1">
    <name>Daily Minimum Temperature</name>
    <value>50</value>
    <value>61</value>
  </temperature>
  <probability-of-precipitation type=;12 hour; units="percent"
    time-layout="k-p12h-n4-2">
    <name>12 Hourly Probability of Precipitation</name>
    <value>0</value>
    <value>11</value>
    <value>32</value>
    <value>46</value>
  </probability-of-precipitation>
  <weather time-layout="k-p24h-n2-1">
    <name>Weather Type, Coverage, and Intensity</name>
    <weather-conditions weather-summary="Increasing Clouds">
    </weather-conditions>
    <weather-conditions weather-summary="Chance Rain Showers">
      <value coverage="chance" intensity="none"
       weather-type="thunderstorms" qualifier="none">
      </value>
      <value coverage="chance" intensity="light"
        weather-type="rain showers" qualifier="none">
      </value>
    </weather-conditions>
  </weather>
```

```
            <conditions-icon type="forecast-NWS" time-layout="k-p24h-n2-1">
              <name>Conditions Icons</name>
              <icon-link>
                http://www.nws.noaa.gov/weather/images/fcicons/bkn.jpg</icon-link>
              <icon-link>
              http://www.nws.noaa.gov/weather/images/fcicons/hi_shwrs.jpg</icon-link>
            </conditions-icon>
          </parameters>
          </data>
          </dwml>
        </dwmlByDayOut>
      </ns1:NDFDgenByDayResponse>
    </SOAP-ENV:Body>
  </SOAP-ENV:Envelope>
```

The response is quite extensive because the service seeks to be very precise about the information it is providing. Note that there are two `time-layout` elements: one providing two start and end times, the other providing four. The first presents the time indices for the minimum and maximum temperatures, and the second is relevant for the probability of precipitation, which is given for 12-hour segments.

Note the `weather-conditions` elements under the `weather` element; they provide detailed information about expected weather for each time segment. This information can be brief, as shown with the first element, which merely states that there will be increasing cloud cover:

```
<value coverage="chance" intensity="none"
weather-type="thunderstorms" qualifier="none"></value>
```

Or the information can be more detailed, as shown in the second element, which indicates that there is a chance of thunderstorms, and also that there is a chance of light showers:

```
<weather-conditions weather-summary="Chance Rain Showers">
  <value coverage="chance" intensity="none" weather-type="thunderstorms"
    qualifier="none">
  </value>
  <value coverage="chance" intensity="light" weather-type="rain showers"
    qualifier="none">
  </value>
</weather-conditions>
```

Depending on the expected weather conditions, a large amount of information can be presented here.

One last item of particular note is the `icon-link` elements under `conditions-icon`. These are links to images hosted by the National Weather Service that graphically represent the expected weather conditions.

Generating the SOAP Request

Thanks to NuSOAP, generating the request is pretty simple, and follows the same structure used for other APIs:

```
require('../lib/nusoap.php');

  $today = date("Y-m-j");

$client =
new soapclient("http://weather.gov/forecasts/xml/DWMLgen/wsdl/ndfdXML.wsdl", true);

 $params = array(
      'latitude'     => "40.7409",
      'longitude'    => "-73.9997",
      'startDate'    => $today,
      'numDays'      => '2',
      'format'       => '24 hourly'
  );

  $result = $client->call('NDFDgenByDay',$params);
  $error = $client->getError();
  if ($error)
  {
    echo "error<pre>";
    print_r($error);
    print_r($result);
    echo "</pre>";
    exit;
  }
```

After the NuSOAP libraries are referenced, today's date is generated in a compatible format. The client is created by referencing the NWS's WSDL document, and the appropriate parameters are set (these are the same values as were used when the request was shown earlier). If an error was encountered, print out the information and exit.

Handling the SOAP Response

Having all that interesting weather data is of little use if you don't do anything with it, and it's pretty easy to display it to the end user in an attractive manner. This section of code will grab some essential data from the SOAP response (relevant dates, min and max temperatures, and the weather icons), then print it out in a simple table:

```
  $xml = simplexml_load_string($result);

  $dayNames = array();
  $weatherDates = array();
  foreach($xml->data->{'time-layout'}->{'start-valid-time'} AS $time)
  {
     $weatherDates[] = (string) $time;
     $dayNames[] = date("l", strtotime($time));
  }
```

Once the response is turned into a SimpleXML object, the dates for the returned data are copied into its own array. Both the full date and name of the day in question (for example, Wednesday) are recorded; the date itself isn't used here but would be the appropriate item to store if this data is going to be stored in a database.

Notice how the `time-layout` *and* `start-valid-time` *elements are encapsulated within the single quotes and curly braces. This is absolutely necessary to refer to an XML element within a SimpleXML object. Write that down.*

Also note the use of casting when populating the `$weatherDates` *array. Without this casting a SimpleXML object containing the appropriate date will be assigned to the* `$weatherDates` *array; with the casting, only the date it contains is assigned. This saves on overhead and helps prevent any "weirdness" later.*

```
$maxTemperature = array();
foreach($xml->data->parameters->temperature[0]->value AS $maxTemp)
{
  $maxTemperature[] = (int) $maxTemp;
}

$minTemperature = array();
foreach($xml->data->parameters->temperature[1]->value AS $minTemp)
{
  $minTemperature[] = (int) $minTemp;
}

$icons = array();
foreach($xml->data->parameters->{'conditions-icon'}->{'icon-link'} as $icon)
{
   $icons[] = (string) $icon;
}
```

No big tricks here — the minimum and maximum temperatures are recorded, as is the URL for the weather icon. Casting is again used to ensure that only the appropriate data is recorded, not the SimpleXML object containing the data.

```
echo "<table>\n<tr>";
$day = 0;
while(isset($weatherDates[$day]))
{
   echo "<th colspan=\"2\">{$dayNames[$day]}</th>";
   $day++;
}
echo "</tr>";

echo "<tr>";
$day = 0;
while(isset($weatherDates[$day]))
{
  echo "<td><b>Low</b>: {$minTemperature[$day]} <br>";
  echo "<b>High</b>:{$maxTemperature[$day]}<br></td>";
  echo "<td><img src=\"{$icons[$day]}\" align=\"right\">\n\n<br></td>";
  $day++;
}
echo "</tr></table>";
```

Finally, the information is printed out in a basic HTML table (if you're one of those anti-table pro-CSS people, just squint really hard and pretend it's CSS).

Take all of that (just raise the number of days you are requesting weather for) and you end up with something like the image in Figure 11-1.

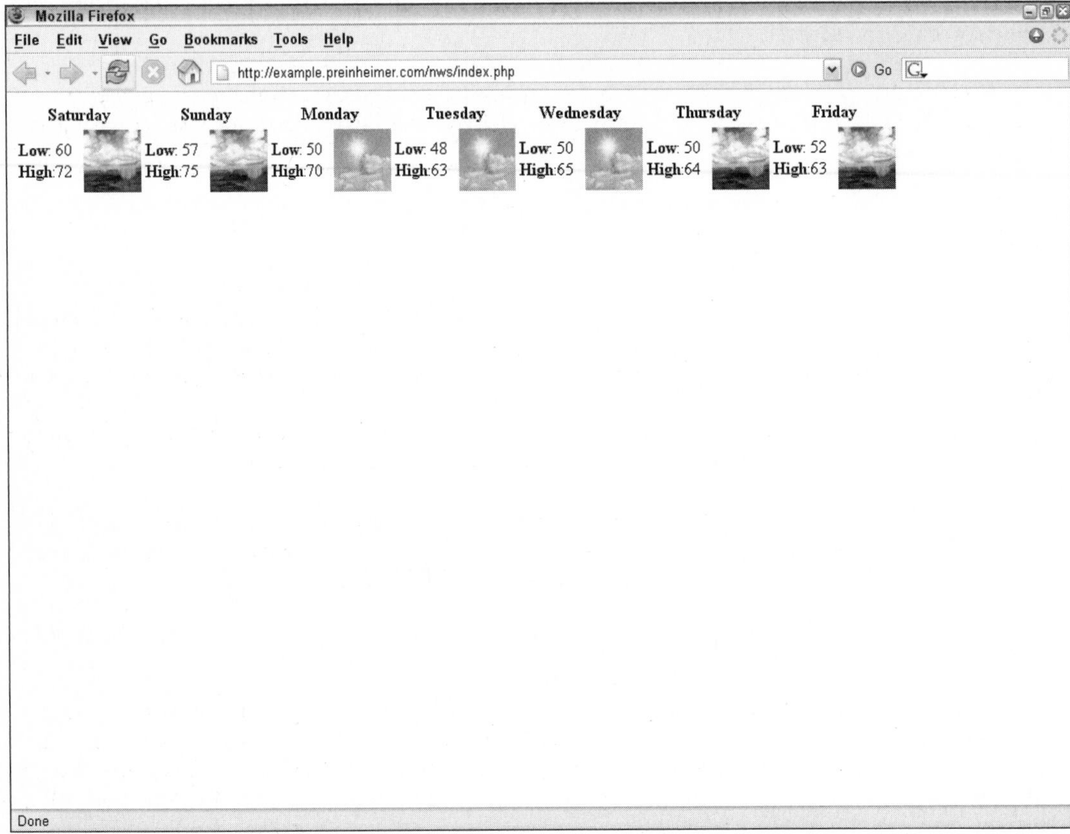

Figure 11-1

Cloudy Conclusions

The NWS API grants easy access to detailed weather forecasts for locations throughout the contiguous United States. In fact, many (if not most) media outlets use the National Weather Service as a primary source for up-to-date weather forecasts. Now your website or firm can be just as up to date and accurate. This information would be well suited for corporate intranets (at which point you may finally be able to convince fellow staffers to uninstall the various spyware utilities that perform a similar service), particularly ones with multiple sites in different geographic locations. In my experience, employees are very curious to learn what the weather is like where their co-workers are.

Flickr

Flickr has fast become *the* site to host images; its easy-to-use feature set combined with easy-to-use web elements to drop photos on blogs or homepages has made it a big hit. Andy Ihnatko of the Chicago Sun Times probably said it best:

> *There are already way too many websites out there where you can upload and display your digital photos, and on the whole, watching these services develop is like watching cavemen trying to figure out fire.*
>
> *But the folks who've created www.Flickr.com get it. They got it, and then they went and beat up some kid on the playground and they took his stuff, too.*

Strong praise, but they deserve it.

One of the API's most attractive options is that it gives you access to all of the (public) images within the archives, rather than just your own. This would allow (for example) a site about horticulture to randomly display images from within the Flickr database that have a particular keyword such as flower (being careful, of course, to credit the images). Though the process of randomly displaying images from the Flickr system is the focus of this brief introduction, the API itself is quite powerful—entire image management applications can be (and have been) built using the Flickr backend.

As seems to be a growing trend, the Flickr API offers both a SOAP and a REST interface; for this section the REST interface is used. The actions performed in this section are all "safe" in that they don't request any changes in Flickr's database, so I am comfortable with this approach.

Obtaining an API Key

Obtaining an API key is relatively easy; it's even an automated process if you are requesting a key for noncommercial use. Once you have logged in to your Flickr account, head to `www.flickr.com/services/api/` (it can be a bit tricky to find via the site's regular navigation; it's listed under the complete sitemap link, toward the bottom). Click the API Keys link, then the application link. You will need to enter a brief description of the application you are planning to build, and you're off to the races.

Determining Your User ID

Flickr associates a user id with every user. This is not the same as the username used to log in to the system. A user id is required to restrict searches to images from a particular user and it's also a very simple query. Here is the request URL:

```
http://www.flickr.com/services/rest/?method=flickr.people.findByUsername&api_key=13
  cff9127a1ceb6da54bd2d21e25d1aa&username=preinheimer
```

Flickr's response looks like this:

```
<?xml version="1.0" encoding="utf-8" ?>
<rsp stat="ok">
 <user id="77964564@N00" nsid="77964564@N00">
      <username>preinheimer</username>
 </user>
</rsp>
```

Although both id and nsid are the same in this case, the API's documentation indicates that the nsid is the value you want to record. The code used to generate this request and show the response is as follows:

```
<?php
$endPoint = "http://www.flickr.com/services/rest/?";

$parameters = array();
$parameters[] = array("method", "flickr.people.findByUsername");
$parameters[] = array("api_key", "13cff9127a1ceb6da54bd2d21e25d1aa");
$parameters[] = array("username", "preinheimer");

foreach ($parameters AS $parameter)
{
 $endPoint .= $parameter[0] . "=" . $parameter[1] . "&";
}

$response = file_get_contents($endPoint);
$xml = simplexml_load_string($response);
echo $response;
$nsid = $xml->user['nsid'];
?>
```

The call's endpoint is given by the API; the parameters change depending on the specific request. The various parameters are saved into an array before being combined to form the final endpoint. There are other ways to accomplish this (the entire URL could just be hard coded, for example), but using this framework should make calling a new method quick and easy. After the endpoint is set, the response document is retrieved and parsed into a SimpleXML object. Finally, the nsid is recorded for possible later use.

Retrieving Images from a Particular User

With the nsid in hand, retrieving images from a particular user is relatively easy:

```
$parameters = array();
$endPoint = "http://www.flickr.com/services/rest/?";
$parameters[] = array("method", "flickr.photos.search");
$parameters[] = array("api_key", "13cff9127a1ceb6da54bd2d21e25d1aa");
$parameters[] = array("user_id", "77964564@N00");

foreach ($parameters AS $parameter)
{
 $endPoint .= $parameter[0] . "=" . $parameter[1] . "&";
}
$response = file_get_contents($endPoint);
$xml = simplexml_load_string($response);
```

This request yields the following (some of the responses have been trimmed for size):

```
<rsp stat="ok">
  <photos page="1" pages="1" perpage="100" total="29">
    <photo id="6742937" owner="77964564@N00" secret="3e5b05764b" server="6"
      title="DCP_0877" ispublic="1" isfriend="1" isfamily="1" />
```

```
    <photo id="4968486" owner="77964564@N00" secret="0b35b20599" server="5"
      title="ForbiddenLove" ispublic="1" isfriend="1" isfamily="1" />
    <photo id="4968483" owner="77964564@N00" secret="67ec4565e6" server="5"
      title="Elegance of Three" ispublic="1" isfriend="1" isfamily="1" />
    <photo id="4968470" owner="77964564@N00" secret="c610053f55" server="4"
      title="WitheringBeauty" ispublic="1" isfriend="1" isfamily="1" />
    <photo id="4968466" owner="77964564@N00" secret="e7b93a7ef4" server="3"
      title="Pink" ispublic="1" isfriend="1" isfamily="1" />
  </photos>
</rsp>
```

As you can see, you get some information about each of the images applicable to the search. Some of the information provided, like `title` or `id`, is pretty self-explanatory, whereas the other information is a bit more arcane. `Owner` is the `nsid` of the owner of the image. Because all of the images are owned by the same person (that was the search performed), these will match all the way through. The `secret` value is required if you want to retrieve the particular image, and it can also be used to give a link to a private image. The `server` indicates which machine the image resides on. This information will be used to generate a link to the image in question. `ispublic`, `isfriend`, and `isfamily` are all binary values stating the permissions of the image: 1 = has access, 0 = does not have access.

Turning Image Information into a URL

Suspiciously absent from the image information is a URL from which the image can be retrieved or viewed. The information given, however, is sufficient to generate the URLs. The form for any URL is as follows:

```
http://static.flickr.com/{server-id}/{id}_{secret}_[stmbo].jpg
```

The `server-id`, `id`, and `secret` values map perfectly to the values returned by the API. The last options [`smstbo`] are used to indicate the desired size of the image:

- `s` — Small square, 75×75px
- `t` — Thumbnail, 100px on the longest side. The other side will be scaled appropriately.
- `m` — Small, 240px on the longest side. The other side will be scaled appropriately.
- `b` — Large, 1,024px on the longest side. This will only be available when the source image is sufficiently large. The other side will be scaled appropriately.
- `o` — Original. The original image, whatever size it is. You must use the appropriate file extension for the image (jpg | png | gif).

Note that when using the `t`, `m`, `b`, or `o` image sizes, the resultant image may or may not be square. It will be a proportionally sized image with the longest side being the indicated length.

Putting It Together

Putting what you know about image URLs together with the information received from the API, you can start sending image tags to the browser:

```
foreach($xml->photos->photo as $photo)
{
  echo "<img src=\"http://static.flickr.com/{$photo['server']}/{$photo['id']}_
    {$photo['secret']}_m.jpg\"><br>\n";
}
```

This comes out looking like the image in Figure 11-2.

Alternatively, for a more visually appealing display of graphics, adding in just a bit of styling, you can get something as shown in Figure 11-3. Here is the code:

```
echo "<img src=\"http://static.flickr.com/{$photo['server']}/{$photo['id']}_
{$photo['secret']}_m.jpg\" style=\"float: left; display: table-cell; width:
  240px; height: 240px; text-align: center; vertical-align: middle;\">\n";
```

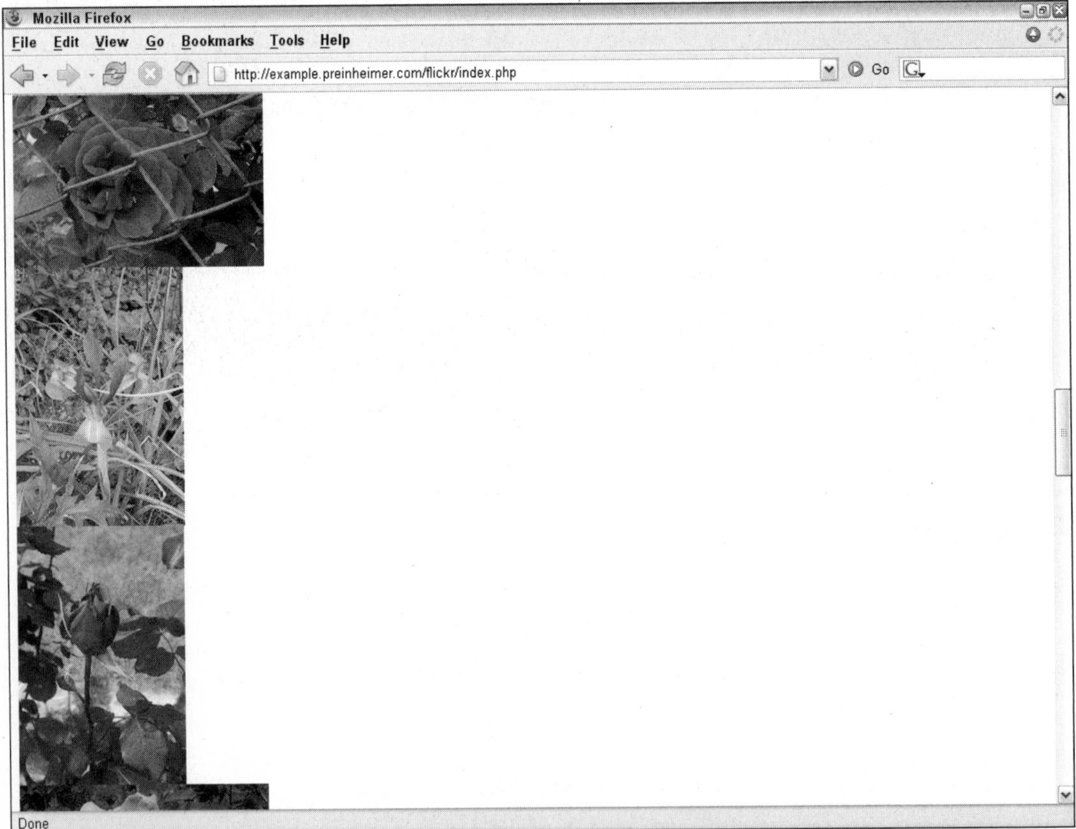

Figure 11-2

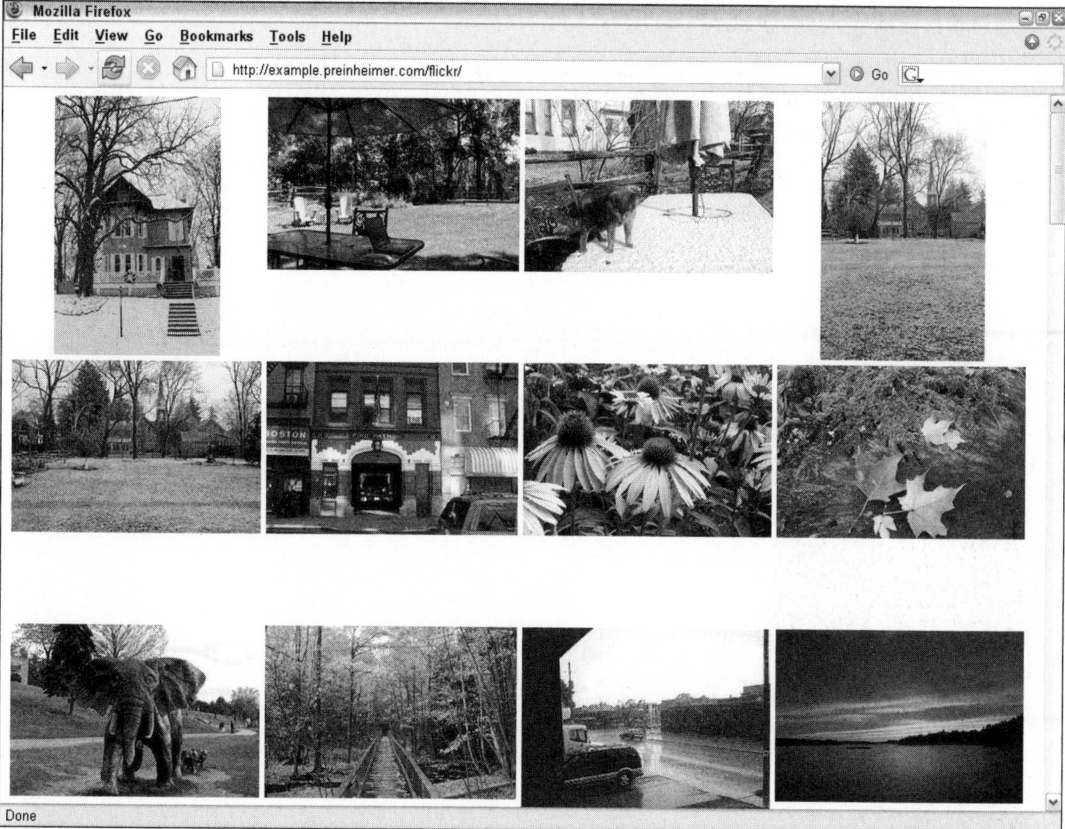

Figure 11-3

Finding Images by Tag

Flickr's system allows users to associate multiple tags with their images. This is a relatively loose system — not all users associate tags with their images, nor is there any required structure for the tags. That being said, the system is large enough that running a search for tags like "flower", "rose", or "puppy" is going to yield many results. Changing the script to search by tags only requires a few changes to the parameters given:

```
$parameters = array();
$parameters[] = array("method", "flickr.photos.search");
$parameters[] = array("api_key", "13cff9127a1ceb6da54bd2d21e25d1aa");
$parameters[] = array("tags", "flower");
```

This returns a number of images that have the tag "flower" associated with them.

Restricting Your Search by License

Flickr also allows users to specify a Creative Commons license (`http://creativecommons.org/`) to distribute their images under. When performing a search, you can restrict your search to images distributed under a specific license. The applicable licenses are as follows:

- 0 — None (All rights reserved)
- 1 — Attribution, noncommercial, share alike
- 2 — Attribution, noncommercial
- 3 — Attribution, noncommercial, no derivatives
- 4 — Attribution license
- 5 — Share-alike license
- 6 — Attribution, no derivatives

So to perform a search, restricting it to a particular license, just add `license` as a parameter:

```
$parameters[] = array("license", "2");
```

This will only return images licensed under the Attribution, noncommercial license.

Flickering Conclusion

The Flickr library is very extensive, containing images posted by users from around the globe. Even though only a percentage of users bother to tag their images with keywords, running a search for most words yields a plethora of results. The ability of users to associate licenses with their images, combined with the ability of the API to filter based on that information, can provide a wealth of images to be used in personal projects, or for dynamic displays on themed websites.

Del.icio.us

Del.icio.us is a social bookmarking tool, through which you can bookmark sites you like, share those bookmarks with friends, and tag those bookmarks to be searchable by all. Del.icio.us also has an API that can be used to access bookmarks already made or to add new bookmarks.

Restrictions on Use

In order to use the API, you must be a registered user of Del.icio.us, and requests must not be performed more than once per second. You should also set a unique User-Agent for your application — something identifying your application and the version. Common User-Agents (like PHP's default setting, for example) are likely to be throttled occasionally as they are abused. Monitor the responses received for a 503 error document and forcefully throttle your application's requests. Finally, ensure that any applications you release based on the site do not add or modify bookmarks without the user's consent, and try emailing the site's owner before you release anything. This will help ensure that your application isn't harmful and doesn't end up getting throttled.

Basic HTTP Authentication

All calls against the Del.icio.us API require the use of basic HTTP authentication. This involves including your credentials along with the HTTP header sent with the request. These are the same credentials (username and password) used to access the Del.icio.us site. In order to properly send your credentials, you need to encode your username and password with Base 64 encoding. Luckily, PHP has a function for this express purpose:

```
$authorization = base64_encode("username:password");
```

The encoded string looks like this:

```
cGt0bG9zczp0d21kZGx
```

This encoding must not be mistaken for encryption; the encoded string can easily be turned back into the original string with the `base64_decode()` function. The username-colon-password format is dictated by the HTTP specification, and is not a requirement of the `base64_encode()` function itself. This authentication information is included in the HTTP headers in this format:

```
Authorization: Basic cGt0bG9zczp0d21kZGx
```

With this authentication information in hand, a request can be successfully sent.

Obtaining Your Own Bookmarks

The API provides the ability to retrieve all of the bookmarks you have set to date. There is special note, however, that this functionality should only be used sparingly. If you plan on integrating your Del.icio.us bookmarks with your own site, ensure you only retrieve the full list of bookmarks you have set sparingly. The API also provides a last update API call, which you can use to determine when you last added a bookmark.

This code is a little different than previous situations where sockets were used to obtain a remote file. The only change this time is the inclusion of the basic authentication header:

```
<?php

  $endpoint = "http://del.icio.us/api/posts/get?";

  $authorization = base64_encode("pktloss:twiddle");

  $url_info = parse_url($endpoint);

  $host = $url_info['host'];
  $path = $url_info['path'] . "?" . $url_info['query'];
  $data = "";
```

The endpoint for the call is set, the username and password are base 64-encoded, and the URL is parsed into its component parts.

```
    $fp=fsockopen($host, 80);
    fputs($fp, "POST " . $path . " HTTP/1.1\r\n");
    fputs($fp, "Host: " . $host ."\r\n");
    fputs($fp, "Authorization: Basic $authorization\r\n");
    fputs($fp, "Accept: text/xml,application/xml,application/xhtml+xml,text/
  html;q=0.9,text/plain\r\n");
    fputs($fp, "Accept-Charset: ISO-8859-1,utf-8;q=0.7,*;q=0.7\r\n");
    fputs($fp, "Connection: close\r\n");
    fputs($fp, "User-Agent: PReinheimer Test App v0.1\r\n");
    fputs($fp, "Content-Type: application/x-www-form-urlencoded\r\n");
    fputs($fp, "Content-Length: " . strlen($data) . "\r\n\r\n");
    fputs($fp, "$data");
```

Here the request itself is sent. Note the `Authorization` header, which is required to access this API, as well as the `User-Agent` header, which identifies the application. The agent string here is pretty meaningless; remember to set something for your own applications, and try to make it more indicative of your application.

```
    $response="";
    while(!feof($fp))
    {
      $response.=fgets($fp, 128);
    }
    fclose($fp);
    list($http_headers, $http_content)=explode("\r\n\r\n", $response);
    echo "Headers: \n" . $http_headers . "\n\n";
    echo "Content: \n" . $http_content;
  ?>
```

Finally, the server's response is pulled from the socket and parsed into its component (header and content) parts. The output is as follows:

```
Headers:
HTTP/1.1 200 OK
Date: Mon, 16 May 2005 19:18:13 GMT
Server: Apache/1.3.33 (Debian GNU/Linux) mod_gzip/1.3.26.1a mod_perl/1.29
    AuthMySQL/4.3.9-2
Vary: *
Connection: close
Transfer-Encoding: chunked
Content-Type: text/xml

Content:
3a4

<?xml version='1.0' standalone='yes'?>
<posts dt="2005-05-16" tag="" user="pktloss">
  <post href="http://bixdata.com/" description="BixData - Performance Monitor,
    Process Viewer, Critical Notifications" hash="d80779ee4c81361239bdb03f608169e0"
    others="1" tag="monitor server software" time="2005-05-16T03:10:20Z" />
```

```
  <post href="http://moonsoar.com/" description="MoonSoar.com"
    hash="4f73d86034dabcd288029a3a7aca4a10" others="2" tag="blogs" time="2005-05-
    16T02:32:03Z" />
  <post href="http://shiflett.org/" description="Chris Shiflett: Home"
    hash="37e86256d39dd6de808d8ab9e8f1f46d" others="33" tag="blogs" time="2005-05-
    16T03:09:01Z" />
  <post href="http://www.acmqueue.org/" description="ACM Queue - Developer Tools,
    Hardware, Security, Open Source, Enterprise Search, Data Management, Virtual
    Machines, Wireless" hash="630611753b9481be8d0e5ec1dda2441d" others="29"
    tag="system:unfiled" time="2005-05-16T03:08:46Z" />
</posts>

0
```

The HTTP headers are pretty standard. The only thing to note here is the response code (`200` in this case; `404 Document not found` is probably the one people are most familiar with). As mentioned earlier, the people who run Del.icio.us would like you to keep your code watching for a `503 Service Unavailable error`, which will indicate that you are using the service too often, and must throttle back. The content contains a nice XML document outlining the Del.icio.us bookmarks I have set up.

> *One of the first things I usually do when I start working with an XML document in code is to stick it into SimpleXML and* `print_r` *the result. This is spectacularly unhelpful this time around because* `print_r` *doesn't reveal attributes when displaying SimpleXML objects. So* `echo'ing` *out the document will need to suffice.*

Getting that code into a SimpleXML object takes a little bit of work. The document starts and ends with some extraneous characters that will prevent the import string from handling the response, so you need to pull that out. The initial characters always appear on the first line, so they can be handled by dumping the first line. The last 0 can be removed by cutting everything off after the final closing brace:

```
$firstLine = strpos($http_content, "\n");
$http_content = substr($http_content, $firstLine + 1);
$lastLine = strrpos($http_content, ">");
$http_content = substr($http_content, 0, $lastLine + 1);
```

The first new line character is located and its position recorded to be used when trimming the start of the string. The final closing brace is located (`strrpos` searches a string in reverse) and the process is repeated.

```
$xml = simplexml_load_string($http_content);

foreach($xml as $post)
{
  echo "Site: {$post['description']} at {$post['href']} has the following tag(s):
    {$post['tag']}\n";
}
```

Finally, the SimpleXML object can be created and iterated through. The output looks like this:

```
Site: BixData - Performance Monitor, Process Viewer, Critical Notifications at
    http://bixdata.com/ has the following tag(s): monitor server software
Site: MoonSoar.com at http://moonsoar.com/ has the following tag(s): blogs
Site: Chris Shiflett: Home at http://shiflett.org/ has the following tag(s): blogs
Site: ACM Queue - Developer Tools, Hardware, Security, Open Source, Enterprise
    Search, Data Management, Virtual Machines, Wireless at http://www.acmqueue.org/
    has the following tag(s): system:unfilled
```

Adding a Caching Layer

Since the owners of Del.icio.us asked so nicely, it would be appropriate to add a small caching layer into any applications built to ensure that both your machine and the Del.icio.us server aren't bogged down with repeated requests. This caching layer will have two functions: At the very bottom sits `baseCall()`, which takes care of actually making needed requests to the API, and returns either the resulting document, the word `THROTTLE` indicating it received a request to slow down incoming requests, or null indicating that it received some other error. Above `baseCall()` sits `callDelicious()`, which looks at each request to call the API, and tries to load the results of a recent identical request from the database. Failing that, it passes the request off to `baseCall()` and records the results.

The `baseCall()` function is remarkably similar to the code already presented:

```
function baseCall($endpoint)
{
  $authorization = base64_encode("pktloss:twiddle");
  $url_info = parse_url($endpoint);
  $host = $url_info['host'];
  $path = $url_info['path'] . "?" . $url_info['query'];
  $data = "";
  $fp=fsockopen($host, 80);
  fputs($fp, "POST " . $path . " HTTP/1.1\r\n");
  fputs($fp, "Host: " . $host ."\r\n");
  fputs($fp, "Authorization: Basic $authorization\r\n");
  fputs($fp, "Accept:
   text/xml,application/xml,application/xhtml+xml,text/html;q=0.9,text/plain\r\n");
  fputs($fp, "Accept-Charset: ISO-8859-1,utf-8;q=0.7,*;q=0.7\r\n");
  fputs($fp, "Connection: close\r\n");
  fputs($fp, "User-Agent: PReinheimer Test App v0.1\r\n");
  fputs($fp, "Content-Type: application/x-www-form-urlencoded\r\n");
  fputs($fp, "Content-Length: " . strlen($data) . "\r\n\r\n");
  fputs($fp, "$data");
  $response="";
  while(!feof($fp))
  {
    $response.=fgets($fp, 128);
  }
  fclose($fp);
  list($http_headers, $http_content)=explode("\r\n\r\n", $response);
  if (strpos($http_headers, "200 OK"))
  {
    $firstLine = strpos($http_content, "\n");
    $http_content = substr($http_content, $firstLine + 1);
```

```
        $lastLine = strrpos($http_content, ">");
        $http_content = substr($http_content, 0, $lastLine + 1);

        $xml = simplexml_load_string($http_content);
        return $xml;
    }else if (strpos($http_headers, "503 Service Unavailable"))
    {
        return "THROTTLE";
    }else
    {
        return NULL;
    }
}
```

The only difference between this code and the code presented earlier is the function encapsulation, and the examination of the response for either the `200 OK` or `503 Service Unavailable` response codes. If the response is `OK`, the document is parsed and returned; on a 503, the word `THROTTLE` is returned, and if neither response is received, `NULL` is returned.

The `callDelicious` function gets a little more complicated, and that should be expected, attempting to handle many of the situations.

```
function callDelicious($endpoint, $parameters)
{
    foreach ($parameters AS $parameter)
    {
            $endPoint .= $parameter[0] . "=" . $parameter[1] . "&";
    }

    $key = md5($endpoint);
    $today = date("Y-m-j H:i:s", time() - 5 * 60);
    $query = "SELECT `key`, `xml` FROM 11_delicious_cache WHERE `key` = '$key' &&
      `tstamp` > '$today' ORDER BY `tstamp` DESC LIMIT 1";
    $result = getAssoc($query, 0);
```

The full endpoint URL for the REST call is determined and then hashed with the MD5 algorithm. Hashing the URL results in a short SQL safe string, which is ideal for this situation. A cached copy of this endpoint is checked for from within the database — this code checks for a copy that was saved 5 minutes ago (5 minutes * 60 seconds). Depending on your needs, you may want to tweak this time up or down. Realistically, if I was using this as a plugin component on my blog, I would probably set the time to 1 hour.

```
    if (isset($result['xml']))
    {
      $xml = simplexml_load_string($result['xml']);
```

If a recent cached copy was found, create the SimpleXML object to be returned later.

```
    }else
    {
       $xml = baseCall($endpoint);
```

Because a cached copy was not located, the `baseCall` function is leaned on to retrieve a recent version.

```
if ($xml == null)
{
  //Record Error?
  $xml = "THROTTLE";
}
```

Unfortunately, it seems that `baseCall` was not able to retrieve a more recent version of that particular endpoint. Depending on how and where your code is used, you may want to note this error for further examination, or cross your fingers and hope that it was a temporary connectivity issue and hope it will resolve itself. Either way, the function will attempt to locate an older version of the endpoint.

```
if ($xml == "THROTTLE")
{
    $query = "SELECT `key`, `xml` FROM 11_delicious_cache WHERE `key` = '$key'
      ORDER BY `tstamp` DESC LIMIT 1";
    $result = getAssoc($query, 0);
    if (isset($result['xml']))
    {
      $safeXML = mysql_real_escape_string($result['xml']);
      $insertQuery = "REPLACE INTO 11_delicious_cache (`key`, `xml`, `tstamp`)
        VALUES (MD5('$endpoint'), '$safeXML', null)";
      insertQuery($insertQuery);
      $xml = simplexml_load_string($result['xml']);
```

If the 503 error was received, the server has requested that the frequency of your connections back off, so the database is checked again for any existing copy of this endpoint. Hopefully there is one in there, even if it is older than 5 minutes. If one is found, it is updated in the database to have a current timestamp. This should prevent any more calls being made to this endpoint for the next 5 minutes. The old cached copy is used to create a SimpleXML object to be returned when the function finishes.

```
    }else
    {
      $xml = null;
    }
```

In this case, either the `THROTTLE` response or an unknown response was received, and unfortunately there was no cached copy of this request in the database. There really isn't anything else to try, so `null` is returned.

```
}else if (is_object($xml))
{
  $safeXML = mysql_real_escape_string($xml->asXML());
  $insertQuery = "REPLACE INTO 11_delicious_cache (`key`, `xml`, `tstamp`)
    VALUES (MD5('$endpoint'), '$safeXML', null)";
  insertQuery($insertQuery);
```

Here, finally, a good response from the API is handled. The XML object returned by `baseCall()` is turned back into a well-formed XML string, escaped for use within a SQL query, and saved to the database.

```
        }else
        {
           $xml = null;
        }
    }
    return $xml;
}
```

This last case should not happen, but it's a good idea to allow for the unexpected within your decision blocks. Finally, `$xml` is returned, which hopefully contains a SimpleXML object.

This caching method has a few pros and cons, which may not be immediately visible when reading the disjoint segments this page layout provides.

Pros:

- Like any good caching layer, this one allows upper layers to completely ignore the fact that they are getting cached in the first place.
- This pair of functions is modular enough that they should work well for any REST-based API.
- Because of the way the database key is generated (including the full endpoint, rather than just the parameters), the same function and database table can be used for multiple REST APIs.

Cons:

- While this pair ensures that identical queries are not run one after another, it is still very easy to run too many queries too quickly: Run different queries. This could be a problem if many queries are called by the same block of code. If this happens, it is probably time to restructure your code so that queries are updated by the clock, not by page load. At the very least, consider changing the cache duration for different endpoints; that way they won't all expire at once.
- Furthermore, with the throttled issue, a better approach than just updating the current endpoint to the current timestamp would be to refresh all endpoints to the present. This would essentially prevent any REST calls that have been made before from happening again for as long as you let caches live.
- MD5 is case sensitive, whereas the API may or may not be. This could result in endpoints the API considers identical to be cached separately (and hence, allowed to be called more often).

Retrieving a List of Used Tags

One of the nice things about Del.icio.us is that it allows you to associate tags with each of your bookmarks. One thing I hate about tags in general is when I accidentally use multiple tags that essentially mean the same thing ("blog" versus "blogs," for example). As such, it is usually a good idea to look at the tag(s) used already before adding a tag to something else. The API provides an endpoint for this call at `http://del.icio.us/api/tags/get?`, and using the functions just created, calling it couldn't be easier:

```
require("../common_db.php");
$endpoint = "http://del.icio.us/api/tags/get?";
$parameters = array();
$xml = callDelicious($endpoint, $parameters);
```

I've snuck the requirement for my database functions in there (it is needed for the caching functions), but other than that, all that has been set is the endpoint. The output looks like this:

```
<?xml version="1.0" standalone="yes"?>
<tags>
  <tag count="2" tag="blogs"/>
  <tag count="1" tag="monitor"/>
  <tag count="1" tag="server"/>
  <tag count="1" tag="software"/>
  <tag count="1" tag="system:unfiled"/>
</tags>
```

That lists each of the tags used, as well as the number of times that specific tag has been used.

Adding a Tag to Del.icio.us

Being able to access all those tags is of little use if you can't add a few of your own. Sure, the Del.icio.us website and bookmarks make this easy, but it's always more fun to do it through code. With a simple form it's easy enough to accomplish:

```
if ($_POST['method'] == "add")
{
  $endPoint = "http://del.icio.us/api/posts/add?";
  $parameters = array();
  $parameters[] = array('url', urlencode($_POST['url']));
  $parameters[] = array('extended', urlencode($_POST['extended']));
  $parameters[] = array('tags', urlencode($_POST['tags']));
  $parameters[] = array('description', urlencode($_POST['description']));
  $parameters[] = array('dt', date("Y-m-jTH:i:sZ"));
  $xml = callDelicious($endPoint, $parameters);
}else
{
  echo <<< htmlCodeBlock
  <form method="post">
  <input type="hidden" name="method" value="add">
  URL: <input type="text" name="url"><br>
  Extended: <input type="text" name="extended"><br>
  Description:<input type="text" name="description"><br>
  Tags:<input type="text" name="tags"><br>
  <br>
  <input type="submit">
  </form>
htmlCodeBlock;
}
```

When the code is first called, a brief form is printed out, which allows the user to enter any desired information about the bookmark they wish to add. The second time around, the parameters are pulled from the `$_POST` variable, URL-encoded, and sent off to the API.

Note the placement of the closing `heredoc` *tag at the very beginning of the line. Remember, you can't have any white space before that tag or it won't work.*

That code works well enough, but why not display the tags already used to the users so they can make more intelligent choices about which tags to use?

```
{
  $endPoint = "http://del.icio.us/api/tags/get?";
  $xml = callDelicious($endPoint, array());
  $usedTags = array();
  foreach($xml as $tag)
  {
    $usedTags[] = $tag['tag'];
  }
  sort($usedTags);
  $usedTags = implode(" ", $usedTags);

  echo <<< htmlCodeBlock
  <form method="post">
  <input type="hidden" name="method" value="add">
  URL: <input type="text" name="url"><br>
  Extended: <input type="text" name="extended"><br>
  Descirption:<input type="text" name="description"><br>
  Tags:<input type="text" name="tags"><br>
  Previously Used Tags: $usedTags<br>
  <br>
  <input type="submit">
  </form>
htmlCodeBlock;
}
```

Using the API, the list of tags used previously is retrieved, sorted alphabetically, and displayed to the user. This will help avoid duplicate nearly similar tag issues. The resulting form looks like the image in Figure 11-4.

Delicious Conclusion

Finally, here is a heading title that looks like a pun. The Del.icio.us social bookmarking tools are becoming wildly popular; particularly, it seems, among PHP programmers. Incorporating portions of your social bookmarks into your website is an easy way to keep fresh and interesting content displayed. The ability to add bookmarks would plug in well with blogging software. Along with looking for a trackback RPC on any URLs entered into a blog entry, the software could offer the user the opportunity to add that URL as a bookmark, if not already present.

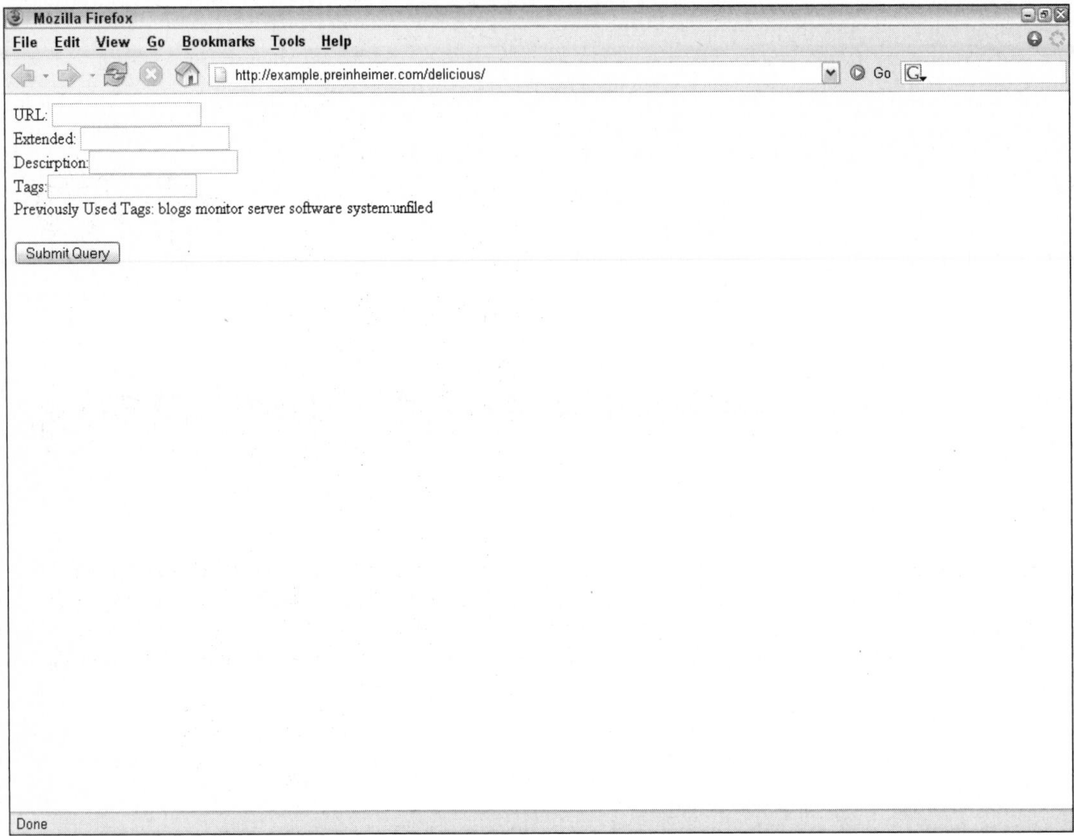

Figure 11-4

Summary

This chapter introduced the following major APIs and examined their use:

- National Weather Service, including information on how to obtain detailed weather forecasts for a specific region.
- Flickr, including information on obtaining images in a variety of different ways.
- Del.icio.us, including information on how to obtain your own bookmarks, and implementing your own caching system to reduce total requests.

This concludes the coverage of existing APIs. The next chapter introduces the major topics of concern when building your own API for others to use, and goes through a series of code examples along those lines.

12

Producing Web APIs

In this chapter, the focus flips from using an API presented by another group to creating one of your own. Creating an API isn't a terribly complicated process; frameworks like NuSOAP handle all the difficult XML processing and generation for you. There are, however, numerous considerations that should be examined before starting a new API project. This chapter covers the following:

- Planning your API
- Enabling authentication and encryption
- Deciding between REST and SOAP
- Working with your community of developers
- Performance considerations
- Error handling

Additionally, the end of this chapter provides two complete examples, one using REST and the other using SOAP.

Planning the API

You have doubtlessly heard the old saying "Fail to plan, and you plan to fail." This is most definitely true in this case. Several critical decisions need to be made before development is begun because, after all, as soon as you put your API out there for others to use, it becomes both difficult for you to implement the changes and troublesome to developers utilizing your API that may be affected by your changes.

Security

There are several options when it comes to the level of security (or lack of security) protecting your API. As is usually the case, additional layers of security introduce additional barriers to use, so a balance must be sought between securing the API, while still making it as easy as possible for the target development community to use the API. Keep in mind that for our purposes, security is for both protecting the data on your server as well as possibly protecting the integrity of the developers themselves by enforcing developer registration (and utilizing a developer "token" for web services). Although this discussion doesn't get deep into code, I'll try to highlight some of the important considerations.

An Open API

Under an open API, absolutely no security or authentication methods are used. A query is received from the wild, and the system makes its best effort to respond to it appropriately. This has several advantages and disadvantages.

Advantages:

- Absolute minimum barrier to use — By not using encryption or special authentication methods, anyone with access to the Internet should be able to begin working with your API quickly.
- Easily distributed code — Login accounts or developer key programs that make use of your API can be widely distributed and used right out of the box.
- Less to worry about — If you aren't managing user accounts or development keys, it's one less thing to keep track of, and your code efforts can concentrate solely on developing the API itself.

Disadvantages:

- No control — Anyone, anywhere, can use the API, and while this may sound like the goal of web services, it drastically limits your response if abuse requests begin pouring in. If those requests are coming from an application on a single machine, it is easy enough to recognize the requests and block them at the firewall. But should an application that behaves poorly reach wide distribution, you will have a very difficult time dealing with the requests.
- No encryption — All requests and responses are visible to anyone between the requesting server and the API server.
- Can't contact developers — Because anyone anywhere can access the API without any prior registration, you are left without any method of directly engaging developers using the API. You may want to contact developers in situations where their application is being abusive, when changes are being made to the API that will affect their application, or to seek suggestions on how to improve the API itself.
- Abuse — Unfortunately today, systems with little or no security or authentication make prime targets for abuse by some less ethical elements out there. Even if you feel that the risk is minimal, you may end up surprised at what others can take advantage of.

With those elements in mind, the only situations in which a completely open API would be appropriate are ones where the API is used only to request information, never to publish it, and where the information being requested is generated (or cached) in a very CPU nonintensive manner. A perfect example would be the National Weather Service API presented in Chapter 11. It only accepts requests for information, and those requests are easily cached for a full hour on the server. In cases where the API allows information to be pushed to it, some authentication is required to determine who is pushing the information, and when requests can be CPU-intensive, the remote application needs to be identifiable so incoming requests can be throttled if necessary.

HTTP Authentication

Authentication can be passed in the HTTP headers of incoming requests. This is the same type of authentication that is used when your browser creates a small login window when attempting to access a site. The authentication information is Base 64-encoded, so it does look like it is encrypted when transmitted over the wire, but in reality it is not. This encoding only ensures that all characters are valid to be passed in the header and is not intended to provide any level of security.

Advantages:

- Easily handled — Because the authentication information is sent in the HTTP headers, it can be handled by some moderately complex routers or gateways. This will allow for hardware-level throttling of abusive clients, or routing based on specific users. On the application side, the authentication will actually be handled by your web server, not your application. Web servers are developed and tested with high performance in mind, so this will likely end up being faster than any attempt to handle authentication in the application itself.
- Transparent — Because the web server is handling the authentication, you may choose to completely ignore what user is logged in, and concentrate solely on handling the request. This is obviously only applicable when requests are user-agnostic (every user receives the same response to the same query).
- Easy to code — Adding an additional HTTP header is relatively easy in most programming languages. It is also pretty universally available even in shared hosting situations (which may prevent things like SSL requests or external libraries).

Disadvantages:

- Authentication is sent in the clear — Base 64 is a two-way algorithm. Anyone who intercepts the request can determine the username and password being used, but they don't even need to; they can just use an identical header themselves.
- Username restriction — When using HTTP authentication, the colon (:) cannot be used in the username. A minor restriction, but one to keep in mind.
- No encryption — All requests and responses are visible to anyone between the requesting server and the API server.
- Slight barrier to use — Those unfamiliar with this method of authentication may shy away from attempting it.

This basic level of authentication is sufficient for many API applications. The presence of some basic authentication allows the API to either be client-aware or client-agnostic, depending on its specific needs, and also allows for throttling or denial to abusive clients. It would be a good idea with this type of authentication to provide some separation between the username and password combo used for the API and the site at large. This way, should the API's authentication information be compromised (by someone with access to the code, or by grabbing it off the wire), the valid user can use their regular information to change the API's credentials.

Server-Side Code

Most of the work is going to be done by the web server, which will handle the authentication from the user. Apache can use a flat file to look up user accounts, but this isn't very practical for an API with a changing user base. Apache can use a Berkeley database instead of a flat file if you use the mod_db or mod_dbm modules. BerkeleyDB is standard under many Linux distributions; under Windows or in situations where it isn't installed, the package can be obtained from www.sleepycat.com. In order to use BerkeleyDB, PHP needs to be configured with the -with-db4 option, and for Apache to support it for authentication, it must be compiled with the --enable-module=auth_db option.

Configuration (either in httpdconf or .htaccess) should look something like this:

```
<Directory /www/domains/api.example.com >
  AuthName "API Requires Registration"
  AuthType Basic
  AuthDBUserFile /www/basicAuth/api.example.com/passwords.dat
  require valid-user
</Directory>
```

The Directory parameter sets the directory on the file system that will be protected by the basic authentication. AuthName sets the message that would be shown to users if they attempted to access the page via a browser. AuthType is basic, the appropriate entry for this type of authentication. AuthDBUserFile sets the path to the Berkeley database that users will be authenticated from; note that it is *outside* the document root—don't be silly and let attackers download your database. Finally, the require statement indicates that users attempting to access the directory must be present in the database.

All of that is useless if users can't be added to the database as required — a feat accomplished by this function:

```
function createUser($username, $password)
{
  $chars = "abcdefghijklmnopqrstuvwxyzABCDEFGHIJKLMNOPQRSTUVWXYZ0123456789";
  $r1 = rand(1, strlen($chars) - 1);
  $r2 = rand(1, strlen($chars) - 1);
  $salt = substr($chars, $r1, 1) . substr($chars, $r2, 1);
  $saltedPassword = crypt($password, $salt);
  $resource = dba_open("/www/basicAuth/api.example.com/passwords.dat", "c", "db4");
  if (dba_insert($username, $saltedPassword, $resource))
  {
    dba_close($resource);
    return true;
  }else
  {
    dba_close($resource);
    return false;
  }
}
```

The essential parts of this function are the opening of the database with the dba_open() function (using the c parameter indicates that the database should be created if it isn't found, and db4 is the database type), inserting the username and encrypted password, and then closing the database connection.

Randomly generated salt is sent to the `crypt` *function with the password to generate an encrypted password resistant to dictionary attacks. Passwords can still be looked up because the* `crypt` *function prepends the salt to the encrypted password.*

Removing a user from the database is similarly easy:

```
function deleteUser($user)
{
  $resource = dba_open("/www/basicAuth/api.example.com/passwords.dat", "c", "db4");
  dba_delete($user, $resource);
  dba_close($resource);
}
```

Finally, should you wish to access the user's information from the API script itself, use this:

```
$username = $_SERVER['PHP_AUTH_USER'];
$password = $_SERVER['PHP_AUTH_PW'];
```

Both variables are stored in the `$_SERVER` global array; the password variable is the clear text version of the password. Remember that the user has already been authenticated by the web server by the time the script is executed, so this information is really only going to be used for recordkeeping purposes.

Client-Side Code

In order to access the API, the client application will need to send an additional HTTP header containing their username and password encoded with Base 64.

```
$authorization = base64_encode("username:password");
```

First the username and password must be encoded with the built-in function. The username-colon-password format is specified by the HTTP specification.

```
fputs($fp, "Authorization: Basic $authorization\r\n");
```

During the socket connection, the Authorization header should be sent along with the regular HTTP headers.

Message-Based Authentication

Client credentials can also be passed along with the regular message payload. This is marginally easier to implement on the client side because adding credentials should be no more difficult than adding another parameter to the request. Remember that even if a secure (SSL) endpoint is used, the URL used for the request is still sent in the clear, so if the credentials are passed on the URL (as is the case with a REST request), they will be visible to any and all intermediaries.

Advantages:

- Easily handled — Authentication should be checked before any other processing, just like a regular page.
- Easy to code — Programmers who wish to access the API need only add an additional parameter.
- Easy to track — Configuring your application to track how many calls during a certain time period, and throttle if necessary, should be easy.

Disadvantages:

- Credentials in the clear — REST APIs will have their credentials sent in the clear whether or not a secure endpoint is used. Nonsecure endpoints will have credentials sent in the clear for both REST and SOAP APIs.
- No encryption — All requests and responses are visible to anyone between the requesting server and the API server.

Message-based authentication is very similar to HTTP authentication in the level of security it provides, the primary difference being the pass off from handling the authentication from the web server to the API application itself. As with HTTP authentication, the API's authentication should be separate from authentication used elsewhere on the site.

Server-Side Code

Once the client's username and password have been made SQL safe, they should be run against your API database. Remember that the authentication information used should be different from authentication used elsewhere on the site.

```
function checkUser($username, $password)
{
  $query = "SELECT `user_level` FROM `users` WHERE `username` = '$username' AND
    `password` = '$password'";
  $results = getAssoc($query, 1);
  return $results['level'];
}
```

This is just your basic authentication function, nothing fancy.

Client-Side Code

The process the client will go through to pass the authentication information depends on whether SOAP or REST is used, and is discussed in the "REST or SOAP?" section, later in this chapter.

SSL Endpoint

Configuring your web server to present the API over an SSL connection adds protection for both the request and response bodies, while requiring little to no additional coding for the API. Remember that the use of a server certificate only authenticates the server for the client, it does nothing to identify the client itself. It is best used layered with one of the previous two examples.

Advantages:

- Encryption — Both request and response bodies are protected from intermediate prying eyes.
- Server authenticated — Clients who record the server's SSL certificate can monitor it to ensure it does not change over time (which could indicate a man-in-the-middle attack). Using a certificate signed by a signing authority can also provide a similar level of assurance for the client application.
- Easy setup — No additional coding required, just configure the web server.

Disadvantages:

- Increased load — Encrypting and decrypting communications is noticeably more CPU-intensive than unencrypted communications. Every request requires additional back and forth communications to set up the secure socket.
- No client identification — Using an SSL
- Additional client-side requirements — Handling SSL from the client side isn't always trivial, and languages may require additional extensions installed (which may or may not be available in a shared host environment).

SSL is an excellent layer to add to any API. It provides security for the request and response payloads, as well as provides some assurance for the client application as to the identity of the server. It is easily combined with either HTTP authentication or message-based authentication. Some care, however, should be taken not to use SSL unnecessarily, because it has additional requirements for the client application that not all developers may be able to meet, and it places additional CPU load on both sides as messages are encrypted and decrypted.

Server-Side Code

No code is required to support being served over SSL. Just configure the web server to present the API over a secure connection.

Client-Side Code

In order to connect to a secure endpoint, PHP will need to be configured with the `--with-openssl` option. You will also recognize SSL support because https will appear under the Registered PHP Streams list in the `phpinfo()` output, and SSL will also show up under Registered Stream Socket Transports.

Client-Side Certificates

The API server can generate a certificate and provide it to the client via a secure channel before any requests are made. This certificate is then used in the authentication process; this confirms the identity of both the client and server before requests are made. Although this method provides the greatest level of security (barring a dedicated VPN connection, which won't be covered here), it also has the most strenuous requirements on both sides: not all modules (say, NuSOAP) can handle client-side certificates.

Advantages:

- Identity confirmed — Both the server and the client can be sure of who they are communicating with.
- Encryption — Both the request and the response are protected from intermediate prying eyes.

Disadvantages:

- Increased load — Encrypting and decrypting communications is noticeably more CPU-intensive than unencrypted communications. Every request requires additional back and forth communications to set up the secure socket.
- Additional server requirements — The server must create a unique client certificate for each client that wishes to access the API. These APIs must be created and stored in a secure location and transmitted to the client via a secure channel.

Client-side certificates are as good as it gets in terms of API security; both the server and client are assured of the other's identity. Just like using an SSL endpoint, client-side certificates stack well with either HTTP authentication or message-based authentication. As with all forms of security, this increased level of security comes with a price: additional CPU load for both the client and the server, and the elimination of several useful client-side tools for interacting with the API.

Server-Side Code

Setting up client-side certificates takes some work. It is unreasonable to expect that anyone wishing to connect to your API will have their own certificate, and doing so would place a noticeable financial burden on anyone wishing to connect. It is much easier to become your own Certificate Authority (CA) and issue client certificates to your users yourself. This method is, however, slightly less secure because it is unlikely that your site is as careful about issuing user credentials as the real CAs. That being said, becoming your own CA is still the easiest method, and the method discussed here:

1. Set up your Certificate Authority. It is a good idea to use a separate machine from your web server for this (particularly any production web server) because the entire process is only as secure as your CA's private keys. Ideally this machine shouldn't be connected to the Internet at all; however, because the API will need to have keys generated regularly, this isn't really feasible. In this case, you can settle for having it inaccessible to the Internet, and preferably only accessible to the machine that will be requesting the new keys for clients.
2. Generate keys for your users and distribute them over a secure connection. A chain is only as strong as its weakest link: If you send the client keys to the user over an insecure HTTP connection, or even worse, email them, there is really no point in generating them at all.
3. Configure your web server to accept your generated CA, and require that users attempting to connect to a resource present a certificate signed by you.
4. Also configure your server to use an SSL certificate, similar to the previous example.

Setting up Your Certificate Authority

OpenSSL is the perfect tool for the job. Source distributions should include two scripts, `CA.pl` and `CA.sh`, which will automate this process for you. There are other tools such as OpenCA or TinyCA designed to provide a more user-friendly solution. Because this is something you are only going to be doing once, it seems slightly overkill for this situation.

First, a slight modification should be made to the CA script. There is a line reading `$DAYS="-days 365"`, which indicates that certificates created with the script will be valid for 1 year (365 days). This is far too short for your purposes, so choose a larger value (say 3,650 for 10 years).

Second, when running the script itself, answer the questions as they relate to your firm. The common name field is important—it should be the hostname users will be connecting to when they access your API. Use a secure password for your PEM pass phrase. The script will generate a directory called demoCA at your current location and place the appropriate files there.

Third, create a server certificate. This process has two steps, first creating a Certificate Signing Request (CSR), then getting that CSR signed by the CA you just created. To create the CSR, use the following options with `openssl`:

```
openssl req -new -key server.key -out server.csr
```

`openSSL` will ask a series of questions to generate your key. For our purposes (and to avoid needing to make configuration changes), these should match the values you used when creating your CA. To sign the server CSR that was generated, first rename the CSR file (`server.csr`) to `newreq.pem`, then use the command

```
CA.sh -signreq
```

This will sign the request. Finally, Apache must be instructed to use this certificate. This configuration should be placed within your `httpd.conf` file, for the VirtualHost that presents the API.

```
SSLEngine On
SSLCertificateFile /etc/http/conf/ssl/server.crt
SSLCertificateKeyFile /etc/http/conf/ssl/server.key
SSLProtocol All -SSLv2
SSLCipherSuite ALL:!EXP:!NULL:!ADH:!LOW
```

The first three lines turn on the SSL Engine and set the locations for both the certificate and the server's private key. The last two lines prevent SSL from using known broken or insecure protocols.

Fourth, generate a client certificate:

```
CA.sh -newreq
CA.sh -signreq
```

Remember to distribute it to the user via a secure channel.

Fifth, configure your web server to require clients attempting to connect to present a certificate, and to ensure that presented certificates were signed (and hence created) by your own CA.

```
SSLCACertificateFile /etc/http/conf/ssl/demoCA.crt
SSLCARevocationFile /etc/http/conf/ssl/demoCA.crl
SSLVerifyClient require
SSLVerifyDepth
```

`SSLCACertificateFile` should point to wherever you placed the CA Certificate File created earlier, and `SSLRevocationFile` should point to the `.crl` file that was generated at the same time as the *.crt. Without this file, you will be unable to revoke certificates from abusive users, or users who no longer wish to make use of your API. `SSLVerifyClient` instructs the web server that all users must present a certificate; users not presenting a certificate will be denied a connection. Finally, `SSLVerifyDepth 1` indicates that all client certificates must have been generated directly by your CA. This prevents other users from creating valid client certificates. Apache will need to be stopped and started again in order for these new certificates to take effect.

For a more in-depth look at SSL and other Apache-related security matters, I would highly recommend Ivan Ristic's book Apache Security.

Client-Side Code

In order to connect to a secure endpoint, PHP will need to be configured with the `--with-openssl` option. You will also recognize SSL support because https will appear under the Registered PHP Streams list in the `phpinfo()` output, and SSL will also show up under Registered Stream Socket Transports.

Because a client certificate must be presented, the cURL library will also be used. This function is appropriate for calling both SOAP and REST APIs. Handling the request and response is identical in either case:

```
function callAPI($endpoint, $requestBody)
{
  $ch = curl_init();
  curl_setopt($ch, CURLOPT_URL, $endpoint);
  curl_setopt($ch, CURLOPT_SSLCERT, "../certs/cert_key_pem-1.txt");
  curl_setopt($ch, CURLOPT_POST, TRUE);
  curl_setopt($ch, CURLOPT_POSTFIELDS, $requestBody);
  ob_start();
  curl_exec($ch);
  $response = ob_get_clean();
  if (curl_error($ch))
 {
   file_put_contents("/tmp/curl_error_log.txt", curl_errno($ch) . ": " .
    curl_error($ch), "a+");
   curl_close($ch);
   return null;
 }else
 {
    curl_close($ch);
    return $response;
 }
}
```

This function (which was basically introduced in the PayPal chapter) sets up the connection using the client certificate, and then uses output buffering to capture the response (cURL sends output directly to the browser). On error, the error is recorded to file for later examination; on success, the response is returned to the calling function. It is important for the client certificate to be stored in a secure location outside the document root.

REST or SOAP?

The two primary architectures for APIs are REST and SOAP. When creating your API, you really have three options: REST, SOAP, or both. REST APIs are known for being easy and quick to develop for, but the entire request is sent in the clear regardless of the type of encryption used. SOAP APIs are more complex, requiring more effort to generate the response and handle the request, but allow for greater flexibility by adding namespace support. Providing APIs of both types may sound like an attractive option, but keep in mind that it will double your maintenance, support, and documentation time for the life of the API.

Both API methods have already been introduced at length; this section concentrates on differences to keep in mind when developing an API.

REST APIs

When receiving a REST request, the information will come in via GET. As such, all the information will need to be URL-encoded during transmission; you will likely want to decode it before subjecting it to any further processing (the exception being usernames and passwords, which are generally processed as-is). Different request types should be addressed to different endpoints (URLs); if you want to use a single script to handle all requests, you can either present it to developers in that manner (all requests go to a single endpoint), or configure your web server to map many endpoints to a single script. I would generally suggest the latter; it's inline with the specification and it allows you to make changes later without affecting the external interfaces developers use.

Consider allowing developers to use a web interface to make requests against the API. This can be of great use when attempting to diagnose a problem; developers will be able to quickly determine if the problem is the request or their code. The more tools you can provide to developers in terms of diagnostics, the easier it will be to develop for your site.

SOAP APIs

When the SOAP request comes in, it should first be checked to ensure that it conforms to the format specified by your WSDL document. If you are using a tool such as NuSOAP, this is done for you. In fact, most SOAP APIs use some framework that takes care of a lot of the grunt work when handling the requests. SOAP APIs use a single endpoint for all requests (as a general rule, some large APIs separate disparate functions onto different endpoints), and as a result you will likely either have a large script at that point, or lots of `require()` calls executed depending on the particular call.

Consider allowing developers to use a web interface where they can paste entire request documents onto a form, and run them against your server. Speaking from direct experience, having something like this available is of great use to developers when trying to diagnose a problem. Providing scripts or functions on your site to allow developers to create requests manually will also be of assistance to developers not using a SOAP framework.

Community Considerations

How the API is presented to the world at large and supported is a great determinant for its success. An example of things done right would be Amazon; it has an API with a large range of functionality. It is supported by an automated registration process, public documentation, development forums, sample code, and perhaps most impressively, regular developer chats where API developers can speak directly with programmers at Amazon responsible for the API. It is my opinion that these community support options have helped bring the API to its current level of popularity. While researching for this book, I have discovered that these features, which sound simple, are not nearly as widespread as they should be.

Automating Registrations

Development projects can be spontaneous and quick. Between end of business on a Friday and start of business on a Monday, projects can start and finish, or (in corporate environments) at least hit the proof of concept stage. If registrations need to be accepted manually because the API is restricted in some manner, consider issuing developers either sandbox or provisional access until the request is either accepted or declined. This is particularly important if it takes several business days for an application to be processed.

Public Documentation

The goal of an API is to allow remote applications to interact with your server. The goal of the team creating the API should be to allow as many people as possible to develop for the API. Hiding documentation behind login prompts, nested menus, or worse (like Non Disclosure Agreements) is counterproductive. Try to use the shortest URL possible for information about your API (api.example.com, for example) so it's easy to access from anywhere, and don't require a login unless the user wishes to access their account.

Development Forums

Developers talk to each other—either they talk to each other on various and disparate forums spread across the Web, or they all find each other on your own forums. The advantages of having all your developers talking in the same place should be obvious: With more eyes looking at the same problems, it's easier for your developers to recognize common problems and resolve them (either through API changes or documentation improvements), and it provides a larger database for searches. Give in-house developers a specific and easily recognizable title or avatar within the forums, so new users can quickly determine which answers are authoritative.

Forums aren't necessarily the only way to accomplish this; use of a mailing list may be an attractive alternative. My personal preference is for forums over mailing lists because it seems to be the easiest way to keep past conversations accessible for new users and Google. It also avoids the constant stream of "How do I get off this list" messages that seem to plague the lists I subscribe to.

Finally, don't underestimate the resource your users represent. I actively participated in the same support forum for a software package for approximately 5 years. It never ceased to amaze me how much effort complete volunteers put into helping fellow users.

Sample Code

In developing your API, you had to test it, so you've already written the code. Why not make it easier on other developers and share it with them? In my experience, development time is split roughly down the middle when interacting with a new API—half of it is spent generating the request and handling the response (namely accessing the data I want), and the other half of it is spent doing stuff with that data. If you can eliminate the first half of that with effective code samples, you have effectively cut your development time in half.

Things to consider before writing the code:

- Publish sample code in as many languages as you can.
- Consider giving users a way to publish their own sample code, particularly in languages you haven't covered.
- Include code that does everything on its own without relying on any external libraries.
- Also include code that uses common libraries such as NuSOAP.
- Demonstrate both sides of your API if it supports both REST and SOAP.
- Include sample requests and responses, at both the HTTP and TCP levels.

Developer Chats

Programmers writing for your API are going to have questions; often these questions can be answered by other development community members, but occasionally not (this is especially true when your API is first released or recently updated). A development presence within the community can be easily accomplished by encouraging participation within the forum or mailing list, but direct communication can be a valuable tool.

Here are a few tips:

- Schedule the chats (rather than using one of the "Live Chat" tools). This will help ensure that users attempt to resolve problems on their own first.

- Schedule multiple times. Remember those things called time zones? There are people in different ones, who may not be too enthusiastic about waking up at 3:00 a.m. to ask why your API is returning some strange data.
- Record the chats, and post them. This information is just as valuable as past forum posts or mailing list archives — try to put them somewhere searchable. Remember to inform users ahead of time that the chat is recorded, and that acceptance of that fact is required for participation (to avoid running afoul of jurisdictions where all parties are required to consent before they can be recorded).
- Be prompt. Ensure that staff members who will be participating in the chat treat the commitment as seriously as a meeting with upper management: arrive on time, give the encounter their full attention, and remain for the entire scheduled time. Anything less and your users will quickly lose respect for the process.

Development Sandbox

A development sandbox is a duplicate of the production sandbox, the difference being that actions taken on the sandbox do not have any permanent effect (for example, placing a bid on the sandbox copy of the eBay API does not require [or allow] you to buy the item in question). Every API where an action taken has a permanent effect (sending money, agreeing to purchase an item, and so on) should have a sandbox, so developers can test their programs without fear of accidentally performing an undesired action. It also allows developers to test edge cases (sending a million dollars, bidding on one thousand items at once) to ensure that their code functions properly.

Even in cases where hitting the API does not create any lasting action (for example, running a query against the Google API), but where there are limits placed on the developer (the number of queries allowed per day, for example), a sandbox should be used. This allows for easy separation between the developer's work and the production programs, and prevents either the production or development version of the code from exhausting the other's resources.

Performance Techniques

Websites are designed to be accessed by individuals, and as such tend to rely on the relatively slow speed of the user to avoid any performance bottlenecks. This technique fails miserably with APIs because they are going to be consumed by other servers with high-speed connections, often designed only with their own performance in mind (they won't cache your responses for you, and will instead make exactly the same request time and time again). Designing your API with performance in mind can help keep the server fast even when many requests are being made, and will help ensure that future hardware upgrades can accomplish their desired tasks.

Many websites are either designed poorly or appear to lack any sort of design whatsoever. I've seen a site that required 10 database queries to start the page, then an additional query for every item in their database. With more than 40 items in their database, there were approximately 50 queries being made every time the index page loaded. This technique was failing horribly for a website receiving relatively few hits. It wouldn't have lasted minutes if it was consumed automatically, and I doubt it would have lasted more than a few seconds under the Slashdot effect. All these database queries were basically pointless as well; the firm's inventory changed slowly, so a static page generated once per week from the same script would have functioned just as well for the end user, but would have been several orders of magnitude faster.

Caching Data

Often both websites and APIs request data from the database each and every time a request is made, even though the data used to populate the response changes rarely. This, combined with the database normalization techniques taught since the beginning of time, means that each of those requests is likely making at least one query joining results from multiple tables, possibly multiple queries. If your data isn't changing that often, consider caching the response.

For example, take the fictional Bob's Video website. Every time someone either views detailed information about a movie on his website or requests it through his API, his server runs three queries: one query that finds the movie's full title, plot line, and rating, another query that runs a joined query to retrieve detailed information on each of the cast members, and a final query to determine the film's rental status. This is a gigantic waste of resources; once a movie is released, the only response that will change is its rental status. Yet, each and every time the page is loaded, the data is requested again from the database. It would make far more sense to either use a static page for released films (populating rental status dynamically), or at the very least cache all the film's information and retrieve the rental status dynamically.

You've probably noticed that, because the cache will likely end up in a database, I've really only reduced the query count from 3 to 2. It doesn't look like a drastic improvement, but it is. The joined query looking up detailed information for the cast members is going an order of magnitude slower than a lookup based on a primary key, so there is a big saving there. You can also cache the movie data in a form close to its final web form, saving on all the processing generally needed to go from database to web page. You will need two caches in this example, one for the website and one for the API.

Smarter Use of Database Queries

Although caching data is an excellent method of reducing the number of queries you use, it isn't always appropriate. Just make sure you are getting the most out of each query you run. Many times duplicate data is requested while handling a single request; this often happens when different functions need the same data, but they don't call each other so they don't share their results. Consider either reworking your script to obtain all required data itself, then pass off data to the functions that require it, or creating an abstraction layer with an object that takes care of obtaining information from the database only when required.

Once you're using your database queries to their fullest, begin work on improving the speed of the queries themselves. Never start queries with `SELECT * FROM`—request only the fields you actually need. Also examine both your queries and your database. Try to ensure that the fields you base your selection on are either primary keys or at least indexed by the database server.

Response Caching

Consider again the case of Bob's Video Store API, which allows users to request information on films. With a small design change (moving rental status to its own query, rather than providing it with each request), many new caching opportunities present themselves. Because the response doesn't change regardless of who requests it, a proxy server can be used server side to handle the response (this is much easier with REST APIs than with SOAP). Setting the appropriate headers for cache life (24 hours for films, and 30 minutes for rental status) will allow the API to shrug off most of its work to the proxy server.

PHP Accelerators

There are a few PHP accelerators available, which can have a drastic effect on the speed of your scripts. Every time a PHP script is executed, it is parsed and compiled into byte code by PHP's scripting engine. Because, generally speaking, the script hasn't changed between executions, this is a huge waste of processing time. PHP accelerators cache the byte code version of the scripts, and execute that copy (being mindful of any changes to the original script). This saves the parse and compilation steps each time the script is executed because your API will be called with great frequency, and changed rarely this can be a significant savings.

It is important to realize how PHP accelerators work to avoid having undue expectations for their results. Consider the parse and compilation time for a script as a fixed cost—every time the script is accessed, regardless of the speed of other resources (databases, for example) or how much processing the finished script requires, this cost must be paid. Caching the byte code copy of the script only saves on that cost; it will not speed your database queries or other CPU-intensive processes.

One of the most prevalent PHP accelerators is from Zend, dutifully titled the Zend PHP [4/5] Accelerator. I found it easy to install and was relatively pleased with its results. Having upgraded to PHP5 shortly after its release, I was unable to test other accelerators that have since become available. One of the other accelerators I did manage to try `sigfault'd` the calling Apache process on a variety of my scripts, so be sure you test whichever accelerator you use extensively before putting it on the production system.

Error Responses

Error messages really are an essential part of any interface; they can either make or break a programmer's heart. Useful error messages can quickly point a programmer to the problem in their code, while cryptic messages or simple numbers cause premature hair loss. As such, a few moments of planning can save your users hours of frustration.

Error Numbers

While error numbers are generally of little use to the general public, they are great for automatic interpretation. Assigning numbers to the various errors your application will generate will help remote applications log any problems they encounter. If you are creating a SOAP API, there are already various error messages defined by the protocol. When planning error numbers, space them out; for example, invalid requests could be given an error number between 100 and 199, properly formatted requests that contain improperly formatted data could be assigned an error number between 200 and 299, and server faults could be assigned a number between 300 and 399. This way, should you decide to be more descriptive in the future by adding more error types, they can still be grouped logically.

Readers who have been programming long enough to remember when line numbers were entered by the programmer, rather than their present state of GUI fluff, will immediately understand this approach. It worked then, and it still makes sense today.

Error Messages

When returning an error message with an API, or any program, there are two key pieces of information to give: what went wrong and why. Again, with SOAP APIs a lot of this may be handled for you (if you are using a prebuilt SOAP toolkit). With REST APIs, for example, if a request doesn't include a required piece of information, don't just return `ERROR: Invalid Request`; instead return `ERROR: Required element username not present`. This way the programmer can quickly see that there is an error, that the error is that a required element was not included, and that the `element` missing was the `username` element.

What Services to Offer

Now that you have determined how you want to authenticate your users, how you will support the programmers, and considered both your REST and SOAP options, it's time to think about what services you want to offer via your API.

Generally, the services offered via the API are a subset of the functionality offered through the traditional website, so you probably already have an idea of what you want to offer. With an API there are a few additional considerations that may affect those offerings.

Processor Load

Even with effective caching methodologies, your API will likely offer services that present a noticeable amount of load on the server. Because these services were designed to be consumed automatically, the amount of load generated may quickly rival that of your site, even though only a small percentage of unique people are using the service. Look at the amount of work required to respond to the different types of requests you are considering. Services that will end up creating significant load should either be documented with warnings (this service is quite CPU-intensive, so don't use it unless you actually need to; instead use otherServiceA or otherServiceB to obtain similar results) or left out of the API.

Competitive Usefulness

Providing your entire product line, including pricing information, may sound like a great boon to your customers or resellers, but consider the value of this information to your competitors. There are a few ways to mitigate these concerns: Limit the number of results to any particular query, restrict your API to known parties (resellers), and limit the amount of information provided in the API.

Generally, these concerns are considered a part of doing business, outweighed by the additional visibility that having an API provides, but they remain issues that should be raised when considering different services.

Example REST API Structure

Supporting REST calls is pretty easy; handling the data has a few sequential steps:

1. Ensure that the user is authenticated. If you are using HTTP Basic Authentication or SSL with client-side certificates, this is already handled. If not, take care of it first.
2. If you are enforcing any sort of limit on the number of requests handled per day, record that the call was made and check to see if the user was throttled.
3. Ensure that the incoming request is valid, in that it contains all the necessary parameters and does not include any unknown parameters. Accepting useless parameters may sound innocuous, but it will only confuse developers who expected that parameter to be applied.
4. Hand the call off to the supporting function, and allow it to return an error or a good response, whichever is appropriate.

User Authentication

Assuming message-based authentication, the calling function would look a little like this.

```
if (!checkUser(mysql_escape_string($_GET['username']),
    mysql_escape_string($_GET['password'])))
{
 echo <<< endquote
<response>
  <error no="001">Invalid Username or Password</error>
</response>
endquote;
 exit;
}
```

The `checkUser()` function called is identical to the one presented earlier; it won't be repeated here. Note that both the username and password are escaped before being passed off; remember that SQL Injection attacks can occur with any user-presented data, so your API is just as vulnerable as any other interface your site presents. Should the user present invalid credentials, an error is returned and the script ends.

Query Limits

Enforcing a limit on the number of queries a particular user can run per day is a big reason to authenticate users in the first place.

```
$queriesPerDay = 2000;
...
$username = mysql_real_escape_string($_GET['username']);
$query = "UPDATE `12_user_throttle` SET queries = queries + 1 WHERE username =
  '$username' AND queries < '$queriesPerDay'";
```

First, at the beginning of the code block, the maximum number of queries a user may run per day is set (for easy access later). Then an update query is generated using the user's credentials and the maximum number of queries a user may run per day. This query will affect one row if the user is still under the max queries per day limit, and zero rows if not, which saves you running two queries: one to increment, and the other to check the present value.

```
if (replaceQuery($query) == 0)
{
echo <<< endquote
<response>
  <error no="2">Query limit reached, please try again tomorrow</error>
</response>
endquote;
 exit;
}
```

Second, the `replaceQuery()` function is called (shown in Appendix A), returning as indicated previously. Should users have already exhausted their max queries per day, an error is returned.

It may be tempting to track other variables, such as the remote user's IP address. This is fine for reporting purposes, but should not be part of your max query enforcement. Multiple developers on a corporate intranet behind proxies may all appear to be a single IP address; the same goes for home users behind similar devices. Should a user's repeated queries become a problem, then and only then do you want to look into blocking their requests on an IP level, but be sure to make appropriate contact information available to innocent users who may have been affected by this action.

In order for this function to work in its desired fashion, you will need to reset the number of queries each user has remaining each night. A cron job or Windows scheduled task can be easily configured to run a small script each night at midnight. Remember to store this script outside the document root. There is no need for it to be accessible to the Internet.

```
<?php
 require("../common_db.php");
 $query = "UPDATE `12_user_throttle` SET `queries` = 0";
 $resetUsers = insertQuery($query);
 echo "$resetUsers users have had their queries reset";
?>
```

With a cron job, the output should be present in your daily reports; under Windows you will need to save the data manually. Using `file_put_contents()` makes this trivial.

To give managing your query limits a bit more granularity, add an additional column to your database to hold the max queries per day for that user, have the reset script set the number of queries remaining to that number each night, and switch the checking query to compare the two columns.

If performance is a key concern, you can easily merge the valid user check and the sufficient queries remaining checks, cutting the number of database hits per call in half. Should the new query return zero rows, you should perform an additional query to determine if the failure was because of invalid credentials or exhausted queries per day so that a meaningful error can be returned.

Request Validity

Checking the request is the first step that actually cares about the API behind the function; as such, to determine if the request is valid, the API itself must be considered. In this format, the API is defined in an array:

```
$API = array();

$expectedValues = array("author", "title");
$optionalValues = array();
$API[] = array("lookup", "lookupCall", $expectedValues, $optionalValues);

$expectedValues = array("keyword");
$optionalValues = array("year", "publisher");

$API[] = array("search", "searchCall", $expectedValues, $optionalValues);
```

This API supports two methods: `lookup` and `search`. `lookup` has two required parameters, `name` and `title`, and no optional parameters. `search` has a single required parameter, `keyword`, and two optional parameters, `year` and `publisher`. The `lookupCall` and `searchCall` values represent the name of the function that will be called if the request is valid.

A function will be used to determine if the request is valid (how it is called is presented next). It will ensure that all of the required parameters are present, and that the request only contains the allowed parameters (the required and optional parameters), nothing else.

```
function checkValues($request, $required, $optional, &$error)
{
  $required[] = "method";
  $required[] = "username";
  $required[] = "password";
```

The function is passed four parameters: the request sent by the user, the required and optional parameters for this type of request, and finally an array passed by reference to contain any errors detected while examining the request. Three elements are added to the required array: `method`, `username`, and `password`; these are present in the request (or an error would have been returned already). They need to be added to avoid raising an error due to unnecessary parameters.

```
  $requestTemp = array();
  $requestTemp = array_diff(array_keys($request), $optional);
  $requestTemp = array_diff($requestTemp, $required);
```

Here the request is checked to ensure that it only contains the required and optional parameters. The `array_keys()` function returns only the keys from the associative array; this is needed to ensure that the comparison occurs between the keys in the request, not the values.

```
  if (count($requestTemp) > 0)
  {
    foreach ($requestTemp as $unknownElement => $unknownValue)
    {
      $error[] = "<error no=\"101\">Unknown Element: $unknownElement</error>";
    }
  }
```

If anything is left over in the `$requestTemp` array, it indicates that there were more parameters passed to the API than allowed. Execution isn't terminated immediately, in an effort to present the developer with as much information about problems with the request as possible.

```
  $requiredTemp = array();
  $requiredTemp = array_diff($required, array_keys($request));
  if (count($requiredTemp) > 0)
  {
    foreach ($requiredTemp as $missingElement)
    {
      $error[] = "<error no=\"102\">Missing required element:
        $missingElement</error>";
    }
  }
```

Identical processing is done to ensure that all required elements are present.

```
  if (count($error) == 0)
  {
    return true;
```

```
    }else
    {
      return false;
    }
  }
```

Assuming all went well, return `true;` if not, return `false`. Remember that the `$error` array was passed by reference; any errors added will be available to the calling function.

This next segment of code will take care of calling the function just introduced:

```
$error = array();
$matchedMethod = false;
$validRequestFormat = false;
foreach($API as $item)
{
  if ($item[0] == $_GET['method'])
  {
     $matchedMethod = true;
     $validRequestFormat = checkValues($_GET, $item[2], $item[3], &$error);
     break;
  }
}
```

Here the API array is iterated through to try and match the method the client is requesting to a method offered by the API. If a match is found, it is passed off to the `checkValues()` function to determine if the other passed parameters are appropriate.

```
if ($matchedMethod == false)
{
          echo <<< endquote
<response>
  <error no="100">Unknown or missing method</error>
</response>
endquote;
         exit;
}else if ($validRequestFormat == false)
{
 echo "<response>\n" . implode("\n",$error) . "\n</response>";
 exit;
}
```

If `matchedMethod` remains false, the method the user requested doesn't exist and an appropriate error is raised. Alternatively, if `validRequestFormat` was set to false by the `checkValues()` function, the parameters passed are invalid (either the required parameters are missing, or there are parameters present that the API does not know how to handle). In this case, the error array that was populated by the `checkValues()` function is imploded and returned.

Finally, if all the previous checks were passed, the appropriate function can be called:

```
call_user_func($item[1], $_GET);
```

Framework Limitations and Notes

This framework has a few built-in limitations that should be kept in mind:

- This framework assumes that the entire API is accessible via a single endpoint, which (while becoming popular) isn't what the spec dictates. If you want to allow for multiple endpoints while still using a single script, save the script without an extension (for example, as `api` rather than `api.php`) and store it on your web server, then configure your web server to present it as shown in the following code. You will then need to explode the `$_SERVER['REQUEST_URI']` value to determine the desired method.

```
<Files api>
  ForceType application/x-httpd-php
</Files>
```

- The framework doesn't look at the data within the request. As long as the appropriate parameters are there, the data is passed off to the appropriate function. Checking is not done to ensure that a value is numeric, for example.
- The data isn't filtered or escaped; it is passed off as-is. This may allow unscrupulous developers to compromise your data in unintended ways.

Using the Framework

The framework only provides the mechanism to receive and pass on requests; you will need to plug in your own authentication function, as well as the functions necessary to return useful data to the end user. Because APIs are generally used to replicate data available through other interfaces, you will likely be implementing a thin interface layer, so both your website and the API can use the same end function to retrieve the data. I would suggest either using the same code to complete the filtering, or performing all the filtering in a single place; too often, data not specifically coming from a website isn't filtered at all.

Here's the code of `restAPI.php` in full:

```
<?php
require("../common_db.php");
//Plug in authentication function here, remember to escape strings if the
//  destination function doesn't do it for you.
if (!checkUser(mysql_escape_string($_GET['username']),
mysql_escape_string($_GET['password'])))
{
 echo <<< endquote
<response>
  <error no="1">Invalid Username or Password</error>
</response>
endquote;
 exit;
}

//Plug in throttling function here if desired
if (userThrottled($_GET['username']))
{
echo <<< endquote
```

```
<response>
  <error no="2">Query limit reached, please try again tommorrow</error>
</response>
endquote;
 exit;
}


//Set up your own array functions here
$API = array();

/* Example:
$expectedValues = array("name", "title");
$optionalValues = array("year", "publisher");
$API[] = array("lookup", "lookupCall", $expectedValues, $optionalValues);

$expectedValues = array("keyword");
$optionalValues = array();
$API[] = array("search", "searchCall", $expectedValues, $optionalValues);
describeAPI($API);
*/



//Framework iterates through array looking to match the requested method
//  with a service the framework provides
$error = array();
$matchedMethod = false;
$validRequestFormat = false;
foreach($API as $item)
{
  if ($item[0] == $_GET['method'])
  {
     $matchedMethod = true;
     $validRequestFormat = checkValues($_GET, $item[2], $item[3], &$error);
     break;
  }
}

//Framework was unable to match method, return an error
if ($matchedMethod == false)
{
        echo <<< endquote
<response>
  <error no="100">Unknown or missing method</error>
</response>
endquote;
        exit;
}else if ($validRequestFormat == false)
{
 echo "<response>\n" . implode("\n",$error) . "</response>";
 exit;
}

//Method was matched, and contained required parameters, call the appropriate
```

```
//  function
call_user_func($item[1], $_GET);


function checkValues($request, $required, $optional, &$error)
{
  $required[] = "method";
  $required[] = "username";
  $required[] = "password";
 // Ensure all elements passed are either required or optional
 $requestTemp = array();
 $requestTemp = array_diff(array_keys($request), $optional);
 $requestTemp = array_diff($requestTemp, $required);
  if (count($requestTemp) > 0)
  {
    print_r($requestTemp);
    foreach ($requestTemp as $unknownElement => $unknownValue)
    {
      $error[] = "<error no=\"101\">Unknown Element: $unknownElement</error>";
    }
  }

 // Ensure all required elements are present
 $requiredTemp = array();
 $requiredTemp = array_diff($required, array_keys($request));
  if (count($requiredTemp) > 0)
  {
    foreach ($requiredTemp as $missingElement)
    {
      $error[] = "<error no=\"102\">Missing required element:
        $missingElement</error>";
    }
  }
  if (count($error) == 0)
  {
    return true;
  }else
  {
    return false;
  }
}

// A quick function for testing, or as a first step to API documentation
function describeAPI($API)
{
  foreach($API as $service)
  {
    echo "<b>Method Name:</b> {$service[0]} <br>";
    echo "<b>Required Parameters:</b> " . implode(",", $service[2]) . "<br>";
    echo "<b>Optional Parameters:</b> " . implode(",", $service[3]) . "<br><br>";
  }
  exit;
}
```

st Conclusion

REST is more popular than SOAP, due in no small part to its simplicity, for both the server and the client. This section introduced a few key steps to keep in mind when developing a REST feed, and presented some sample code to help quickly flesh out any new REST server.

Example SOAP Structure

Supporting a SOAP server can be a bit more complex. The incoming requests are going to encapsulate the data within an XML document, which can make accessing the data a bit more difficult. Fortunately, tools like NuSOAP provide an easy framework to work with. Because the NuSOAP modules provide a lot of the functionality for you, the processes used when developing a server are slightly different.

First, create your SOAP server and register your methods:

```
$server = new soap_server();

$server->configureWSDL('basicwsdl', 'urn:ratingwsdl');
$server->register('movieRating',                            // Service Method
  array('name' => 'xsd:string'),                           // Expected parameters
  array('return' => 'xsd:string'),                         // Returned parameters
  'urn:ratingwsdl',                                        // Namespace
  'urn:ratingwsdl#movieRate',                              // Soap Action
  'rpc',                                                   // Style
  'encoded',                                               // Use
  'Returns a rating for the movie specified'               // Description of the service
);
```

Here the server is configured to present a `wsdl` document if requested, and a `movieRating` method is added. This is the name of the operation the client will call, as well as the name of the function that will receive the parameters sent with the request. Both the expected and returned parameters are arrays, so any number of values can be entered.

Second, create the functions that will receive the requests. These functions will only receive the parameters, not the entire request.

```
function movieRating($name)
{
  return "$name was great!";
}
```

The functions must return data in the format indicated earlier (`xsd:string` in this example). More complicated data types are introduced shortly.

NuSOAP can also generate documentation pages for the various methods offered; to offer this, you will need to add a bit more code at the end of the file:

```
$HTTP_RAW_POST_DATA = isset($HTTP_RAW_POST_DATA) ? $HTTP_RAW_POST_DATA : '';
$server->service($HTTP_RAW_POST_DATA);
```

With that in place, pointing your web browser at the SOAP server, you should see something as shown in Figure 12-1.

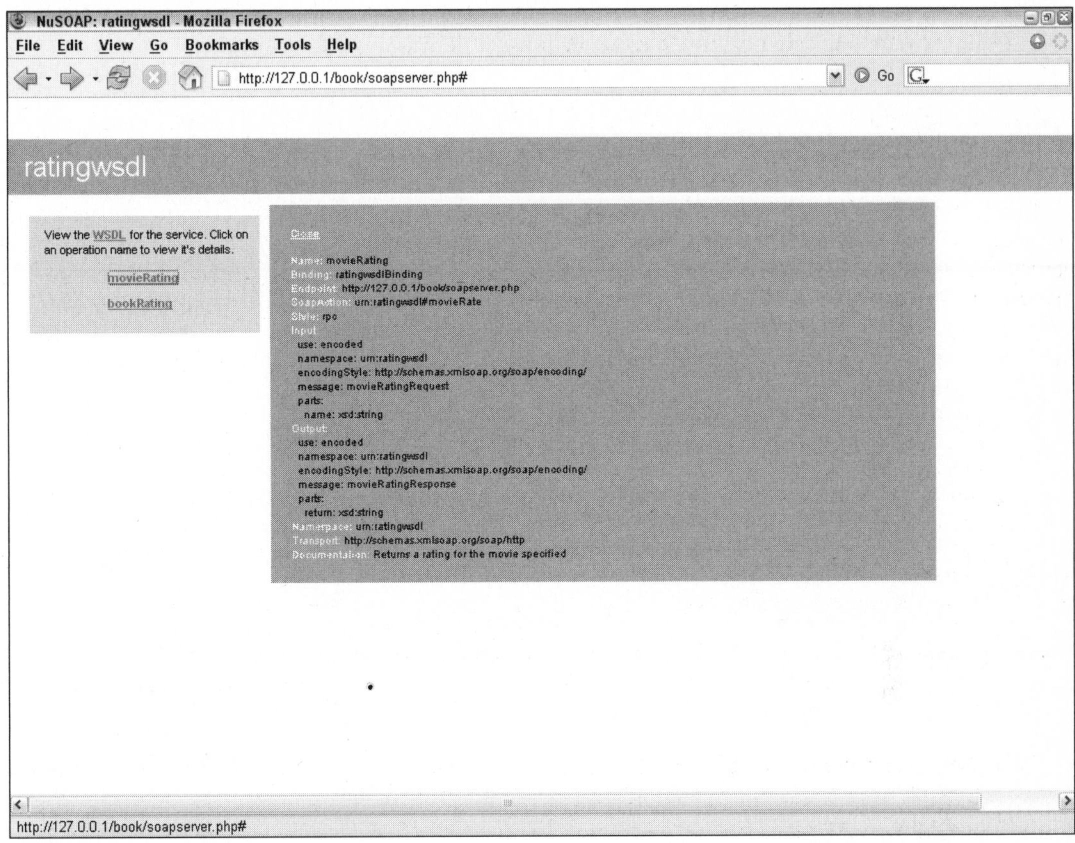

Figure 12-1

Clicking the `wsdl` link presented on that page will yield the `wsdl` document for the service:

```
<?xml version="1.0" encoding="ISO-8859-1"?>
<definitions xmlns:SOAP-ENV="http://schemas.xmlsoap.org/soap/envelope/"
  xmlns:xsd="http://www.w3.org/2001/XMLSchema"
  xmlns:xsi="http://www.w3.org/2001/XMLSchema-instance"
  xmlns:SOAP-ENC="http://schemas.xmlsoap.org/soap/encoding/"
  xmlns:si="http://soapinterop.org/xsd"
  xmlns:tns="urn:ratingwsdl"
  xmlns:soap="http://schemas.xmlsoap.org/wsdl/soap/"
  xmlns:wsdl="http://schemas.xmlsoap.org/wsdl/"
  xmlns="http://schemas.xmlsoap.org/wsdl/"
  targetNamespace="urn:ratingwsdl">
<types>
  <xsd:schema targetNamespace="urn:ratingwsdl">
   <xsd:import namespace="http://schemas.xmlsoap.org/soap/encoding/" />
   <xsd:import namespace="http://schemas.xmlsoap.org/wsdl/" />
```

```
    </xsd:schema>
  </types>
  <message name="movieRatingRequest">
    <part name="name" type="xsd:string" />
  </message>
  <message name="movieRatingResponse">
    <part name="return" type="xsd:string" />
  </message>
  <message name="bookRatingRequest">
    <part name="name" type="xsd:string" />
  </message>
  <message name="bookRatingResponse">
    <part name="return" type="xsd:string" />
  </message>
  <portType name="ratingwsdlPortType">
    <operation name="movieRating">
      <documentation>Returns a rating for the movie specified</documentation>
      <input message="tns:movieRatingRequest"/>
      <output message="tns:movieRatingResponse"/>
    </operation>
    <operation name="bookRating">
      <documentation>Returns a rating for the book specified</documentation>
      <input message="tns:bookRatingRequest"/>
      <output message="tns:bookRatingResponse"/>
    </operation>
  </portType>
  <binding name="ratingwsdlBinding" type="tns:ratingwsdlPortType">
    <soap:binding style="rpc" transport="http://schemas.xmlsoap.org/soap/http"/>
    <operation name="movieRating">
      <soap:operation soapAction="urn:ratingwsdl#movieRate" style="rpc"/>
      <input>
        <soap:body use="encoded" namespace="urn:ratingwsdl"
          encodingStyle="http://schemas.xmlsoap.org/soap/encoding/"/>
      </input>
      <output>
        <soap:body use="encoded" namespace="urn:ratingwsdl"
          encodingStyle="http://schemas.xmlsoap.org/soap/encoding/"/>
      </output>
    </operation>
    <operation name="bookRating">
    <soap:operation soapAction="urn:ratingwsdl#bookRate" style="rpc"/>
      <input>
        <soap:body use="encoded" namespace="urn:ratingwsdl"
          encodingStyle="http://schemas.xmlsoap.org/soap/encoding/"/>
      </input>
      <output>
        <soap:body use="encoded" namespace="urn:ratingwsdl"
          encodingStyle="http://schemas.xmlsoap.org/soap/encoding/"/>
      </output>
    </operation>
  </binding>
  <service name="ratingwsdl">
    <port name="ratingwsdlPort" binding="tns:ratingwsdlBinding">
      <soap:address location="http://127.0.0.1/book/soapserver.php"/>
```

```
  </port>
</service>
</definitions>
```

Considering the small amount of code required to generate it, the WSDL document looks quite impressive.

Although it may not take much code on your part to generate the WSDL document and the human-readable documentation, it took a lot of work on NuSOAP's part. As such, these are excellent candidates for caching.

Complex Data Types

The previous example works great as long as you're satisfied receiving only basic data types and returning single values, but it isn't really feasible for a production API. Complex data types can be created to allow different structures to be passed to and from the server.

Here a more complex data type is created to return a more detailed movie review:

```
$server->wsdl->addComplexType(
'MovieReview',      // Type Name
'complexType',      // What we are adding
'struct',           // Given
'all',              // Given
'',                 //
array(
  'rating'   => array('name' => 'rating', 'type' => 'xsd:string'),
  'reviewer' => array('name' => 'reviewer', 'type' => 'xsd:string'),
  'stars'    => array('name' => 'stars', 'type' => 'xsd:int')
  )
);
```

Only the `MovieReview` item and the array are of interest. `MovieReview` is the name of the complex type; this will be referred to later in the chapter. The array defines all the elements that will combine to form the `MovieReview` type. In this case, each of the items is a basic type, but you can nest complex types within each other, or use more advanced types like arrays.

A small change is required to the definition of the `MovieRating` function to make use of this new data type:

```
$server->register('movieRating',
 array('name' => 'xsd:string'),
 array('return' => 'tns:MovieReview'),
 'urn:ratingwsdl',
 'urn:ratingwsdl#movieRate',
 'rpc',
 'encoded',
 'Returns a rating for the movie specified'
);
```

The only change here is to the return type, your new complex type. Within the function itself, the appropriate type must be returned:

```
function movieRating($name)
{
  $review = array(
  'rating' => "It was great!",
  'reviewer' => "Paul",
  'stars' => "5");
  return $review;
}
```

The format of the response looks quite similar to the definition; an associative array containing three elements, the names here must match the names used earlier. Because PHP is loosely typed, you must be careful to ensure you return the appropriate data type. You may want to look into the `ctype_*()` functions to ensure this.

Though this example used the complex type to return data, it could have just as easily required a different type. Just make the complex type the required element when the function is registered.

SOAP Conclusions

SOAP's more robust protocol and encapsulation can make it appear intimidating, but fortunately tools like NuSOAP take the pain out of implementation. This section provided an example SOAP server using the NuSOAP toolkit. By adding your own complex types to the service, you can require or return data in a format of your choosing.

Summary

This chapter focused more on the things that you should consider when creating a new API than on the API code itself; this was a deliberate decision. These considerations include the following:

- Methods of securing your API from a completely open API, open for the world to use (and abuse), to the protected and authenticated server functioning over SSL with client-side certificates.
- The tradeoffs in choosing between utilizing REST and SOAP APIs from a server prospective was discussed briefly, along with additional considerations or functionality that should be made present to assist developers using the API.
- Considerations in assisting the development community.
- Managing the growth and evolution of your API.
- Proactively enabling error handing to help both you and your developers improve the overall usefulness of your web services.
- Deciding on the types of functions you may want to make available.

Finally, the chapter ended with example code for both REST and SOAP APIs. The REST coverage was slightly more exhaustive because a framework was developed from scratch, whereas the SOAP examples used the already robust NuSOAP framework.

Supporting Functions

Throughout this book, a series of functions are used, particularly when it comes to database access. Because these functions are not intrinsically tied to any of the chapters and not really the purpose of the book, they are covered here. I have also included some brief code snippets that I believe to be of use while working on the topics covered here.

common_db.php

These functions are used to facilitate database access, MySQL in particular. The first few are either similar or identical to functions presented in other PHP books from Wrox.

```
<?php
  $dbhost = 'localhost';
  $dbusername = 'example';
  $dbuserpassword = 'example';
  $default_dbname = 'example';
  $MYSQL_ERRNO = '';
  $MYSQL_ERROR = '';

  $default_sort_order = 'ASC';
  $default_order_by = 'uid';
  $records_per_page = 5;
```

Here default values are initialized, including the username and password for the database. Remember: Do not save include files within the document root files with an .inc or any other extension that will show their contents to remote users (passwords and all). Allowing remote users to run includes at a whim could have unexpected consequences. The best solution is to store your include files in a separate directory outside the web root and reference them from your script using their fully qualified path.

```
function db_connect()
{
 global $dbhost, $dbusername, $dbuserpassword, $default_dbname;
 global $MYSQL_ERRNO, $MYSQL_ERROR;
 $link_id = mysql_connect($dbhost, $dbusername, $dbuserpassword);
 if(!$link_id)
 {
    $MYSQL_ERRNO = 0;
    $MYSQL_ERROR = "Connection failed to the host $dbhost.";
    return 0;
  }
  else if(empty($dbname) && !mysql_select_db($default_dbname))
{
    $MYSQL_ERRNO = mysql_errno();
    $MYSQL_ERROR = mysql_error();
    return 0;
}
else return $link_id;
}
```

This function handles connecting to the database and returning a connection ID. It is used by many other functions within this file, and is called frequently from the including files as well.

```
function sql_error()
{
global $MYSQL_ERRNO, $MYSQL_ERROR;
if(empty($MYSQL_ERROR))
{
    $MYSQL_ERRNO = mysql_errno();
    $MYSQL_ERROR = mysql_error();
}
return "$MYSQL_ERRNO: $MYSQL_ERROR";
}
```

Should an error be encountered during database access, this function will provide the information necessary to diagnose the problem.

```
function getAssoc($query, $force_array = 0)
{
// Force Array
// 0 = Accept Default
// 1 = Force Single Row
// 2 = Force Multi Row (may have only one item)

  /* There are 6 Possibilities for this function to deal with
   Force Array      Results    Desired Action
   0                   =1       Push first row directly
   0                   >1       Loop through results
   1                   =1       Push first row directly
   1                   >1       Push first row directly
   2                   =1       Loop through results
   2                   >1       Loop through results

   So, If there is more than 1 result, and force array = 0 OR force array = 2, loop
  through the results, otherwise, just push the first row.
```

```
  */

  $link_id = db_connect();
  $result = mysql_query($query);
  if (mysql_num_rows($result) == 1)
  {
   $SingleResult = TRUE;
  }else
  {
   $SingleResult = FALSE;
  }
  if (($SingleResult == FALSE && $force_array == 0) || ($force_array == 2))
  {
   $results = array();
   while ($query_data = mysql_fetch_assoc($result))
   {
    array_push($results, $query_data);
   }
  }else
  {
   $results = mysql_fetch_assoc($result);
  }
  return $results;
}
```

This is one of my favorite functions for database access. I use it essentially every time I want to run a query. The logic can be a bit confusing, but the point of the function is relatively simple: to run the specified query and return the result(s) in an associative array. Setting the `force_array` option allows the calling function to specify that it would always like an array of arrays as a result, or that it would always like just a single associative array as a result, or finally (the default setting) that the way results are returned should depend on the number of rows the query returns.

```
function rowCount($query)
{
 $link_id = db_connect();
 $result = mysql_query($query);
 $rowCount = mysql_num_rows($result);
 return $rowCount;
}
```

This is just your basic row counting function.

```
function insertQuery($query)
{
$link_id = db_connect();
$messages = mysql_query($query, $link_id);
return $messages;
}

function insertQueryReturnID($query)
{
$link_id = db_connect();
$messages = mysql_query($query, $link_id);
```

```
return mysql_insert_id($link_id);
}

?>
```

These last two functions are closely tied, as they are both designed to be used to `INSERT`, `UPDATE`, or `REPLACE` type operations. The first function is appropriate for use under most circumstances; it returns the number of rows affected. The second function is appropriate when inserting a row with a query that allows the database to specify the primary key; it returns the primary key assigned by the database to the inserted row (assuming the primary key is set to auto increment).

Dates

From a MySQL internal date format (like timestamp or datetime) to RFC 822 Format (used in RSS), this would be used within a MySQL query:

```
DATE_FORMAT(<Field Name>,'%a, %d %b %Y %T EST')
```

From the present date according to the server to RFC 822:

```
date("r")
```

From a MySQL internal date format to W3C's date-time format & ISO 8601 (used in Atom):

```
DATE_FORMAT(<Field Name>,'%Y-%c-%dT%H:%i:%S-04:00')
```

From the present date according to the server clock to W3C's required date format / ISO 8601:

```
echo date("c")                        // PHP 5 Only
echo date("Y-m-d\TH:i:sO")            // PHP 4 and previous
```

Complete Feed Specifications

This appendix reveals the specifications of the various versions of RSS and Atom feeds. The first part of the appendix shows an XML template for each specification, which provides an easy reference for the elements in each version, and the second half of the appendix defines each of the elements and provides an example of how each element is used.

Specifications

RSS 0.91

```
<?xml version="1.0"?>
<rss version="2.0">
<channel>
  <title></title>
  <link></link>
  <description></description>
  <language></language>
  <copyright></copyright>
  <managingEditor></managingEditor>
  <webMaster></webMaster>
  <pubDate></pubDate>
  <lastBuildDate></lastBuildDate>
  <docs></docs>
  <image>
    <url></url>
    <title></title>
    <link></link>
    <width></width>
    <height></height>
```

```
    <description></description>
  </image>
  <rating></rating>
  <textInput></textInput>
    <title></title>
    <description></description>
    <name><name>
    <link></link>
  </textInput>
  <skipHours></skipHours>
  <skipDays></skipDays>
  <item>*
    <title></title>
    <link></link>
    <description></description>
  </item>
</channel>
```

RSS 1.0

```
<?xml version="1.0"?>
<rss version="1.0">
<channel>
  <title></title>
  <link></link>
  <description></description>
  <image>
    <url></url>
    <title></title>
    <link></link>
  </image>
  <textInput></textInput>
    <title></title>
    <description></description>
    <name><name>
    <link></link>
  </textInput>
  <item>*
    <title></title>
    <link></link>
    <description></description>
  </item>
</channel>
```

RSS 2.0

```
<?xml version="1.0"?>
<rss version="2.0">
<channel>
  <title></title>
  <link></link>
  <description></description>
  <language></language>
```

```
  <copyright></copyright>
  <managingEditor></managingEditor>
  <webMaster></webMaster>
  <pubDate></pubDate>
  <lastBuildDate></lastBuildDate>
  <category></category>
  <generator></generator>
  <docs></docs>
  <cloud domain="" port="" path="" registerProcedure="" protocol="" />
  <ttl></ttl>
  <image>
    <url></url>
    <title></title>
    <link></link>
    <width></width>
    <height></height>
    <description></description>
  </image>
  <rating></rating>
  <textInput></textInput>
    <title></title>
    <description></description>
    <name><name>
    <link></link>
  </textInput>
  <skipHours></skipHours>
  <skipDays></skipDays>
  <item>*
    <title></title>
    <link></link>
    <description></description>
    <author></author>
    <category domain=""> </category>
    <comments></comments>
    <enclosure url="" length="" type="" />
    <guid></guid>
    <pubDate></pubDate>
    <source url=""></source>
  </item>
</channel>
```

Atom

```
<?xml version="1.0" encoding="utf-8"?>
<feed version="0.3" xmlns="http://purl.org/atom/ns#">
  <title>dive into mark</title>
  <link rel="alternate" type="text/html"
   href="http://diveintomark.org/"/>
  <modified>2003-12-13T18:30:02Z</modified>
  <author>
    <name>Mark Pilgrim</name>
  </author>
  <entry>
    <title>Atom 0.3 snapshot</title>
```

```
    <link rel="alternate" type="text/html"
     href="http://diveintomark.org/2003/12/13/atom03"/>
    <id>tag:diveintomark.org,2003:3.2397</id>
    <issued>2003-12-13T08:29:29-04:00</issued>
    <modified>2003-12-13T18:30:02Z</modified>
  </entry>
</feed>
```

Definitions

RSS 0.91

Code	Example	Description
`<?xml version="1.0"?>`	N/A	Defines the document as XML 1.0.
`<rss version="0.91">`	N/A	Defines the document as RSS 2.0, and begins the RSS namespace.
`*channel`	N/A	Begins the channel namespace.
`*title`	`Recipes`	Title of the feed. It often matches the title of the originating HTML document.
`*link`	`http://www.example.com`	The URL back to the corresponding HTML page.
`*description`	`Recipes for the computer hacker and culinary slacker`	Phrase or sentence describing the channel.
`*language`	`en`	Defines the language the feed will be provided in. For a full listing of appropriate codes, see `http://www.w3.org/TR/REC-html40/struct/dirlang.html#langcodes`.
`copyright`	`2005 Paul Reinheimer`	Defines the copyright restrictions on the document.
`managingEditor`	`paul@preinheimer.com (Paul Reinheimer)`	The email address for the managing editor for the feed. Note that this element must contain a valid email address if present.

Code	Example	Description
`webMaster`	`webMaster@preinheimer.com (Jon Doe)`	Address for the webmaster of the feed. Note that this element must contain a valid address if present.
`pubDate`	`Sat, 07 Sep 2002 00:00:01 GMT`	The publication date for the data within the channel. Date should be in the format specified in RFC 822; four year date preferred.
`lastBuildDate`	`Sat, 07 Sep 2002 09:42:31 GMT`	The last time content in the channel was modified.
`docs`	`http://my.netscape.com/publish/formats/rss-spec-0.91.html`	URL that points to the documentation to the feed.
`image`		Parent for the next five elements.
`*url`	`http://example.org/logo.png`	Address where the image can be located.
`*title`	`Our Logo`	Title for the image, just like HTML.
`*link`	`http://example.org/`	Address where users should be sent after clicking on the image.
`description`	`Stylized PHP logo`	Description of the image.
`width`	`88`	Width of the image, maximum of 144.
`height`	`25`	Height of the image, maximum of 400.
`rating`		The PICS rating for the channel, see `http://www.w3.org/TR/rdf-pics` for more information.
`textInput`		Parent for the next four elements, most aggregators ignore this.
`title`	`Submit`	Label for the Submit button.
`description`	`Enter comments here`	Explains the text input area.
`name`	`txtComments`	Name for the text input area.

Table continued on following page

Code	Example	Description
link	http://example.org/scripts/comments.php	Address of the script that processes the input.
skipHours	<hour>0</hour><hour>1</hour>	A set of up to 24 integers (0–24) indicating which hours aggregators may skip reading the feed.
skipDays	<day>Saturday</day> <day>Sunday</day>	A set of up to seven days (Sunday–Saturday) indicating which days aggregators may skip reading the feed.
Item		Parent for the next set of elements.
title	PHP 5.0.3 Released	Title for the element.
link	http://example.org/news/story.php?item=142	Link to the story in question. Note that it should link to the story, not the root page for the site.
description	The PHP team is proud to announce the release of PHP 5.0.3, which contains several important bug fixes and security updates	Description for the element in question.

RSS 1.0

Code	Example	Description
<?xml version="1.0"?>	N/A	Defines the document as XML 1.0.
<rdf:RDF>	N/A	Defines the document as RSS 2.0, and begins the RSS namespace.
<channel>	N/A	Begins the channel namespace.
<title>	Recipes	Title of the feed. It often matches the title of the originating HTML document.

Code	Example	Description
`<link>`	`http://www.example.com`	The URL back to the corresponding HTML page.
`<description>`	`Recipes for the computer hacker and culinary slacker`	Phrase or sentence describing the channel.
`image`		Parent for the next five elements.
`url`	`http://example.org/logo.png`	Address where the image can be located.
`title`	`Our Logo`	Title for the image, just like HTML.
`Link`	`http://example.org/`	Address where users should be sent after clicking on the image.
`textInput`		Parent for the next four elements. Most aggregators ignore this.
`title`	`Submit`	Label for the submit button.
`description`	`Enter comments here`	Explains the text input area.
`name`	`txtComments`	Name for the text input area.
`link`	`http://example.org/scripts/comments.php`	Address of the script that processes the input.
`Item`		Parent for the next set of elements
`title`	`PHP 5.0.3 Released`	Title for the element.
`link`	`http://example.org/news/story.php?item=142`	Link to the story in question; note that it should link to the story, not the root page for the site.
`description`	`The PHP team is proud to announce the release of PHP 5.0.3, which contains several important bug fixes and security updates`	Description for the element in question.

RSS 2.0

Code	Example	Description
`<?xml version="1.0"?>`	N/A	Defines the document as XML 1.0.
`<rss version="2.0">`	N/A	Defines the document as RSS 2.0, and begins the RSS namespace.
`<channel>`	N/A	Begins the channel namespace.
`<title>`	`Recipes`	Title of the feed; it often matches the title of the originating HTML document.
`<link>`	`http://www.example.com`	The URL back to the corresponding HTML page.
`<description>`	`Recipes for the computer hacker and culinary slacker`	Phrase or sentence describing the channel.
`<language>`	`en`	Defines the language the feed will be provided in. For a full listing of appropriate codes, see `http://www.w3.org/TR/REC-html40/struct/dirlang.html#langcodes`.
`<copyright>`	`2005 Paul Reinheimer`	Defines the copyright restrictions on the document.
`managingEditor`	`paul@preinheimer.com (Paul Reinheimer)`	The email address for the managing editor for the feed. Note that this element must contain a valid email address if present.
`webMaster`	`webmasater@preinheimer.com (Jon Doe)`	Address for the webmaster of the feed. Note that this element must contain a valid address if present.
`pubDate`	`Sat, 07 Sep 2002 00:00:01 GMT`	The publication date for the data within the channel. Date should be in the format specified in RFC 822; four year date preferred.
`lastBuildDate`	`Sat, 07 Sep 2002 09:42:31 GMT`	The last time content in the channel was modified.

Code	Example	Description
`category`	`News`	Defines the category the feed belongs to, one optional attribute domain, used with forward slashes either to define the location of the category within a hierarchy, or to define the root page for the category in question.
`generator`	`Serendipity 0.7.1 - http://www.s9y.org/`	Defines the program used to generate the feed.
`docs`	`http://blogs.law.harvard .edu/tech/rss#syndic8`	URL that points to the documentation to the feed.
`cloud`	`cloud domain="rpc.sys .com" port="80" path="/ RPC2" registerProcedure= "pingMe" protocol="soap"`	Allows a process to register itself to be informed when the feed is updated.
`ttl`	`60`	Amount of time, in minutes, a channel can be cached before refreshing from the source.
`image`		Parent for the next five elements.
`url`	`http://example.org/ logo.png`	Address where the image can be located.
`title`	`Our Logo`	Title for the image, just like HTML.
`Link`	`http://example.org/`	Address where users should be sent after clicking on the image.
`Width`	`88`	Width of the image, maximum of 144.
`Height`	`25`	Height of the image, maximum of 400.
`Rating`		The PICS rating for the channel; see `www.w3.org/TR/ rdf-pics` for more information.
`textInput`		Parent for the next four elements. Most aggregators ignore this.

Table continued on following page

Code	Example	Description
title	Submit	Label for the submit button.
description	Enter comments here	Explains the text input area.
name	txtComments	Name for the text input area.
link	http://example.org/scripts/comments.php	Address of the script that processes the input.
skipHours	<hour>0</hour><hour>1 </hour>	A set of up to 24 integers (0–24) indicating which hours aggregators may skip reading the feed.
skipDays	<day>Saturday</day> <day>Sunday</day>	A set of up to seven days (Sunday–Saturday) indicating which days aggregators may skip reading the feed.
Item		Parent for the next set of elements.
title	PHP 5.0.3 Released	Title for the element.
link	http://example.org/news/story.php?item=142	Link to the story in question; note that it should link to the story, not the root page for the site.
description	The PHP team is proud to announce the release of PHP 5.0.3, which contains several important bug fixes and security updates	Description for the element in question.
Author	PHP Team	Author of the item.
Category	Releases	Defines the category the item belongs to, one optional attribute domain, used with forward slashes either to define the location of the category within a hierarchy, or to define the root page for the category in question.
Comments	http://example.org/comments.php?story=142	URL for a page containing comments for the item.

Code	Example	Description
Enclosure	url="http://www.wroxnews.com/feedusage.pdf" length="38642" type="application/pdf"	Attaches a file to a specific item within the channel. url is the address for the resource, length is the length of the resource in bytes, and type is the media type for the resource.
Guid	<guid isPermaLink="true"> http://example.org/story.php?story=142</guid>	Stands for globally unique identifier. This value should be unique across all items on the blog. Often the URL of the site or the feed is used as a portion of the value for two reasons: first, to ensure that it is unique across feeds, and second, when the isPermaLink attribute is set to true, to provide a permanent link to the item.
pubDate	Sat, 07 Sep 2002 06:12:11 GMT	Publication date for the item, same format as previous date elements.
source	<source url="http://example.net/story"> example.net</source>	Reference a source for the item in question, optionally include a URL for that source.

ATOM 0.3

Code	Example	Description
<?xml version="1.0"?>		Defines the document as XML 1.0.
<feed version="0.3" xmlns="http://purl.org/atom/ns#">		Declares the document as a version 0.3 feed, and includes the root level xml atom namespace.
title	Example.com's New Feed	Title for the feed.
link	<link rel="alternate" type="text/html" href="http://example.org/"/>	Link to root page for the site providing the feed.

Table continued on following page

Code	Example	Description
*modified	2005-1-9T19:14:15Z	Date and time the feed was last modified GMT, reading (year)-(month)-(day)T(24 hour):(minute):(second)Z, with the T standing for time, and the Z for Zulu, or GMT.
*author	Paul Reinheimer	Author of the feed, required unless every entry element contains an author element.
contributor	Chris Shiflett	Lists people who contributed to the feed; feed may have multiple contributor elements.
tagline	Cool Example Feed	Human-readable description or tagline for the feed.
generator	<generator url="http://example.org/generator/" version="2.1">Example Feed Generator</generator>	Lists information on the software used to generate the feed.
copyright	Copyright (C) 2004, Paul Reinheimer	Lists copyright information for the feed.
info	ATOM 0.3 Feed	Human-readable information about the feed format.
entry		Parent for the next ##TODO## children.
*title	New Feed Launched	Title for the entry.
*link	<link rel="alternate" type="text/html" href="http://example.org/feed.php?entry=1"/>	Link for URL associated with the entry; an entry may contain multiple link elements, as long as the "type" attribute differs.
author	Paul Reinheimer	Author of the entry, required if there is no root author element. Must not be present if there is a root author element.
contributor	Chris Shiflett	Lists people who contributed to the feed; feed may have multiple contributor elements.

Code	Example	Description
`id`	`1`	Globally unique identifier for the entry; must be unique for the feed and may not change over time.
`*modified`	`2005-1-9T19:14:15Z`	Date and time the entry was last modified, same format as root modified element.
`*issued`	`2005-1-9T17:14:15Z`	Date and time the entry was first published.
`created`	`2005-1-9T17:14:15Z`	Date and time the entry was created, if not present it is assumed to match `issued`.
`summary`	`Example.org is pleased to announce the publication of a new feed in the ATOM format.`	A short summary of the entry.
`content`	`Example.org is pleased to announce the publication of a new feed in the ATOM format. We will be using this feed to keep our loyal users in the loop with all of our new developments.`	Full content of the entry.

C

Development System

Several examples presented in this book require extensions or external programs not provided with PHP by default. This appendix has been included to explain which extensions were used. A selection of the output of `phpinfo()` from our development system is presented first. Compare this with the output of `phpinfo()` on your system; missing packages may need to be added for some of the examples in this book.

> *Our development system was a fairly standard Linux system. That said, if your paths don't line up with ours or your version numbers aren't exactly the same as ours, don't panic. Things may still work perfectly. Also, if you are developing on another OS such as Windows, Mac OS, or another flavor of *nix, things may be missing or different. Generally, if a package isn't available for a specific OS, there is a suitable replacement. This listing should be used as a guide, not an absolute.*

Following the `phpinfo()` output, build information for the relevant libraries is presented, with Apache and PHP being presented last because they depend on the other packages.

phpinfo()

PHP Version 5.0.4	
System	Linux myserver.myhost.com 2.4.21-27.0.2.EL #1 Wed Jan 12 23:46:37 EST 2005 i686
Build Date	Apr 9 2005 16:09:23

Table continued on following page

PHP Version 5.0.4	
Configure Command	'./configure' '—with-mysql=/usr/local/mysql' '--with-apxs=/etc/httpd/bin/apxs' '--with-gd' '--with-png' '--with-zlib-dir=/usr/local/lib/zlib-1.2.2' '--enable-gd-native-ttf' '--with-ttf' '--with-jpeg-dir=/usr/local/lib/jpeg-6b/' '--with-freetype-dir=/usr/local/lib/freetype-2.1.9/' '--with-xpm-dir=/usr/X11R6/' '--with-tidy' '--with-curl' '--with-openssl=/usr/local/'
Server API	Apache
Virtual Directory Support	disabled
Configuration File (php.ini) Path	/usr/local/lib/php.ini
PHP API	20031224
PHP Extension	20041030
Zend Extension	220040412
Debug Build	No
Thread Safety	disabled
IPv6 Support	enabled
Registered PHP Streams	php, file, http, ftp, compress.zlib, https, ftps
Registered Stream Socket Transports	tcp, udp, unix, udg, ssl, sslv3, sslv2, tls

Apache	
APACHE_INCLUDE	no value
APACHE_TARGET	no value
Apache Version	Apache/1.3.33 (Unix) mod_ssl/2.8.22 OpenSSL/ 0.9.7f
Apache Release	10333100
Apache API Version	19990320
Hostname:Port	admin.myhost.com:80
User/Group	apache(48)/48

Apache	
Max Requests	Per Child: 0 - Keep Alive: on - Max Per Connection: 100
Timeouts	Connection: 300 - Keep-Alive: 15
Server Root	/etc/httpd
Loaded Modules	mod_security, mod_php5, mod_ssl, mod_setenvif, mod_so, mod_auth, mod_access, mod_alias, mod_userdir, mod_actions, mod_imap, mod_asis, mod_cgi, mod_dir, mod_autoindex, mod_include, mod_status, mod_negotiation, mod_mime, mod_log_config, mod_env, http_core

Curl	
CURL support	enabled
CURL Information	libcurl/7.13.0 OpenSSL/0.9.7f zlib/1.2.2

Gd	
GD Support	enabled
GD Version	bundled (2.0.28 compatible)
FreeType Support	enabled
FreeType Linkage	with freetype
FreeType Version	2.1.4
GIF Read Support	enabled
GIF Create Support	enabled
JPG Support	enabled
PNG Support	enabled
WBMP Support	enabled
XPM Support	enabled
XBM Support	enabled

Openssl	
OpenSSL support	enabled
OpenSSL Version	OpenSSL 0.9.7f 22 Mar 2005

SimpleXML	
Simplexml support	enabled
Revision	$Revision: 1.139.2.4 $
Schema support	enabled

tidy	
Tidy support	enabled
libTidy Release	1st December 2004
Extension Version	2.0 ($Id: tidy.c,v 1.56.2.5 2005/02/08 05:29:48 rasmus Exp $)

zlib	
ZLib Support	enabled
Compiled Version	1.2.2
Linked Version	1.2.2

Building Dependencies

Before you start building all of these packages, check your system for existing versions and also check if there are any precompiled binaries made for your specific system. Overwriting an existing library that is used elsewhere in your system could have unfortunate results.

Zlib

Name: zlib
Version: 1.2.2
Source: `www.gzip.org/zlib/`
Configure Command: `./configure`
Reasoning: Zlib is needed for PNG, which is needed for PNG support within GD, which is used to generate some CAPTCHA images.

Jpeg

Name: Jpeg
Version: 6b
Source: `www.ijg.org/`
Configure Command: `./configure --enable-static --enable-shared`
Reasoning: Jpeg is a common image format; adding jpeg support to GD will come in useful when manipulating user images or images supplied by web services.

Freetype

Name: Freetype
Version: 2.1.9
Source: `www.freetype.org/`
Configure Command: `./configure`
Reasoning: Freetype is needed to manipulate text with the GD libraries, which is done in order to create CAPTCHA images.

Gd

Name: GD Graphics Library
Version: 2.0.28
Source: `www.boutell.com/gd/`
Configure Command: `./configure`
Reasoning: GD provides image interrogation (height, width, size, and so on) and manipulation capabilities to PHP. The image information capabilities are useful when retrieving or receiving images (when downloading images specified in a feed or API, or when receiving them as the result of form input), while the manipulation capabilities are used extensively to create CAPTCHAs, or to resize images received.

OpenSSL

Name: Open Source toolkit for SSL/TLS
Version: 0.97f
Source: `www.openssl.org/`
Configure Command: `./Configure --shared --prefix=/usr/local linux-pentium`
Reasoning: OpenSSL is required by both cURL and `mod_ssl` in order to access secure streams. `mod_ssl` was used to connect to https:// hosts for secure API access, and `mod_ssl` was used to provide an https:// host for PayPal to connect to.

The preceding site does not have any information for Windows users; however, the official Apache HTTP Server Windows Binary is precompiled with OpenSSL support built in. There should be no additional work required for you.

WARNING!: Be very careful when building OpenSSL from source when you are using a binary-based (for example, RPM) Linux distribution. Removing the built-in functions may cause all manner of programs to stop working (lynx, mail, sftp, ssh, and so on). This is particularly true for RedHat systems.

Curl

Name: cURL
Version: 7.13.0
Source: `http://curl.haxx.se/`
Configure Command: `./configure`
Reasoning: cURL provides excellent support for communicating with a remote server over virtually any protocol. Its support of client-side certificates was needed for several of the secure APIs presented in this book. It also provides an alternative to `fsockopen()` when dealing with raw streams.

mod_ssl

Name: mod_ssl
Version: 2.8.22
Source: `www.modssl.org/`
Reasoning: `mod_ssl` provides access to the OpenSSL library to Apache. This allows Apache to serve pages over SSL.

Apache

Name: Apache
Version: 1.3.33
Source: `http://httpd.apache.org/`
Configure Command: `/configure --prefix=/etc/httpd/ --enable-module=so --enable-module=ssl`
Reasoning: Apache is an excellent, stable, mature web server that works perfectly with PHP. You may have noticed that the `phpinfo()` output indicated `mod_security`. It isn't used at all within this book (and hence not covered here), but it is an excellent security tool to look into.

PHP

Name: PHP: Hypertext Preprocessor
Version: 5.0.3
Source: `http://php.net/`
Configure Command:

```
'./configure' '--with-mysql=/usr/local/mysql' '--with-
apxs=/etc/httpd/bin/apxs' '--with-gd' '--with-png' '--with-zlib-
dir=/usr/local/lib/zlib-1.2.2' '--enable-gd-native-ttf' '--with-ttf'
'--with-jpeg-dir=/usr/local/lib/jpeg-6b/' '--with-freetype-
dir=/usr/local/lib/freetype-2.1.9/' '--with-freetype-dir' '--with-xpm-
dir=/usr/X11R6/' '--with-tidy' '--with-curl' '--with-openssl=/usr/local/'
```

Reasoning: All of the options are required, either directly for some of the examples in this book, or for related code that was explored while this book was in development. Note the `'--with-tidy'` stuck in there; it is shipped with PHP, but not enabled by default.

Index

Index

SYMBOLS AND NUMERICS

A

D

E

F

G

Q

R

S

V

W